POPULATION
Demography and Policy

POPULATION
Demography and Policy

Robert H. Weller
Florida State University

Leon F. Bouvier
Population Reference Bureau

St. Martin's Press
New York

Library of Congress Catalog Card Number: 80–52385

Manufactured in the United States of America.
54321
fedcba
For information, write St. Martin's Press, Inc.,
175 Fifth Avenue, New York, N. Y. 10010

cover design: Mies Hora
typography: Caliber

ISBN: 0–312–63114–6

To my wife, Jean; my children, Angie and Chuck; my parents, Robert M. and Mary Jane Weller; and my grandparents, George S. and Mary Catherine Ridgely and Martin L. and Bertha M. Weller—all of whom provided love and support during critical stages of my life—*Robert H. Weller*

To my wife, Terry; my children, Tommy, Lynne, Linda, and Kenny; and my eight grandchildren, who will provide pleasure and love in the later stages of my life—*Leon F. Bouvier*

Preface

The issues involved in population dynamics are being discovered by policy makers and academics alike. As a result, courses in population and problems of population are being offered more and more frequently. We take this burgeoning of population studies to be an encouraging sign. For too long, the sole public concern with population was the potential growth rate and what that might imply for the inhabitants of our planet. While growth is still a very important aspect of population study, more people are now realizing how crucial *all* demographic behavior is to social life.

Population behavior is the basic frame of reference for this text. Changes in demographic rates reflect changes in the demographic behavior of individual people as they give birth, move or do not move, and eventually die. By approaching this study through the individual "population actor," we believe that the reader will better appreciate the individual's role within the broader context of population change.

Population: Demography and Policy, intended for the undergraduate as well as the graduate student taking a first course in demography, is sociologically oriented. The emphasis is on the demographic rather than the environmental or ecological aspects of the population-resources question. Part I opens with the microdemographic perspective of the individual population actor, followed by an overview on how to study population. In part II, we examine past, current, and future trends in national and global population patterns and distributions. Part III explains the importance of the three major demographic variables—fertility, mortality, and migration. A chapter on contraceptive technology (chapter 6) is included because we are convinced that contraceptive technology is an integral part of the changing fertility behavior occurring throughout the world. Part IV covers the determinants and consequences of age and sex composition, including the effects of age composition on various social issues. All of part V, the concluding section, is devoted to the various policies that affect population behavior, so that students will be able to relate demography to the means of controlling or encouraging population growth and changing behavior.

The basic techniques needed to understand the application of these demographic policies are explained and illustrated where appropriate. For students interested in pursuing the subject in greater depth, boxed inserts have been included to explain some of the finer technical points.

As an aid to our readers, we have provided a comprehensive glossary. Terms defined in the glossary are printed in **boldface type** the first time they appear in the text.

Many people have been instrumental in the writing and production of this book. We have benefited greatly from discussions with colleagues at our past and present places of employment. We are grateful as well to Walter Kossmann, senior editor of the College Division at St. Martin's Press, who was very supportive at a crucial stage of the manuscript's development and made numerous helpful suggestions; Jinny Joyner, the developmental editor, who did an excellent job of rewriting and reorganizing our sometimes jumbled prose; Elaine Romano, our superb copy editor, who corrected all those points we forgot or overlooked; Michael Weber, the project editor, who put all the pieces together and oversaw the editing process; Ann Fountain, who faithfully and tirelessly typed (and retyped) the manuscript without complaining; Charles B. Nam, who supplied many needed references; Richard Ames, Kenneth C. W. Kammeyer, Dudley L. Poston, Jr., Ronald Rindfuss, Kent Schwirian, Edward G. Stockwell, and Livia S. Wan, M.D., who served as reviewers and whose advice we invariably accepted; and colleagues Joseph Chamie and Mary Chamie, who offered critical but helpful suggestions for our work. Of course, we accept responsibility for any remaining shortcomings.

Robert H. Weller
Leon F. Bouvier

Contents

I

II

Chapter 6
BIRTH PREVENTION METHODS 150

Chapter 7
MORTALITY 175

POPULATION
Demography
and Policy

Part I

Chapter 1 INTRODUCTION

The Study of Population

Along with every living person you are part of a population. You are both actor and acted upon. Your living, moving, procreating, and dying all affect your environment. At the same time your social, cultural, and economic environments affect your population (or demographic) behavior. Your life is also influenced by demographic trends in other societies.

Some of these connections are illustrated in part I. We have concentrated on the relationship between rapid population growth and several problems facing the earth's population. By doing so, we hope you will gain an appreciation or awareness of the extent to which population is a relevant concept for you, and why it is important to study it systematically.

1
Introduction

All of us are population actors. As such, we can perform only three types of acts: (1) we can have children (or not have them); (2) we can move from one place to another (or not move); and (3) we can die. Collectively, our population acts have a tremendous effect on our society, as well as on other societies and the world itself. It is important to know the demographic characteristics of a population in order to make decisions regarding the quality of life in that population. For instance, in order to plan the future supply of schools, highways, hospitals, courts, and so forth policy makers must know if the population is decreasing or increasing. Areas with a large proportion of elderly or poor persons need to provide a different mixture of social services than do areas with predominantly middle-aged or upper-class persons. Later in this book we will look at how some factors such as these relate to collective population acts. But right now let us look more closely at individual acts.

INDIVIDUAL POPULATION ACTS

The three population acts of having children, moving, and dying make up what are commonly known as the basic **demographic variables:**[1] fertility, migration, and mortality. Why these factors are variables can be illustrated by asking yourself some questions.

Having Children: Fertility

How many children are there in the family headed by your parents? (Be sure to include yourself as well as any brothers and sisters who may have died.) How many children do you expect to have during your lifetime? If the answers were tabulated for the entire class, you would see that not everyone gave the same answer. You would also probably find out that the average number of children your classmates expect to have is smaller than the average number of children their parents had. This provides an example of variations in **fertility**—that is, the birth rate of a population. The many factors that contribute to differences in fertility behavior are discussed at length in chapter 5.

Changing Residence: Migration

In what state (or country) were you born? In how many different states or countries have you lived? Where would you like to live five years from now? Again, if the answers were tabulated for your class, you would find wide variations in **migration** behavior. Some people are born in one city or state and remain there throughout their lives. This demographic "act" consists of not moving. Many other people will

[1]Words in **boldface type** are defined in the glossary at the back of the book.

move on numerous occasions—on entering college, beginning a new career, changing jobs, or perhaps retiring. Their decisions to move result in adding people to one area and subtracting them from another area.

Dying: Mortality

Are you a male or a female? How old are you now? Gender and age are each related to the number of years you should expect to live.

Mortality refers to the number of people who die in a specific period of time. Death is not a variable in the sense that we can choose whether or not we will die eventually. The timing of death is a variable, however. Some of us will die much earlier than others. As you will see in chapter 7, numerous factors come into play that partially determine how many years we live.

In summary, then, we are all population actors. Yet we all "act" somewhat differently. Some of us have large families; some of us move many times; some of us will die young. Others will show just the opposite behavior. Our demographic behavior is "caused" by various social, religious, economic, cultural, and biological factors. In turn, these different types of demographic behavior have fairly predictable consequences for the individual actor and for the society in which he or she lives.

As a result of our demographic acts, the **population composition** changes. By composition, we mean in part the age and sex distribution—the proportion of young to old; the proportion of males to females. Population composition also includes such variables as race, education, marital status, and religion. Throughout this text reference will be made to this all-important aspect of demography.

HOW TO STUDY POPULATION: DEMOGRAPHY

The matters we have discussed need to be studied systematically. The systematic study of population is called **demography.** Demography emphasizes the study of: (1) the size, composition, and distribution of the population in a given area; (2) changes in population size, composition, and distribution; (3) the components of these changes; (4) the factors that affect these components; and (5) the consequences of changes in population size, composition, and distribution or in the components themselves.

Population Change and Its Components

The size of a population can change only through fertility, mortality, or migration. As people are born, die, and move, they are continuously entering or leaving a population.

There are two methods of entering a population—being born or moving into it. Similarly there are two methods of leaving a population—moving out or dying. Demographers have portrayed this by constructing a **demographic equation.** The demographic equation is used to explain statistically the change in size of a population, *P,* between two different points in time, P_1 and P_2. Formally, the equation reads

$$P_2 - P_1 = (B - D)_{12} + (I - O)_{12}$$

The equation states that the difference between P_2 and P_1 is the amount of change in population size between time 1 and time 2. $(B-D)_{12}$ is the number of births minus the number of deaths between times 1 and 2; it is called reproduction change, or **natural increase.** $(I-O)_{12}$ is the difference between the number of persons moving into an area and the number of persons moving out between times 1 and 2; it is called **net migration.**[2]

As you can see from examining this equation, a population can change its size *if, and only if,* the sum of the demographic variables is not zero. If the number of births exactly equals the number of deaths but there is net **in-migration,** or movement into an area, the population will still increase in size. Of course, this increase would be larger if the number of births also exceeded the number of deaths. This latter pattern (net in-migration and positive reproductive change) characterizes population change for the United States as a whole today. However, certain areas of the nation exhibit different patterns. For example, the central cities of large metropolitan areas are characterized by a net **out-migration.** These cities will decrease in population if their reproductive change is not large enough to counterbalance the net out-migration of persons to suburbs. For instance, between 1970 and 1976 the population of Washington, D.C., decreased by about 54,900 persons. The net out-migration of 77,000 persons offset the positive reproductive change of 22,100 persons. By contrast, the entire Washington metropolitan area (which includes the District of Columbia and neighboring counties in Virginia and Maryland) increased by about 110,000 persons between 1970 and 1976 because the net out-migration of 45,800 persons from this area was not enough to offset the positive reproductive change of 155,800 persons (U.S. Bureau of the Census 1978, p. 23).

Some populations exhibit negative reproductive change. They have more deaths than births because of a high proportion of elderly persons. One example of this is the Tampa–St. Petersburg, Florida, metropolitan area. Between 1970 and 1976 there were 2,700 more deaths than births. Still the population grew because of a net in-migration of 220,800 persons. Thus, having more deaths than births does not automatically mean population decline. Indeed, some of the fastest

[2]See box 1.1 for an application of the equation to the U.S. population.

Box 1.1 The Demographic Equation

The demographic equation for the United States covering the period April 1, 1970, to January 1, 1979, may be calculated as follows:

P_2, or population size on January 1, 1979	=	219,530,000
P_1, or population size on April 1, 1970	=	204,335,000
$P_2 - P_1$, or change in population size	=	15,195,000
B_{12}, or births between 4/1/70 and 1/1/79	=	28,905,000
D_{12}, or deaths between 4/1/70 and 1/1/79	=	16,850,000
$(B - D)_{12} = B_{12} - D_{12}$	=	12,055,000
$(I - O)_{12}$, or net migration between 4/1/70 and 1/1/79	=	3,140,000

$$\begin{aligned} P_2 - P_1 &= (B - D)_{12} + (I - O)_{12} \\ &= 12{,}055{,}000 + 3{,}140{,}000 \\ &= 15{,}195{,}000 \end{aligned}$$

Thus, the U.S. population increased by over 15 million persons between April 1, 1970, and January 1, 1979. Of this increase, about 12 million (or 80 percent) was due to reproductive change. The remaining 3 million (or 20 percent) was due to net migration.

The growth of the U.S. population and the demographic components of this increase are examined in greater detail in chapter 3.

Source: U.S. Bureau of the Census 1979.

---

growing counties in the United States since 1970 have exhibited negative reproductive change, which has been offset by net in-migration.

In populations with both net out-migration and negative reproductive change, a decline in population size is inevitable. For instance, ten counties in Iowa lost population between 1970 and 1976 because there were more deaths than births at the same time that there was net out-migration (U.S. Bureau of the Census 1978, pp. 48–49).

The patterns of population change and the factors that produce them can and do vary from situation to situation, and all the demographic variables—fertility, migration, and mortality—play an important role. Change in the variables is the result of demographic acts performed by all of us. This is the heart of demography—understanding how the many factors that cause changes in demographic behavior and that are the consequences of this behavior are interrelated.

Population Composition

Demographers are interested in the characteristics of a population—what its composition is. For example, what are the numbers and proportion of males and females, young and old people? Marital status, socioeconomic status, religion, education, and race are also variables in population composition that are of interest to demographers. But it is age and sex that interest them most because they are both strongly related to the three demographic variables. A population's **age-sex composition**—the relative number of males and females in each age category of a population—reflects past levels of fertility, mortality, and migration. At the same time, current and future levels of fertility, mortality, and migration will depend partly upon the existing age-sex composition. The age and sex composition of a population has a number of other effects on society. For instance, two-thirds of the arrests in 1975 were of people between the ages of thirteen and twenty-nine. Because of recent declines in fertility, the absolute size of this age group should begin to decline in 1980. This may produce reductions in crime rates. Also, because of the increasing proportion of elderly persons in the United States, the federal budget is "graying"—that is, it contains increased spending for the aged. Age composition has an important role in demography, which we will study in chapter 9.

The other composition variables are of interest because they are related to at least one of the three demographic variables. For instance, marital status is important in studying fertility because married persons do most of the childbearing. Marital status can also influence some of the other variables which indirectly affect fertility levels, such as the labor force participation and educational level of women. At the same time, fertility can affect marital status. Conceptions occasionally lead to marriage; the presence of young children may contribute to emotional and economic stress within the family and to marital instability. Migration and mortality also vary according to marital status. We will discuss these connections in later chapters.

In the United States, race is an important compositional factor. Blacks have higher fertility, move locally more often, and have higher levels of mortality than whites. There are genetic differences between the races, but the demographic differences exist because race is also a social variable. Thus, race is strongly related to socioeconomic status (SES). For a variety of reasons blacks in the United States have a lower SES than whites on average. Consequently they have different life styles and different value systems. When differences in SES are controlled, most of the demographic differences between blacks and whites are reduced or even disappear. The same explanation applies to the differences in demographic behavior between whites and other ethnic groups, such as Indians or Hispanic-Americans. Immigrants to this country historically have had higher fertility than Americans who settled here earlier because the immigrants were raised in societies with high fertility. However, as the offspring of the immigrants were assimilated into American society their fertility has become virtually identical.

Education is an important compositional factor because it is an indicator of SES and because it affects a person's life style, which influences demographic behavior. At the same time, the ability of a government to educate its citizens is affected by demographic factors. Because of the post–World War II baby boom, school enrollments increased rapidly during the 1950s and 1960s. This resulted in overcrowded schools and a shortage of qualified teachers. Lately, school enrollments have been falling due to a decline in fertility on the national level. But, migration patterns affect the demand for schooling on the local and state levels. Because Americans tend to move to suburban or urban areas and to the South and the West, school enrollments in these areas will show less decline than schools in other areas. Moreover, schools in some areas will lose enrollment at faster than average rates because their populations are aging. In some suburbs housing costs have become too high for younger couples to move in. In some cities many of the in-migrants are singles or childless couples.

We have selected only a few of the compositional variables for discussion. The number of possible variables is practically infinite, which gives demographers a wide field to study since they are interested in *anything* that is related to demographic behavior. Also, remember that compositional variables should be viewed as both cause and effect. They affect the demographic variables and thereby influence population changes; in turn, demographic behavior can affect many of the compositional variables.

Population Distribution

How people are spatially dispersed over an area—population distribution—reflects local levels of fertility, mortality, and migration. Large cities are losing population because reproductive change is insufficient to offset a large net out-migration. The Sunbelt in the South and West is growing very rapidly because of a massive in-migration of persons born in other parts of the country. At the same time, the type of area a person lives in may affect demographic behavior. This may be due to the environment. For instance, until the last part of the nineteenth century, mortality levels were higher in cities than in rural areas because of crowded, unsanitary living conditions and because of the prevalence of infectious, communicable diseases in cities. Often demographic differences by residence reflect socioeconomic status. Cities have higher death rates among infants than do suburbs because the inner portions of cities have disproportionately more poor people. Some types of people may be more likely than other types to move to certain areas, such as to cities. Chapter 4 deals at length with rural-urban and metropolitan-nonmetropolitan residence.

Sources of Demographic Data

Where do demographers get most of their data? The three major sources are censuses, special **sample surveys,** and **population registers.** The United Nations defines a **population census** as "the total process of collecting, compiling and publishing demographic, economic and social data pertaining, at a specified time or times, to all persons in a country or delimited territory" (United Nations 1958, p. 3). Within a population a sample survey may be taken on various topics of interest, such as fertility or migration behavior, or it may be used to estimate the size of the population living in an area. Finally, a registration system records all births and deaths through some central government agency. Data may also be recorded on arrivals and departures at international boundaries.

The Census

Most censuses aim at a complete count or listing of the inhabitants and certain of their characteristics. For instance, in the 1980 census of the U.S. population, information was obtained from all persons on their address, name, relationship to householder, sex, race/ethnicity, age, month and year of birth, marital status, and whether they are of Spanish/Hispanic origin or descent. Several housing characteristics were also ascertained. For some items information is obtained on a sample basis; that is, only a representative section of the population is asked certain questions. In the 1980 census sampling was used to ascertain such disparate information as state or country of birth, educational attainment, children ever born (for women only), employment and occupational characteristics, length of commute to work, residence in 1975, income, ancestry, veteran status, health impairments, migration history, and the date of first marriage if married more than once. Of course, the contents of a census are not static. Items are added and deleted according to how useful the government believes they would be (see box 1.2, page 14). In general, however, the typical scope of a census is the size, distribution, and characteristics of the population.

The Survey

The distinction between a census and a survey is not clear-cut, but surveys tend to concentrate on the characteristics of the population. Occasionally they are also used to estimate population size or distribution. In countries without adequate registration of births and deaths, a population survey may include questions about births or deaths of household members in the preceding year. Even when fairly adequate registration systems exist, the survey may include questions on fertility (such as children ever born, number of children still living, and the date of birth of each child) because this information cannot be obtained readily from the registration certificates. Sometimes surveys are combined with registration systems to collect special information. For instance, the U.S. National Center for Health Statistics mails questionnaires to a sample of mothers identified from birth certificates in a given year. In this fashion the center obtains particulars concerning the pregnancy and characteristics of the parents.

Registration Systems

Registration systems have been in use a long time. The recording of marriages, baptisms, and deaths in parish registers developed for religious purposes early in history. Gradually it evolved into a secular system for the compulsory registration of births, marriages, and deaths of the whole population. The events that are registered may include live births, deaths, stillbirths, marriages, divorces, annulments, legal separations, and adoptions. Not all countries with a civil registration system record all these events or publish statistics on their numbers. The statistics on births and deaths are called **vital statistics.**

In the United States the collection of data about individual births, deaths, marriages, and divorces is primarily the responsibility of each state. The federal government sets standards for their accuracy and completeness of coverage and publishes statistical reports using the data that the states collect. Birth and death certificates are collected from local registrars by each state, which then transmits them to the National Center for Health Statistics.

A registration system that collects information on a continuing basis is called a continuous population register. More formally, the United Nations defines it as "a mechanism which will provide for the continuous recording of information about the population in such a manner that data on particular events that occur to the individual, as well as selected characteristics describing him, are maintained on a current basis" (1962, p. 3). There are two types of continuous population registers.

Universal population registers attempt to cover the entire population on a permanent basis. They are relatively rare and occur primarily in some Scandinavian countries, the Far East, and Eastern Europe. Much more common are *partial* population registers, which are established for specific administrative purposes, and which restrict coverage to those persons directly affected by the particular administrative program. Examples of common partial population registers include national social security systems, lists of persons eligible for a military draft, welfare rolls, voter registration lists, tax office records, and city directories (Shryock and Siegel 1971, pp. 15–37).

Most countries also collect information on the number of persons arriving and departing from their borders. These records tend to be complete for aliens arriving for the purposes of settlement. They tend to be less complete for arrivals and departures of a country's own citizens.

Sources of Error

Because demographers rely on their data so extensively, it is important that the data be as complete and accurate as possible. But no system of collecting demographic data is completely free of error. Some people are missed completely. Other people give inaccurate responses or

Box 1.2 The United States Census

In 1980 the U.S. Bureau of the Census undertook the largest and most expensive count of the population in history. It cost about $1 billion to complete this massive operation of enumerating, either through personal interviews or by mailed questionnaires, the over 226 million people residing in the United States on April 1, 1980.

Why does the government undertake a census? First and foremost, the Constitution mandates such a count every ten years. In 1982 the House of Representatives as well as most state legislatures will be reapportioned to ensure that the one person–one vote principle is maintained. Second, the census is the basis for enormous transfers of funds from the federal to the state and local governments for a wide array of social programs. Third, the census is the basic statistical source for all sorts of activities. Census data of all types are crucial for analyzing markets, planning new services and facilities, carrying out affirmative action programs, studying environmental impact, and conducting basic research in many academic fields. These three points help explain why certain questions are asked in some years and not in others, and why the length of the schedule has tended to increase over time.

What is asked in the census? The first census in 1790 was very brief. It counted only the number of white males over and under the age of sixteen, the number of white females, all other free persons (including any Indians who paid taxes), and slaves. The first inquiry on manufactured goods was made in 1810; questions on agriculture, mining, and fisheries were added in 1840; and in 1850 the census included inquiries on social statistics for the first time.

The range of the population censuses grew in the nineteenth and early twentieth centuries, as the following list of topics indicates:

Age and sex, 1790–present (but only for free whites until 1820)
Slave status, 1790–1860
Color or race, 1790–present
Citizenship, 1820–1830, 1870, 1890–present
Physical or mental handicap, 1830–1930, 1970–present
Education or literacy, 1840–present
Married in past year, 1850–1890 (but only for free whites until 1870)
Occupation, 1950–present
Crime, 1850–1910
Mortality, 1850–1890
Place of birth, 1950–present
Pauperism, 1850–1910
Parents' birthplace, 1870–1970
Prisoners, 1880–1910
Marital status, 1880–present
Employment status, 1880–present (except 1920)

continued

The United States Census (continued)

Year of immigration, 1890–1930; 1970–present
Number of children ever born, 1890–1910; 1940–present
Language (or whether the person could speak English), 1890–present (except 1950)

Were you counted in 1980? Recent censuses have missed about 2.5 percent of the total population. The 1980 census was apparently even more successful in counting the population. Thus the chances are extremely high that you were counted, even if you were not aware of it. Someone in your family undoubtedly completed the required short form (or the long form if they fell into the sample). If you lived in a dormitory or some other institutional quarters, the dormitory director undoubtedly completed the required form. So, rest assured that it is very likely that you were among the 226 million people enumerated as residents (though not necessarily citizens) of the United States as of April 1, 1980.

---

fail to answer all the items. Moreover, these errors often are systematic—that is, some types of people are more likely than other types to be missed or to give inaccurate information.

Errors in coverage by the census may be attributable to the design of the census itself, the field operations, the respondents, or the way the data are handled after they are received. Sometimes the instructions are inadequate or confusing. Maps may be inaccurate; listings of residences may be incomplete. Some respondents may lose their census schedules or may not fill them out completely. The census form may be lost after it is received by the census personnel, or errors may be made in transcribing the data to a form suitable for data processing. The U.S. Bureau of the Census has developed several techniques to reduce the number of such errors. In 1970 an estimated 97.5 percent of the U.S. population was enumerated in the census (Siegel et al. 1977, p. 12). The bureau attempted to do even better in the 1980 census. Census data in other countries, particularly the less developed countries, often are less complete.

Sample surveys are subject to sampling error and sampling bias, in addition to all the kinds of errors to which censuses are subject. But people may be more likely to respond to a sample survey than to a census, particularly if the survey is not sponsored by the government. These persons may believe the government is invading their privacy or will somehow use their responses against them.

Errors in population registers arise from a failure to report births, deaths, or moves to the authorities, or from a failure to record these events properly even when they are reported. Sometimes the data reported are inaccurate or imprecise. For instance, the cause of death may be described as "old age." Some events are not registered at all because people do not wish to bring themselves to the attention of the authorities or because they do not know such events are supposed to be registered. Like errors in censuses and sample surveys, errors in population registers are frequently systematic (Shryock and Siegel 1971, pp. 34–35).

SUMMARY

You are a population actor. All population change results from your acts, combined with those of other persons. These population acts consist of giving birth or not giving birth, moving or not moving, and dying. We have called these the three demographic variables of fertility, migration, and mortality. Each of these is affected by a variety of social, economic, psychological, and biological factors. Each also has consequences for the individuals involved and for the larger society.

The systematic study of population is called demography. It encompasses the study of population size, composition, and distribution; changes in these; the components of population change (reproductive change and net migration); the factors that affect these components; and the consequences of changes in population size, composition, or distribution or in the components themselves.

The principal sources of demographic data are population censuses, special sample surveys, and registration systems. Each of these contains some built-in sources of error.

REFERENCES AND SUGGESTED READINGS

Shryock, Henry S., and Siegel, Jacob S. 1971. *The methods and materials of demography.* Washington, D.C.: Government Printing Office.

Siegel, Jacob S., et al. 1977. Developmental estimates of the coverage of the population of states in the 1970 census: demographic analysis. *Current population reports,* series P-23, no. 65. Washington, D.C.: Government Printing Office.

United Nations. 1958. *Principles and recommendations for national population censuses.* New York: United Nations.

———. 1962. *Methodology and evaluation of continuous population registers.* New York: United Nations.

U.S. Bureau of the Census. 1978. Estimates of the population of counties and metropolitan areas: July 1, 1975 and 1976. *Current population reports,* series P-25, no. 739. Washington, D.C.: Government Printing Office.

———. 1979. Popstan: A case study for the 1980 censuses of population and housing. Washington, D.C.: Government Printing Office.

Part II

Population Growth and Distribution

Part II describes the growth of the world's population, some of the major consequences of this growth, and the distribution of population throughout the earth. The current rate of world population growth is high, and most of this growth is taking place in the less economically developed countries of the world.

Chapter 2 shows that the high rate of world population growth is a recent phenomenon and is likely to continue in the near future. Indeed, the world's population will become at least twice as large as it is now and possibly close to four times its present size. This rapid population growth is aggravating several problems facing humans—chronic malnutrition in many parts of the world, low standards of living, and pressure on available energy supplies.

Chapter 3 looks at the pattern of population growth in the United States. Currently the rate of population growth here is relatively low, but this period follows one of the most explosive epochs in American demographic history—the increase in births following World War II. Because of that increase the U.S. population will continue to increase until the middle of the twenty-first century—even if the birth rate remains low. The chapter also examines some of the consequences of population growth for you personally and for the society in which you live.

Chapter 4 examines another aspect of population—its distribution by geographic region, level of economic development, and community type. Using the deconcentration of the metropolitan population in the United States as an example, we examine some consequences of trends in population redistribution. This chapter also shows some ways that you as a population actor can affect your community and be affected by the demographic acts of other people.

2

Patterns of World Population Change

Throughout most of human history the population has increased very slowly and sporadically. Its current rate of over 1.7 percent a year is high and cannot continue indefinitely, but it is unlikely that the population will stop growing in the near future. In this chapter we examine the present and past patterns of world population change, and we use projections to get some idea of what the future holds in store. The chapter also discusses some of the major consequences of the rapid growth currently being experienced by the world's population.

CURRENT PATTERNS

The world's population did not reach the 1 billion mark until A.D. 1850. The second billion was added by 1930—just eighty years later. It took only thirty more years to reach 3 billion, and a mere sixteen years for the world's population to increase to 4 billion.[1] By the middle of 1980 it was about 4.4 billion.

This growth is occurring because the **crude birth rate** (the number of births in any given year per 1,000 population) is 28 and the **crude death rate** (the number of deaths in any given year per 1,000 population) is only 11 (Population Reference Bureau 1980). The **growth rate** can be measured by subtracting the death rate from the birth rate. This gives a difference of 17 per 1,000 population, which is equivalent to a 1.7 percent rate of annual population growth. If this rate of population growth continues, the world's population will double in size every forty-one years. Thus, by the year 2021 there would be over 8.8 billion people and by the year 2062 almost 17.6 billion people!

The rate of world population growth has declined since the early 1970s, when it was about 2 percent annually. The growth rate of the world is projected to decline to about 1.5 percent by the year 2000. At that rate of growth the world's population would double every forty-six years.

The growth of the world's population through time is shown in figure 2.1 on page 24. The figure clearly shows that the recent population growth is unprecedented in magnitude. This rapid rate of world population growth is produced by high growth rates in the less economically developed countries (which contain about three-fourths of the world's population) and by low to moderate growth in the more developed countries.

A growth rate of 1.7 percent may seem like a small figure, but

[1]As a point of information, the Population Reference Bureau, a private, nonprofit educational organization, estimates that the world's population reached 4 billion on March 21, 1976, at 7:00 P.M. As the bureau recognized at the time, such estimates should not be taken too seriously, for our knowledge concerning the world's population is far from accurate.

Box 2.1 Crude Rates

Crude birth and death rates are computed by dividing the number of births or deaths in a given year by the estimated midyear population and multiplying the quotient by 1,000. We use the midyear (July 1) population because it roughly corresponds to the number of people exposed to the risk of giving birth or dying throughout the entire year. The number of persons alive at the beginning of the year would be too small and the number alive at the end of the year would be too large. So we use the midyear population.

For example, in 1977 there were 3,326,632 births and 1,889,597 deaths in the United States. The population on July 1 was estimated to be 215,500,000.

The crude birth rate is calculated as follows:

$$\text{CBR} = \frac{\text{Births}}{\text{Midyear Population}} \times 1{,}000 = \left(\frac{3{,}326{,}632}{215{,}500{,}000}\right) 1{,}000 = (.0154)\ 1{,}000 = 15.4$$

The crude death rate is calculated in the same way.

$$\text{CDR} = \frac{\text{Deaths}}{\text{Midyear Population}} \times 1{,}000 = \left(\frac{1{,}889{,}000}{215{,}500{,}000}\right) 1{,}000 = (.008)\ 1{,}000 = 8.8$$

These are called "crude" rates because the denominator in the equation consists of the total population of the area being studied. Ideally, the denominator should only include the population "at risk" of performing the act in the numerator. This is not the case with crude birth rates (which ignore the fact that only females of certain ages can give birth) and crude death rates (which disregard the fact that babies and the elderly are much more likely to die than youths and young adults). As we will see later, demographers have devised many other more sophisticated measures of the actual rate.

applied to a base of 4.4 billion persons it produces astonishing figures. In absolute terms this means an increase of over 75 million people in one year—an addition to the world's population larger than the 1980 population of Mexico.

In dealing with such figures two things must be remembered. First, they represent *additional* people to be fed, clothed, housed, and otherwise sustained. Second, these figures are now calculated on a base of 4.4 billion, but growth is cumulative. The base gets bigger every year. For instance, after only three years the total population would have increased to 4.7 billion people. The fourth year's growth would increase the population by 80 million rather than 75 million persons.

The cumulative nature of population growth can produce figures that stagger the imagination. Lincoln Gordon, a prominent resource economist, wrote in 1976 that "continuation of recent world popula-

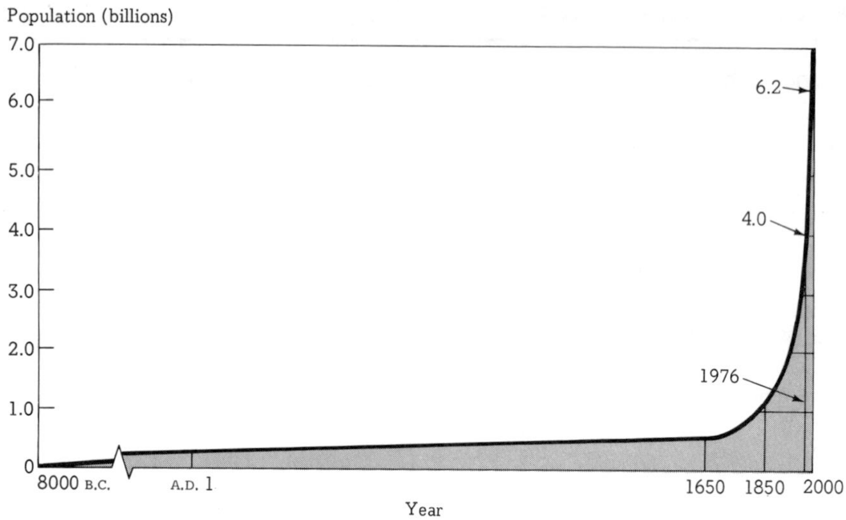

Figure 2.1 Historical Growth of the World's Population
Source: Population Reference Bureau (1976).

tion growth rates of 2 percent a year would bring today's figure of about 4 billion to . . . 48 billion by the year 2100 and 344 billion by the year 2200" (1976, p. 3).

It is unlikely that such figures will actually be reached. At some point in the future, the population must stop growing. If birth rates are not reduced, death rates will simply increase. The question is: what combination of fertility and mortality will produce this nongrowth? The possibilities range from very high fertility and very high mortality to low fertility and low mortality. Most people feel the second combination is preferable to the first.

Indeed, many population planners have been heartened by recent declines in the rate of population growth. As stated earlier, in 1980 it was estimated at 1.7 percent annually, as contrasted to 2.0 percent annually during the early 1970s. This decline occurred because fertility rates have declined more than mortality rates during this interval. A further cause for optimism is that significant fertility declines have recently been noted in a number of key developing countries: China, South Korea, Malaysia, Indonesia, Thailand, the Philippines, Sri Lanka, Costa Rica, Colombia, and Mexico. Further declines in the rate of world population growth are anticipated.

Several factors offset these reasons for optimism. First, growth rates in many developing countries of Africa, Asia, and Latin America have remained unchanged despite efforts to lower them (Haupt 1979). Second, our knowledge concerning past fertility levels in many of these developing countries is incomplete. It is possible that our estimates have overstated the amount of actual decline in fertility that has taken place. Finally, the world's population is still continuing to grow. Even if the growth rate of the world's population declines to the projected 1.5 percent by the year 2000, the absolute number of persons will continue to rise—by an estimated 95 million per year by then.

HISTORY OF WORLD POPULATION CHANGE

Since 1962 over 2 billion additional persons have been born. Thus, the current world population of 4.4 billion people represents more than 5 percent of the people who have *ever* lived on earth. Why was population growth so slow in the past? Let us take a look at past patterns.

Population Change Before A.D. 1650

Estimates of past population size are risky because we have so little information. There may have been some 8 million people alive in 8000 B.C., the approximate date when agriculture and the domestication of animals began. These two developments allowed the support of larger populations at greater densities than were possible within a hunting and gathering society. The pace of population growth accelerated slightly, so that by the year A.D. 1 there were some 250 or 300 million people alive. Again, this is only a general figure. It is based on sources as diverse as ancient Chinese censuses and modern estimates of the populations of the major ancient nations.[2]

After A.D. 1 the population continued to increase slowly. It did not double in size until about the year 1650—at an annual average rate of growth of .04 percent. Growth rates were low because high death rates canceled out high birth rates. For instance, the infant mortality rates were frequently 250 per 1,000, or greater. This means that as many as one out of every four persons died before the first birthday. The chances of dying during childhood and early adulthood were also very high compared with today's standards. Consequently, the average length of life was between twenty and thirty-five years. It was rare for a person to survive past age fifty.

Of course, population growth was uneven. Changes in climate and the occurrence of famine, other natural disasters, war, and the plague and other epidemic diseases made the death rate fluctuate. Under these conditions a high birth rate just barely led to the replacement of the population that died. In fact, during some time periods more people died than were born, and the population actually declined in size. For instance, during both the sixth and the fourteenth centuries Europe experienced plagues that reduced its population by 40 percent (Russell 1958, p. 41). Other areas also experienced high

[2]Those readers seeking greater detail concerning the methodology of making these estimates should consult John Durand (1967 and 1977) and Colin Clark (1968).

mortality because of epidemics of the plague and other infectious diseases.[3]

These periods of very high mortality were often followed by periods of relatively low mortality and increased fertility. This produced population growth in the short run, but over the long run the population grew very slowly before 1650.

Population Change Between 1650 and 1930

Only 200 years were required for the population to double from 500 million in 1650 to 1 billion in 1850—and 80 more years for it to double again to 2 billion by 1930. The accelerated growth, caused primarily by lower death rates, was concentrated in countries that were experiencing industrialization. The improved standards of living accompanying industrialization brought about substantial declines in mortality beginning in the early nineteenth century. Countries that did not undergo industrialization during this period—that is, almost all of today's developing countries—were growing much more slowly because their death rates were still high.

Initially industrialization may have caused the birth rate in Western Europe to increase slightly. The principle that a man might not marry until his living was assured had previously served as a check on fertility. Industrialization meant that more men could marry at younger ages than before, which probably caused fertility to increase during the early stages of industrialization. (Habakkuk 1953 and Petersen 1960 contain examples.) However, a decline in mortality was soon followed by a decline in fertility. By 1930 the rate of population growth began to approach zero again—except that this time the nongrowth was produced by *low* birth rates and *low* death rates. This change from *high* birth and death rates to *low* birth and death rates has been called the **demographic transition** (see figure 2.2).

The Demographic Transition

As we have seen, both birth rates and death rates—that is, vital rates—were very high before the transition began, but very little population growth took place in the long run. This pretransitional stage has been named **high growth potential** because of the potential for growth if mortality were lowered (Notestein 1945). Its important characteristic was that birth and death rates were high and showed no downward trends. This stage probably lasted for thousands of years. It is shown in the left portion of figure 2.2.

For a number of reasons (discussed in the next section), mortality began to decline around 1800—gradually at first and then in an accel-

[3]Barbara Tuchman (1978) contains a popularized account of the plague and its impact on the world's population.

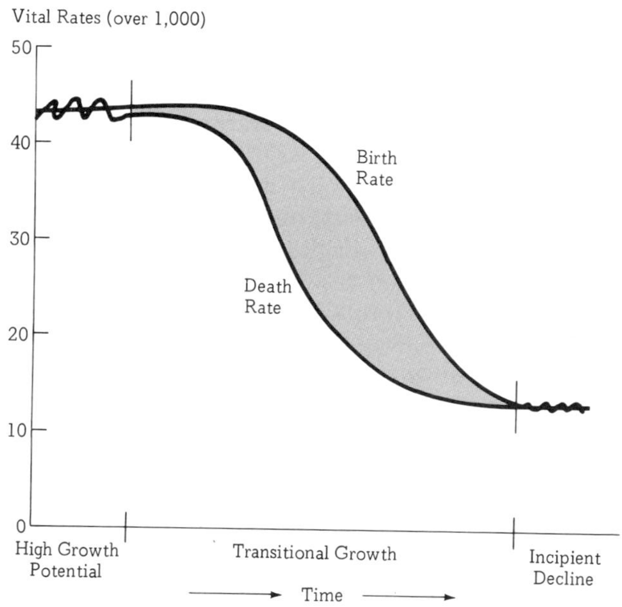

Figure 2.2 The Demographic Transition

erated fashion. The birth rate did not drop as early as the death rate, and the initial declines in fertility did not keep pace with the declines in mortality. During this period, called **transitional growth,** the population increased rapidly. This is depicted by the shaded portion of figure 2.2. Eventually, as the death rate ceased to decline and the birth rate also approached a low level, population growth almost ceased.

This third stage of the demographic transition has been called **incipient decline.** It is characterized by low birth and death rates and is shown in the right portion of figure 2.2. It is not possible to forecast how long this stage will last. Any population growth that occurs is caused by fluctuations in fertility from year to year. Mortality rates are almost as low as can be expected. Fertility rates may even decline to levels lower than the mortality rates, which is what is happening in some European countries today. If this difference persists for a long period of time, the population will actually decrease in size, unless offset by in-migration.

The demographic transition is a model of population change. As such, it depicts in *general* terms the change from relatively uncontrolled high fertility and mortality to relatively controlled low fertility and mortality that took place in most of the industrializing countries during their period of economic expansion and growth. However, the timing and pace of the transition certainly have varied among countries. It is also debatable whether the model of demographic transition is applicable to conditions in today's developing countries (Notestein, Kirk, and Segal 1969, pp. 144–145; Kirk 1971; and Coale 1978).

Causes of the Mortality Decline

The decline in mortality in the industrializing countries was the direct result of the improved standards of living that accompanied industrialization. The death rate fell slowly (although erratically) during the eighteenth and early nineteenth centuries, as the food supply increased and famines occurred less frequently because of improvements in agricultural techniques. New foods introduced into Europe from the Americas improved the quality of the diet. Also, technological advances in transportation facilitated the movement of food from areas of surplus to areas of scarcity. More adequate housing was constructed and better clothing became available.

After the middle of the nineteenth century, the decline in mortality accelerated as a result of sanitary reform and public health movements. Not until the twentieth century did improved medical practices make a significant contribution (McKeown 1976; and United Nations 1973, pp. 146–152). All these factors will be discussed in greater detail in chapter 7.

Causes of the Fertility Decline

The falling birth rate in these societies is not as easy to explain as the falling death rate. The historic decline of fertility is generally attributed to a complex set of factors related to economic development and societal modernization, but the relative importance of these factors is difficult to assess. Consequently, what follows should be regarded as a set of generalizations.

As urbanization and industrialization took place, the family lost importance as an economic unit of production. Impersonal systems like the factory took over the allocation of jobs. The occupational structure shifted away from primary industries such as agriculture (associated with high fertility levels) and toward white-collar and skilled industries (associated with lower fertility). Children who were useful as a cheap supply of labor in farming families were not as useful in industrial working-class families, particularly when child labor was abolished and compulsory education laws were passed. In fact, children began to be a financial burden as the costs of child rearing increased.

The decrease in infant and childhood mortality meant that more children lived. The parents saw that it was no longer necessary to have extra births to assure the survival to adulthood of the desired number of offspring.

Increased educational attainment among females may also have contributed to declines in fertility. Economic roles for women developed outside of the home. These factors, along with the declining importance of the family as a production unit and the growth of impersonal systems for the allocation of jobs, tended to increase the possibility of economic mobility that could be better achieved with small families and tended to decrease the economic advantages of a large family (Coale and Hoover 1958, pp. 11–12; and United Nations 1973, pp. 86–92).

Of course, numerous exceptions may be made to these general statements. For instance, the nationwide decline in fertility began in France nearly a century before it began in England, even though England was the leader in the Industrial Revolution. Moreover, there are many instances in which declines in fertility either coincided with declines in mortality or preceded them (Coale 1975, p. 353). Despite these departures from the pattern of population change predicted by demographic transition, the model still has value as an overall generalization.

Population Change Since 1930

Between 1930 and 1976, the world's population doubled to 4 billion people. Most of this growth occurred in relatively nonindustrialized countries where fertility remained high while mortality declined rapidly. Added to this source of growth was the population increase caused by the **baby boom,** a high birth rate that occurred during the late 1940s and the 1950s in North America and, more briefly, in many Western European countries. The causes of the baby boom are discussed in the next chapter.

During the eighteenth and nineteenth centuries mortality remained high in countries that did not industrialize. However, in the period from 1920 to 1950 mortality levels in many of those countries declined drastically. Often the declines were so great that they equaled in magnitude the declines that had taken place in the industrialized countries over a period of 100 to 150 years. By current estimates the average length of life in the developing countries increased from thirty-two years in 1940 to fifty or more years in 1975.

The decreases in mortality in the developing countries have been generated externally. That is, relatively little change in the social and economic structure of the society was needed to produce these mortality declines. Instead, external factors, including modern medical technology developed in Western countries and public health measures such as the massive spraying of insecticide and inoculation against various infectious diseases, accounted for the changes. Standards of living have not increased significantly in many of these developing countries.[4] Nor have declines in mortality been accompanied by equally large declines in fertility. Although the average length of life

[4]Although these statements are generally valid, the relative importance of the various factors may vary from country to country. For treatments of the factors causing the rapid mortality decline in Sri Lanka, for example, see Harold Fredericksen (1960 and 1961), S. A. Meegama (1967), Peter Newman (1970), R. H. Gray (1974), and Alberto Palloni (1975).

in the developing countries increased by 56 percent between 1940 and 1970, the birth rate declined a mere 7.8 percent (Coale 1974, p. 51). Consequently, extremely rapid population growth, often more than 3 percent annually, has taken place.

It would be comforting to believe that the developing countries have entered into the second stage of the demographic transition, in which declines in mortality precede similar declines in fertility. It also would be comforting to believe that these countries will progress to the third stage, in which birth and death rates are low and in balance, producing low rates of population growth. As we noted earlier a number of key developing nations have, in fact, experienced a significant decrease in fertility. In many of those nations the decline in fertility even seems to be gaining momentum (Tsui and Bogue 1978). But there are also a number of developing countries in which fertility has not declined significantly. The area sweeping from the Bay of Bengal to Asia Minor (Iran, Iraq, Afghanistan, India, Pakistan, and Bangladesh) contains about one-fifth of the world's population. Fertility has remained quite high in this area, despite efforts by several of the governments to lower fertility through family planning programs. Moreover, these countries contain a relatively high proportion of young people, which increases their potential for growth. For the most part those countries in which fertility has declined sharply are also the ones that have experienced rapid economic growth. For a variety of political, economic, and environmental reasons, the prospects for economic growth in most of the other developing countries are not as good. (Exceptions are certain Middle Eastern oil-producing countries, such as Kuwait, Qatar, and the United Arab Emirates.) Some demographers wonder if those countries will be able to enter the third stage of the demographic transition. They may revert instead to the first stage, in which high death rates offset high birth rates.

Population growth such as we have experienced since 1930 will continue for some time and can greatly affect the future geographic distribution of the world's population. It will also create pressures on the prevailing food supply, contribute to continued pressure on the supply of nonrenewable natural resources, and inhibit economic growth in developing countries. Those effects will be discussed later in this chapter.

THE FUTURE POPULATION

No one knows how much more the world's population will grow. Eventually it may even decrease in size. Future population change depends on future levels of fertility and mortality, and we can make only educated guesses about these. But we can use such educated guesses to make **population projections.** If our guesses on future levels of fertility and mortality are accurate, then the future population will coincide with the projected one. Demographers have learned the hard way that choosing the "right" set of birth and death rates is nearly impossible. So, instead of using only one set, they use different combinations of birth and death rates to project a number of possible future population sizes.

Use of Population Projections

There are several methods of making population projections. The most accepted is the cohort-component method. In this method the size and age-sex composition of the existing population are used as starting points. A series of death rates are applied to each age and sex category. That allows us to estimate how many people currently alive will survive until the date being projected. The number of births in each year is estimated by applying a series of fertility rates to the estimated number of potential mothers in that year. After allowances have been made for infant mortality, the projected births are added to the surviving population. The result is a new population, with its own age-sex composition and size. Note that in using this method a number of combinations of fertility and mortality rates must be applied.

Until we start colonizing the moon or accepting outer-space visitors, it is safe to assume that there is no net migration on the global level. However, net migration patterns are a factor when projecting local or national populations.

The U.S. Bureau of the Census has used the cohort-component method to project the world's population to the year 2000. Depending on which combination of birth and death rates is used, their projections range from 5.9 billion to 6.8 billion (U.S. Bureau of the Census 1979).

An interesting approach to projecting the world's population has been made by Tomas Frejka (1973*a* and 1973*b*). Rather than applying constant birth and death rates, Frejka started with current levels of fertility and mortality and varied the length of time it would take to arrive at **replacement level fertility (RLF)**—the level of fertility needed so that a child is born to replace each person in the parents' generation. It should not be confused with **zero population growth (ZPG)**, which means that in a given period of time, such as a year, the overall population does not change its size. In the long run the continuous occurrence of replacement level fertility will produce zero population growth in the global population, but in the short run it may not.

The reason that it may not is the age distribution. Populations with high fertility tend to have a relatively large proportion of young persons. This increases the **reproductive potential** of the population. Each young person is a potential future parent. Because of the relatively large number of young people, there will be more births than deaths. Thus, relatively young populations have a built-in potential for short-term growth. Even if each generation merely replaces itself, the population will continue to grow for some time.

This principle explains why the global population is unlikely to stop growing in the near future. Thirty-six percent of the earth's population was under the age of fifteen in 1979, so that even the immediate achievement of replacement level fertility would not result in zero population growth in the short run. Indeed, Frejka has shown that even if fertility had reached replacement level in the early 1970s, the earth's population still would have increased by 80 percent by the year 2050 simply because of the young age composition of the population.

Some characteristics of Frejka's projections of the world's population are shown in figure 2.3. In addition to offering alternative dates for the attainment of replacement level fertility, Frejka made the assumption that world mortality levels would gradually decline to the low levels currently present in the industrialized countries. You can see that the projected populations in the year 2100 vary considerably. Projections 1 and 2 are clearly impossible, for world fertility levels could not achieve replacement by 1985. Indeed, even given the most

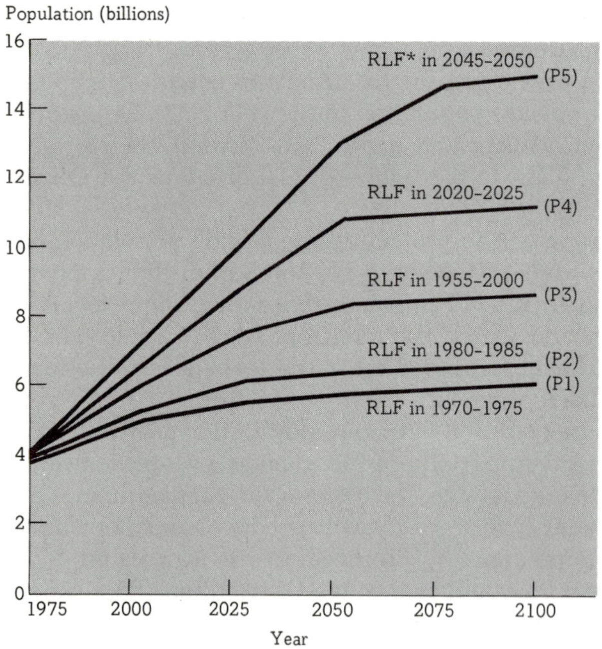

Figure 2.3 Projections of World Population Size, 1975–2100
Source: From "The Prospects for a Stationary World Population" by Tomas Frejka.

promising demographic developments possible, it is doubtful that world fertility could reach the replacement level before the end of the century. This brings us to projection 3. If this projection is realized, then the global population will be 8.2 billion by the middle of the next century, and the earth's population will not stop growing until it contains 8.4 billion people (roughly twice the number alive now).

In order for that projection to be realized, **completed family size** (the total number of live births to a woman who has finished childbearing) must decline significantly from current levels, especially in the developing countries. This is possible, but not very likely. Thus, projection 3 probably understates the future size of the world's population. Projection 4 or 5 may be more realistic. Projection 4 would produce a total population size of 10.5 billion persons by the middle of the next century. Eventually the population would stop growing around the year 2100, when there would be 11.2 billion people. Projection 5 results in an even larger population—13 billion by the year 2050 and 15.2 billion people in the year 2125, when the population stops growing.

Of course, these are only projections; they are not predictions. They are intended to point out a range of possibilities. We do not know exactly when replacement level fertility will be achieved, or even how it will occur. Mortality plays as important a role as fertility in producing population change. Most population projections assume constant or declining mortality. Almost none assume an increase in mortality. Yet this is a real possibility in several of the less developed regions of the world. Another development that is usually not considered is an increase in fertility in the developed countries, such as the one during our baby boom.

Despite these uncertainties demographers are sure of one thing: future population growth will be substantial. Moreover, this growth will not be distributed evenly throughout the world.

The developing countries are expected to account for 90 percent of the world population growth between now and the end of the century. One reason for this is the large number of people there under the age of fifteen who represent future parents. Another reason is that the gap between birth and death rates is much higher there than in the developed countries. Table 2.1 shows how populations will vary by region according to Frejka's projections 3, 4, and and 5.[5]

[5]Projections 1 and 2 have been omitted from this table to save space and make it easier to read and because they are impossible to attain on a global level. However, levels of childbearing in several European countries, Japan, and the United States are already at or below replacement levels. Hence, discounting the effects of net migration, projections 1 or 2 would be more realistic for those countries than projections 3, 4, or 5, which overstate the amount of population growth that will occur in highly modernized countries. The basic point remains, however: most future population growth will occur in the developing regions of the world.

Table 2.1 Projected Population of Major Regions of the World

REGION*	EST. 1980 POPULATION (MILLIONS)	PROJECTED POPULATION IN 2000			PROJECTED POPULATION IN 2050			PROJECTED POPULATION IN 2100		
		Proj. 3	Proj. 4	Proj. 5	Proj. 3	Proj. 4	Proj. 5	Proj. 3	Proj. 4	Proj. 5
East Asia	1,173	1,485	1,592	1,646	2,002	2,487	3,011	2,062	2,467	3,448
South Asia	1,390	2,079	2,339	2,469	3,077	4,350	5,916	3,166	4,711	7,170
Europe	484	561	572	578	641	692	739	645	708	778
U.S.S.R.	266	314	318	320	353	371	387	355	376	401
Africa	472	620	693	729	899	1,244	1,664	934	1,351	2,003
North America	247	302	310	315	368	406	444	372	418	475
Latin America	360	540	598	626	797	1,077	1,396	823	1,172	1,683
Oceania	23	27	28	29	35	41	47	36	43	52
World Total	4,414	5,928	6,450	6,712	8,172	10,668	13,025	8,393	11,426	15,102

*Regions containing a number of developing countries are italicized.

Sources: Frejka (1973*a*), pp. 86–87; and Population Reference Bureau (1980).

SOME CONSEQUENCES OF WORLD POPULATION GROWTH

During the past forty years the world's population has grown very rapidly. Although the rate of population growth has declined slightly since the early 1970s, we have noted that the world's population will continue to increase for quite a while. This growth has a number of social, economic, and ecological consequences. For instance, the world's population is currently increasing faster than the amount of available usable energy. Energy is a basic need of any population. And, while often overlooked as a form of energy, food is the most fundamental energy requirement.

Population Growth and the Food Supply

Food requirements are very difficult to establish. They vary according to the body size, age, and activity of a person. In the late 1960s the President's Science Advisory Committee estimated that each person in the world needs at a minimum 2,354 calories daily (Ehrlich and Ehrlich 1970, p. 69). An examination of available data shows that in numerous countries the average number of calories available **per capita** (or per person) is lower than this figure. Indeed, in only half of the 162 countries for which data are available did the average number of calories per person in the period from 1972 to 1974 equal this minimum (United Nations 1978*a*, pp. 241–242).[6] The range of figures is from 1,728 (Upper Volta) to 3,637 (Belgium-Luxembourg). These are averages, so they conceal the even lower caloric intake of those persons in the lower socioeconomic classes of the various countries. Also, these figures do not take into account the large number of people whose diet lacks sufficient amounts of such essential nutrients as protein. Altogether, perhaps 2 billion people in the developing countries are chronically undernourished, resulting in low vitality, vulnerability to disease, and high mortality (Department of State 1978).

The prevailing distribution system is partly responsible for this situation. Food is unequally distributed at several levels—between the economically developed and developing countries, among regions within the developed countries, among economic classes within a given society, and even within families themselves. Some countries of the world grow so much food that they can export the surplus to other countries. The United States illustrates the importance of the distribution system. It is a major exporter of food on the world market and in the past has even paid some of its farmers not to grow certain types of grain in order to prevent a surplus. Nevertheless, an estimated 10

[6]Obtaining current data for the various countries in the world is very difficult. Occasionally the authors are forced to use data that appear to be out of date but are the most recent data available to them.

million Americans are undernourished (Hearings of Select Committee on Nutrition and Human Needs 1977).

Even if the world did have a perfect distribution system, there can be little doubt that the global population would strain the means of subsistence. If population continues to increase at current rates, bumper crop years and technological breakthroughs such as the **Green Revolution** (a term coined in 1968 to describe the introduction and rapid adoption world wide of high-yielding wheat and rice) will merely postpone the inevitable—food shortages and even massive hunger and starvation in some areas. This position is compatible with that of Thomas Malthus, who painted a grim picture of population growth and food supply.

The Malthusian Principle

In 1798 Thomas Malthus, an English clergyman and scholar, wrote "An Essay on the Principle of Population," which proposed that population, when unchecked, tends to double once every generation. Food shortages arise because, while the population doubles geometrically (1, 2, 4, 8, 16, . . .), the "means of subsistence" tend to increase at an arithmetic rate (1, 2, 3, 4, 5, . . .).

According to Malthus there are two ways to halt human population growth—preventive checks and positive checks. The only acceptable preventive check to Malthus was "moral restraint"—refraining from premarital intercourse and postponing marriage. Malthus classified other types of preventive checks (homosexuality, contraception, and abortion) as "vice." The positive checks include war, famine, and disease.

By definition, in the long run population cannot exceed the food supply. So there *have* to be some checks. Malthus doubted the ability of people to apply moral restraint, and he viewed the other types of preventive checks as unacceptable because they were "immoral." That left the positive checks to limit population growth in the future.

The Situation Today

Today major portions of Malthus's line of reasoning are suspect, particularly his doubts concerning people's ability (and willingness) to practice "moral restraint" and his rejection of contraception and abortion as immoral (though the latter view is still held by some people). Several elements in his work are highly regarded, however.

Malthus was concerned not with the ultimate carrying capacity of the earth but with the tendency for population to grow faster than food supplies. This is a valid concern. It is easy to see that the world could eventually feed a population several times larger than the present one. And unquestionably the present distribution system could be improved. But changing the current distribution system and providing for a population that is larger than the current one are quite different matters from *continually* increasing food supplies to keep pace with rapid population growth (Abercrombie 1976).

Regarding food production there have been swings between optimism and pessimism since World War II. The war itself caused optimism because of the benefits achieved by international cooperation and because people believed that the new technologies could be used to produce all the food that might be needed to meet foreseeable population increases. During the early 1960s, however, new sources of data revealed that a population explosion was taking place in the developing countries and that, in some of these, food shortages did exist. Since then, there have been additional swings between optimism and pessimism, depending on the weather (prolonged droughts produced gloom) and changes in technology (the Green Revolution produced cheer).

On the global level food production has kept ahead of population growth since World War II because large gains in population have been offset by large gains in total food production. This means that per capita food production did not decline. But a somewhat different impression is obtained when data are examined for specific regions, rather than for the world as a whole. In the industrialized nations food production increased an average of 2.7 percent per year during the 1968–1977 interval, while population increased an average of 1 percent annually. This means that per capita food production gained an average of 1.7 percent a year. However, in the developing countries (excluding communist Asia, for which data are lacking), a food production increase of 2.95 percent a year was largely offset by a population increase of 2.6 percent a year.

The result may be seen in figure 2.4, which contains data for grain production between 1960 and 1977. Per capita production increased in the developed countries but not in the developing ones. A 1977 survey by the Food and Agriculture Organization (FAO) found that per capita daily caloric supplies actually declined in forty-four countries between 1961 and 1963 and between 1972 and 1974 (United Nations 1977, p. 17). What makes this per capita decrease particularly meaningful is that levels of food consumption were already low in those countries.

More recently a preliminary report of a presidental commission on world hunger concluded that the world's food situation is getting worse rather than better. Even with the good world harvests of the late 1970s, the report states that the number of the world's hungry has grown from 740 million to 800 million (President's Commission on World Hunger 1979). The only hope for the developing countries is to import food from the developed countries, but as the 1979 report points out, "The better-off developing countries, the OPEC countries, and the USSR are today the chief customers in the grain market, with the result that the poorest of the poor are being priced out of the market" (*Christian Science Monitor* 1979, p. 22).

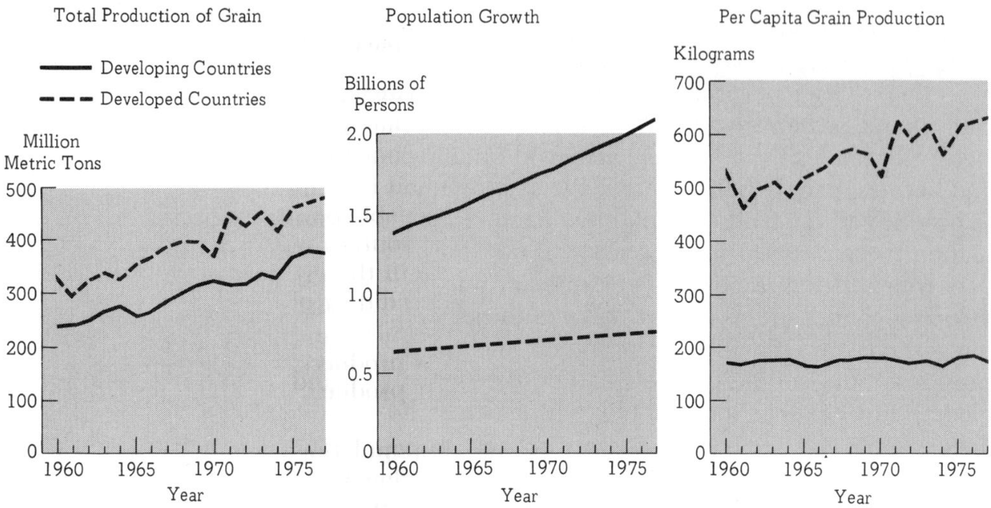

Figure 2.4. Population Growth and Grain Production, 1960–1977, Excluding Centrally Planned Economies

Note: Grain production comprises on the average 35 percent of total food production in developed countries and 64 percent in developing countries. The greater variations in total and per capita grain production in developed than in developing countries are attributable to greater weather variations in temperate than in tropical farming zones and to more extensive policy interventions by developed than developing country governments in farm acreage and production levels.

Source: Department of State (1978), p. 15.

The Example of India

The growth of demand for food is mainly determined by growth of population and increases in per capita income, which make it possible for each person to spend more on food (Brown 1973). Needless to say, in almost all the developing countries, the population effect is greater than the income effect. India, for example, has increased its total food production considerably, but its per capita consumption of food has not increased because there have been equally great increases in population. In 1964–1966 there were 2,457 calories available for each person's consumption, a level roughly equal to the minimum standards. This has not changed significantly. Although food production increased by 27 percent over the next decade, population size increased by over 25 percent.

India's food situation is fluctuating. In the mid-1960s, the government redesigned its food policies and priorities, which gave Indian agriculture a big boost. Grain imports dropped considerably, and India was on the brink of self-sufficiency (as far as grain was concerned) by 1972. Since then there have been several poor harvests, while India's population has continued to grow. India has been forced to rely increasingly on grain imports, most of which come from North America.

Future Prospects

What are the prospects for increasing the availability of food? Food could be made more available in several ways: increasing the amount of land under cultivation, increasing the yield of each unit of land, altering dietary habits, exploiting new sources of food supply (such as the ocean), and reducing food losses due to spoilage and rodents (Ehrlich and Ehrlich 1970, pp. 101–103). But even though major breakthroughs in any of these areas could occur in the future, they are all short-term solutions.

It is extremely difficult to increase the available food supply as rapidly as the population increases. As of now, such increases are barely keeping pace with population growth. Moreover, some of the poorer countries are growing so rapidly that their population can be expected to double within the next twenty to twenty-five years, but they cannot be expected to increase their food production that much. Given the currently inadequate nutritional levels in these countries, the available food supply would have to be increased by a *greater* amount than the population to prevent widespread malnutrition and periodic starvation.

Population Growth and Other Sources of Energy

Of course, food is only one type of energy. We need other types of energy to manufacture fertilizers, run machinery, operate factories, travel from one place to another, construct buildings, and maintain a given life style. The rapid population growth being experienced by the world's population has definite effects on the availability of these other forms of energy.

The Consumption Explosion

Given present rates of world population growth, the amount of material goods produced must be doubled every forty-one years just to maintain today's levels of consumption. Part of this increase will be possible because production is being made more efficient. However, increased pressure on the available natural resources is practically unavoidable. More than half of the world's total consumption of energy from fossil fuels (oil, coal, gas) since the beginning of historical time has taken place since 1947. Fossil fuels are being used currently at rates that may lead to their depletion within a few decades.

Efforts of the existing population to improve its standard of living will only compound the pressure on natural resources. Currently, any pressure is attributable more to rapidly increasing levels of consumption per capita than to population growth per se. However, population growth interacts with consumption levels by producing *more* people with *higher* levels of consumption (United Nations 1973, pp. 389–397).

The total world needs for energy will increase significantly for the rest of this century, partly in response to population growth.

The consumption explosion raises grave doubts about how long current sources of energy can produce adequate supplies at reasonable prices. It is clear we need to develop alternative sources of energy. Nuclear power is already being used, but it may have harmful effects on the environment. Other sources, such as tidal, wind, and geothermal power, may be more limited in scope. Solar energy is perhaps the most promising major alternative to conventional energy sources. Yet currently, the installation of solar equipment is very expensive, and solar energy is not suited for widespread use in some regions of the world. It will be some time before these alternative sources of energy are readily available.

In the meantime present sources of energy could be used more efficiently. We could conserve by developing and expanding mass transit systems; producing smaller, more economical cars; improving insulation and heating systems; reclaiming and recycling more materials such as aluminum; improving the efficiency of home appliances; and reducing heating and lighting levels (Population Reference Bureau 1977). Without such conservation measures energy will be used needlessly and wastefully. Even with such measures the pressures on the available energy supplies will be severe, and we may have to alter our current patterns of energy consumption considerably.

Variations in Consumption Patterns

The differences in energy consumption between the developed countries and the developing countries may be seen in figure 2.5. Latin America, Asia, and Africa (which contain almost all the world's developing countries) have much lower levels of energy consumption per person than do the other regions of the world. Moreover, energy consumption has not increased as much since 1950 in these regions as in the more economically developed countries. The developed countries of the world consume about 80 percent of the world's energy each year, even though they contain only one-fourth of the world's population.

The amount of energy consumed also varies by income level within a given country. For instance, in the United States households in the highest income group use almost four times as much energy (on the average) as those in the lowest group (Freeman 1975).

Despite the relatively low amounts of energy consumed by lower-class Americans, the overall level of consumption in America is very high compared to the rest of the world. This makes ecologists very sensitive to the American consumption level and the impact it has on the world's supply of energy.

For instance, the United States represents only 5 percent of the world's population, yet it consumes about 35 percent of its natural resources and produces about 50 percent of its pollution. By contrast, In-

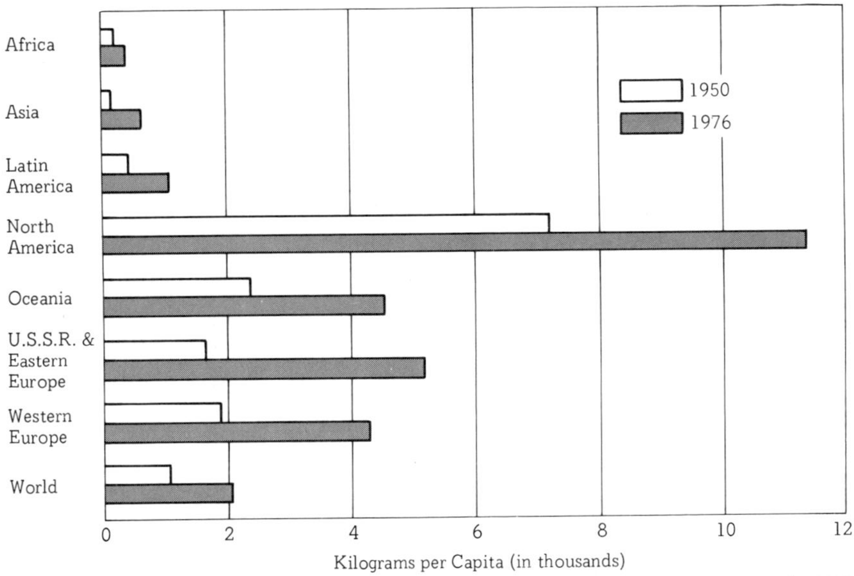

Figure 2.5 Per Capita Energy Consumption by World Regions, 1950 and 1976
Sources: United Nations (1978); and Population Reference Bureau (1977).

dia, which contains about 15 percent of the world's population, uses only about 1.5 percent of the total energy consumed each year. The average American uses 50 times as much steel, 56 times as much energy, 170 times as much synthetic rubber and newsprint, 250 times as much motor fuel, and 300 times as much plastic as the average citizen of India (Ehrlich and Holdren 1971; and Population Reference Bureau 1977). Indeed, based on environmental impact, some people assert that the United States is the most overpopulated country in the world. As G. Tyler Miller has stated, "With an impact factor of 25 to 50 times that of poorer countries, our population of 214 million is equivalent to a pollution population of somewhere between 5 and 10 billion" (1975, p. 15).

The international differences in levels of energy consumption result more from differences in the ability to pay for energy than from differences in tastes. The differences in per capita income among various countries are startling. For instance, in 1975 per capita income in the United States was $6,291, while it was $390 in Africa, $1,060 in Latin America, $1,440 in the Middle East, and $540 in eastern and southern Asia (United Nations 1978*b*, pp. 745–749). Of course, these are average figures; income is seldom distributed evenly within a population. Nevertheless, the low levels of per capita income among two-thirds of the world's population cause great concern among economists and developmental planners, and a great deal of attention has been given to how these nations will be able to improve their per capita incomes and standards of living in the future.

The outlook for future economic growth in these developing countries depends on several factors, among them, availability (and cost) of scarce resources, technological advances, and the rate of population growth. As mentioned earlier, the developing countries have relatively high rates of population growth, which may limit the possibilities of economic growth.

The Effect of Rapid Population Growth on Economic Development

Rapid population growth in the developing countries is produced by a combination of high birth rates and low death rates. This population growth adversely affects economic growth in two ways—by increasing the total size of the population and by producing a population that is relatively young.

Table 2.2 shows the number of years it takes to double the population for various rates of growth. The higher the rate of population growth, the shorter the doubling time. As the population grows, additional services must be provided; more houses, jobs, and food are needed; more roads must be built; and so forth. Otherwise the standard of living will decline, because there will be fewer services, houses, job opportunities, and the like per person. Just to maintain the standard of living, then, costs money, and rapid population growth reduces the amount of time needed to save this money (or capital). If there were no population growth, this capital could be used to increase standards of living.

The amount of capital absorbed by population growth is difficult to estimate. Economists generally say that every percent of population growth requires a 3 or 4 percent growth in the gross national product (GNP)—the total market value of all goods and services a country produces. Thus, a population growing at 1 percent a year needs to reinvest 3 to 4 percent of the GNP in order to prevent the standard of living from declining. Countries whose populations are growing at 3 percent a year need to reinvest between 9 and 12 percent of their

Table 2.2 Doubling Time for Various Rates of Population Growth

PERCENT OF ANNUAL GROWTH RATE	YEARS TO DOUBLE POPULATION
1.0	69
1.5	46
2.0	35
2.5	28
3.0	23
3.5	20
4.0	17

GNP. Even greater reinvestment is needed to increase standards of living instead of merely maintaining current ones. Yet developing countries generally have a severe shortage of reinvestment capital.

The combination of high birth rates and low death rates present in most developing countries increases the ratio of young dependents (under age fifteen) to persons in the economically active ages (fifteen to sixty-four). This may be seen in figure 2.7, which compares the **age-sex pyramid** of a developing country (Pakistan) to one for a developed country (Sweden) in 1975. (The construction of an age-sex pyramid is described in box 2.2). Note that the pyramid for Pakistan is very broad at the base; about 45 percent of the population is under age fifteen. By contrast, the pyramid for Sweden has a narrower base; less than 25 percent of its population is under age fifteen.

These differences are typical of those present throughout the world, as can be seen in figure 2.6. Notice that in most developing re-

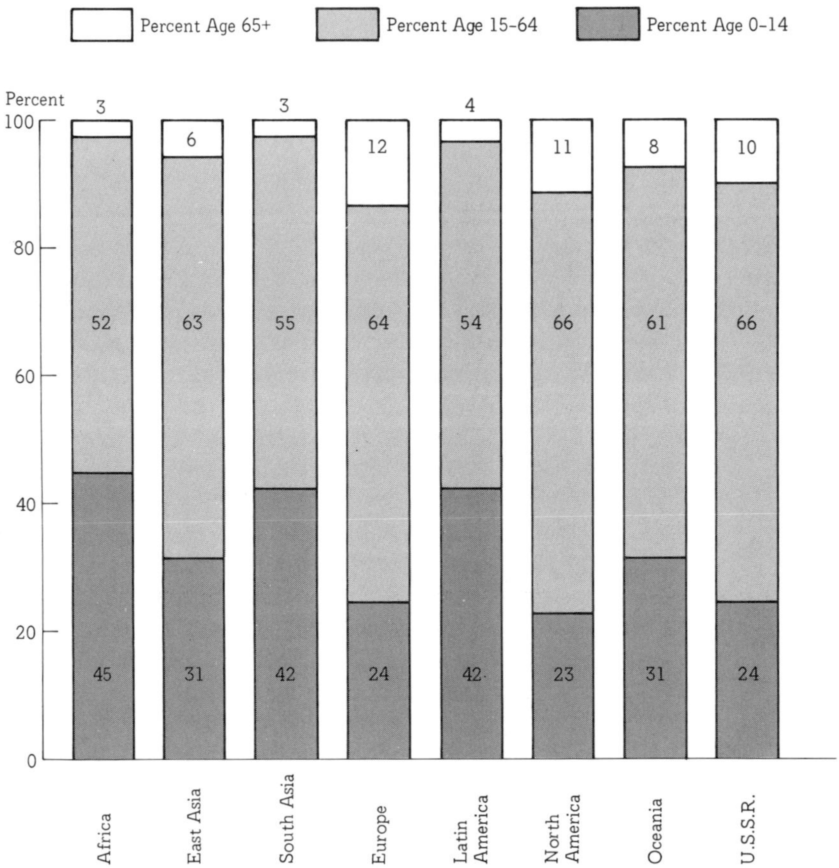

Figure 2.6 Population of Major Regions of the World by Age, 1980
Source: Population Reference Bureau (1980).

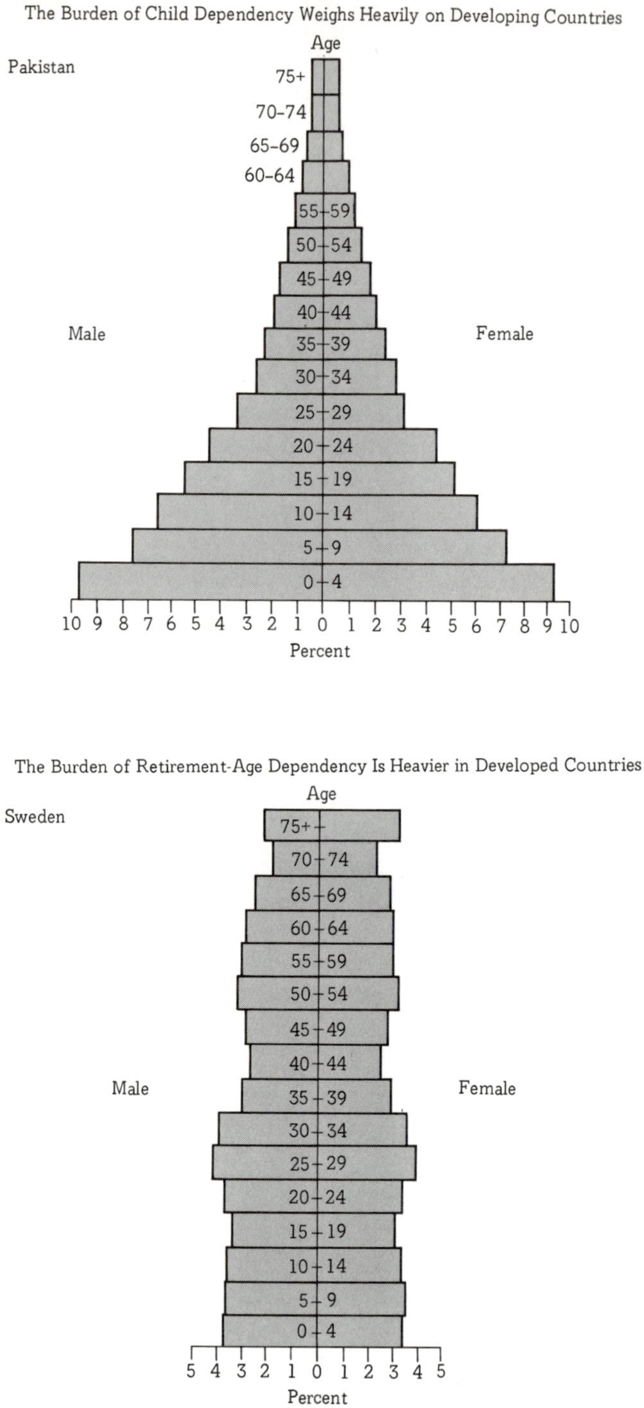

Figure 2.7 Age-Sex Pyramids for Pakistan and Sweden, 1975

Source: Department of State (1978), p. 6.

Box 2.2 Constructing an Age-Sex Pyramid

An age-sex pyramid is a bar graph which depicts the proportion (or number) of persons in each age and sex category. It is called a pyramid because it often resembles one, and it tends to be smaller at the top (which contains the older age groups) than at the bottom (which contains the younger ones). An age-sex pyramid gives a picture of population composition with respect to age and sex at any given point in time and shows the effect of past levels of fertility, mortality, and migration.

Constructing one is simple. Place every member of the population being studied into mutually exclusive age-sex categories. Usually five-year spans for each age group are used—0–4, 5–9, 10–14, and so forth—until the upper limit of 75+ or 85+ is reached. Males appear on the left side and females on the right side of the pyramid. Age-sex pyramids may be constructed either by using the actual number of persons in each of the age-sex categories or by calculating the percent of the total population in each category. We have used the latter form of construction, which is useful for comparing different populations.

An age-sex pyramid for the population of the United States in 1979 may be constructed as follows:

Estimated Population of the United States, July 1, 1979 (in thousands)

AGE	MALE	FEMALE	TOTAL
0–4	8,003	7,646	15,649
5–9	8,424	8,069	16,493
10–14	9,212	8,859	18,071
15–19	10,633	10,285	20,918
20–24	10,435	10,292	20,726
25–29	9,181	9,260	18,441
30–34	8,221	8,362	16,583
35–39	6,661	6,954	13,615
40–44	5,612	5,909	11,521
45–49	5,476	5,746	11,222
50–54	5,667	6,068	11,735
55–59	5,428	5,939	11,367
60–64	4,487	5,098	9,585
65–69	3,865	4,823	8,688
70–74	2,777	3,807	6,584
75–79	1,678	2,596	4,274
80–84	977	1,803	2,780
85	720	1,612	2,332
Total	107,457	113,128	220,584

$$\text{Percent Male 0–4} = \left(\frac{8{,}003}{220{,}584}\right) 100 = 3.6$$

$$\text{Percent Female 0–4} = \left(\frac{7{,}646}{220{,}584}\right) 100 = 3.5$$

You should then proceed to calculate the proportions of the *total* population in each age-sex group.

gions at least 40 percent of the population is under age fifteen, compared to 24–31 percent in the other regions of the world. The developed regions have a greater proportion of elderly persons (age sixty-five and older). But these differences at the older ages are much smaller than the differences at the younger ages. Consequently, the developed regions have about 10 percent more of their population in the potentially productive ages between fifteen and sixty-four.

The large number of dependent children relative to the size of the labor force promotes spending for immediate consumption, restricts private and public saving, and absorbs resources needed for investment in economic development. Moreover, when the children reach working age, they create severe pressures on the ability of the urban and rural labor markets to absorb them. This increases levels of unemployment and underemployment and further contributes to lower standards of living. Other things being equal, a population in which the percent of the population under fifteen drops from 40 to 25 would increase its per capita income by approximately 25 percent (United Nations 1973, p. 442). The developing countries can attain such a goal only through dramatic reductions in fertility or, less happily, increased levels of infant and child mortality.

WILL STOPPING POPULATION GROWTH SOLVE OUR PROBLEMS?

Planet Earth is beset with countless problems: the threat of nuclear war; famine and malnutrition in some parts of the world; an unequal distribution of income; racial, religious, and sex discrimination; assorted types of crime (on the street, in big business, and in politics); the potential exhaustion of nonrenewable resources; and deterioration of the environment. Some people claim that a **population explosion** has created these various problems and that the way to solve them is simply to stop population growth, but this vastly oversimplifies the matter.

For one thing, there are ways to handle these problems without having to stop population growth. Nuclear war is avoidable. Famine and malnutrition can be eradicated (in the short run, at least) if the wealthy nations share with the poorer ones, and if distribution systems are improved. Unequal distribution of income among nations and within them could be ameliorated independent of any changes in rates of population growth. Discrimination and crime can be minimized by the development of a greater social conscience and a better enforcement of existing laws.

This is not to say that population growth has absolutely no relation to the problems facing people. But we must realize that there is no single "cause" or "solution" for our social difficulties. The problems facing humans result from the very complicated interaction of a number of factors. Population growth is one of these factors, especially when it is rapid. Of course, while stopping world population growth would not completely solve the world's problems, it would certainly make it *easier* to solve some of them. In any case, it is clear that eventually the world population will *have* to stop growing.

The Ultimate Need for Zero Population Growth

The earth is finite. Prolonged growth *at any rate* will eventually fill this finite space. For instance, in 1974 Ansley Coale noted that if the then current rate of population growth (2 percent) continued, in less than 700 years there would be one person for every square foot on the earth's surface (Coale 1974, p. 51). Obviously there are limits to growth. When they are reached, the earth's population will have to stop growing because of an increase in the death rate and/or a decrease in the birth rate. We do not know when this will happen, what size the earth's population will be, what the prevailing standards of living will be, or what combination of birth and death rates will produce this nongrowth. But it will happen.

These comments do not mean that at some point in the distant future the population will suddenly stop growing and never again increase its size. More likely, the rate of population growth will gradually approach zero and the size of the population will fluctuate. Increases will be followed by decreases, and vice versa. However, the *average* rate of growth will, of necessity, be zero. This demographic situation would be very similar to the one in prehistoric times, except that the absolute number of people involved would be much larger.

Nongrowth need not be produced by the combination of high birth and death rates that prevailed in prehistoric times. Instead, it could result from a combination of low birth and death rates. Additionally, the global population may stop growing before the limits to growth are reached, due perhaps to dramatic declines in the birth rate or to some catastrophe (such as a nuclear war) that obliterates a significant proportion of the population.

Given a choice between lowering fertility and raising mortality, we do not really have much choice. Fertility should be reduced. As noted earlier, populations with high fertility have a built-in potential for continued growth because of their relatively young age composition. Thus, the sooner fertility is reduced, the more likely continued survival becomes. But how can the birth rate be reduced? A number of people believe that making contraceptives and abortion freely available to everyone will be sufficient. Other persons disagree; they believe that demographic behavior reflects the social, cultural, and economic environment in which it occurs, and so the way to alter demographic behavior is to change that environment. Instead of giving the highest priority to birth control programs, they propose institutional change and economic development. These divergent approaches to lowering fertility are discussed at length in chapter 11.

SUMMARY

Throughout most of human existence the population has grown very slowly. Both high death rates and high birth rates prevailed. World population growth began to accelerate after 1650, when death rates began to fall faster than birth rates.

Until 1900 world population growth was concentrated in the relatively industrialized countries. However, as these countries experienced the demographic transition, their birth rates declined to balance their low death rates. Since 1920 world population growth has been concentrated in the developing countries, a trend that will continue in the foreseeable future. In these countries death rates have declined significantly, while the birth rates have remained high.

Some of the developing countries have experienced declines in fertility since 1970, but the world's population is increasing at an annual rate of 1.7 percent. It can be expected to double in size every forty-one years if this rate of growth continues. Unless death rates suddenly increase, population projections show there will be at least 6 billion people alive by the end of the century, partly because of the relatively young age composition of the present global population.

The rapid growth of the world's population contributes significantly to several problems facing humans: massive malnutrition in some parts of the world, pressures on nonrenewable natural resources, and low standards of living in many countries. Stopping growth would not completely solve these problems, but it would make it easier to solve them.

Eventually the world's population must stop growing because we inhabit a finite space. Nongrowth can come about because of a combination of high death rates that balance high birth rates or because of a combination of low birth and death rates. The latter alternative is preferable. Thus, the birth rate must be lowered, especially in developing countries. Two approaches to lowering fertility are to institute massive family planning programs and to make institutional changes that will bring about the desired changes in fertility behavior.

REFERENCES AND SUGGESTED READINGS

Abercrombie, K. C. 1976. Population and food. In *Population growth and economic development in the Third World,* ed. Leon Tabah, pp. 345–389. Liege: Ordina Editions.

Brown, Lester R. 1973. Population and affluence: growing pressures on world food resources. *Population bulletin* 29.

Christian Science Monitor. 1979. Hunger—a sober report. (December 12):22.

Clark, Colin, 1968. *Population growth and land use.* New York: St. Martin's Press.

Coale, Ansley J. 1974. The history of the human population. *Scientific American* 231 (September):41–51.

———. 1975. The demographic transition. In *The population debate: dimensions and perspectives,* vol. I, pp. 347–355. New York: United Nations.

———. 1978. Population growth and economic development: the case of Mexico. *Foreign affairs* 56 (January):415–429.

Coale, Ansley, and Hoover, Edgar M. 1958. *Population growth and economic development in low-income countries.* Princeton, N.J.: Princeton University Press.

Department of State. 1978. Silent explosion. *Department of State bulletin* (Fall). Washington, D.C.: Government Printing Office.

Durand, John D. 1967. The modern expansion of world population. *Proceedings of the American Philosophical Society* 111 (June): 136–159.

———. 1977. Historical estimates of world population: an evaluation. *Population and development review* 3 (September):253–296.

Ehrlich, Paul R., and Ehrlich, Anne H. 1970. *Population, resources, environment.* San Francisco: W. H. Freeman.

Ehrlich, Paul R. and Holdren, John. 1971. Impact of population growth. *Science* 171 (March 26):1212–1217.

Fredericksen, Harold. 1960. Malaria control and population pressure in Ceylon. *Public health reports* 75 (October):865–868.

———. 1961. Determinants and consequences of population trends in Ceylon. *Public health reports* 76 (August):659–663.

Freeman, S. David. 1975. Energy: a time to choose. *Interchange* 4 (February): 1–2.

Frejka, Tomas. 1973*a*. *The future of population growth: alternative paths to equilibrium.* New York: John Wiley & Sons.

———. 1973*b*. The prospects for a stationary world population. *Scientific American* 228 (March):15–23.

Gordon, Lincoln. 1976. Limits to growth debate. *Resources* 52 (Summer):1–6.

Gray, R. H. 1974. The decline of mortality in Ceylon and the demographic effects of malaria control. *Population studies* 28 (July):205–229.

Habakkuk, H. J. 1953. English population in the eighteenth century. *Economic history review* 6 (December):117–133.

Haupt, Arthur. 1979. World population growth in 1979: still soaring. *Intercom* 7 (April):1, 4–5.

Hearings of Select Committee on Nutrition and Human Needs. 1977. U.S. House of Representatives, February 2, 1977.

Kirk, Dudley. 1971. A new demographic transition? In *Rapid population growth,* ed. National Academy of Sciences, pp. 123–147. Baltimore: Johns Hopkins Press.

May, David A, and Heer, David M. 1968. Son survivorship motivation and family size in India: a computer simulation. *Population studies* 22 (July):199–210.

McKeown, Thomas. 1976. *The modern rise of population.* New York: Academic Press.

Meegama, S. A. 1967. Malaria eradication and its effect on mortality levels. *Population studies* 21 (November):207–237.

Miller, G. Tyler, Jr. 1975. *Living in the environment: concepts, problems, and alternatives.* Belmont, Calif.: Wadsworth Publishing.

Newman, Peter. 1970. Malaria control and population growth. *The journal of developmental studies* 6 (January):133–158.

Notestein, Frank W. 1945. Population—the long view. In *Food for the world,* ed. Theodore W. Schultz, pp. 36–57. Chicago: University of Chicago Press.

Notestein, Frank W., Kirk, Dudley, and Segal, Sheldon. 1969. The problem of population control. In *The population dilemma,* 2nd ed., ed. Philip M. Hauser, pp. 139–167. Englewood Cliffs, N.J.: Prentice-Hall.

Palloni, Alberto. 1975. Comments on R. H. Gray's "The decline in mortality in Ceylon and the demographic effects of malaria control." *Population studies* 29 (November):497–499.

Petersen, William. 1960. The demographic transition in the Netherlands. *American sociological review* 25 (June):334–347.

Population Reference Bureau. 1962. How many people have ever lived on earth? *Population bulletin* 18 (February):1–18.

———. 1976. *World population growth.* Washington, D.C.: Population Reference Bureau.

———. 1977. Energy: increasing consumption, decreasing resources. *Interchange* 6 (January):1–2.

———. 1978. *1978 world population data sheet.* Washington, D.C.: Population Reference Bureau.

———. 1980. *1980 world population data sheet.* Washington, D.C.: Population Reference Bureau.

President's Commission on World Hunger. 1979. *A preliminary report.* Washington, D.C.: Government Printing Office.

Russell, J. C. 1958. Late ancient and medieval population. *Transactions of the American Philosophical Society* 48, new series (June).

Tsui, Amy Ong, and Bogue, Donald J. 1978. Declining world fertility: trends, causes, implications. *Population bulletin* 33 (October).

Tuchman, Barbara W. 1978. *A distant mirror.* New York: Alfred A. Knopf.

United Nations. 1973. *The determinants and consequences of population change,* vol. I. New York: United Nations.

———. 1977. *The Fourth World food survey.* Rome: Food and Agricultural Organization of the United Nations.

———. 1978*a*. *FAO production yearbook, 1977.* Rome: Food and Agricultural Organization of the United Nations.

———. 1978*b*. *Statistical yearbook, 1977.* New York: United Nations.

U.S. Bureau of the Census. 1979. Illustrative projections of world populations to the 21st century. *Current population reports,* series P-23, no. 79. Washington, D.C.: Government Printing Office.

3
Population Change in the United States

The less developed countries in Asia, South America, and Africa have a population explosion; the United States does not. However, we have earned a position of unique demographic importance within the world because we are the world's fourth largest nation (after China, India, and the Soviet Union) and because our levels of consumption are so high. As we saw in chapter 2, per capita consumption of scarce resources is much higher in the United States than in other countries. Thus, any signs of population growth in the United States are potentially of great concern to ecologists and planners, and many of them have contended that it should be limited at all costs.

This chapter traces the pattern of population growth from colonial to modern times and then examines some projections of the future population of the United States. In doing so, it shows how dramatically the patterns of fertility, mortality, and migration have changed during the past one hundred years. It also demonstrates how variations in fertility can greatly affect our future.

HISTORY OF POPULATION CHANGE IN THE UNITED STATES

By the time Columbus approached the North American continent, there were perhaps over 1 million persons already living in what is now called the United States. The number of Native Americans declined considerably over the next 400 years, until in 1890 there were only about 250,000 of them. This decline probably resulted from attrition during the course of the continuous warfare they conducted in defense of their tribal lands as well as from the unusual hardships imposed and diseases introduced by white settlers (Bogue 1969, pp. 127–129). The number of American Indians has increased during this century. (About 800,000 were enumerated in the 1970 census.) Still, they comprise less than .5 percent of the total population of the United States. Obviously the substantial growth of the U.S. population has occurred among the non-Indians (and perhaps even at the expense of the Indians).

The Colonial Period, 1607–1790

The first permanent colonial settlement was at Jamestown, Virginia, which had over one hundred colonists when it was founded on May 14, 1607. Although the number of surviving colonists was reduced to forty by December of that year, new colonists arrived from England, and the population grew. By 1610 Virginia contained 350 settlers. New colonies were founded. The non-Indian population of the colonies was over 2,000 in 1620 and is estimated to have been 50,000 in 1650. By 1790, when the first U.S. census was taken, there were almost 4 million persons enumerated. The eightyfold increase from 1650 to 1790 is surely one of the most spectacular examples of population growth in history.

During the decades immediately following settlement, **immigration** (the migration of persons into a country) played a major role in producing population growth. Reproductive change apparently played the major role during the latter portions of the colonial period. Our knowledge of demographic conditions during this period is very rough. It is believed that fertility was quite high and mortality was only moderately high. In fact, two noted demographers have estimated that at the end of the eighteenth century the crude birth rate was about 55 per 1,000 and the crude death rate was about 25 per 1,000 population (Thompson and Whelpton 1933, p. 263). This rate of reproductive change alone would increase the population by 3 percent annually. Massive immigration compounded this growth.

Whatever the cause, the non-Indian population of the United States grew to almost 4 million persons in 1790. About four out of five of these persons were whites. Most of these were of English or Irish birth or ancestry; others came from Holland, Sweden, Spain, and France. About one out of five was black. Most of these were slaves who had involuntarily immigrated to the United States from Africa. Their forced migration began slowly in the seventeenth century and increased in the eighteenth and early ninteenth centuries; the settlement of blacks was concentrated in the South (Taeuber and Taeuber 1971, pp.3–4).

The Nineteenth Century

Figure 3.1 shows total population increase during the nineteenth century by decades. By 1800 there were 5.3 million, which represents an increase of 35 percent over the population of 4 million just a decade earlier. This rate of growth was repeated in each decade to 1850—but always on a larger base. By mid-century there were 23.2 million Americans—almost a fivefold increase in only fifty years.

Most of the population increase between 1800 and 1850 took place on the Atlantic seaboard. That is why the **population density,** or number of persons per unit of land, actually increased from 6.1 persons per square mile in 1800 to 7.9 persons per square mile in 1850, even though the nation's land area had grown significantly to cover the size of the continental United States. The western portion of the country remained empty—except for the Indians, most of whom were not counted in the census until 1890.

After 1850 the rate of population growth slowed somewhat, although the population still managed to triple in size by 1900. About 76 million Americans were counted in the 1900 census. By then there were 25.6 persons per square mile.

In the last half of the century the Industrial Revolution acceler-

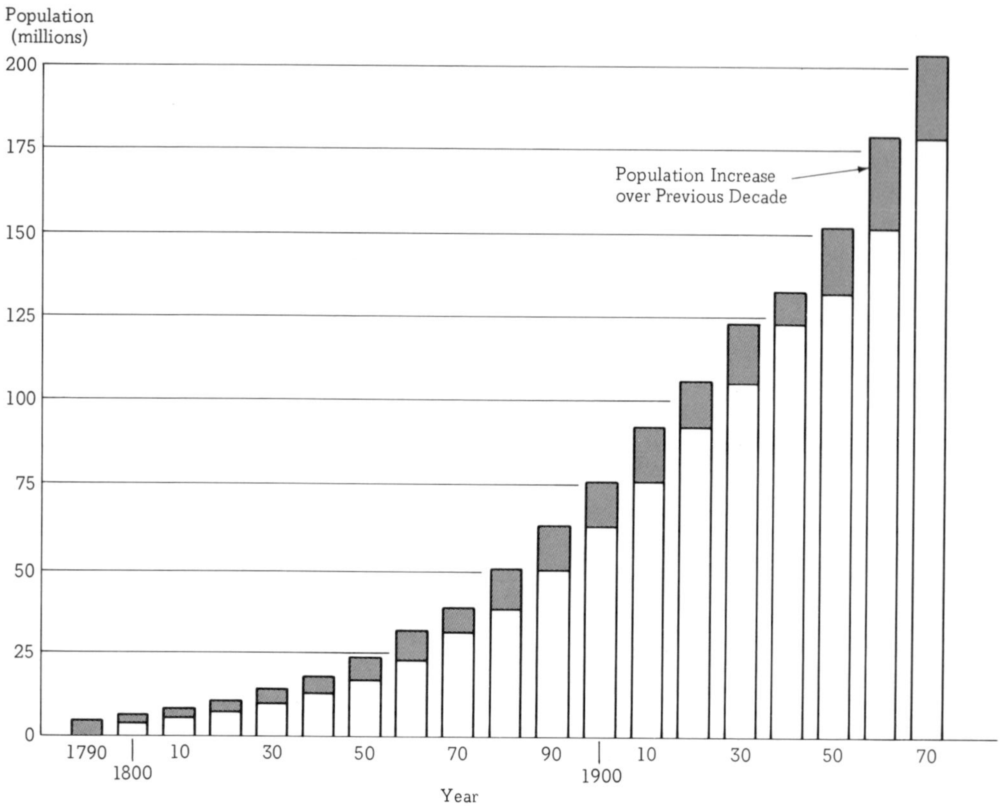

Figure 3.1 Total Population and Increase in Population by Decade, 1790–1970
Source: Kaplan and Van Valey (1980), p. 196.

ated and urbanization intensified. By the end of the century almost 40 percent of the people lived in urban areas, compared to a mere 15 percent in 1850. The society also became increasingly heterogeneous. Until the middle of the nineteenth century, most of the population was white and of Anglo-Saxon ancestry. These persons, along with the blacks and the few Indians that were enumerated, comprised the American population. However, new waves of immigration during the latter decades of the nineteenth century brought people from southern Europe and from Asia, particularly China and Japan. By 1900 the U.S. population could no longer be classified as predominantly white, Anglo-Saxon, and Protestant (WASP).

The black population provides an interesting case study during this period. The number of blacks increased from 1 million in 1800 to 8.8 million in 1900. Yet the proportion of the population that was black declined from almost 19 percent in 1800 to 11.6 percent in 1900. That proportion has not changed significantly since then. One reason for this decline is that the mortality rate for blacks was higher than for whites. Another reason is that large numbers of whites came from Europe to the United States, while few blacks migrated from Africa to the United States, particularly after the African slave trade was abolished in 1808.[1]

The Twentieth Century

The rate of change in population size between 1900 and 1950 was slower compared to earlier rates of growth. The population merely doubled—from 76 million Americans in 1900 to 151.6 million in 1950. Two events then greatly affected the growth of the U.S. population. First, the baby boom began in 1947. Fertility rates rose to levels well above those found in other industrialized countries and did not decline until the late 1950s. The causes of the baby boom will be discussed in a later section in this chapter. The demographic effects were startling. About 30 million people were added to the U.S. population between 1950 and 1960, compared to only 19 million during the 1940s and 9 million during the 1930s. The second demographic surprise came in the late 1960s and early 1970s when fertility declined sharply. By 1975 the crude birth rate had reached 14.8—an all-time low. In 1979 the rate of growth due to reproductive change (crude birth rate minus crude death rate) was only .7 percent. By 1980 the population of the United States was about 226 million.

The population continued to settle in and around cities during the first half of this century, a trend discussed in the next chapter. By World War II about 66 percent of the population lived in urban areas, compared to only 40 percent in 1900. The percent of the population classified as urban is shown in figure 3.2 for the period from 1790 to 1979. Note the steady increase in each decade except 1810–1820 and 1930–1940.

Immigration dwindled after World War I. As a consequence, the population became more homogeneous culturally. In 1900 over 34 percent of the population of the United States was of **foreign stock** (either foreign-born or born in the United States of at least one foreign parent). By 1950 this figure had declined to 22.5 percent. In 1970 only 16 percent of the U.S. population was of foreign stock.

To sum up, in the 190 years following the first census in 1790, the United States experienced major demographic changes. Among those changes were the following:

1. Population increased from almost 4 million to over 226 million.
2. The proportion of the population classified as urban increased from 5 percent to over 70 percent.
3. The population became more heterogeneous.
4. The percentage of blacks decreased from 19 percent to about 12 percent of the population.

[1] The U.S. Bureau of the Census (1975) is an invaluable source of information for persons interested in the demographic aspects of nineteenth-century life in America.

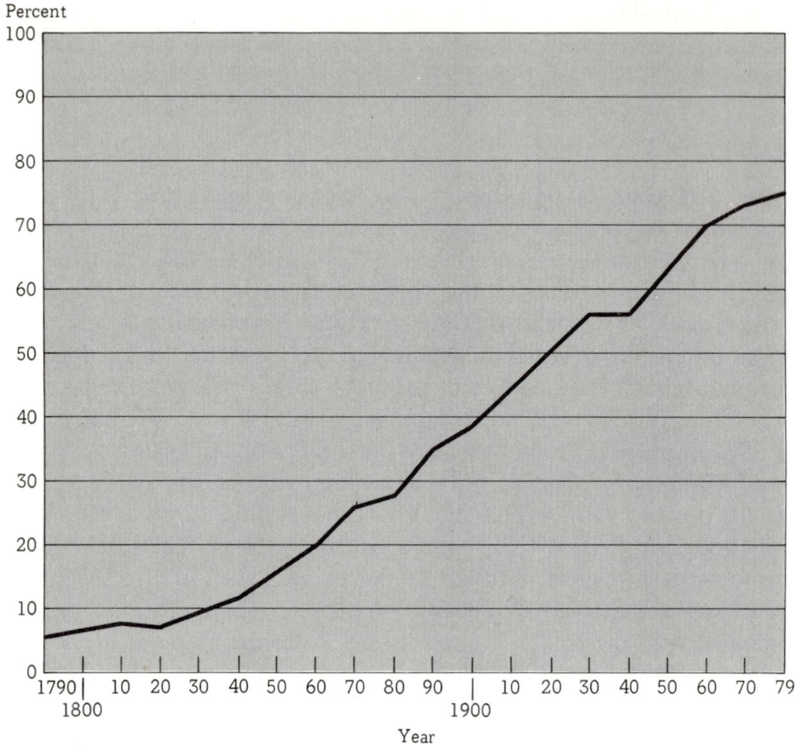

Figure 3.2 Percent of the Population Classified as Urban, 1790–1979
Sources: U.S. Bureau of the Census (1971), p. 32; and Population Reference Bureau (1979).

COMPONENTS OF CHANGE

As we saw in chapter 1, a change in any of the basic demographic variables—fertility, mortality, and migration—can affect population size. There have been significant historical trends affecting each of these variables in the United States, and each has contributed to the growth of the U.S. population.

Fertility

Fertility was high during the colonial period. Women averaged eight to ten live births, making the crude birth rate about 55. Fertility has declined gradually since then. By 1850, when the crude birth rate was 44.3, women were averaging 5.5 live births. In 1900 the crude birth rate was 29.8; the **total fertility rate**—the average number of children a woman will have if throughout her childbearing years she has children at the rate that prevailed in each age group in the year in question—was 3.6.[2] This drop in fertility continued until after the Great Depression in the 1930s. In 1937 the crude birth rate was 17.4, and the total fertility rate was 2.2. This pattern of declining fertility is typical of societies experiencing rapid industrialization. As such, it illustrates part of the model of demographic transition discussed in chapter 2.

The birth rate began to increase during the early 1940s. The period after World War II was characterized by spectacular increases in fertility, as can be seen in figure 3.3 on page 60. The relatively high fertility immediately following the war was expected. Historically, fertility has increased during demobilization as men return home and renew the process of family formation interrupted during wartime. Moreover, the nation had just experienced a depression, which had caused many persons to postpone childbearing. However, most demographers did not expect fertility to remain high for so long. Instead of dropping after a few years, fertility climbed steadily for more than a decade. The crude birth rate of 25.3 in 1954 and 1957 was the highest that had been recorded since 1924. The total fertility rate in 1957 was 3.7, a figure 60 percent higher than the total fertility rate in 1940. What caused the baby boom?

Viewing the baby boom as a "catching up" by men who had been at war or by persons who had delayed marriage and/or childbearing in response to the economic insecurities created by the depression is only a partial explanation. A number of other factors were at work, including the following:

1. The proportion of women in the childbearing years during this time was greater than normal. This resulted from the high fertility of the 1920s relative to that of the 1930s.
2. The percentage of women who remained single dropped significantly in this period.
3. Childlessness declined to a new low.
4. The three- or four-child family became the norm, as people moved to the suburbs and had more space to raise children.
5. The prosperous postwar economic situation encouraged parents to have an extra child.
6. The average age at marriage decreased, and people began having their children sooner after marriage and closer together.

All these factors contributed to the baby boom. The people born in the period between 1945 and 1960 will represent a bulge in the age-sex composition of the nation's population throughout their lives. Some of the consequences of this bulge will be discussed later in this chapter.

A long-term decline in fertility has followed the baby boom. The

[2]See box 3.1 for further discussion of the total fertility rate and how it is calculated.

Box 3.1: The Total Fertility Rate

The total fertility rate (TFR) tells us how many children a woman would have if her childbearing was the same as that which prevailed in each age group at the time of observation. For example, the total fertility rate of 3.6 in 1900 means that if a hypothetical group of 1,000 women were to have the same birth rate as each age group observed in the actual childbearing population in 1900, these women would then have had 3,600 live births (or an average of 3.6 per woman) by the time they had reached the end of their reproductive period, assuming that all survived that long. The total fertility rate may differ from the actual average completed family size because the age-specific birth rates may change through time.

Calculating the TFR involves determining the fertility rate for various age groups of potential childbearers (from age fifteen to nineteen through age forty-five to forty-nine); summing these; and multiplying by the size of the age interval (usually five).The fertility rate for each group is referred to as an **age-specific rate** and it represents the probability that a woman in a given age group will give birth.

Let us try to determine the total fertility rate for the United States in 1977. To do this, we must first determine the age-specific fertility rate. This is given by the formula:

$$\text{Age-Specific Fertility Rate} = \frac{\text{Number of Births to Women of an Age Group}}{\text{Total Women of That Age Group}}$$

The table below applies this formula to 1977 data.

(1) AGE	(2) NUMBER OF WOMEN	(3) NUMBER OF BIRTHS (PER THOUSAND)	(4) AGE-SPECIFIC RATE
15–19	10,412,500	570,609*	.0548
20–24	9,943,500	1,146,491	.1152
25–29	8,898,700	1,016,231	.1142
30–34	7,772,850	446,939	.0575
35–39	6,296,900	120,900	.0192
40–44	5,742,150	24,117	.0042
45–49	6,725,000	1,345	.0002

*This includes 11,455 births to women under age fifteen.

To arrive at the total fertility rate, all we must do is add the figures in column 4 and multiply by five.

Thus the TFR for the United States in 1977 was .3563 times 5, or 1.826 per 1,000 women. If the age-specific fertility for that year did not change in the future, women would average 1.8 live births in their reproductive years.

Two other important measures of reproduction are derived from the

continued

Total Fertility Rate (continued)

total fertility rate: the **gross reproduction rate** and the **net reproduction rate.** The gross reproduction rate indicates how many *female* births a woman (or 1,000 women) would have if throughout her reproductive years she had female births at the age-sex specific rate noted for a particular year.

If the **sex ratio** at birth (or number of males per hundred females) is known, calculating the gross reproduction rate is quite simple. First we determine the proportion of all births that were female, and then we apply that to the total fertility rate.

Thus, in 1977 the sex ratio at birth in the United States was 105. To calculate the proportion of male births, we divide 105 by 205 (100 + 105) = .512. Therefore, the proportion of female births was 1 − .512 = .488. The total fertility rate was 1.826. Thus the gross reproduction rate was 1.826 × .488 = .891.

The net reproduction rate goes one step further than the gross reproduction rate by taking into consideration the fact that not all women live to enter and complete the reproductive phase of the life cycle. It indicates how many female births a woman would have if that woman experienced through her reproductive years the same age-sex specific fertility rates and the same age-specific mortality rates as the women of a particular calendar year. Thus, the net reproduction rate measures population replacement. If one woman lives to give birth to one female, the population is replacing itself. To calculate the net reproduction rate, it is first necessary to learn how to construct a life table. This will be discussed in chapter 7.

crude birth rate decreased slightly from 1957 to 1961. Then a pronounced decline occurred. In 1961 the crude birth rate was 23.5; by 1968 it was 17.6. The birth rate increased slightly between 1968 and 1970. This was partly due to the increasing proportion of the population comprised of females in the prime childbearing ages (twenty to thirty-four), a direct result of the earlier baby boom. However, even though this proportion continued to increase, the crude birth rate began to decrease after 1970. By 1975 it was 14.8, the lowest rate in American history. In 1978 it was 15.2. The total fertility rate also declined spectacularly from its high 1957 level of 3.7. By 1968 the total fertility rate had declined to 2.5. It reached 2.0 in 1972 and since then has been under 2. In 1978 it was only 1.8, a figure well below replacement.

It is too early to determine the causes of this decline in fertility. In view of the increasing number of women in the prime childbearing ages, the decreases in fertility since 1967 have been remarkable. Perhaps the unsettled economic conditions that began in the late 1960s

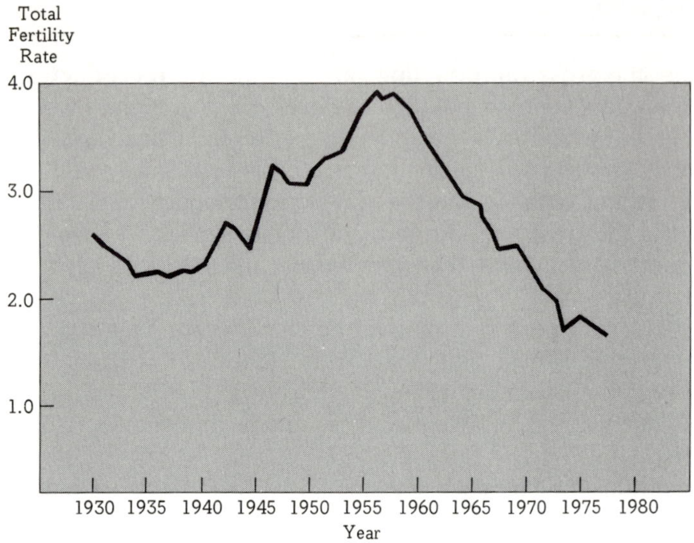

Figure 3.3 Total Fertility Rate, 1930–1978
Source: U.S. Bureau of the Census (1977*a*), p. 4, and U.S. Bureau of the Census (1979*b*), p. 3.

led people to postpone marriage and/or childbearing. They also could have led to the belief that people could not afford to have as many children as their parents had. Because of the size of the baby boom **cohort** (a group of people experiencing a major event at the same time), the competition for employment has been intense among persons in their twenties, which certainly could heighten feelings of economic insecurity. In turn, this could lead to postponement of marriage and/or childbearing and decrease the likelihood of having an "extra" child (Easterlin, Wachter, and Wachter 1978). In addition, more effective contraceptives are available, sterilization of males as well as females is generally acceptable, and abortion laws have been liberalized. Finally, more women are completing college, more women are in the labor force, and more women have meaningful careers than ever before. Each of these factors could have led to reduced fertility.

Whatever the causes, fertility is now at an all-time low. The United States fertility level is among the lowest in the world. Predicting future fertility is almost impossible. Norms could change, or the economy could improve. Because of the declines in fertility that occurred in the 1960s and 1970s, during the 1980s a growing scarcity of young workers will develop. This condition favors earlier marriage, earlier childbearing, and increased fertility. On the other hand, it is quite possible that we will continue our current pattern of low fertility and that the two-child family will remain the norm.

Mortality

Data for the early decades are rough, but it is estimated that the crude death rate averaged about 25 between 1800 and 1820. From that high, mortality dropped steadily throughout the nineteenth century. By 1900 the crude death rate was 17.2, and newly born Americans could expect to live for forty-seven years. In 1950 the crude death rate was 9.6 and **life expectancy** (the average number of additional years a person can be expected to live) at birth was 68.2. By 1979 the crude death rate had reached a record low (8.7), and life expectancy at birth had attained a record high of 73.5.

Certain molecular biologists are convinced that we are on the verge of major new discoveries that will increase life expectancy to over one hundred years in the near future (Endres 1975, pp. 132–146). Although no one can say for sure that this will not occur, there are two reasons to believe it may not. First, there is little real evidence that dramatic improvement in disease elimination will come to pass. Second, the demographic effects of the elimination of a specific disease may be rather small. For instance, Nathan Keyfitz (1977) estimates that eliminating all cancer deaths would increase life expectancy at birth by just 3 percent. This is because deaths from other causes would increase, and the major causes of death today are clustered largely in the same age groups.

Migration

About 50 million people are believed to have migrated to the United States since its independence. Some 80 percent of these have remained. There is quite a lot of guesswork involved in these figures since the U.S. Immigration and Naturalization Service did not begin to gather statistics on legal immigration until 1819, and these data reveal nothing about illegal immigration. Moreover, there are few reliable estimates of **emigration**—the number of people who leave the United States permanently.

Between 1819 and 1850 about 2.5 million persons immigrated to the United States, mostly from England, Ireland, and Germany. Between 1850 and 1900 there were about 17 million **immigrants.** The countries of origin of these new immigrants differed considerably from those of the old immigrants, as can be seen in figure 3.4. By 1880 the emphasis had shifted from northern and western Europe to southern and eastern Europe—particularly Italy, Poland, and Greece. The old WASP immigrants tended to look down on these new immigrants who were swarthier, spoke strange languages, and very often looked to the Roman Catholic Church for religious guidance.

The volume of immigration to the United States reached its peak at this time. The 6.3 million immigrants who came between 1900 and

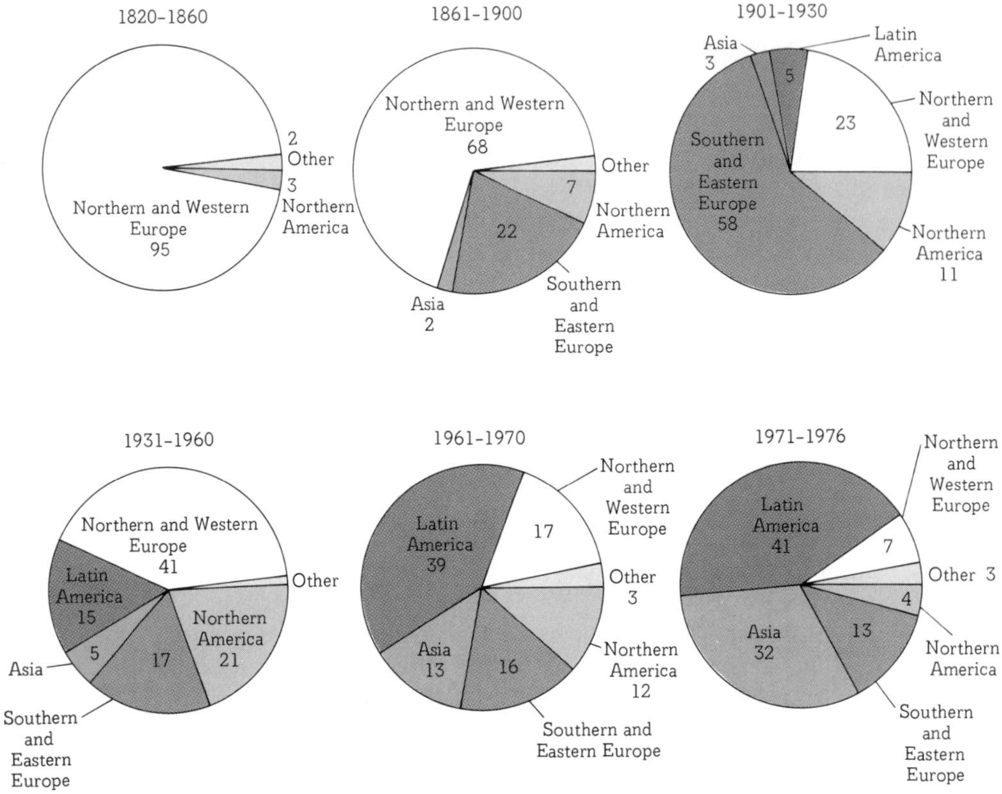

Figure 3.4 U.S. Immigrants by Region of Origin, 1820–1976
Source: Bouvier, Shryock, and Henderson (1977), pp. 24–25.

1910 represented 8 percent of the 1900 population. Immigration dropped sharply after that: only 2.5 million came during the 1910–1920 interval, 3.2 million during the 1920s, and 0.1 million during the depression years of the 1930s. Since then, however, immigration has increased in each successive decade—from 1.8 million during the 1940s to 3 million during the 1950s to 3.9 million during the 1960s and to almost 5 million in the 1970s (U.S. Bureau of the Census 1974 and 1979*b*). The majority of these immigrants came from Latin America and Asia, particularly Southeast Asia. Less than 10 percent came from northern or western Europe, regions that supplied 95 percent of the immigrants during the early part of the nineteenth century.

Future levels of legal immigration are difficult to forecast. The level of immigration into the United States depends on economic conditions in the sending countries as well as in the United States and on the policies of the U.S. government about the number of immigrants who may enter in a given year and from what countries these immigrants may come. The existence of emigration policies in other countries is also important. Unless current U.S. laws setting a worldwide limit and requiring needed occupational skills by some of the immigrants are changed, the future level of legal immigration into the country probably will be about the same as that during the 1970s.

Contributions to Growth

In the long run immigration has been the principal cause of population growth in the United States. Descendants of the original inhabitants (the American Indians) now represent a small fraction of the population, as noted earlier. Thus, everyone else is either an immigrant or the descendant of one. Nevertheless, if you look at relatively short periods of time, such as a decade, you would reach a different conclusion. This is especially true if you isolate the direct effects of immigration in population size during a given period.

For example, population size increased by 18 million persons between 1800 and 1850. Only about 2 million of this can be attributed directly to immigration. During most of those years the **rate of reproductive change** (crude birth rate minus the crude death rate) fluctuated between 25 and 30. This alone would have been sufficient to double the population size every twenty-five years. Thus, the 5.3 million Americans in 1800 would have reproduced to form 21.2 million Americans in 1850 even if there had been no immigration during this interval. Instead, there were 23.2 million Americans enumerated in the 1850 census.

In another instance, between 1850 and 1900, the population increased by 53 million persons, but no more than one-third of this can be directly attributed to immigration. The rate of reproductive change was about 20 during this interval. This would have increased the population at an annual rate of 2 percent and caused it to double every thirty-five years.

Looked at in another way, though, immigration did have *indirect* effects on population size. Young female immigrants were likely to bear children after their arrival in the United States. These children were counted as native born and thus contributed to the rate of reproductive change. Likewise, immigrants to the United States were likely to die in the United States. This increased the number of deaths and further affected the rate of reproductive change. Campbell Gibson (1975, p. 165) has estimated that taking into account both the indirect and direct effects of immigration, we could attribute about 42 percent of the U.S. population in 1900 to immigration during the preceding century—a larger role than is traditionally granted it, but still secondary to reproductive change as a component of growth in the nineteenth century.

Immigration was a more important component in the period from 1900 to 1950, when there were 20 million immigrants. The rate of reproductive change averaged about 10, which would have produced an annual rate of growth equal to 1 percent, enough to double the population every sixty-nine years. Instead, the population doubled in fifty years. Thus, the direct effect of immigration was to speed up the doubling time of the population by nineteen years, even though immigration itself was negligible between 1920 and 1946.

During the past two decades immigration has become an even more important contributor to the growth of the U.S. population (see figure 3.5). But this is not due to any major increases in the volume of immigration. Rates of immigration are no larger now than they were in the late 1950s. And yet immigration accounted for only 10 percent of the population growth in 1958, while in 1978 it accounted for 20 percent. How can this be?

The solution to this seeming paradox lies in the way population

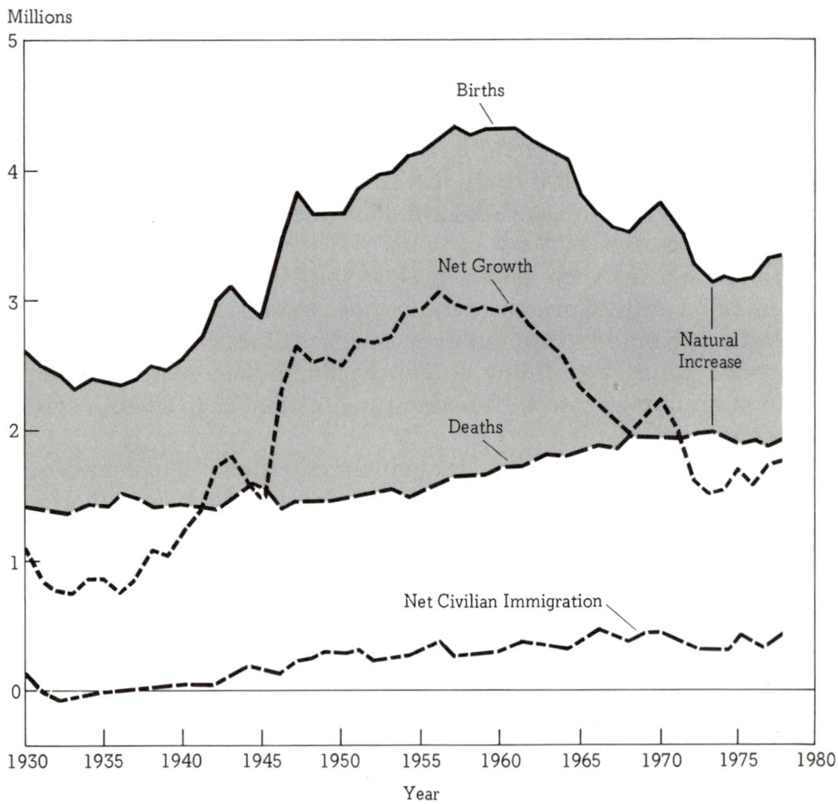

Figure 3.5 Annual Levels of Net Growth, Births, Deaths, and Net Immigration, 1930–1978
Source: U.S. Bureau of the Census (1979*b*), cover.

growth is produced. Remember the demographic equation that was discussed in chapter 1. This equation depicts population change as a *combination* of reproductive change and net migration. Net migration does not have to increase in order to become a more important component of change—reproductive change can decrease. This is exactly what has happened in the United States since the late 1950s. The birth rate was high then (24.5 in 1958) and the death rate low (9.5), producing a rate of reproductive change of 15. This combined with the rate of civilian immigration to produce a total rate of change equal to 16—90 percent of which was attributable to reproductive change and 10 percent to immigration. Although the death rate has declined only slightly and the rate of civilian immigration has remained fairly constant since 1958 (8.8 and 1.6, respectively, in 1978), the crude birth rate has decreased to 15.2). This means that the rate of reproductive change was only 6.4 in 1978. The total rate of change was 8.0. Of this, reproductive change accounted for 80 percent and net immigration 20 percent.

So far, we have discussed only legal immigration. Many persons enter the United States illegally, without going through inspections or by using fraudulent documents. It is unlikely that the number of such **illegal** (or undocumented) **immigrants** exceeds 500,000 per year. Net illegal immigration would be much smaller, for a number of the persons would not settle permanently in the United States. Nevertheless, because it is illegal, the volume of illegal immigration is difficult to estimate with any degree of confidence (Keely 1979).

To the extent that illegal immigration occurs, the figures cited earlier underestimate the importance of immigration as a factor producing change in the size of the U.S. population. Nevertheless, reproductive change remains the most important component in current U.S. population change. Many demographers believe that levels of immigration and mortality are not likely to change much in the near future. Thus, any future changes in the pattern of population growth will be produced by fluctuations in fertility. If fertility increases, then immigration will play a less important role than it does now in producing U.S. population growth. If fertility decreases further, then immigration will play a more important role. In any event, the future levels of all three demographic variables—fertility, mortality, and migration—will determine the size of the U.S. population in the future.

THE FUTURE POPULATION OF THE UNITED STATES

The unexpected population growth that occurred as a result of the baby boom led to many doomsday predictions about the nation's future. Much was made of the fact that by the late 1960s the first cohorts born during the baby boom would themselves begin entering the prime years of childbearing (twenty to twenty-nine). Sample surveys conducted during the 1950s showed that women expected to have an average of over three children. If the baby boom cohorts also bore children at this level, the baby boom itself would have paled into insignificance compared to the aftereffects. In the late 1950s predictions were made of a total population size of more than 350 million Americans by the end of the century. Fortunately, these predictions overstated the case.

Still earlier forecasts had seriously *understated* the amount of population growth that has taken place. In 1938, Warren Thompson and P. K. Whelpton forecast a maximum population size of 158 million for the year 1980. Yet by 1980 the actual population was over 226 million and still growing. The demographers of the 1930s, as well as those of the 1950s and the 1970s, based their projections on known behavior at that time. Those of the 1930s had no way of predicting the baby boom that followed World War II.

The utility of any population projection depends on the validity of the assumptions about the three variables that contribute to population change—fertility, mortality, and migration. The U.S. Bureau of the Census has made certain assumptions in its projections of U.S. population from 1977 to 2050. These projections have taken into account the recent declines in age-specific death rates among middle-aged and older adults and recent research on future trends in mortality. Thus, average life expectancy at birth is assumed to increase from 69.1 to 71.8 years for males and from 77.0 to 81.0 for females between 1976 and 2050. The assumed level of net immigration (that is, immigration minus emigration) is 400,000 per year, which reflects the recorded level of legal immigration in recent years. Fertility is the component of population change that is most difficult to predict. Therefore, the Bureau of the Census has made a number of alternate assumptions about completed family size. Each one yields a different projected population size.

The Series I projection assumes an average of 2.7 children per woman. Under this assumption the population would increase by 30 percent between 1976 and 2000. Population would total 282 million in 2000 and 488 million in 2050. The annual rate of population growth would be 1.0 percent in 2000 and 1.1 percent in 2050 (see table 3.1). The Series II projection assumes that women will average 2.1 children. This corresponds closely to the level of future fertility suggested by recent sample survey data on birth expectations. The Series II projection indicates the total population of the United States would increase to 260 million by the end of the century and to 316 million by the year 2050. By this latter date, the annual rate of population growth would be only 0.2 percent.

The Series III projection assumes that women will average 1.7 children. Under this projection the U.S. population would increase by 13 percent by the end of the century (to 246 million). Shortly after the

Table 3.1 Projections of the United States Population, 1977–2050

	AVERAGE FAMILY SIZE	1977	2000	2050
Population Size (millions)				
Series I	2.7	217	282	488
Series II	2.1	217	260	316
Series III	1.7	217	246	231
Percent Change since Preceding Date				
Series I	—	—	30	73
Series II	—	—	20	18
Series III	—	—	13	-6
Annual Rate of Population Change				
Series I	—	1.0	1.0	1.1
Series II	—	0.8	0.5	0.2
Series III	—	0.6	0.2	-0.4

Source: U.S. Bureau of the Census (1977*b*), pp. 22–24.

turn of the century there would be a negative amount of reproductive change—that is, deaths would exceed births. This would be offset for a few years by the assumed level of net immigration, but after the year 2020, when the population would peak at 253 million, the assumed level of net immigration would not be sufficient to offset the sizable negative reproductive change. Consequently, by the year 2050, the U.S. population would be about 231 million, a figure 6 percent *smaller* than the population size at the beginning of the century (U.S. Bureau of the Census 1977*b*, pp. 4–5).

We do not know what the total size of the U.S. population will be in the future. The projections suggest that the population will continue to grow throughout the remainder of the twentieth century at rates that are well below those of the 1950s and 1960s. Based upon available evidence, it is unlikely that future fertility levels will be higher than 2.7 children per woman or lower than 1.7 children per woman. Given current levels of fertility, the Series I projection seems relatively unlikely. If fertility remains at its low level of the late 1970s, and if the assumptions about mortality and net immigration are correct, then Series III projections should be close to the observed population size. However, recent survey data suggest that fertility may increase in the future to reach replacement level, so that Series II projections should not be discounted.

The assumptions about mortality and net immigration are the same for each series. Differences in assumptions about fertility levels account for the variations in future population size. The effects of these differences are startling. There is a difference of only one child per woman between Series I (2.7) and Series III (1.7), yet Series I produces a population that is 36 million persons larger than the Series III population by the year 2000 and 257 million larger by the year 2050. Even the effects of a difference of 0.4 children can be substantial. Thus, Series II produces a population that is 14 million persons more than the Series III population by the year 2000 and 85 million larger than the Series III projections for the year 2050. These projections illustrate the extent to which fluctuations in one demographic variable—in this instance, fertility—can significantly affect our future.

The Magic Number 2.1

There is a certain undeserved magic in the number 2.1, the fertility replacement level in the United States today (given prevailing mortality).[3] To many people, this figure means **zero population growth (ZPG)**. They believe that if all couples have only about 2 children that population growth will immediately cease. However, attaining zero population growth is far more complicated than that. The recent experience of the United States illustrates that. Fertility has been *below* replacement level since 1972, yet the population has still grown.

How can the population increase if fertility is below replacement? Two factors must be considered—the age structure and net immigration. As we have seen, the baby boom created a relatively high proportion of persons in the prime childbearing ages during the late 1960s and the 1970s. Those persons provide a momentum for population growth that is independent of the levels of fertility, mortality, or immigration. For instance, the number of females aged twenty to twenty-nine (when fertility rates are highest) increased by 3 percent between 1976 and 1978. In fact, the number of "baby boom" women in the prime childbearing ages is expected to increase for some time. Thus, replacement level fertility, in the short run, does not necessarily produce zero population growth.

Even in the long run the attainment of replacement level fertility does not mean zero population growth if there is sufficient immigration. The Series II projections discussed earlier assumed replacement level fertility and a net annual immigration rate of 400,000 persons.

[3]The 2.1 refers to the average number of births to all women. Yet not all women marry, so the level of fertility by married persons that corresponds to replacement level is higher than 2.1. According to the proportion of females in the United States who do marry, replacement level fertility translates to about 2.3 births per married woman. Because the proportion of females that marry may vary through time, and because some unmarried women also are fertile, in our text we measure replacement level fertility based upon the experience of *all* women, regardless of marital status.

In measuring replacement level fertility, one female must replace herself with another female. Because there are slightly more male births than female births and because not all females survive to bear children, the average number of live births per woman that is needed to ensure that one female will be born and will live to replace herself is 2.1 instead of the 2.0 many people expect it to be.

Under these assumptions the population would be 316 million in the year 2050. The Census Bureau also did a projection (Series II-X) assuming replacement level fertility and *zero* net immigration. Under these assumptions the population in the year 2050 would be only 269 million. Thus the net effect of maintaining current legal immigration levels is about 47 million additional persons by the middle of the next century.

Because of the effect of immigration patterns on U.S. population growth, many people have urged that we eliminate immigration completely. They argue, correctly, that averaging 2.1 children will never result in ZPG as long as there is net immigration. However, these persons overlook the fact that fertility has been *below* replacement since the early 1970s and that, under these conditions, a certain volume of immigration is compatible with the eventual attainment of zero population growth. Indeed, Charles Westoff (1978) concludes that, under current fertility conditions, even with 800,000 immigrants a year, we could still have zero population growth in the United States (see also Coale 1972; and Keely 1979).

Instant ZPG?

What would it take to achieve zero population growth immediately? Since the current age structure provides its own momentum for growth, women would have to limit themselves to fertility far below replacement and immigration would have to come to an immediate halt. In the absence of immigration, fertility below replacement could not continue indefinitely or the population would actually start to decline. Sooner or later women would have to bear more children to compensate for this earlier behavior. As Tomas Frejka has explained:

> Individual families and persons would have to accept very strange attitudes to childbearing in order to maintain a non-growing population starting with the initial year. . . . Each family would have to limit its average number of children to a value of about 1.2 for the next 20 years or so, and thereafter the mean number of children per family would have to increase gradually, reaching a maximum of 2.8 children in the period 2030–35 (1968, p. 382).

Later still, fertility would have to decrease, and women could average only 1.4 children beginning about 2055. The fluctuations in fertility that would have to be present in order for instant ZPG to occur are shown in figure 3.6.

Although Frejka's starting point was 1965, his basic conclusions remain valid. Because of the age structure produced by the baby boom, the attainment of instant ZPG would require fertility to fall far below replacement level, then increase far above it (to avoid population loss), then decline below replacement, and so forth, for a considerable period of time. Indeed, figure 3.6 shows that these fluctuations

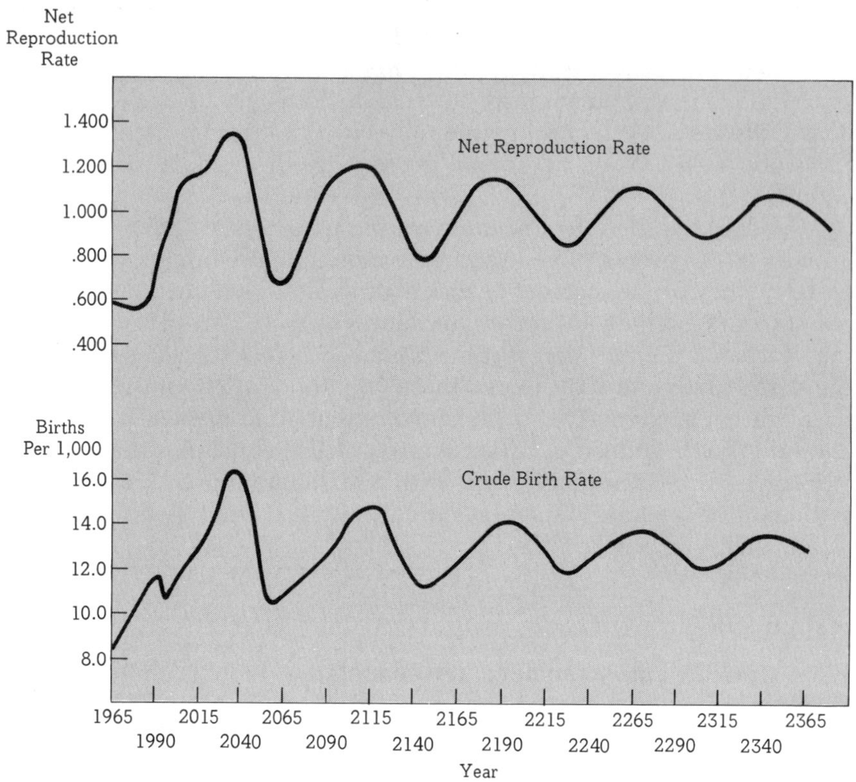

Figure 3.6 Fluctuations in the Crude Birth Rate and Net Reproduction Rate Necessary to Achieve Instant Zero Population Growth, 1965–2365
Source: Frejka (1968), p. 383.

would still have to occur through the year 2365, although the later fluctuations would be a great deal less pronounced than the earlier ones. These fluctuations in fertility would produce alterations in the age structure of the population that would be almost as great as those produced by the baby boom. Although the attainment of ZPG would be beneficial for the society, such fluctuations in the age structure would probably have some adverse effects for the persons in these age groups and perhaps also for the society as a whole. (This will be discussed in chapter 10.) Gradual attainment of ZPG would not involve these sharp fluctuations in fertility (and cohort size), which is why many demographers believe it is preferable to instant attainment of ZPG.

CONSEQUENCES OF POPULATION CHANGE

Different forms of population change produce various consequences. It is to these effects that we now turn.

Unanticipated Growth

The baby boom is an excellent example of unanticipated growth. Its effects are readily observed in education. Beginning in the 1950s our schools and colleges experienced a "population explosion" of students that lasted for over twenty years. Between 1950 and 1970 the number of children age five to seventeen increased by 70 percent. The resulting increases in school enrollments created a shortage of qualified teachers, large classes and crowded classrooms, double sessions, and inadequate physical plants. Many local communities were faced with the prospects of building new schools and greatly increasing their pool of teachers. The nation's colleges also experienced significant increases in enrollment. For example, in 1960 there were slightly more than 3 million persons enrolled in colleges and universities. By 1978 enrollments had soared to 9.8 million—over three times the level seventeen years earlier. Although part of the increased enrollments at the college and high-school levels was due to the desire on the part of many to stay in school longer to receive more education, there can be no doubt that the sheer size of the baby boom placed severe strains upon the ability of the educational system to provide quality education for our nation's youth.

Currently the educational system is facing another challenge—declining enrollments. The school-age population (age five to seventeen) declined by about 11 percent during the 1970s and is expected to decline by another 10 percent during the 1980s. Consequently, elementary and secondary schools are now having to cope with smaller enrollments and a surplus of qualified teachers. Many communities are closing schools that they rushed to open during the 1950s and early 1960s in response to the baby boom. Many teachers have had to find other occupations because there are not enough jobs for them as teachers. College enrollments are more difficult to predict than elementary and secondary enrollments. Not everyone decides to go to college. Those in the eighteen to twenty-one age group will decline in number by about 25 percent nationally between 1979 and 1994. College enrollments may not decline as much as elementary and secondary school enrollments, because colleges will tend to expand their continuing education programs for older persons and to attract foreign students. Nevertheless, they cannot realistically expect to experience increases in enrollment similar to those caused by the baby boom.[4]

Education is not the only area to feel the disequilibrium of the baby boom. In nearly every stage of life people born in that period will feel some effect. The baby boom will have a particularly severe impact on employment prospects and on social security programs.

[4]For a special treatment of the challenges to higher education during the rest of this century posed by demographic change, see the June 1979 issue of *American Demographics.*

As those born during the baby boom graduate from college or high school, they will create a greater demand for employment. The highest rates of unemployment are traditionally found among the young. Large influxes of young and inexperienced new workers into the labor force may increase the overall level of unemployment if there are not enough jobs in the economy that meet the aspirations of the young entrants. Because of the inexperience of younger workers, productivity may be lower. There are signs that this has indeed happened. Not all of the high unemployment and low productivity growth of the past ten years can be blamed on the poor health of the economy. The entry of the baby boom cohorts into the work force must be considered (Waking up 1979, p. 32).

During the 1970s an average of 3.5 million persons made their initial entry into the labor force each year. This exceeded the annual average for the 1960s by about 700,000 persons. Although part of this growth is due to increasing participation in the labor force, most of it is due to accelerated population growth produced by the baby boom.

The baby boom cohorts will continue to have a heavy impact upon American society as they move from one age group to the next. Beginning in the year 2015, they will reach age sixty-five—the customary age for retirement. In 1980 there were about 25 million Americans age sixty-five or older. By the year 2015 there will be over 40 million persons in that age group. This will have an adverse effect upon the social security system (which is having difficulties anyway). The system is a pay-as-you-go one, in which workers pay the benefits of the retired. In the year 2015 a large pool of beneficiaries (the product of the baby boom) will be depending on a much smaller pool of workers (the product of the recent fertility decline) to generate their social security payments. One recent estimate is that if benefits were to remain at current levels, the total tax burden on the employed by the 2020s would be close to 50 percent of wages (Waking up 1979, p. 47). Of course, there are alternatives to such higher future tax rates—such as lower benefits and later retirement ages. Congress has already moved in the latter direction by abolishing age sixty-five as the mandatory retirement age for most classes of workers. Nevertheless, this will ease the pressure only partially: we will still be faced with the choice between higher taxes for social security or decreased benefits. This issue is discussed in greater detail in chapter 10.

Two Versus Three Children

Another way to estimate the consequences of population growth is to examine the effects of having different average-size families. The Commission on Population Growth and the American Future has done just this. The commission was a panel of politicians, prominent citizens, scholars, housewives, and students that was formed by President Nixon in 1969 to examine the probable extent of population growth and internal migration in the United States between 1970 and 2000 and to assess the impact that such population change would have upon American society. The commission gathered expert opinions on the societal implications of an average of two children per family versus an average of three children per family between 1970 and 2000. These averages can be made up by many possible combinations of family sizes, ranging from childless couples to those with many children. They do not assume that everyone has the same number of children.

The commission found that if families average three children rather than two children, these consequences may follow:

1. There will be an additional 51 million people by the year 2000.
2. There will be 46 percent more persons of elementary and secondary school age and 36 percent more persons of college age in the year 2000.
3. Food prices will be about 30 to 50 percent higher.
4. Expenditures for health care during the 1970–2000 interval will be $20 billion greater.

On the other hand, if families average two children rather than three, these effects are likely:

1. The **dependency ratio**[5] (the ratio of the number of persons under fifteen years of age and sixty-five or older to all other persons) will be 22 percent lower.
2. Per capita income may be as much as 15 percent higher in the year 2000.
3. The amount of minerals consumed in the year 2000 will be about 9 percent lower.
4. The volume of polluting emissions will be about 5 to 12 percent less.
5. Potential demands for many governmental services will be smaller. At the same time the potential resources to finance governmental activities will be larger because of higher per capita income (see Commission on Population Growth and the American Future 1972; Parke 1973; and Population Reference Bureau 1973).

Of course, many of these estimates are very rough. Over a decade has passed since the beginning of the interval studied by the commission. These estimates should not be taken literally. Rather, they should be viewed as illustrating the magnitude of change for some sectors of our society that may result from population growth during the last quarter of this century.

[5]For calculation of this ratio, see box 3.2.

Box 3.2 The Dependency Ratio

The dependency ratio is the number of persons under fifteen and sixty-five or older per one hundred persons fifteen to sixty-five years of age. It is calculated as follows:

$$\text{Dependency Ratio} = \left(\frac{P_{0-14} + P_{65+}}{P_{15-64}}\right)100$$

P_{0-14} is the number of persons under fifteen
P_{65+} is the number of persons over 65 and over
P_{15-64} is the number of persons between these two age brackets

In mid-1978 the dependency ratio for the United States could be calculated as:

$$P_{0-14} = 50{,}823{,}000$$
$$P_{65+} = 24{,}054{,}000$$
$$P_{15-64} = 143{,}671{,}000$$

$$\text{Dependency Ratio} = \left(\frac{50{,}823{,}000 + 24{,}054{,}000}{143{,}671{,}000}\right)100$$

$$= \left(\frac{74{,}877{,}000}{143{,}671{,}000}\right)100$$

$$= (.5212)\ 100 = 52.12$$

In other words, in the United States on July 1, 1978 there were about fifty-two persons under fifteen or sixty-five and older for every hundred persons fifteen to sixty-four years of age.

The age groups used to calculate the dependency ratio roughly correspond to the various stages of the **life cycle** (the stages through which a person evolves from infancy to old age). Thus, persons under fifteen are young dependents, those sixty-five and older are elderly dependents, and those in between represent the population's potential labor force. Of course this is an oversimplification. In economically advanced countries few persons under age eighteen contribute substantially to the economy (except as consumers) and many persons over age sixty-five are economically self-sufficient. Moreover, not everyone between these ages can work, or even wishes to be employed. In some countries many persons under fifteen are employed. Despite these limitations, this age division is useful for those who wish a general indicator of the proportion of the population which is "young," "potentially productive," or "old," and who are aware of the measure's limitations.

Some demographers have attempted to refine the division by using different age ranges (e.g., twenty to sixty-four or eighteen to sixty-four), but this is not always possible. For instance, if data are available only in ten-year intervals (zero to nine, ten to nineteen, etc.), then the breakdown using ages eighteen to sixty-four is not very feasible.

Slow or No Growth

Despite the arguments against rapid population growth, some demographers have expressed reservations about the social and economic consequences of slow growth or nongrowth (often called "stationarity"). The results of a zero population growth rate arise from the absence of growth itself as well as from the age and sex structure associated with this absence of growth. The age structure of the United States will become much older if replacement level fertility is maintained. As recently as 1960, only 9 percent of the population was age sixty-five or older. In 1980 this figure was 11 percent, and the median age of the population was about thirty years. If fertility were to remain at replacement level, by the middle of the next century the median age of the population would be about thirty-eight and over 16 percent of the population would be age sixty-five or older.

Some people have maintained that such an "old" population would be more likely than a "young" population to resist social change and to be more conservative (Coale 1968; and Sauvy 1976). But aging does not necessarily bring with it conservatism (Cutler and Kaufman 1975). Moreover, Sweden and Great Britain have older age structures than the United States, yet they are not known for being politically conservative. New power blocs which stress the interests of the elderly could be expected to emerge. Indeed, there are signs that this is occurring already, as, for example, in the work of the Gray Panthers, an organization that lobbies on issues of importance to the elderly.

Health services would probably be geared toward the adult and the elderly rather than the young. For instance, we could expect a lowered demand for pediatricians and special health facilities for children. The incidence of certain types of diseases and mental disorders might increase. However, aging is as much a social and a psychological process as a biological one. Thus, alterations in our health care system and in our attitude toward the elderly might change many of these effects and make generalizations impossible (Day 1978).

What about the economic consequences of reduced population growth? The Commission on Population Growth and the American Future concluded that a reduction in the rate of population growth would bring important economic benefits. Remember that per capita income would be about 15 percent higher in the two-child family situation than it would be in the three-child family scenario. This in itself would be an important benefit. More important, the commission concluded that a lower population growth rate would not cause serious problems for any industry or its employees. There are four reasons for this:

1. Regardless of the rate of population growth, total income (and hence demand) will rise.
2. Slower population growth will cause total as well as per capita in-

come to be higher over the next ten years than would a more rapid rate of population growth.

3. Because of the baby boom the population will have a relatively high concentration of persons in the prime childbearing ages for the rest of the century. Under the assumption of replacement level fertility, this means that there is no year in which there would be fewer births than there were in 1971. Thus, the slower population growth implied by replacement level fertility would not reduce demand from 1970 levels for any of the numerous industries studied.
4. Beyond the next ten to fifteen years the adjustments that businesses must make to changes in consumer tastes and technological developments should far exceed the problems of adjusting to a lower population growth rate.

For these reasons, the commission concluded: "We find no convincing economic argument for continued national population growth. On the contrary, most of the pluses are on the side of slower growth" (1972, p. 40).

This response may be unsatisfactory to local retailers, because it seems "obvious" that more people mean more customers. However, it is necessary to examine the kind of growth that means more business. More business results chiefly from net in-migration, not from reproductive change. As the commission (1972, p. 41) points out, adults moving into a community make ready customers and ready employees. They have grown up elsewhere, their education has been paid for elsewhere, and they impose few of the demands of the dependent aged. Moreover, the nongrowth of the national population does not mean that local populations will not change their population size through net migration patterns. And the demand for services could also increase because each member of the population has increased purchasing power.

Some nations that have had low birth rates longer than the United States have experienced labor force shortages, but this is not an inevitable consequence. The labor force can be expanded by bringing more women into the labor force, by delaying retirement, by bringing youth into the labor force at an earlier age, or by importing labor (Ford 1977). Ansley Coale (1970) has suggested that occupational advancement will be reduced under stationarity. But, although older people will have seniority and hold their positions longer, there will always be competition among industries for talented workers, and new occupations and industries will constantly be providing a new start for workers.

Adverse economic effects of reduced population growth (or even nongrowth), such as a strain on the social security system, are difficult to document (see, for example, Serow and Espenshade 1977). Adverse social consequences are even more difficult to ascertain. Social and economic phenomena have a variety of causes. Some of these are demographic; some are nondemographic. As the Commission on Population Growth and the American Future concluded:

> Slower population growth can contribute to the nation's ability to solve its problems . . . by providing an opportunity to devote resources to the quality of life rather than its quantity, and by "buying time"—that is, slowing the pace at which problems accumulate so as to provide opportunity for the development of orderly and democratic solutions (1972, p. 25).

Thus, although eliminating population growth through sustained low fertility will not eliminate many of the problems confronting American society, it would make the solution of some of them easier and less costly. As Lincoln Day (1978, p. 15) has stated, a nongrowing population would only make the "good life" more attainable; it would not, in itself, produce it. Ultimately, of course, a zero rate of population growth is necessary if we are to survive.

SUMMARY

Since the first census was conducted in 1790, the population of the United States has increased from under 4 million to over 226 million persons. The proportion of the population classified as urban has increased from 5 percent to over 70 percent. The population has become more heterogeneous ethnically, although the percentage of blacks has decreased from 19 percent to about 12 percent.

Immigration has been an important source of this growth in the national population. Indeed, the Native Americans (Indians) now comprise less than 1 percent of the total population. However, during any relatively short period of time reproductive change has been the principal component of population change.

Both birth rates and death rates declined steadily during the nineteenth and early twentieth centuries. The death rate has reached a very low level and is unlikely to become much lower in the foreseeable future. The birth rate has fluctuated widely during the past forty years. It increased dramatically during the late 1940s and the 1950s. This baby boom has caused a number of social and economic problems. Since the mid-1960s the birth rate has declined dramatically. Currently, fertility is actually below replacement level. However, this does not mean the population will stop growing in the near future. There is a considerable volume of immigration into our country. Moreover, the baby boom has produced a relatively high proportion of our population in the prime childbearing ages, resulting in a momentum for growth. This effect will probably continue until late in the century, unless fertility declines to even lower levels.

The population of the United States will continue to grow

throughout the remainder of the twentieth century at rates that are well below those of the 1950s and 1960s. The achievement of instant zero population growth through the elimination of immigration and further reductions in fertility is not likely.

The rapid population growth that would result from an average of three children per family as opposed to two children per family has demonstrable negative effects. It is difficult to establish that low rates of population growth (or even zero population growth) would have an adverse effect upon the social and economic well-being of the American population. The opposite appears to be the case. But social and economic phenomena are complex; any social or economic problems that exist will not disappear just because the population stops growing. Slow or no growth will only make the solution of some of these problems easier and less costly.

REFERENCES AND SUGGESTED READINGS

Bogue, Donald J. 1969. *Principles of demography.* New York: John Wiley and Sons.

Bouvier, Leon F. 1980. America's baby boom generation: the fateful bulge. *Population bulletin* 35 (April).

Bouvier, Leon F., Shryock, Henry S., and Henderson, Harry W. 1977. International migration: yesterday, today, and tomorrow. *Population bulletin* 30 (September).

Coale, Ansley J. 1968. Low U.S. birth rate not entirely desirable. *University: a Princeton quarterly* 39 (Winter):29–44.

———. 1970. Man and his environment. *Science* 170 (9 October):132–136.

———. 1972. Alternative paths to a stationary population. In *Demographic and social aspects of population growth,* eds. Charles F. Westoff and Robert Parke, Jr., pp. 589–603. Washington, D.C.: Government Printing Office.

Commission on Population Growth and the American Future. 1972. *Population and the American future.* Washington, D.C.: Government Printing Office.

Cutler, Stephen J., and Kaufman, R. L. 1975. Cohort changes in political attitudes: tolerance of ideological nonconformity. *The public opinion* 39 (Spring):69–81.

Day, Lincoln H. 1978. What will a ZPG society be like? *Population bulletin* 33 (June).

Easterlin, Richard A., Wachter, Michael L., and Wachter, Susan M. 1978. Demographic influences on economic stability: the United States experience. *Population and development review* 4 (March):1–22.

Endres, Michael E. 1975. *On diffusing the population bomb.* New York: John Wiley and Sons.

Ford, Thomas R. 1977. Social implications of sustained low fertility in the United States. Paper presented at annual meetings of the Southern Regional Demographic Group.

Francese, Peter K. 1979. The 1980 census: the counting of America. *Population bulletin* 34 (September).

Frejka, Tomas. 1968. Reflections on the demographic conditions needed to establish a U.S. stationary population growth. *Population studies* 22 (November):379–397.

Gibson, Campbell. 1975. The contribution of immigrants to the U.S. population growth: 1790–1970. *International migration review* 9 (Summer): 157–176.

Kaplan, Charles, and Van Valey, Thomas L. 1980. *Census '80: continuing the fact-finder tradition.* U.S. Bureau of the Census. Washington, D.C.: Government Printing Office.

Keely, Charles B. 1979. *U.S. immigration: a policy analysis.* New York: The Population Council.

Keyfitz, Nathan. 1977. What difference would it make if cancer were eradicated? An examination of the Taeuber paradox. *Demography* 14 (November):411–418.

National Center for Health Statistics. 1980. Provisional statistics, 1979. *Monthly vital statistics,* report 28, number 12.

Parke, Robert. 1973. The impact of population growth on government and society. In *Toward the end of growth,* by Charles F. Westoff et al., pp. 121–132. Englewood Cliffs, N.J.: Prentice-Hall.

Population Reference Bureau. 1973. *Options.* Washington, D.C.: Population Reference Bureau.

———. *1979. World population data sheet.* Washington, D.C.: Population Reference Bureau.

Sauvy, Alfred. 1976. *Zero growth?* New York: Praeger.

Serow, William J., and Espenshade, Thomas J. 1977. The economics of declining population growth: an assessment of the literature. Paper presented at the General Conference of the International Union for the Scientific Study of Population.

Taeuber, Irene B., and Taeuber, Conrad. 1971. *People of the United States in the 20th century.* Washington, D.C.: Government Printing Office.

Thompson, Warren S., and Whelpton, P. K. 1933. *Population trends in the United States.* New York: McGraw-Hill.

———. 1938. *The problems of a changing population.* Washington, D.C.: Government Printing Office.

U.S. Bureau of the Census. 1971. *1970 census of population, number of inhabitants,* Final Report PC(1)-A1, United States summary. Washington, D.C.: Government Printing Office.

———. 1974. Population of the United States, trends and prospects: 1950–90. *Current population reports,* series P-23, no. 49. Washington, D.C.: Government Printing Office.

———. 1975. *Historical statistics of the United States, colonial times to 1970.* Washington, D.C.: Government Printing Office.

———. 1977*a*. Estimates of the population of the United States and components of change: 1940 to 1976. *Current population reports,* series P-25, no. 706. Washington, D.C.: Government Printing Office.

———. 1977*b*. Projections of the population of the United States: 1977 to 2050. *Current population reports,* series P-25, no. 704. Washington, D.C.: Government Printing Office.

———. 1979*a*. Estimates of the population of the United States, by age, sex, and race: 1976 to 1978. *Current population reports,* series P-25, no. 800. Washington, D.C.: Government Printing Office.

———. 1979*b*. Population profile of the United States: 1978. *Current population reports,* series P-20, no. 336. Washington, D.C.: Government Printing Office.

Waking Up. 1979. *American demographics* 1 (May):30–33, 47.

Wells, Robert V. 1975. *The population of the British colonies in America before 1790.* Princeton, N.J.: Princeton University Press.

Westoff, Charles F. 1978. Marriage and fertility in the developed countries. *Scientific american* 239 (December):51–57.

4
Population Distribution

The human population is not evenly distributed. Some geographic areas in the world contain more people than others. In some countries more people live in urban than in rural areas. And more people live in less economically developed countries than in those with higher levels of economic development. The first part of this chapter looks at these geographic, residential, and economic patterns of population distribution in the world.

This chapter also examines the geographic and residential distribution of the U.S. population. Patterns of population redistribution are examined. We conclude by examining the major consequences of the prevailing patterns of population redistribution.

DISTRIBUTION OF THE GLOBAL POPULATION

The population is very unevenly distributed geographically. Some countries have very large populations; some very small populations. Some countries and regions are very densely settled, while others have a very low population density.

Geographic Distribution

About 30 percent of the earth's land is permanently inhabited. This does not mean that 70 percent of the land awaits settlement. Areas like the Arctic and Antarctic, vast deserts, and rugged mountains are totally unfit for human living. The geographic distribution of the global population is shown in table 4.1. The area known as East Asia has the largest population; Oceania (Australia, Fiji, New Zealand, Papua-New Guinea, Western Somoa, and the Solomon Islands) has the smallest population. As of 1980 four countries had more than 200 million inhabitants: China (975 million), India (676 million), the Soviet Union (266 million), and the United States (226 million). Indonesia (144 million), Brazil (122 million), Japan (117 million), Bangladesh (91 million), Pakistan (86 million), and Nigeria (77 million) complete the list of the ten largest national populations in the world. In 1930 Great Britain, France, Germany, and Italy were all among the ten largest nations of the world. The change in the list reflects the rapid population growth that has taken place in the developing countries, while the more economically developed countries in Europe have experienced much slower growth.

Regional population figures do not take into account differences in the size of the areas. For instance, Asia's land area is five times larger than Europe's land area, so it stands to reason that more people live in Asia than in Europe. A more descriptive figure is an estimate of pop-

Table 4.1 Distribution of the World Population by Region, 1980

MAJOR AREAS AND REGIONS	ESTIMATED MIDYEAR POPULATION (MILLIONS)	
Africa		472
Northern Africa	110	
Western Africa	141	
Eastern Africa	135	
Middle Africa	54	
Southern Africa	32	
Asia		2,563
Southwest Asia	98	
Middle South Asia	938	
Southeast Asia	354	
East Asia	1,173	
North America		247
Latin America		360
Middle America	91	
Caribbean	30	
Tropical South America	198	
Temperate South America	41	
Europe		484
Northern Europe	82	
Western Europe	153	
Eastern Europe	110	
Southern Europe	140	
U.S.S.R.		266
Oceania		23
World		4,414

Source: Population Reference Bureau (1980).

ulation density, measured as the number of persons per square kilometer (or sometimes, square mile).[1] When this is done, Europe (96) is seen to be more densely settled than Asia (86). Of course, considerable variations in population density exist among countries in the various regions, and even greater differences exist within a particular country (see box 4.1).

The major features that influence population distribution are: (1) geographical factors, such as climate, terrain, soils and natural resources; (2) economic, social, and political factors, such as the type of economic activity and the form of social organization; and (3) demographic factors, such as the different rates of growth that exist between areas (United Nations 1973, pp. 162–172). As we saw in chapter 2, current patterns of population distribution will also have a major influence upon the future distribution of the world's population.

[1]A kilometer equals 1.609344 miles.

Box 4.1 Population Density

Population density may be defined mathematically by means of the following formula:

$$\text{Population density} = \frac{\text{Total Population}}{\text{Land Area (square miles or square kilometers)}}$$

An example of the variation in population density within a country may be seen by looking at the United States. The population density in 1978 for the nation as a whole and its four regions is shown below:

REGION	POPULATION	SQUARE MILES	DENSITY
Northeast	49,981,000	163,269	306
North Central	58,251,000	751,831	77
South	70,627,000	873,743	81
West	40,100,000	1,712,187	23
Nation	218,059,000	3,501,030	62

Source: U.S. Bureau of the Census (1978*a* and 1979).

Residential Distribution

In addition to the obvious fact that the economy of rural areas is largely agricultural, while the economy of urban areas is more diversified and nonagricultural, there are several other important differences between rural and urban areas. Sociologists maintain that rural residents have different attitudes and values and different life styles than urban residents. The urban areas have a greater population density, which necessitates a different, more impersonal form of social organization than is effective in rural areas. Finally, there have been sharp demographic differences traditionally between rural and urban areas. Although the pervasiveness of the mass media (magazines, radio, and television) and the access of both rural and urban residents to public education have blurred these distinctions recently in the United States and some other industrialized countries, they have not disappeared completely. Moreover, they remain very pronounced in the developing countries.

Throughout most of their history, humans have been rural dwellers. Large-scale **urbanization**—or increase in the percent of the population that dwells in cities—is a modern development. Widespread urbanization was not possible until recently because three conditions must be present for it to develop:

1. A surplus of farm products
2. A means of transporting these products to the urban areas, where they can be processed into items of food, clothing, and shelter

3. A sufficiently developed technology to utilize the surplus of farm products and to provide employment for the urban residents

By 1800 only 3 percent of the global population could be classified as urban. After that, however, technological advances and changes in the world's economic system made possible large agricultural surpluses, releasing large numbers of people from direct dependence upon the land. As people migrated to jobs in factories located in and around cities, massive urbanization got under way (see figure 4.1).

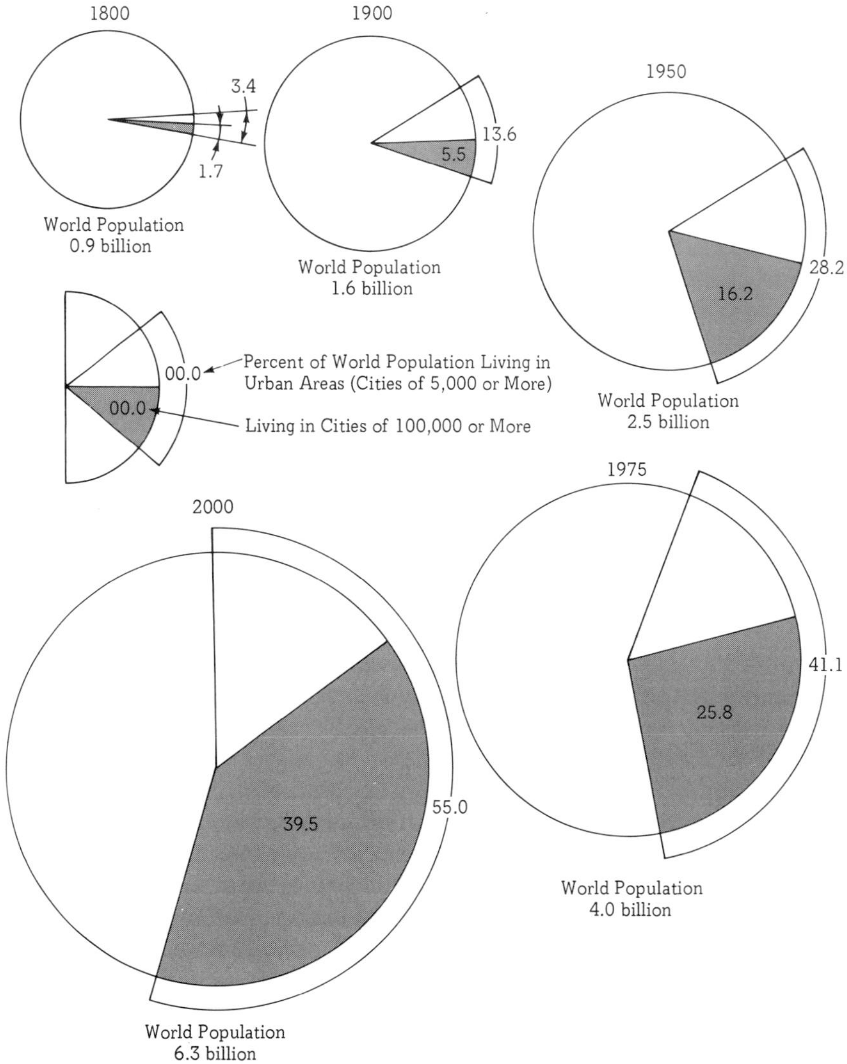

Figure 4.1 Degree of World Urbanization, 1800–2000
Source: Population Reference Bureau (1975).

Large-scale urbanization began in Europe at the time of the Industrial Revolution and spread to other areas as they industrialized. Today it is spreading to the developing countries, which are still relatively rural (United Nations 1973, p. 191). Some people have grown alarmed over the rapid urbanization apparently taking place there. They believe that rapid population growth in the rural areas has created surpluses of population, which the rural economy is unable to absorb, and they wonder if the developing countries will be able to support their urban areas. However, a recent study of world urbanization questions these common assumptions. Samuel Preston (1979) notes that the rate of change in the proportion of the population that is urban in developing countries is not exceptionally rapid by historical standards. For example, during the interval from 1950 to 1975 the level of urbanization went from 16.7 percent to 28.0 percent in developing countries. This increase is similar to the one that occurred in the more developed countries during the last quarter of the nineteenth century (where the level went from 17.2 percent to 26.1 percent between 1875 and 1900).

The mistaken notion that urbanization is occurring very rapidly in the developing countries arises from confusing urbanization with urban growth. As stated earlier, urbanization refers to an increase in the *percent* of the population that is urban. Urban growth refers to an increase in the *number* of persons living in urban areas. It is urban growth in the developing countries that is proceeding at unprecedented rates. Between 1875 and 1900 urban populations in the now developed countries grew by 100 percent (and rural populations by 18 percent). In comparison, between 1950 and 1975 the urban populations of the developing countries grew by 188 percent (and their rural ones by 49 percent). It is this unprecedented rapid urban growth in the developing countries that is so startling and that is so often confused with rapid urbanization. At the same time the rapid urban growth in the developing countries is caused primarily by reproductive change among the urban populations and is an integral part of the rapid population growth being experienced by the entire population in those countries.

Actually, the enormous growth of large urban areas has been a recent development. Although large cities existed in ancient times—the population of Rome in the second century A.D. may have been well over 1 million persons—such cities were not common. Most urban areas were much smaller. Even as late as 1800 only forty-five cities in the entire world had 100,000 or more inhabitants; at most there were only two (Hangchow in China and Tokyo in Japan) with 1 million or more inhabitants (United Nations 1973, p. 191). Today an estimated 229 cities have 1 million or more inhabitants, and about one-seventh of the world's population lives in a city of this size (Goldstein and Sly 1977, p. 59).

Table 4.2 Percent of Population Living in Large Cities (over 1 million) in Major World Regions and Areas, 1980

MAJOR AREAS AND REGIONS	PERCENT
Africa	7.0
Northern Africa	14.3
Western Africa	3.0
Eastern Africa	2.3
Middle Africa	4.3
Southern Africa	20.7
Asia	10.9
East Asia	14.8
South Asia	8.0
North America	34.9
Latin America	24.9
Middle America	20.0
Caribbean	15.6
Tropical South America	27.0
Temperate South America	34.0
Europe	20.1
Northern Europe	30.2
Western Europe	24.7
Eastern Europe	16.4
Southern Europe	10.7
U.S.S.R.	14.4
Oceania	37.5
World	14.5

Source: Goldstein and Sly (1977), p. 59.

Table 4.2 shows the percent of the total population of each world region that lived in large cities (of more than 1 million) in 1980. The smallest percentages are in parts of Africa and South Asia. The largest percentages occur in Oceania, North America, temperate South America, and northern Europe. In general, large cities are concentrated in the more industrialized countries. For instance, the more developed countries contain only about one-fourth of the world's population, yet they contain almost half of its large cities.

Economic Distribution

Another way of describing the distribution of the world's population is to classify people according to their country's level of economic development. This concept is extremely difficult to measure. Two common measures are per capita income and per capita energy consumption. Each yields similar results: about three-fourths of the world's population live in developing countries and one-fourth lives in developed countries. It must be emphasized that economic development is a relative term. Countries are classified as developing or developed only in comparison to each other.

This proportion is expected to increase in the next fifty years. The rates of population growth are much higher in the developing countries than they are in the developed countries. These high rates of growth are produced by an imbalance between birth and death rates. For instance, in 1980 the rate of reproductive change in Africa was 29, reflecting a birth rate of 46 and a death rate of 17. If maintained through time, this rate would double the size of the African population in twenty-four years. By contrast, the rate of reproductive change in the United States in 1980 was 7 (a birth rate of 16 and a death rate of 9), which would double the U.S. population in 99 years (Population Reference Bureau 1980). Massive migration from the developing countries into the developed countries is unlikely because of political barriers erected by the latter to prevent this type of migration (see in chapter 12). Unless birth rates decline or death rates increase there, the developing countries will have an increasingly larger share of the global population in the future.

DISTRIBUTION OF U.S. POPULATION

Several major trends have shaped the distribution of the U.S. population. There has been a westward movement of people. Lately there has also been net migration into the Sunbelt states in the Southwest and the South. For most of our history, the population was concentrated in large metropolitan areas, but since 1950 the trend has been toward deconcentration of the population.

A Shift to the West and South

The population of the United States is concentrated in the eastern third of the nation's land area, and vast portions of the nation's land area remain sparsely settled. Nevertheless, the long-term trend in geographic distribution may be described in one word—westward. This may be seen in figure 4.2, which shows, for each census date, the **center of population.** That refers to the point at which a flat rigid map of the United States would balance if weights of identical value were placed on it, each weight corresponding to the location of one person on April 1 of the census year. In 1790 the center of population was located in the upper portion of the Chesapeake Bay. Since then, there has been a steady westward movement of the population. The population of the East Central states (which border the Great Lakes) began to grow rapidly in 1800. By about 1820 the entire middle section of the country started its growth as agricultural and grazing lands were developed in the prairie states immediately west of the Mississippi.

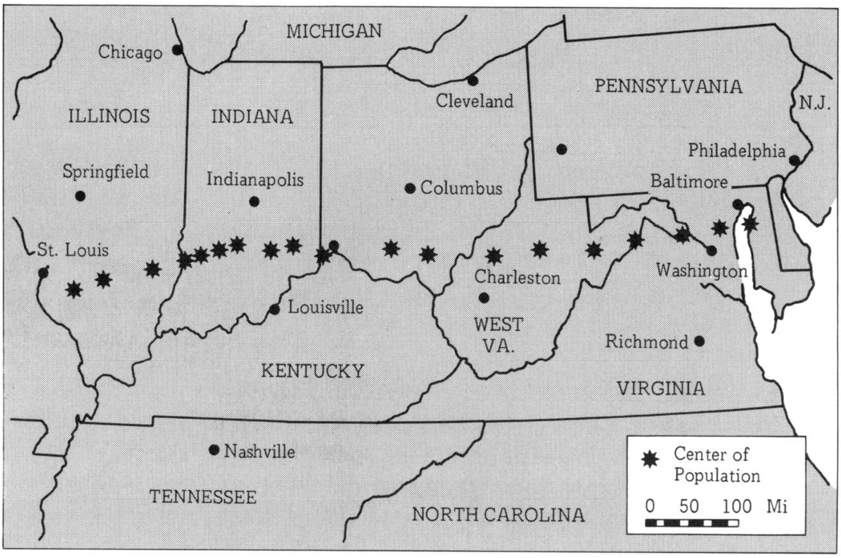

Figure 4.2 Center of Population for the United States, 1790–1970
Source: U.S. Bureau of the Census (1971), p. 14.

The West began to grow about 1850 as the frontier became more accessible to settlers, rich ore deposits were located, and cheap land became scarcer in the East. As a result of this westward expansion, the center of population has moved further west with each census. In 1970 it was located in St. Clair County, Illinois, at a point about five miles southeast of the city of Miscoutah. Since 1970 the population has continued its movement to the west, helped along by a vast movement of population into the Sunbelt—the Southwest and South. Consequently, by 1980 the center of population had crossed the Mississippi for the first time in history.

Most regional variations in growth have been due to streams of migration from one part of the country to another, not to immigration from outside the country or regional differences in the amount of reproductive change. Internal migration will continue to be an important factor affecting the future geographic distribution of the U.S. population.

The role of internal migration in causing a redistribution of the population is illustrated by the recent resurgence of the South (see figure 4.3). Historically, more people have migrated from the South than into it. Yet since 1970 this migration flow has been reversed. During the decade the South gained almost 4 million net migrants, while the Northeast and North Central regions experienced net out-migration.

The turnaround from net out-migration to in-migration into the South has several causes. A lot of the in-migrants are retirees, attracted by the South's mild climate, lower taxes, and lower cost of living. Con-

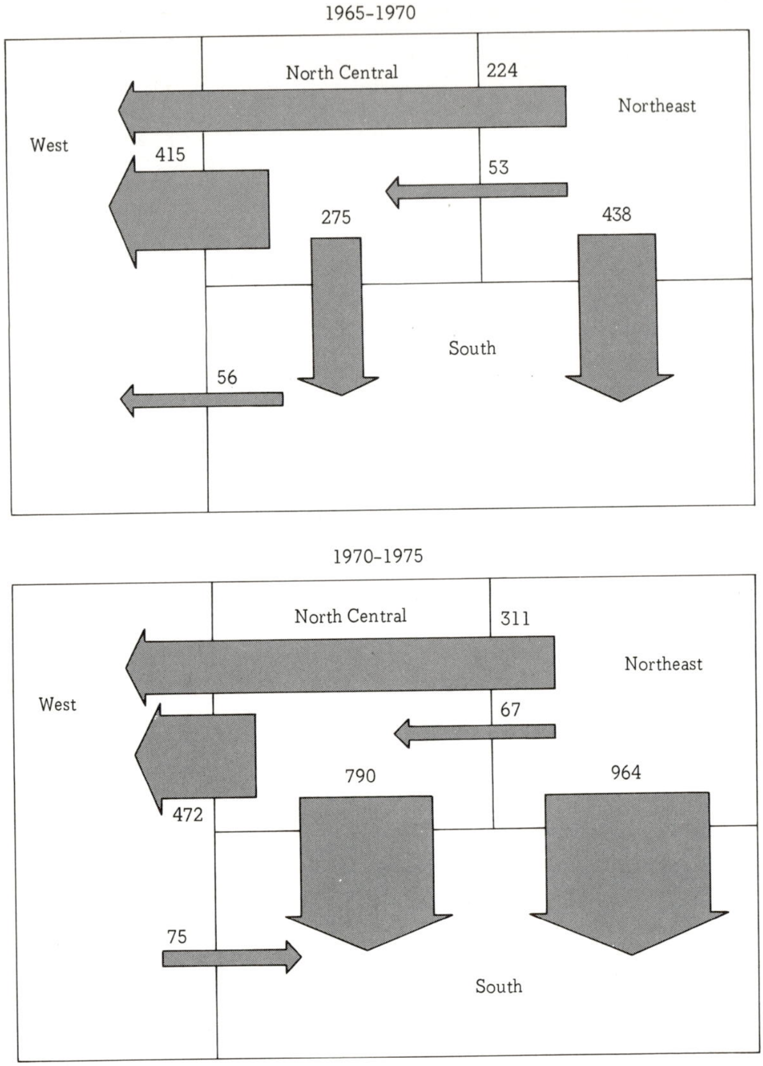

Figure 4.3 Net Interregional Migration, 1965–1970 and 1970–1975

Note: Width of arrows is proportional to volume of net interregional migration flows. Figures accompanying arrows indicate numbers of net interregional migrants in thousands.

Source: Reprinted with the permission of The Population Council from Brian Berry and D. Dahmann, "Population Redistribution in the United States in the 1970s," *Population and Development Review* 3, no. 4 (December 1977): p. 458.

sequently, there is a concentration of elderly persons in the South. The turnaround can also be attributed to a smaller volume of out-migration from the South—particularly among blacks—and the phenomenon of **return migration,** which involves people migrating back to some place where they were born or lived earlier. Many of the in-migrants during the 1970s were southerners who had migrated out of the South during preceding decades. At the same time the volume of migration out of the South has declined. The South has experienced a significant economic expansion during the 1960s and 1970s and now offers employment opportunities that are comparable to those of the other regions. Indeed, part of the industrial growth in the South has taken place because of the relocation of industries attracted to the South from the Northeast and North Central regions due to lower wage levels and cheaper supplies of energy.

Because of this migration turnaround, instead of growing more slowly than the rest of the nation, the South is now growing more rapidly. This rate of growth will continue unless prevailing patterns of internal migration—that is, migration within the nation—change significantly (Poston and Weller 1980).

Metropolitanization

Perhaps even more dramatic than the westward shift of the population has been its concentration into urban areas. The U.S. Census Bureau recognizes many different ways of defining urban populations. These include:

Urban places: These are areas with a minimum population of 2,500 and may be either incorporated or unincorporated.

Cities: These are places that are incorporated and have been granted certain powers, as defined in their charters, by the state in which they are located.

Urbanized areas: The major objective of defining urbanized areas is to separate the urban and rural population in the vicinity of the larger cities. They consist of a **central city** of 50,000 or more inhabitants (or twin cities within contiguous boundaries with that combined population) and surrounding, closely settled territory. The U.S. Bureau of the Census defines "closely settled" as a population density of around 2,000 persons per square mile or a housing density of approximately 500 houses per square mile (Hawley 1971, p. 152).

Metropolitan areas: In our discussion of urbanization in the United States we will focus on population distribution in metropolitan areas, which in general refers to large cities and areas that surround them. However, the term has undergone changes in definition over time. The U.S. Bureau of the Census first attempted to delimit places as metropolitan in 1910, when the term "metropolitan district" was used. This referred to urban units having aggregate populations of at least 100,000 persons and containing one or more central cities of 50,000 or more persons. In 1950 the Census Bureau officially adopted the Standard Metropolitan Area (SMA) to replace the metropolitan district. In the 1960 and 1970 censuses, the nomenclature was changed to Standard Metropol-

> itan Statistical Area (SMSA), but the criteria for inclusion remained quite similar to those used in 1950.

The SMSAs consist of one or more contiguous counties that (1) contain at least one large city with a population of at least 50,000 (or twin cities with a combined population of at least 50,000), and (2) are socially and economically integrated with the central city. Economic integration takes into consideration factors such as residence and employment patterns, the extent to which the labor force consists of nonagricultural workers, per capita telephone calls between the county and the central city, newspaper circulation reports, official traffic counts, and the extent of retail trade in the central city by residents of the contiguous county. The persons living within a SMSA are referred to as the metropolitan population, which is divided into two parts. Those living in the large city are classified as residents of the central city. All other persons are classified as noncentral-city residents. They may live in suburbs, in smaller cities located within metropolitan areas, or on farms located within the outlying areas of the SMSA. The rest of the nation's population is classified as nonmetropolitan.

In the 1980 census the bureau changed the nomenclature to Metropolitan Statistical Area (MSA) and changed the definition to make it harder for cities to qualify for metropolitan status. The area must contain a minimum population of 100,000, whereas there was no minimum SMSA size—only a minimum size for the central city. The new definition retains the concept of a metropolitan area as consisting of a central city and surrounding counties that are integrated with it socially and economically, but it is harder for the outlying counties to qualify for inclusion. Commuting patterns have been deemphasized in the new definition, and nonagricultural land use has assumed more importance in determining which outlying counties should be included in a particular metropolitan area.

These changes took place in response to criticisms that the SMSAs tended to include too much sparsely settled territory simply on the basis of high commuting. They illustrate the way in which census terminology and items change in response to changing social and political conditions.

Growth of the Metropolitan Population

Because the criteria for designating metropolitan areas have changed over time, it is advisable to use some constant definition in order to see how the metropolitan population has grown. In 1900 there were 61 areas that would have qualified as SMAs under the 1950 definition. By 1960 the number of such areas had tripled to 189, and 202 areas would have been classified as SMAs in 1970. During this same interval the proportion of the U.S. population living in areas classifiable as SMAs increased from about one-third in 1900 to two-thirds in 1960. From 1900 to 1950 this increase was caused by both the expansion of existing metropolitan areas and the growth of other areas into a size classified as "metropolitan," but since 1960 an increasingly important source of growth has been the addition of adjacent counties to preexisting areas (Hawley, Duncan, and Goldberg 1964; and Hawley 1971). The number of SMSAs increased from 212 in 1960 to 243 in 1970 and to 264 in 1977, and the total population living in metropolitan areas increased by 26 million persons between 1960 and 1977.[2] In 1977 more than 153 million persons—72 percent of the total population—were classified as living in SMSAs.

The proportion of the national population living in metropolitan areas has remained fairly constant since 1970. There are only two states that contain no metropolitan areas—Vermont and Wyoming. The growth of the metropolitan population slowed considerably in the 1970s. Between 1970 and 1978 the population in metropolitan areas increased by only 4.4 percent, while the nonmetropolitan population increased by 12.2 percent (U.S. Bureau of the Census 1979). In fact, one out of every seven SMSAs is actually declining in population size. Because these tend to be the larger, older SMSAs, one out of every three Americans lives in an SMSA whose population is declining (Morrison 1976*a*).

The declines in population size are primarily occurring in the SMSAs in the Middle Atlantic, Northeast, and East North Central states. More and more migrants are leaving the larger and older urban centers located in these regions and moving into metropolitan areas in the Sunbelt. As mentioned earlier, many of these migrants are retirees and many others are southerners who are "returning home" after living in the North for some time. All fifteen of the fastest growing SMSAs in the nation are located in the South and West. Nine are in one state—Florida.

Megalopolis—A Super Metropolis?

Recently a great deal of attention has been given to the possible emergence of a new community form—the **megalopolis**. Presumably it represents a stage of urban development that follows extensive metropolitanization of the population. A megalopolis is viewed as a chain of contiguous and interrelated metropolitan areas. The example most frequently used is "Boswash," an area extending from southern New Hampshire (the Boston area) to northern Virginia (the Washington area) and inland for thirty to one hundred miles from the Atlantic Ocean (Gottmann 1961). This vast concentration of people, goods, and services functions as an "economic hinge" for the United States, linking the North American continent with the foreign markets accessible via the Atlantic.

But does this megalopolis have the essential characteristics of a

[2]At the end of 1979, there were 288 SMSAs, including 4 in Puerto Rico.

community? It certainly has one such characteristic—a common geographic area which is distinguishable from other areas. However, its people must be linked in a system characterized by a division of labor, increasing differentiation of economic activity, and functional interdependence. Unless such a pattern of interaction exists between the metropolitan areas of a megalopolis, and unless the differentiation of economic activity has *increased* through time, it is difficult to conceive of a megalopolis as anything other than a grouping of contiguous metropolitan areas sharing a common, heavily populated geographic area.

Robert Weller (1967) conducted a test of the megalopolis as an emergent community form. He used data from the 1950 and 1960 censuses to examine the amount of specialization in various types of economic activities among the SMSAs in the areas Gottmann identified as Megalopolis. He reports that the economic activities of metropolitan areas have generally become more similar rather than more differentiated.

This does not prove that a megalopolis is not a community. There is, in fact, considerable evidence of interdependence among metropolitan areas in most types of economic activity at a given point in time. But there is no evidence of *increasing* differentiation—and therefore increasing interdependence—through time. Such differentiation has already taken place *within* each of the respective metropolitan communities. The absence of differentiation *among* the metropolitan communities between 1950 and 1960 raises grave doubts about the value of megalopolis as a community form—unless it had already fully evolved before 1950, which seems unlikely. Although "megalopolis" is an eye-catching term to use when discussing urban development in the United States, there is no evidence to suggest that it is replacing the metropolis as the focal point of American life.

Trends Toward Deconcentration

At the same time that the population has become concentrated into metropolitan areas, a process of deconcentration within metropolitan areas has occurred. This is popularly known as suburbanization. It represents a shift from higher-density central cities to lower-density, noncentral-city (or ring) portions of the SMSAs. Another form of deconcentration is the shift of population from metropolitan to nonmetropolitan areas. We will consider each of these shifts separately.

Shift to the Suburbs

Since 1900 the proportion of the U.S. population classified as metropolitan has increased in each decade until 1970, and yet since 1930 the proportion of the population living in central cities of metropolitan areas has decreased slightly (see table 4.3). Indeed, the pace of this decrease has accelerated since 1970. Thus the metropolitanization of the

Table 4.3 Population Distribution by Metropolitan Residence in the United States, 1900–1977*

YEAR	TOTAL	PERCENT METROPOLITAN CENTRAL CITY	RING	PERCENT NONMETROPOLITAN
1900	41.9	26.0	15.9	58.1
1910	45.7	29.5	16.2	54.3
1920	49.7	32.8	16.9	50.3
1930	54.3	35.1	19.2	45.7
1940	55.1	34.5	20.6	44.9
1950	59.0	34.6	24.4	41.0
1960	63.0	32.4	30.6	37.0
1970	68.6	31.4	37.2	31.4
1977	67.3	28.2	39.1	32.7

*SMSAs did not exist in official terminology until 1960. Figures for dates before then are based upon areas that would have been SMSAs by 1960 definitions.

Sources: Bogue (1969), p. 534; U.S. Bureau of the Census (1971), pp. 180, 206; and U.S. Bureau of the Census (1978*d*), p. 4.

population in recent years has occurred primarily within the ring portions of the SMSAs.

This does not mean that the population of the central cities has not increased in absolute numbers. On the contrary, between 1930 and 1970 the combined central-city population of the various SMSAs grew from 43.1 to 62.9 million persons. But this population increased less rapidly than the population in the metropolitan rings. In this way the *percentage* of the population living in these areas declined.

Most of the growth in the central-city population that occurred between 1950 and 1970 was accomplished by annexation—that is, by placing outlying areas under the jurisdiction of the central city for one reason or another. When this factor is controlled, the population of the central cities increased by a mere 1.5 percent between 1950 and 1960 and by only 0.1 percent between 1960 and 1970; this amounts to nongrowth. Likewise, without annexation the growth of the ring population would have been even larger during this interval (Bogue 1969, p. 534; and U.S. Bureau of the Census 1971, p. 192).

Since 1970 the combined population of the central cities of the SMSAs has declined in absolute numbers by over 3 million persons. At the same time the noncentral-city portions have continued to grow at a considerably higher rate than the national average.

Why have the central cities lost population since 1970? One reason is what has been called "white flight." As more and more poor nonwhites have settled in the central cities, more and more affluent whites have left the cities to escape conditions brought on by poverty and overcrowding—crime, drug addiction, slum areas, and the like. Some white flight is simply a matter of out-and-out racism and takes place to avoid sending children to the same schools as blacks or living in the same neighborhood. But part of it takes place because of the attractiveness of living in the **suburbs**—owning a piece of land, having a yard, sending children to "nice" schools, owning a second car, and leading a middle-class life style. Indeed, the declining population size of the central cities cannot be ascribed solely to racial fear, because black migration to the suburbs appears to be accelerating.

For whatever the reasons, between 1970 and 1977 the white population in central cities declined by a greater amount (3.9 million) than the amount of increase by the nonwhite population (1.1 million). In the 1960s the white population in central cities remained fairly constant, but in the 1970s it decreased at an annual rate of 1.2 percent. Although the number of nonwhites in central cities has continued to increase, the rate of increase was considerably lower during the 1970s than during the 1960s. Indeed, the black population living in central cities did not grow significantly after 1974. Meanwhile black migration to the suburbs has accelerated, and the suburban black population has grown at a faster rate than the white suburban population since 1970, although the suburbs are still predominantly white (93 percent). During the 1980s the central cities may experience declines in the black as well as the white population (U.S. Bureau of the Census 1978*d*).

Another reason for the cessation of population growth in the central cities is a change in immigration patterns. Earlier in this century there was a considerable amount of legal immigration (see chapter 3). The immigrants tended to settle in the central cities of existing metropolitan areas. Since then, however, the volume of legal immigration has become much smaller, and the immigration stream has contained a large number of illegal immigrants. Illegal immigrants are extremely difficult to enumerate in a census or population survey. Many who settle in central cities are not counted, and this overstates the amount of population decline in those areas. And some of them are engaged in economic activities, such as agriculture or small industry, which are located outside the central cities. However, even if all the illegal immigrants were counted and even if all of the immigrants had settled in central cities, the population of the central cities would still have declined during the 1970s because of the pattern of internal migration.

Internal migration used to be predominantly from nonmetropolitan areas to central cities. But this sort of migration is limited now, because so many people already live in metropolitan areas. Instead, population movement tends to occur within and among metropolitan areas or out of metropolitan areas altogether. Those who migrate from one metropolitan area to another are likely to move directly into a suburban area instead of first settling in the central city. Those who move within a metropolitan area tend to go from central city to ring. Finally, those who move *out* of a metropolitan area tend to settle in a nonmetropolitan, nonfarm area. In this way the central cities have continued to experience net out-migration. The pattern of net movement be-

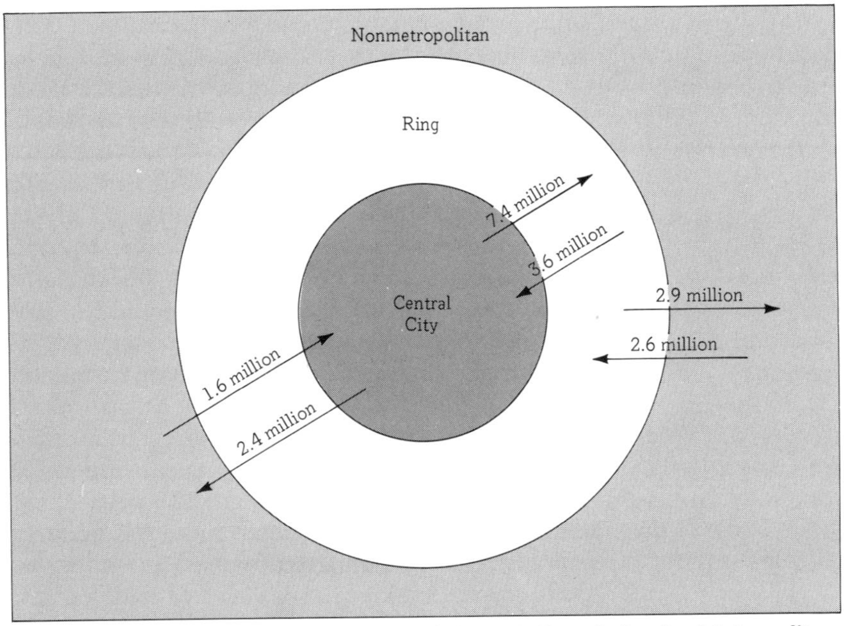

Figure 4.4 Internal Mobility Patterns of the U.S. Population by Metropolitan Status, 1975–1977
Source: U.S. Bureau of the Census (1978*c*), p. 5.

tween 1975 and 1977 may be seen in figure 4.4. Central cities lost 9.8 million out-migrants and gained only 5.2 million in-migrants—a loss of 4.6 million people. Of those persons leaving the central cities, 7.4 million moved into the rings and 2.4 million moved into nonmetropolitan areas. Overall, 5.3 million persons moved from metropolitan areas to nonmetropolitan areas, and 4.2 million moved in the opposite direction—a loss of 1.1 million persons by the metropolitan areas.

By contrast, during this same interval the ring portions of SMSAs experienced a net in-migration of 3.5 million persons. A total of 10 million moved in while 6.5 million moved out. Of those persons leaving the rings, 3.6 million moved into central cities, and 2.9 million moved into nonmetropolitan areas.

The impact of mobility patterns on metropolitan change is even greater when indirect effects are considered. Those who move tend to be concentrated in the young-adult age brackets, when marriage and/or child-bearing are most likely. Thus, an area experiencing net in-migration gains population in two ways: (1) by the net number of movers (direct effect), and (2) by the number of children born to movers after their arrival (indirect effect).

In summary, then, prevailing patterns of population mobility are not conducive to the growth of the central-city population. Indeed, the central cities have been experiencing net out-migration since 1960. During the 1960s, however, the central cities did not lose population because there was a sufficient amount of reproductive change to offset the out-migration. (Remember the demographic equation in chapter 1.) However, during the 1970s the amount of reproductive change in the central cities was not as large as the volume of net out-migration, and consequently the central cities declined in size.

We have been discussing aggregate trends for the various portions of the U.S. population. Of course, we should bear in mind that certain individual SMSAs are growing rapidly. Net in-migration contributes significantly to the growth of most of these areas. For instance, the population of the Fort Myers, Florida, SMSA increased by 52.9 percent between 1970 and 1976, as the population grew from 105,216 persons to 160,900 persons. The total growth was 55,700 persons, and 54,300 of this was produced by net in-migration (U.S. Bureau of the Census 1978*b*, p.11). Likewise, certain central cities are continuing to grow—partly because of net in-migration and partly because of reproductive change. But these are exceptions to the rule. The general pattern is one of deconcentration, with a massive net migration from the central cities of the nation's metropolitan areas.

Consequences

What are the consequences of this shift to the suburbs? One consequence is that particular types of economic activity (e.g., manufacturing and retail and personal services) have also relocated in the ring portions of metropolitan areas. This removes from the central city important sources of tax revenue and jobs.

But the social and economic implications for the metropolitan population are much greater than this. The composition of the population of central cities has changed radically. The out-migrating middle class has been replaced by relatively disadvantaged segments of the population—poor minority groups, the chronically unemployed, the aged, and the socially disadvantaged. Compared to the ring portions of metropolitan areas, the central cities contain a disproportionate share of blacks and other minority groups, female heads of household, persons with minimal levels of education, families with incomes less than the poverty level, and elderly persons (see table 4.4).

The significance of this concentration of economically and socially disadvantaged persons in central cities is twofold. First, the increasing proportion of such persons has added to the demand for related social services—welfare, health, public housing, sanitation, police protection, and so on. At the same time the economic status of the resident population is lowered, because more families move out of central cities than move into them and because the average income of the out-migrants is higher than the income of the in-migrants. For example, the U.S. Bureau of the Census (1978*d*, p. 2) estimates that $18 billion less income was available to persons living in central cities in 1977 than would have been the case if there had been no migration in and out of cities between 1975 and 1977. The lowered economic status of

Table 4.4 Selected Characteristics of Central-City and Ring Populations of SMSAs, 1977

SELECTED CHARACTERISTIC	CENTRAL CITY	RING
Percent of population with black or Spanish heritage	30.3	11.5
Percent 65+ years old	11.4	8.4
Percent of households with female heads	20.7	10.9
Percent of males (25+) with seven or fewer years of schooling	11.9	7.2
Percent of families receiving public assistance income	12.4	5.3
Percent of families with income less than poverty level	15.8	6.9
Mean family income	$16,017	$19,405
Unemployment rate for white males (20–34)	9.2	8.1
Unemployment rate for black males (20–34)	20.45	15.2

Source: U.S. Bureau of the Census (1978*d*).

the resident population and the loss of industry and business activity through deconcentration combine to reduce the tax base and cause declines in the financial ability of the central-city government to support the increased need for services brought about by the relative concentration of the disadvantaged. Thus, central cities are confronted with a financial crisis: demands for services are increasing at the same time that taxable resources are diminishing. To meet the demands, the central city has been forced to increase greatly the property tax rate, which has had the effect of forcing *more* homeowners and industries to move out of the central city, again lowering the tax base. It is a vicious circle.

At the same time suburban portions of metropolitan areas tend to have lower levels of expenditures while having higher levels of taxable resources and lower tax rates. In a sense they may be characterized as achieving an American goal—having their cake and eating it too.

John Riew (1970) has conducted a detailed case study of Milwaukee that illustrates these fiscal disparities between central cities and suburbs. Some of his major findings are presented in table 4.5. Although he uses data for the 1960–1966 interval, his conclusions can apply to many metropolitan areas today. Riew distinguishes three types of suburbs—primarily residential, primarily industrial, and those containing a balance of residential and industrial land use. Riew further classifies the residential suburbs according to whether their inhabitants have high-income, medium-income, or low-income levels.

Notice that in all cases the property values are higher in the suburbs than for the city of Milwaukee, with low-income suburbs having

Table 4.5 Fiscal Characteristics of Municipalities in the Milwaukee Urban Area

	PER CAPITA PROPERTY VALUES	PERCENT CHANGE 1960–1966	FULL-VALUE TAX RATE (Mills)*	PERCENT CHANGE 1957–1966
Central city	$ 5,454	3.8	40.7	48.0
Urban area suburb	9,219		28.4	31.3
Balanced	8,982	9.0	29.5	29.8
Industrial	25,239	7.0	24.3	22.6
Residential				
High income	10,937	16.0	29.4	34.6
Medium income	7,180	15.0	28.4	29.4
Low income	5,799	13.0	27.9	33.9

*A mill is equal to one-tenth of a cent.

Source: "Metropolitan Disparities and Fiscal Federalism" by John Riew, vol. 4 of Urban Affairs Annual Reviews, John P. Crecine, Editor, copyright 1970, pp. 137–161, by permission of the publisher, Sage Publications, Inc. (Beverly Hills/London).

only slightly higher values and the industrial suburbs having property values over four times as great as the city. Moreover, between the period 1960–1966 the increases in per capita property values were greater in all classes of suburbs than in the central city.

Faced with an economic base that was not expanding very much, the central city has been forced to cope with the greater demands for expenditures by markedly increasing rates at which properties are taxed. Thus central Milwaukee tax rates are at least 43 percent higher than the rates for all types of suburbs and increased at a much faster rate during the study period. This encourages people and industries to move out of the central city, which starts the cycle of migration all over again.

The implications of "tax revolts," such as California's adoption of Proposition 13, on the fiscal and demographic structure of metropolitan communities is hard to tell. Other things being equal, by reducing the property tax, the disposable income of inhabitants is increased and the amount of money available to municipal governments is decreased. These governemnts are then faced with the choice of raising revenue from some other source (such as increasing the sales tax or imposing a local income tax) or reducing the level of "free" services provided to the population. These services then become available for a "fee" to the users, who pay for them directly instead of indirectly through a local property tax.

Traditionally, the central city has provided facilities and services to many suburban residents, who paid only minimal, if any, taxes to the central-city government. This greatly increased the cost of municipal services in the central city and therefore the need for increased revenue (Zimmer 1975, p. 83). To the extent that this pattern remains valid today, tax revolts such as Proposition 13 might be expected to ease the financial pressure on central-city governments by forcing all users of services to pay for them directly. To the extent that the tax structure affects out-migration from the central city, one incentive to migrate to the suburbs would be removed.

However, two types of persons have used central-city services and facilities without paying for them—(1) nonresidents and (2) residents who are too poor to pay. The central cities contain a disproportionate share of the latter. Unless the poor are to be deprived of services, Proposition 13 can do little to ease the burden they represent for central-city governments.

Moreover, the traditional pattern of a central city providing services and facilities to an entire metropolitan area may no longer be as applicable as it once was. Partly in response to changes in transportation and communication, which have made possible the easy movement of goods and information, jobs, retail shops, service industries, sports, and entertainment have been decentralized and are now located in the rings. The rings are being asked to provide services and facilities to an increasingly large number of nonresidents. More and more people, including some central-city residents, now work in the rings. This decentralization is likely to lead to many different types of problems for suburban municipal governments. In turn, this will lead to further increases in the municipal budgets of the rings.

Eventually the ring residents must pay higher taxes, which could be a factor in the migration of persons out of the metropolitan area completely. Likewise, the property tax revolts would fail without strong support from the ring residents, for these people are a plurality of the population in most states facing this issue and certainly are more active politically than the disadvantaged of the central cities. To the extent that high taxes were a factor which led to a decline of cities and to the extent that these high taxes resulted from the use of city facilities and services by nonresidents, then suburban areas may very well face a similar situation in the future (Sly and Tayman 1980).

Are There Solutions?

One means of more evenly distributing some of the demands for social services would be to disperse some of the low-income populations to the outer metropolitan areas. However, most suburban areas have effectively resisted such attempts. The high service demands and low tax revenues of the inhabitants of public housing constitute a fiscal drain on any community. Instead, suburban communities seek highly priced housing and "clean" industries and commercial services. These tend to yield more tax value relative to the level of expenditure.

The most common means that local governments use to impose these limitations has been "fiscal zoning." Laws are passed to require large lot sizes for building, specify minimum house sizes, or prohibit multifamily dwellings. Stringent building codes and extensive subdivision regulations also increase the cost of construction, effectively discriminating against lower- and lower-middle-class groups. Reinforcing these factors are the practices of many local real estate, building, and financial institutions, which discriminate against certain segments of the population.

All these fiscal disparities and exclusionary practices affect the residential patterns not only of lower income groups in general, but also of blacks in particular. A greater percentage of blacks than whites within metropolitan areas are economically disadvantaged. Indeed, some people believe that fiscal zoning and other discriminatory techniques may be intended more to exclude racial minorities than to exclude lower-income groups in general. These exclusions have had a secondary effect on levels of employment and income levels of the black population. The industrial employment opportunities in suburban locations are relatively inaccessible to central-city blacks, since the transportation system in most major cities is organized to service the central city rather than the suburbs (Kasarda 1977). Transportation from center city to remote suburban locations is time consuming and costly, and it usually necessitates the use of a private automobile. The relative remoteness of suburban job locations also means that many potential employment opportunities go unrecognized. Many suburban jobs are not posted in central-city newspapers. At the same time employment opportunities in central cities are frequently in low-paying service jobs, in marginal industries requiring cheap labor, or in clerical and administrative positions for which the low-skilled, undereducated black worker may be unsuited. Hence, many central-city blacks are locked into low-paying, dead-end jobs, thereby contributing to low levels of median income in the black population and high rates of unemployment.

The Shift to Nonmetropolitan Areas

Another major shift of population has been from metropolitan to nonmetropolitan counties. Since 1970 the nonmetropolitan counties in the United States have been receiving in-migrants from the metropolitan counties, reversing a pattern which has been present throughout almost all of this century. Partly as a consequence, since 1970 the nation's nonmetropolitan counties have grown much more rapidly than the metropolitan counties. Part of this shift to nonmetropolitan counties is due to metropolitan spillover, as persons relocate in the fringe areas immediately outside of existing SMSAs. This has been facilitated by improved transportation networks (e.g., the interstate highway system) and the decentralization of employment within metropolitan areas, which have made it possible for people to live in rural areas and commute to metropolitan labor markets. But population growth in the nonmetropolitan areas is not simply the latest manifestation of urban sprawl. Even counties nonadjacent to SMSAs have experienced inmigration since 1970 (Beale 1976; and Morrison 1976*b*).

Three factors appear to be facilitating this "rural renaissance"—

industrial trends, life style changes, and the growth of colleges in nonmetropolitan areas. The industrial trends that have had the most noteworthy effect upon nonmetropolitan areas are the decentralization of manufacturing into nonmetropolitan areas in response to reduced transportation costs, inexpensive land and low wage rates in those areas, development of the trucking industry, and the revival or expansion of mining. The South Appalachian coal region provides an example. During the 1960s those counties in the coal fields that were not adjacent to metropolitan areas experienced a 2.6 percent out-migration of persons. However, petroleum costs have risen so rapidly since then that new employment opportunities in coal extraction have risen, and during the 1970s there was a 0.8 percent inflow of population into these counties (McCarthy and Morrison 1979).

The trend toward earlier retirement and semiretirement has multiplied the ranks of retirees and lengthened the interval between retirement and death. Retirees have become more affluent and mobile and have assumed increased importance as consumers. They are no longer forced to remain in the communities where they worked, and many retirees are attracted to nonmetropolitan areas by the lower costs of living and the life style there. This generates employment for other persons in those areas. At the same time there has been an increased emphasis at all ages on those leisure activities and recreation that are more readily available in nonmetropolitan areas—fishing, camping, hiking, and the like. Thus, retirement and recreation have emerged as important growth-related activities in nonmetropolitan areas and have contributed to the so-called rural renaissance.

Note that we are discussing nonfarm areas. Farm areas are still losing population. Farming has become increasingly capital intensive and less labor intensive. Thus, farm employment opportunities have continued to decline, which has caused the farm population to decline.

One additional qualification: the rural renaissance or rural revival does not mean that the nation's metropolitan areas are losing population. Some of them are, especially the larger ones. However, in the aggregate, the metropolitan population increased by 0.7 percent annually between 1970 and 1977. By comparison, the nonmetropolitan population increased by 1.2 percent per year during this interval. Yet the numerical base of the metropolitan population (150 million in 1970) is so much larger than the numerical base of the nonmetropolitan population (53 million in 1970) that the absolute numerical growth of the metropolitan population was almost twice as large as the growth of the nonmetropolitan population between 1970 and 1977. Thus, as a nation we hardly need to worry about deserted metropolises in the near future. We are a nation of metropolitanites and will remain that way for some time, even though the percentage of the national population living in metropolitan areas leveled off during the 1970s and may actually decline during the 1980s.

Consequences

The revival of population growth in nonmetropolitan areas has important implications for the future. Small governmental jurisdictions will experience population growth with which they are not prepared to cope and which their residents may oppose vigorously. For instance, Kimberling City, Missouri, had only about 600 people in 1970 but has almost doubled in size since then. A local planning official estimates that the town's population will reach 4,000 by the end of the century. Mountain Home, Arkansas, increased its population from 3,900 in 1970 to 6,300 in 1976—a jump of about 60 percent in six years.

Growth can cause problems. Often the newcomers demand services such as paved roads and other conveniences the town cannot afford. Shopping malls, fast-food outlets, and traffic jams develop. (The results may not be all bad. According to news reports, a would-be bank robber was arrested in the growing town of Navastota, Texas, because he could not get out of the bank parking lot in time.) The housing market is often strained. As a result, concern mounts and attempts to slow this growth sometimes are made. But other communities have attempted to exploit this growth. We will discuss strategies for controlling growth in chapter 12.

SUMMARY

The earth's population is not distributed evenly across its surface. In general the developed areas contain a third of the global population. The developing countries are experiencing more rapid population growth than the developed countries are experiencing. The reason is that their death rates have fallen faster than their birth rates. Because of this more rapid rate of growth, the proportion of the world's population that lives in developing countries is expected to increase for at least the remainder of this century.

Urbanization is a modern phenomenon. Historically it was made possible by industrialization and technological change, although in today's developing countries urbanization appears to be taking place independently of these factors. The urbanization of the world's population is expected to continue.

Three trends have characterized the distribution of the U.S. population. One has been the westward shift of the population, and more recently, the movement to the South as well. The second has been its concentration into metropolitan areas. The third has been the deconcentration of the metropolitan population. The last has taken the form of a shift from central-city to ring portions of the areas, and since 1970 a shift from metropolitan to nonmetropolitan areas. These trends are expected to continue.

The metropolitanization and deconcentration of the U.S. population are the products of prevailing patterns of population movement and reproductive change. Initially, increase in the metropolitan population was caused primarily by the migration of persons from nonmetropolitan to metropolitan areas. However, between 1940 and 1970 the importance of net migration as a component of metropolitan population change diminished and the influence of reproductive change increased. If American fertility levels remain low, the importance of net migration is expected to increase.

The central cities of metropolitan areas may be characterized as having a net loss of migrants and an excess of births to deaths. By contrast, the ring portions of the metropolitan areas are experiencing a net gain from migration as well as growth from reproductive change. The importance of reproductive change as a component of growth in the ring population seems to have increased through time.

One result of deconcentration of the metropolitan population has been a relative concentration of economically disadvantaged persons in the central cities. Consequently the demand for public expenditures has increased while the financial capacity of the central city to provide them has decreased. These problems are intensified by the fragmented character of local government in metropolitan areas and by practices such as fiscal zoning.

The shift to nonmetropolitan areas began during the 1970s and was facilitated by improved transportation networks, changes in the location of industrial and commercial activities, changes in the life styles of Americans (particularly increased retirement and emphasis on recreational pursuits), and the growth of colleges in nonmetropolitan areas. However, this growth was confined to nonfarm areas, for the population of farm areas continued to decrease.

REFERENCES AND SUGGESTED READINGS

Beale, Calvin L. 1976. A further look at nonmetropolitan growth since 1970. *American journal of agricultural economics* 58 (December):953–958.

Berry, Brian J. L., and Dahmann, Donald D. 1977. Population redistribution in the United States in the 1970s. *Population and development review* 3 (December):443–471.

Bogue, Donald J. 1969. *Principles of demography.* New York: John Wiley and Sons.

Goldstein, Sidney, and Sly, David F. 1977. Recent and projected trends in world urbanization. In *Patterns of urbanization: comparative country studies,* eds. Sidney Goldstein and David F. Sly, pp. 41–92. Bolhain: Ordina Editions.

Gottmann, Jean. 1961. *Megalopolis: the urbanized northeastern seaboard of the United States.* New York: Twentieth Century Fund.

Hawley, Amos H. 1971. *Urban society.* New York: The Ronald Press.

Hawley, Amos H., Duncan, Beverly, and Goldberg, David. 1964. Some observations of changes in metropolitan population in the United States. *Demography* 1:148–155.

Kasarda, John D. 1977. Metropolitan deconcentration and the urban fiscal crises. Paper presented at the annual meetings of the Population Association of America.

McCarthy, Kevin, and Morrison, Peter A. 1979. *The changing demographic and economic structure of nonmetropolitan areas in the United States.* Santa Monica: Rand Corporation.

Morrison, Peter A. 1976*a*. *Demographic trends that will shape future housing demand.* Santa Monica: Rand Corporation.

———. 1976*b*. Rural renaissance in America? *Population bulletin* 31 (October).

Population Reference Bureau. 1975. *World urbanization 1800–2000.* Washington, D.C.: Population Reference Bureau.

———. 1980. *1980 world population data sheet.* Washington, D.C.: Population Reference Bureau.

Poston, Dudley L., and Weller, Robert H., eds. 1980. *The population of the South: structure and change in social demographic context.* Austin: University of Texas Press.

Preston, Samuel H. 1979. Urban growth in developing countries: a demographic reappraisal. *Population and development review* 5 (June):195–215.

Riew, John. 1970. Metropolitan disparities and fiscal federalism. In *Financing the metropolis,* ed. John P. Crecine, pp. 137–161. Beverly Hills: Sage Publications.

Sly, David F., and Tayman, Jeffrey. 1980. Changing metropolitan morphology and municipal service expenditures in cities and rings. *Social science quarterly* (Summer).

United Nations. 1973. *The determinants and consequences of population change,* vol. I. New York: United Nations.

U. S. Bureau of the Census. 1971. *1970 census of population, number of inhabitants,* Final Report PC (1)-A1, United States summary. Washington, D.C.: Government Printing Office.

———. 1978*a*. *County and city data book, 1977.* Washington, D.C.: Government Printing Office.

———. 1978*b*. Estimates of the population of counties and metropolitan areas: July 1, 1975 and 1976. *Current population reports,* series P-25, no. 739. Washington, D.C.: Government Printing Office.

———. 1978*c*. Geographical mobility: March 1975 to March 1978. *Current population reports,* series P-20, no. 331. Washington, D.C.: Government Printing Office.

———. 1978*d*. Social and economic characteristics of the metropolitan population: 1977 and 1970. *Current population reports,* series P-23, no. 75. Washington, D.C.: Government Printing Office.

———. 1979. Population profile of the United States: 1978. *Current population reports,* series P-20, no. 336. Washington, D.C.: Government Printing Office.

Weller, Robert H. 1967. An empirical examination of megalopitan structure. *Demography* 4:734–743.

Zimmer, Basil. 1975. The urban centrifugal drift. In *Metropolitan America in contemporary perspective,* eds. Amos Hawley and Vincent Rock, pp. 23–92. New York: John Wiley and Sons.

Part III

Three Demographic Variables

Fertility, mortality, and migration are the three key demographic variables. They combine to produce changes in population size, distribution, and composition. A complex interaction of social, economic, cultural, and physiological factors affects levels of fertility, mortality, and migration. In turn, prevailing (and past) levels of these three demographic variables affect our society and the world in which we live.

This part examines world patterns of fertility, mortality, and migration, the major determinants of each of these variables, and the chief differences in fertility, mortality, and migration within countries. In doing so it illustrates the interconnections that exist between demographic behavior and social, economic, and cultural factors.

We have also included here a chapter on methods of birth prevention. Fertility behavior is largely determined by the way in which the social, economic, and cultural system is structured, but use of some means of birth prevention is one of the major mechanisms producing differences in fertility, especially in the more economically developed countries. Furthermore, technological advances in contraception have influenced the marked decline in fertility in recent decades. Many varied means of birth prevention are available. Each has its own advantages and disadvantages, and some are more effective than others. We believe that as a demographic actor you should be aware of these features.

5
Fertility

Fertility results from a biological process. It takes place because a man and a woman have sexual intercourse, the woman conceives, and this conception results in a **live birth.** Yet we know that fertility is affected by a person's social, economic, and cultural environment. The key to this seeming paradox is that having intercourse, conceiving, and giving birth are themselves variables and are influenced by other factors. Thus, a person's social, economic, and cultural environment (and physiological variables such as age) influence how often he or she has sexual intercourse, whether this intercourse results in a conception, and whether a live birth is the outcome. In turn, these latter variables directly determine how many children a person has.

Fertility can be studied cross-sectionally to give us period measures that show the number of births women have in a certain calendar date, regardless of their age, and whether they will have any more births in the future; or it can be studied through time to give us measures revealing the number and spacing of births to various cohorts of women as they pass through the life cycle as well as information from a number of different years in the women's past. Not all women begin their childbearing at the same time or have intervals of equal length between births, so fertility must be measured on a cohort as well as a period basis. Variations in the timing and spacing of births can cause the cohort and period approaches to yield different results (see box 5.1).

A third way to study fertility is to take a macro approach—that is, determine the rate at which births occur in a population or subpopulation within a given period of time. Demographers measure fertility on the macro level in order to compare it with mortality and compute rates of reproductive change. They also use it to compare the fertility levels of different types of subpopulations or fertility levels over time. Finally, demographers sometimes take an individual, or micro-level, approach to examine different numbers of births among different types of women. There are three primary ways of studying fertility at the individual level. They involve determining (1) the number of births that a woman has borne by a given point in time, such as the date of a census or survey; (2) the number of births a woman has by the time she finishes childbearing; and (3) the timing and spacing of births at various stages of the life cycle (e.g., age twenty-five or thirty).

This chapter looks at world fertility patterns as well as the major differences in fertility among people within societies. It also examines the extent to which women are successful in controlling the number and spacing of their births. We pay particular attention to two types of births that are relatively unplanned—births to unmarried women and births to teen-agers. First, though, let us look at the three steps that lead to giving birth—sexual intercourse, conception, and successful **gestation** (the carrying of young in the uterus) and **parturition** (the process of giving birth). *(Text continues on page 116.)*

Box 5.1 Period and Cohort Rates of Fertility

Period analysis of fertility measures the fertility of a population during a given period of time, such as a year. One such measure, the crude birth rate, tells us how many live births occur in a given year per 1,000 population. As we have seen earlier, the crude birth rate is based upon the total population and includes in its denominator males, children, and elderly persons who are unable to give birth. The **general fertility rate (GFR)*** is an improvement on the crude birth rate because it is based on the number of women in the reproductive years (age fifteen to forty-four). The general fertility rate measures the number of births in a calendar year per 1,000 women of childbearing age. Thus:

$$\text{General Fertility Rate} = \frac{\text{Number of Live Births}}{\text{Number of Females 15–44}} \times 1{,}000$$

In 1977 there were 3,326,632 live births registered in the United States. In that same year there were about 49,100,000 females of childbearing age in the United States population. Substituting these values in the above formula,

$$\text{GFR} = \left(\frac{3{,}326{,}632}{49{,}100{,}000}\right) 1{,}000 = 67.8$$

Thus, for every 1,000 women in their reproductive years in the U.S. population, there were 67.8 births in 1977.

Another period measure is the **child-woman ratio**. It indicates the number of children under age five per 1,000 women age fifteen to forty-four in a particular year. Thus it serves as an indirect measure of fertility over a five-year period.

Although each of these measures is useful in measuring fertility at one point in time, neither measure tells us the number of children women will have by the time they complete their childbearing and the tempo (or timing and spacing) of these births.

We use **cohort analysis** of fertility to follow women through their reproductive years. By counting the number of births that a cohort of women has by the time the women complete their childbearing (usually age forty-four although some people use age forty-nine as the cutoff age), we have a measure of completed family size for that cohort. This measure can be compared with the completed family size of other cohorts to determine whether fertility is changing.

Cohort measures of fertility are very similar to the total fertility rate, which was explained earlier in box 3.1 (p. 58). The total fertility rate is not considered a cohort measure of fertility because it uses age-specific birth rates for one point in time (for example, 1977), while cohort measures are based on the actual experiences of a cohort of women as they pass through

*Official U.S. government publications refer to it simply as the fertility rate. We will use the adjective "general" to avoid confusion with the crude birth rate and because that is conventional.

continued

Period and Cohort Rates of Fertility (continued)

the reproductive years (fifteen through forty-four). Thus, cohort measures use data from a number of different calendar years. Because age-specific rates frequently change through time, the total fertility rate may differ from cohort measures of fertility. This difference may be seen by examining the accompanying table, which presents data for each cohort of women who entered the childbearing years between 1920 and 1974.

Age-Specific Birth Rates for Women Ages Fifteen to Forty-four, 1920–1924 to 1970–1974*

RACE AND YEAR	15–19 YEARS	20–24 YEARS	25–29 YEARS	30–34 YEARS	35–39 YEARS	40–44 YEARS
White						
1970–1974	53	131	121	60	24	6
1965–1969	59	169	142	78	38	10
1960–1964	77	227	184	106	52	14
1955–1959	85	239	191	113	57	15
1950–1954	76	205	176	109	55	15
1945–1949	60	176	160	104	55	16
1940–1944	49	143	136	89	48	15
1935–1939	45	122	114	78	48	17
1930–1934	46	124	120	87	57	21
1925–1929	53	146	142	105	72	27
1920–1924	57	162	164	122	86	33
Black and Other Races						
1970–1974	124	165	119	70	35	10
1965–1969	133	203	145	93	51	17
1960–1964	142	256	199	126	70	21
1955–1959	154	269	201	130	73	21
1950–1954	148	232	176	111	66	20
1945–1949	128	192	140	90	58	18
1940–1944	114	164	117	75	52	19
1935–1939	105	150	105	68	55	20
1930–1934	97	147	109	79	62	24
1925–1929	106	165	135	93	77	29
1920–1924	107	186	154	102		36

*Rates are live births per 1,000 women in specified age group.
Source: U.S. Bureau of the Census (1978), p. 10.

To compute the total fertility rate during the 1970–1974 interval,* we must add across the row for 1970–1974, multiply the sum by 5 (the number of years in each age group), and then divide by 1,000 (because the rates are presented per 1,000 women). Doing this for whites, we get:

Sum of Row 1970–1974	=	395
Multiplied by 5	=	1975
Divided by 1,000	=	1.975

*Sometimes we use five-year averages instead of single-year data in order to reduce random fluctuations or because they are more convenient to analyze and present to the reader.

continued

Period and Cohort Rates of Fertility (continued)

The total fertility rate is 1,975 per 1,000 or an average of 1.975 births per woman. Thus, if women in the age group fifteen to nineteen in 1970–1974 had children according to the age-specific birth rates that existed in that time span, they would have averaged 1.975 births by the time they left their reproductive years (around 1995–1999).

Of course, age-specific rates do change through time. When this happens the total fertility rate provides a poor estimate of completed family size, which is why we also use cohort measures of fertility.

Cohort measures are calculated by following a group of women through their reproductive years. In the table presented above, we may do so by reading diagonally upward. The cohort of women fifteen to nineteen years of age in 1945–1949 were age twenty to twenty-four in 1950–1954, age twenty-five to twenty-nine in 1955–1959, and so forth, until they reached age forty to forty-four in 1970–1974. Because very few women are capable of giving birth past age forty-four, if we counted the number of births to this cohort of women by 1970–1974, we would have a measure of completed family size for that cohort. The age-specific birth rates for women we have selected, using data for whites, are:

Fifteen to nineteen years in 1945–1949	60
Twenty to twenty-four years in 1950–1954	205
Twenty-five to twenty-nine years in 1955–1959	191
Thirty to thirty-four years in 1960–1964	106
Thirty-five to thirty-nine years in 1965–1969	38
Forty to forty-four years in 1970–1974	6

The sum is 606. As in computing the total fertility rate, we have to multiply the sum of the age-specific birth rates by 5 and then divide by 1,000 to get the completed family size per woman. Thus:

$$\frac{606(5)}{1{,}000} = \frac{3{,}030}{1{,}000} = 3.03$$

In other words, women who were fifteen to nineteen in 1945–1949 (which means they were born in 1930–1934) averaged 3.03 births by the time they completed childbearing. By contrast, the total fertility rate for the 1945–1949 calendar years was 2.855. (Add across the 1945–1949 row, multiply by 5, and divide by 1,000.)

Cohort fertility measures also have shortcomings. They do not reflect current fertility but rather the fertility of past years. Indeed, the completed fertility rate tells us how many children women had fifteen to twenty-five years ago. By comparing cohort and period measures over time, certain trends can be noted and better projections of future fertility are possible.

Sources: U.S. Bureau of the Census (1979); and National Center for Health Statistics (1979).

DETERMINANTS OF FAMILY SIZE: THE "INTERMEDIATE" VARIABLES

The three variables intercourse, conception, and gestation/parturition may be looked at as "intermediate" to the social, economic, and cultural environment and the biological process of having children. Nonbiological factors can be related to family size only if they affect one or more of these intermediate variables. For instance, later in this chapter we will see that the more years a person has attended school, the smaller that person's family size tends to be. One reason is that persons who are in school longer tend to marry later and start a family later. Kingsley Davis and Judith Blake (1956) have classified the various ways that the intermediate variables can affect fertility, and their work is used as the basis of discussion in this section. Briefly stated, their work posits that: (1) the amount of intercourse is affected by the proportion of persons who marry, how long these persons are married, and their frequency of sexual intercourse while they are married; (2) the probability of conception is affected by contraception and voluntary or involuntary **infecundity** (or inability to conceive); and (3) the probability of a birth resulting from a given conception depends upon whether it is involuntarily or voluntarily aborted.

Davis and Blake emphasize that each intermediate variable can operate to increase as well as decrease family size. Not all of them need to operate in the same direction. The observed level of fertility depends upon the net balance of *all* the intermediate variables.

Exposure to Intercourse

Most sexual intercourse involves a male and female living in a stable **conjugal union**—a marriage or consensual (common law) union. Thus the factors affecting exposure to intercourse may be divided into two classes—those associated with the length of time a person is married and those affecting the rate at which intercourse occurs within a given marriage. Let us look now at the variables that affect these factors.

Age at Marriage

The age at marriage affects the length of time spent in a conjugal union. Ireland and India represent extremes, with Ireland having a pattern of late marriage and India one of early marriage. In 1973 Irish males married at an average of 26.0 years and females averaged 23.5 years. In India the figures in 1971 were 22.2 and 17.2, respectively (United Nations 1977; and Goyal 1975). Considerably greater differences between these countries are reported for earlier dates.

Extent of Nonmarriage

Another factor affecting the length of time spent within a conjugal union is the extent to which people do not marry at all. In Rwanda,

Iran, and South Korea less than 1 percent of the males and females remain single through ages forty-five to forty-nine. On the other hand, in Ireland and the Dominican Republic about one-fourth of the males and one-sixth of the females in that age bracket report they have never married (United Nations 1977, table 25).

Time Spent After and Between Marriages

A person's exposure to intercourse can be affected by the amount of time during the potentially reproductive years that is spent after or between conjugal unions. Not all people remarry upon being widowed or divorced. And many men prefer to marry never-married females, especially in societies where female virginity is highly valued. The years spent outside legal marriages also lessen a person's lifetime exposure to intercourse. Perhaps the best-known example—on a societal level—occurs in the Caribbean, where the incidence of consensual unions (without marriage) is relatively high. These unions are more unstable than legal unions. Some demographers have argued that this instability reduces fertility levels in these areas.

Voluntary Abstinence

Some societies have special ceremonial occasions or periods of time during which sexual intercourse is prohibited. For example, in the Singur area of West Bengal, Hindu religious beliefs condemn sexual intercourse nearly one hundred days annually (Nag 1967, p. 161). Almost all societies have a period of abstinence during late pregnancy and for a period following the birth (called **postpartum**). Abstinence during late pregnancy would, of course, have no effect, and any effects of abstaining during early postpartum would be minimal because few women are capable of conceiving then. However, in some societies postpartum abstinence is relatively long, even lasting for two or three years in some cases (Nag 1962, p. 77). For women who give birth to three or four children such periods of abstinence can remove them from intercourse for a substantial proportion of their reproductive lives.

Involuntary Abstinence

In a few societies a large proportion of the males must absent themselves periodically to obtain gainful employment. For instance, in the Peruvian highlands many males migrate to the coastal region during the sugar cane harvesting season. A similar phenomenon takes place in some African countries. These males tend to be in the age brackets where family formation normally is highest. Also, some persons may have sales jobs which necessitate frequent absence from home. Others are institutionalized and unable to have sexual intercourse with the opposite sex.

Frequency of Intercourse

A final factor affecting exposure to intercourse is coital frequency during periods of nonabstinence. It is not known if the frequency of intercourse varies enough between societies to affect fertility levels, but on the individual level it can be an important determinant of family size among those who do not try to prevent conception and/or birth. Christopher Tietze (1960) has estimated that conception will result from a single act of unprotected coition in two to four out of one hundred couples. Thus, persons with a low frequency are less likely to conceive during a given period of time (see box 5.2).

Exposure to Conception

If intercourse has occurred, the second intermediate variable, conception, must be considered. Conception may or may not take place, depending upon a number of factors. One of these, of course, is chance. There are, in fact, three nonrandom factors that determine whether conception occurs, and we shall turn to these next.

Involuntary Infecundity

One reason that conception may not occur is that at least one of the persons may be involuntarily sterile, or infecund. On a global level a major factor contributing to the incidence of involuntary sterility and reproductive impairments is venereal disease, particularly gonorrhea. Venereal disease reduces the **fecundity** of males as well as females. Studies have shown it to be a frequent cause of childlessness in parts of tropical Africa. Several other diseases also increase infecundity. For instance, men with African sleeping sickness or leprosy often become impotent. Any infection that is accompanied by high fevers may alter the process of sperm formation. And pelvic inflammation in women may result in permanent reductions in the ability to conceive. Infecundity may also be caused by genetic factors, psychological conditions which cause coital inability and/or pregnancy loss, nutritional deficiencies, and environmental factors such as radiation and exposure to toxic chemicals (McFalls 1979).

Data collected in the 1970 National Fertility Study indicate that about 13 percent of the couples in the United States in which the wife is under age forty-five are involuntarily sterile or have difficulty conceiving (Westoff 1973, p. 20). In industrialized countries medical science is making considerable progress in its efforts to reduce the incidence of involuntary childlessness. The use of antibiotics to cure venereal disease has already been effective in this respect. Another advance has been the use of artificial insemination to impregnate women whose husbands are sterile. Moreover, drugs have been developed which stimulate ovulation and allow some women to conceive who otherwise probably would not be able to do so. Finally, several "test

Box 5.2 The Effect of Coital Frequency on the Risk of Conception

In an effort to estimate the effects of coital frequency upon the probability of impregnation within a given length of time, John Barrett (1971) collected data on 241 British couples who already had at least one child and who were not using contraceptives. The following table presents his results:

COITUS EVERY *N*TH DAY	*P**	1/*P*†	*R*‡
$N = 7$	.16	6.48	0.57
$N = 6$	.18	5.68	0.63
$N = 5$	.21	4.71	0.70
$N = 4$	.26	3.83	0.78
$N = 3$	.33	3.02	0.87
$N = 2$	.45	2.23	0.95
$N = 1$	.71	1.41	1.00

**P* = The probability of impregnation within a given menstrual cycle.

†1/*P* = The mean number of months from ovulation to conception for a couple having sexual intercourse every *N*th day.

‡*R* = The probability of impregnation within a six-month interval.

One-sixth of the couples having unprotected coitus every seventh day may expect impregnation within one month. About five out of ten can expect conception within half a year. Seven out of ten couples having intercourse every day can expect conception within one month. The likelihood of impregnation within six months is 100 percent. The probability of conception gets progressively greater as coital frequency is increased. Thus, the effect of changing from a schedule of intercourse every seventh day to coitus every sixth day is not nearly as large as the effect of changing from every fourth to every third day.

These data pertain only to women age thirty or younger. Barrett states that for those women over age thirty, the value of *P*, upon which the other figures are based, are about .7 of the corresponding value for the younger women. It is not known to what extent Barrett's estimates may be generalized to other populations. In addition, they apparently do not take into account the fact that sperm count declines with an increase in coital frequency. Thus, the figures on chances of impregnation among those having intercourse every day may be a little high. Nevertheless, the differences shown are of such magnitude that the basic conclusion is clear. In a population that does not use contraceptives, frequency of sexual intercourse may have a significant effect upon family size.

tube" babies have been conceived outside the wombs of women unable to conceive normally. However, this procedure may not be feasible on a large scale.

Voluntary Infecundity

Surgical sterilization of either the male or the female results in permanent freedom from the risk of conception without altering personality or posing a threat to health. Sterilization has long been a popular method of limiting family size in several countries—for instance, Puerto Rico and Japan (Presser 1970)—and since the 1960s it has become very popular in the United States. By 1976 one out of every five American couples with a husband present and a wife under age forty-five had chosen sterilization as a means of preventing further conceptions. Among those couples with a wife age thirty to forty-four, voluntary sterilization has become the most popular method of birth prevention (Ford 1978; and Westoff 1976).

The probability of conception may be reduced (although not eliminated) by prolonged lactation, or breast feeding, which increases the length of postpartum sterility. Among women who do not nurse their newborn infants, the mean length of the sterile period after birth is about four months. Sterility results from a delayed return of menstruation (called amenorrhea), followed by one or more menstrual cycles during which ovulation does not occur. Among nursing women the length of amenorrhea increases in proportion to the amount of time the infant is nursed and usually lasts about three-fourths of the nursing time (Tietze 1961). Historical studies of European populations and more recent sample surveys in India and Taiwan have indicated that among women not practicing **birth control,** prolonged lactation increases the length of the interval between births by 15 to 33 percent (Van Ginnekan 1974, p. 201).

Use of Contraception

In many societies large proportions of the population use contraception. Some methods work better than others. The relative effectiveness of various contraceptives will be discussed in chapter 6.

There are significant differences among societies in the level of contraceptive use. In general, the more modernized the country the greater the extent of contraceptive use. Within societies various categories of people differ in whether they use contraceptives, the kinds of contraceptives used, and how early in the family formation process they begin using contraception. Some persons wait until they have all the children they want before they begin use. Others begin using contraception right after marriage to control the timing and spacing of their births. These differentials in contraceptive use help to explain several major differences in fertility.

Likelihood of Having a Live Birth

Even though intercourse has occurred and conception has resulted, a third intermediate variable, birth, must be considered. A live birth may or may not take place. The outcome depends upon two forms of fetal mortality—spontaneous and induced abortion.

Spontaneous Abortion

When a pregnancy is aborted involuntarily, it is called a spontaneous abortion. It is estimated that about 50 percent of all fertilized ova are lost (Kerr 1971, p. 236). One analysis suggests that 35 percent of all fertilized ova are lost before the first menstrual period and another 14 percent are lost between the first missed period and delivery (James 1970). Losses early in pregnancy are due mainly to genetically defective sperm or ova and to errors in fertilization and early cell divisions. In later pregnancy factors external to the physiology of the fetus become more important—poor maternal nutrition and body build, Rh incompatibility (a blood disorder), transmission of communicable disease from the mother to the fetus, and abnormal position at delivery (Nortman 1974, p. 22). The tendency to abort spontaneously varies greatly from one person to another, but the fetus of a younger woman has a much better chance of survival than that of an older woman.

Induced Abortion

When a pregnancy is aborted voluntarily, it is called an induced abortion. Primitive and often hazardous methods of inducing abortion have been practiced throughout history. Today medical technology has made induced abortion an extremely safe procedure, but it is illegal in many countries and is often not available to women who cannot purchase proper medical supervision. For them abortion may represent a severe threat to their health. Nevertheless, it is estimated that between 20 and 30 percent of all known pregnancies in some cities in Latin America (where abortion is proscribed) are deliberately aborted (Requena and Monreal 1968; and Mendoza-Hoyos 1968). In the United States about 1 million abortions are performed annually. The proportion of pregnancies intentionally terminated is extremely high in most of central and eastern Europe.[1] In Hungary abortions have outnumbered live births in each year since 1959 (David 1970, pp. 19–23).

The eleven variables discussed above that affect exposure to intercourse, conception, and having a live birth are the direct determinants of fertility. As mentioned earlier, social, economic, and cultural variables can increase or decrease fertility only if they influence one or more of these eleven variables. The observed level of fertility with-

[1]See box 5.3 for the means of measuring the extent of induced abortions.

Box 5.3 Abortion Rates and Ratios

There are two conventional ways of measuring the extent of induced abortions—rates and ratios. **Abortion rates** refer to the number of induced abortions per 1,000 women age fifteen to forty-four in a given calendar year, or, more formally expressed:

$$\text{Abortion Rate} = \frac{\text{Number of Abortions}}{\text{Number of Women Fifteen to Forty-four}} \times 1{,}000$$

In the United States an estimated 1,000,000 induced abortions took place in 1978. In that same year there were 50,060,000 females in the appropriate age bracket. So, in 1978 the abortion rate in the United States was:

$$\left(\frac{1{,}000{,}000}{50{,}060{,}000}\right)1{,}000 = (.0200)\ 1{,}000 = 20$$

The **abortion ratio** calculates the number of induced abortions per 1,000 live births in a given year. This can be expressed in the following formula:

$$\text{Abortion Ratio} = \frac{\text{Number of Abortions}}{\text{Number of Live Births}} \times 1{,}000$$

In the United States in 1978 there were about 3,328,000 live births. Substituting this figure into the formula for the abortion ratio, we get:

$$\left(\frac{1{,}000{,}000}{3{,}328{,}000}\right)1{,}000 = (.3005)\ 1{,}000 = 300.5$$

These figures could be used to make statements such as the following: (1) for every 1,000 women of childbearing age in the United States there were 20 induced abortions; or (2) for every 1,000 live births in the United States in 1978 there were also about 300 induced abortions.

in a group or population depends upon the net balance of *all* the intermediate variables. Since they can combine in a number of different ways, it is not surprising that there are wide differences in fertility among the various countries of the world and among different types of persons.

WORLD PATTERNS

The world's crude birth rate in 1980 was about 28 per 1,000 population. In the developed countries it was lower (16) than in the developing countries (32). The crude birth rates for the various regions of the world are shown in table 5.1. High birth rates are found almost exclusively in Africa, Asia, and Middle and South America, although within these regions certain countries have relatively low birth rates. The countries with low fertility may be divided into three subgroups, based on the pattern of declining fertility. The first includes most of the countries in northern and western Europe as well as Argentina, Australia, Canada, New Zealand, and the United States. These countries had declining fertility rates in the twentieth century until the 1930s and then fertility either leveled off or declined, except for places where the baby boom occurred. The second group of low-fertility countries includes those of southern and eastern Europe. These nations had fairly consistent declines in fertility throughout the 1930s, 1940s, and 1950s. The third group includes Japan, Taiwan, and Singapore, which were characterized by relatively high fertility rates until the end of World War II but very sharp declines subsequently.

Birth rates in the **developing countries** are relatively high but not as high as biologically possible. Crude birth rates have probably never been higher than 65 (Kuczynski 1936). In prerevolutionary Russia the birth rate in several provinces was over 60 (United Nations 1973, p. 73). Rates approaching this level are possible only when almost everyone is engaged in frequent sexual intercourse and does nothing to prevent births, childbearing begins at a young age, and families have

Table 5.1 Crude Birth Rates in Major World Regions, 1980

Africa		46
Northern Africa	42	
Western Africa	49	
Eastern Africa	48	
Middle Africa	45	
Southern Africa	37	
Asia		28
Southwest Asia	40	
Middle South Asia	37	
Southeast Asia	36	
East Asia	18	
North America		16
Latin America		34
Middle America	38	
Caribbean	28	
Tropical South America	36	
Temperate South America	24	
Europe		14
Northern Europe	13	
Western Europe	12	
Eastern Europe	18	
Southern Europe	15	
U.S.S.R.		18
Oceania		20
World		28

Source: Population Reference Bureau (1980).

a large number of children. There are documented cases of women having twenty or more births. However, the largest *average* family size that seems possible ranges from nine to thirteen children, and then only in societies in which marriage occurs at an early age and birth prevention is not practiced. For instance, rural Irish women who married under age twenty and who had completed childbearing by the 1911 census averaged 8.8 live births (Glass and Grebenik 1954). And T. E. Smith (1960) reports that Cocos Island women marrying at age fourteen or fifteen had averaged 10.8 children at age forty-five. Among the Hutterites, a Protestant religious sect living in small agricultural settlements in the Dakotas, Montana, and the adjacent portions of Canada, data collected in the 1950s show an average of 11.9 confinements among women whose last child was born when they were forty-five or older (Tietze 1957). Currently the highest national birth rate is in Gaza (53). A number of African countries have birth rates in the low 50s. The total fertility rate exceeds seven children per woman in Algeria, Libya, Nigeria, Kenya, Honduras, Saudi Arabia, South Yemen, and some of the small sheikdoms near the Arabian sea (Population Reference Bureau 1980).

As mentioned earlier, fertility has been declining in a number of developing countries since the early 1970s. However, some of those countries show no decreases at all, and others show increases in fertility. In general, fertility is high in developing countries and will remain so during the 1980s. But the recent declines in some countries suggest that the situation is not hopeless.

In addition to significant differences in the level of fertility between societies, there are equally important differences in family size within a given population. Most of these differences are examined in the next section.

DIFFERENCES IN FAMILY SIZE

Differences in family size can help us understand the determinants and consequences of fertility. For one thing, they are frequently useful in explaining past fertility trends and predicting future ones in a population. For another, an attempt to explain family size differences uses linkages between fertility behavior and a variety of social, economic, psychological, and biological variables. The discovery of such linkages allows demographers to look at more than the intermediate variables mentioned previously in studying fertility. Finally, by comparing predicted differences with those that are actually observed, the adequacy of competing theoretical models can be partially tested.

The remainder of this section deals with some of the major social and economic variables that appear to be associated with differences in family size. In reading about them you should remember that the causal direction of these associations is not always clear. In some cases, the social and economic variables affect fertility (through the intermediate variables). In other cases fertility may affect the social and economic variables.

Socioeconomic Status (SES)

One of the most consistently observed differences in family size involves socioeconomic status, or SES. Generally, the higher a person's SES, the fewer children that person tends to have. The three primary indicators of SES are education, occupation, and income.

Education

Table 5.2 presents data collected by the U.S. Bureau of the Census from a 1978 survey which related the number of children ever born to women of a certain age group to their educational attainment. This table refers only to women thirty-five to forty-four years old, since most will have completed childbearing by that age in the United States. Because different women get married at different ages, begin having children at different ages, and space their births differently, including younger women who have not completed their childbearing yet might have produced misleading results.

Note that the number of births becomes smaller with each increase in educational attainment, and college graduates have only 57 percent as many children as those with less than an eighth-grade education. Similar results have been observed in other countries (Abu-Lughod 1975; and Arnold 1970) and also when the male's schooling is considered instead of or in conjunction with the female's education (Bouvier and Macisco 1968).

One reason that educational attainment and family size are inversely related is that the probability of never marrying increases with education, as does the average age at marriage. Also, less educated

Table 5.2 Average Number of Children Ever Born to U.S. Women Ages Thirty-five to Forty-four by Educational Attainment, 1978

YEARS OF SCHOOL COMPLETED	AVERAGE NUMBER OF CHILDREN BORN	NUMBER OF WOMEN (THOUSANDS)
0–7	3.74	635
8	3.57	519
9–11	3.54	1,999
12	2.78	5,697
13–15	2.59	1,840
16	2.26	1,063
17+	1.93	637
All women	2.87	12,391

Source: U.S. Bureau of the Census (1979*b*), p. 36.

persons tend to desire more children than persons with more education, although recent survey data indicate that the difference is relatively small.

However, beyond these simple statements there are some gaps in our knowledge of exactly why family size and education are so strongly related. Increased education certainly increases a person's general store of knowledge and exposure to communications. It is also probably true that a person's knowledge of the existence, relative effectiveness, and cultural acceptability of a variety of contraceptive methods also increases.

Occupation

The more prestigious the husband's occupation, the lower the family size tends to be. In general, white-collar workers have the smallest families. Farm workers have the largest. This ordering is not strict. Operatives, a category which includes transport equipment operatives, tend to have somewhat larger families than service workers or nonfarm laborers (see table 5.3).

Occupational groups differ substantially in family size. Some of the differences in family size among the various occupations are connected with the life styles and incomes associated with each occupation. And they undoubtedly also reflect the varying levels of educational attainment characteristic of each occupational group.

Income

The relationship between income and family size is even more complex. Income changes throughout a person's lifetime. Persons having high incomes at the end of the reproductive period may not have had the same high level at its beginning. One might expect that greater in-

Table 5.3 Children Ever Born to U.S. Women Ages Thirty-five to Forty-four by Major Occupation Group of Employed Civilian Husband, 1978

MAJOR OCCUPATION GROUP	AVERAGE NUMBER OF CHILDREN BORN	NUMBER OF WOMEN (THOUSANDS)
Professional, technical	2.56	1,498
Managers and administrators, except farm	2.76	1,663
Sales workers	2.78	547
Clerical workers	2.87	437
Craft workers	2.94	1,948
Operatives	3.28	1,436
Service workers	3.08	494
Laborers, except farm	3.13	393
Farm workers	3.44	320
All women	2.92	8,735

Source: U.S. Bureau of the Census (1979*b*), p.52.

Table 5.4 Children Ever Born to U.S. Women Ages Forty-five to Forty-nine by Husband's Income, 1970

INCOME (1969)	AVERAGE NUMBER OF CHILDREN BORN	NUMBER OF WOMEN (THOUSANDS)
None	3.23	140
$1,000–1,999	3.40	762
2,000–2,999	3.41	453
3,000–3,999	3.41	622
4,000–4,999	3.18	714
5,000–6,999	2.91	1,954
7,000–9,999	2.75	3,614
10,000–14,999	2.71	3,344
15,000–24,999	2.74	1,612
25,000+	2.81	707

Source: U.S. Bureau of the Census (1973), pp. 246, 252.

come would mean a greater ability to afford children, but this is not necessarily true. The costs of childbearing may increase with income because expectations for the child are greater. Realization of these expectations means spending more money per child.

As table 5.4 shows, the husband's income and family size are inversely related. Wives whose husbands' incomes were less than $4,000 in 1969 reported having about .6 more children than wives in the highest income category. However, data collected in the National Fertility Study reveal only small differences in **desired family size** by husband's income (Ryder and Westoff 1971, p. 60).

Female Labor Force Participation

Differences in family size are also related to the participation of females in the paid labor force. Studies conducted in the developed countries have usually shown that the greater the participation of women in the labor force, the lower the fertility. Moreover, the higher the wage rate a female worker can obtain, the lower her fertility. In the developing countries female employment and fertility may not be inversely related. Within these countries the probability of observing a decline in fertility with employment is greater (1) in urban areas than in rural areas, (2) if the wife works for pay rather than as an unpaid or self-employed worker, (3) if she works away from home rather than at home, and (4) if she has a white-collar occupation rather than some other occupation. Thus, the labor force participation of women and fertility tend to be inversely related only under specific conditions—conditions which do not prevail in most developing countries (Weller 1977).

The causes of this relationship are very complex. One obvious possibility is that women's family size affects their labor force participation. Women who are incapable of having as many children as they want find it easier to work away from home than women with larger families. But it is also possible that women's labor force participation affects fertility. Certainly this is the case when employment delays marriage. Moreover, to the extent that employment and fertility are incompatible activities, a woman can participate intensively in her employment only by engaging in motherhood less intensively. Some women find the rewards associated with working greater than the rewards associated with motherhood. They may deliberately restrict their family size in order to maximize their time in the labor force. Labor force participation also affects fertility by influencing how women define their role and how they perceive themselves. They become less inclined to devote themselves solely to home and children. This effect is heightened if the women have prestigious, well-paid jobs that require extensive skills or preparation and that provide psychological satisfaction.

The pattern of familial decision making may be altered by female participation in the labor force. The gainfully employed wife often contributes substantially to family income, so she is in a better position to have greater influence over family size decisions than is the wife who does not work outside the home. Employment may also affect fertility because of the potential income that must be forgone if the woman is not employed (called an "opportunity cost"). The opportunity cost of children increases when employable women must give up income in order to rear children. The opportunity cost of motherhood is less for women who could not earn much money than it is for women who could receive high wages if they were working. This—along with different amounts of schooling—probably accounts for some of the occupational differences that have been observed. The opportunity cost is also less for women for whom child care is available at little or no cost. Finally, employment affects fertility by delaying marriage. However, fertility can also affect female labor force participation (Smith-Lovin and Tickamyer 1978; and Waite and Stolzenberg 1976). The presence of young children in the household may prevent women from being employed outside the home, because they believe it would be improper for a mother with small children to work or because acceptable child care arrangements cannot be made or are too expensive.

Because of the complexity of the relationship, most researchers have simply concluded that female labor force participation and fertility affect each other. Not all causal mechanisms operate in a given instance. Which ones are operating depends upon the situation of the woman, her family, and the employment opportunities available in her society. Differences in these factors explain why the relationship between female employment and fertility is so strong in the industrialized countries and so weak in the developing countries.

Rural-Urban Residence

People living in urban areas tend to have fewer children than do those living in rural areas. Moreover, the average number of children ever born tends to decrease as the community size increases (United Nations 1973, p. 97).

It is logical that rural families should have more children than urban families. Single-family homes typical of rural areas permit expansion more easily than city dwellings. When at least a portion of the food is produced at home, children are less expensive to raise than when everything has to be bought. Farm children may help to earn their keep from a very young age by doing chores. Urban parents receive no such financial returns from their young offspring. Finally, urban females are more likely to find alternative roles to being a housewife. Thus, they may postpone childbearing or even put it off altogether (Petersen 1969, p. 496). Given this line of reasoning, differences in fertility by size of community would reflect relative job opportunities for women, the relative costs of living, and differences in housing arrangements (Grabill, Kiser, and Whelpton 1958, p. 85).

Table 5.5 presents data for the United States in 1978. Within each age group the persons living in nonmetropolitan areas have more children than the women living within metropolitan areas. Central-city and ring residents of metropolitan areas have virtually identical fertility. Data from the 1970 census show that the size of the central city itself is irrelevant. Historically, size of community and fertility in the United States have been inversely related, but that pattern virtually disappeared by 1970.

Rural fertility is not always higher than urban fertility in the developing countries. Although data collected in Latin America, Sri Lanka, the Philippines, Thailand, and Taiwan generally support the pattern of higher rural fertility, sample survey data collected in a number of African countries show no consistent difference between urban and rural fertility (United Nations 1973, pp. 97–98). Some of these regional disparities may be due to regional differences in the nature of urbanization or in the migration streams to cities from the rural areas.

Table 5.5 Number of Children Ever Born to U.S. Women by Age and Metropolitan-Nonmetropolitan Residence, 1978

RESIDENCE	20–24 YEARS	25–34 YEARS	35–44 YEARS
Metropolitan	0.50	1.50	2.78
In central cities	0.54	1.46	2.78
Outside central cities (rings)	0.48	1.53	2.78
Nonmetropolitan	0.67	1.83	3.06

Source: U.S. Bureau of the Census (1979*b*), p. 36.

Race

Studies in the United States since 1920 have shown that nonwhite (predominantly black) fertility has followed the same trends as white fertility. For both, fertility declined until the mid-1930s, remained at a low level for several years, rose dramatically with the baby boom, and did not start to decline again until after 1957. But consistently fertility has been higher for nonwhites.

Between 1936 and 1957 the general fertility rate (births per 1,000 women of childbearing age) increased by 61 percent among whites and 70 percent among nonwhites. The result was that nonwhites had a general fertility rate 39 percent higher than whites in 1957, compared to 29 percent higher in 1936. Figure 5.1 shows that between 1957 and 1965 fertility declined more among whites than among nonwhites, increasing the general fertility rate difference by race to 46 percent. Since then fertility has decreased more among nonwhites than among whites, and in 1978 blacks had a general fertility rate only 40 percent higher than the rate for whites. Differences in the total fertility rate were of similar magnitude.

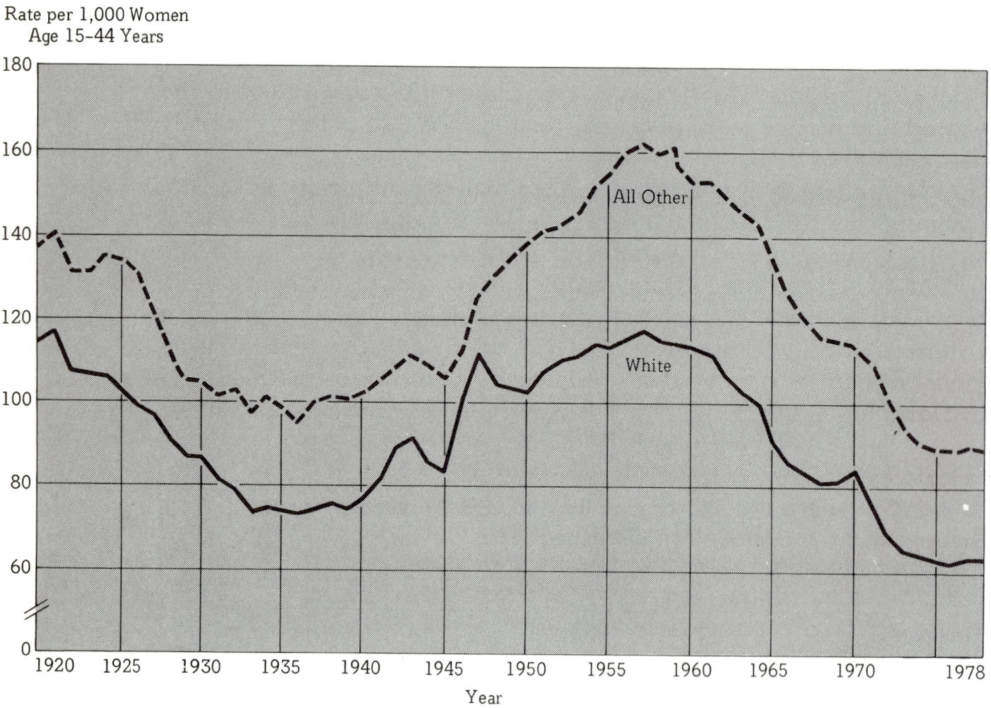

Figure 5.1 General Fertility Rates in the United States by Race, 1920-1980

Note: Beginning in 1959, trend lines are based on registered live births; trend lines for 1920–1959 are based on live births adjusted for underregistration.

Source: Taffel (1977), p. 3; and National Center for Health Statistics (1980), p. 9.

Some attempts to explain why blacks have more children than whites have concentrated upon the socioeconomic differences of the two groups. Blacks tend to be less educated, have less prestigious occupations, and receive less income than whites. Because SES is strongly related to family size, these differences alone could be why blacks have more children than whites. If so, then simultaneously controlling for differences in education, occupation, and income should eliminate any family size differences between blacks and whites. To date, most investigators have controlled only one or two of these variables and have reached differing conclusions about whether race is related to family size in a manner independent of differences in SES (Goldscheider and Uhlenberg 1969; Sly 1970; and Roberts and Lee 1974).

Data from several national surveys conducted in the United States indicate that blacks have higher fertility rates than whites primarily because they have more unwanted births (Ryder and Westoff 1971; Westoff and Ryder 1977; and Weller 1979).[2] Blacks have more unwanted births than whites because they tend to start having children earlier. They also are exposed to the risk of having unwanted children for a longer time than whites because there is a longer period of time between the birth of the last wanted child and the onset of involuntary sterility. The fact that blacks are less likely to use birth prevention practices and that the methods used have been slightly less effective among blacks than among whites only adds to the differences in unwanted childbearing (Ryder and Westoff 1971, p. 306; and Ryder and Westoff 1972, p. 480). Today racial patterns of contraceptive use are more similar than they were during the 1950s and 1960s. So there is some evidence that racial differences in unwanted childbearing are declining.

Religious Preference

Differences in fertility may exist among religious groups because of pronatalist ideologies in one group, because the use of effective means of birth prevention is discouraged, or because of differences in socioeconomic characteristics or residence patterns. In the United States all three factors may be used to explain fertility differences between Catholics and non-Catholics.

Catholics

Catholic ideology is pronatalist in two respects. Catholics are encouraged to have as many children as they can properly educate and support. And the only morally acceptable means by which married couples may prevent births is to use the rhythm method, based upon abstinence from coition when the woman is believed to be fertile, which frequently is relatively ineffective and results in unplanned con-

[2]For a precise definition of the term "unwanted birth," see box 5.4 on p. 36.

ceptions. A number of studies in the 1950s and 1960s showed Catholics as having substantially more children than non-Catholics. Among the non-Catholics Jewish couples had smaller families than Protestants, and among the Protestants the fundamentalists had relatively high fertility. When the pronounced differences in SES among these various non-Catholic religious groups were controlled, most of the fertility differences disappeared. However, the differences in fertility between Catholics and non-Catholics did not disappear (Freedman, Whelpton, and Smit 1961; and Stokes 1972). Moreover, the greater the Catholic couple's involvement in religious activities, the larger the family size, while among non-Catholics there was only a slight association between the woman's perception of the importance of religion in her life and her fertility level (Westoff and Ryder 1977, p. 284). And the greater the proportion of a Catholic's education in Catholic schools, the larger the family size tended to be. The religious commitment of the woman and her home environment rather than the educational experience per se produced this pattern. Protestant-Catholic marriages tended to have fertility rates much closer to the Protestant than to the Catholic levels because Catholics involved in mixed marriages are less religiously involved than those in all-Catholic unions. (Ryder and Westoff 1971, pp. 70–77; and Westoff and Potvin 1967).

Since 1965, however, Catholic and non-Catholic fertility rates have become much closer to one another. Degree of devoutness no longer makes a difference in the fertility of Catholics, and Catholics have become very similar to non-Catholics in their use of birth prevention practices. What has caused this convergence?

The rates of fertility of Catholics and non-Catholics had started to converge before the baby boom. However, during the baby boom the fertility of Catholics increased more than the fertility of non-Catholics increased. Some persons argue that the Great Depression during the 1930s and then World War II reduced Catholic fertility to lower than normal levels because of their very cataclysmic nature. The relatively high levels of economic well-being during the late 1940s and 1950s thus enabled Catholics to achieve a high fertility potential that had been contained (but not realized) in the preceding periods (Goldberg 1967, p. 137). Whatever the cause of the disproportionately large increase in Catholic fertility during the baby boom, since then the fertility of American Catholics has declined more sharply than that of non-Catholics, and by 1975 these two groups had virtually identical fertility rates (Westoff and Jones 1979). Thus, in some respects the present convergence may be viewed as a continuation of a trend that had started earlier but was interrupted by the baby boom (Bouvier and Rao 1975).

We also know that Catholics have been assimilated into American culture to an extent greater than ever before. In terms of social, economic, and residential characteristics, there are only minor differences between Catholics and non-Catholics. And although Catholic educational institutions persist, the extent to which they contribute to a separate group consciousness seems less and less (Greeley, McCready, and McCourt 1976).

Traditionally, Catholics have been more likely than non-Catholics either to use no contraceptive method at all or to use the rhythm method. However, since the mid-1960s there has been a massive departure among Catholics from the formal church doctrine on birth prevention. For instance, among Catholic women married fifteen to nineteen years, the proportion using either no method at all or the rhythm method declined from 67 percent among women married in the 1936–1940 interval to 16 percent among women married during the 1956–1960 interval (Westoff and Jones 1979, pp. 209–210). This convergence between Catholics and non-Catholics on the matter of contraceptive use has taken place among the more devout Catholics as well as among those who receive Communion less frequently.

Thus, fundamental changes have taken place in the birth prevention practices of Catholics, despite the issuance of a papal encyclical in 1968 which condemned use of the pill and other artificial methods of birth prevention and reaffirmed the traditional teaching of the church that the rhythm method is the only acceptable means of preventing conception.

Some people believe that these changes were facilitated by the moral ambiguity about use of the pill which existed for several years *before* issuance of the encyclical. Many persons believed that the church would change its traditional stance and endorse the pill as an acceptable means of regulating the ovulatory cycles. Indeed, the Papal Commission on Population and Birth Control even made a recommendation to that effect. Although the commission's position was subsequently rejected in the encyclical, a large number of Catholics had already adopted the pill. In fact, about one-third of American Catholic couples were using it by the time the encyclical was issued (Westoff and Ryder 1977, p. 209). The change was underway, and issuance of an encyclical espousing an unpopular point of view only served to cause many to question the moral authority of the church in this matter (Westoff and Jones 1979, pp. 215–216).

In other countries the average level of childbearing among Catholics ranges from 18 to 30 percent higher than the level among non-Catholics (Population Council 1968, p. 5). But there are variations from one country to another. Lincoln Day (1968) has pointed out that the fertility level among Catholics in developed countries where they represent a *minority* of the population exceeds that of Catholics living in developed countries in which they form a majority. He concludes that Catholic pronatalism increases family size only in those situations in which Catholics see themselves as a numerically and politically important minority group.

Numerous studies in developing countries show only small or nonexistent differences in the family size of Catholic and non-Catholic couples. Research conducted in Latin American cities, for example, shows no clear relationship between religiousness and fertility (Miro 1966, p. 627). Within the Catholic population in these areas, family size differences tend to follow the expected relationships, being higher in rural areas and among the less educated than in the urban areas and among persons with higher educational levels (Miro 1964; and Population Council 1968, p. 6).

Moslems

Moslem fertility is high almost universally. It is generally higher than that of neighboring peoples of other religions (Kirk 1966, p. 567). Several studies examining fertility differences among Moslem and non-Moslem groups in the same country suggest that such differences are slight in the more backward sectors but are more pronounced in the more developed sectors (United Nations 1973, p. 105). A recent study in Lebanon noted that Moslem sects had the highest fertility while Christians had the lowest. This fact, however, may have reflected the substantial socioeconomic differences between the two groups, with non-Catholic Christians and Catholics at the top and Sunnite and Shiite Moslems at the bottom (Chamie 1976, p. 180).

All Moslem countries are in the category of developing nations. Most of them display relatively low levels of economic development, although the oil shortage is changing this rapidly in some of the Moslem nations. Because of the lack of extensive economic development, infant mortality has tended to be high, which, as we saw in chapter 2, encourages high fertility, especially when the gender of the surviving children is important. Moslems value sons for many purposes: continuity of the family line and land ownership, their contribution to agricultural labor, support in old age, and for religious intervention at or after death.

Yet Moslem views on the central issues involved in family planning have always been progressive and modern. While the Koran sees wealth and children as the joy of life, it does not enjoin begetting children. Indeed, the use of contraceptives "was both approved by the Prophet Muhammed and practised by his followers during his lifetime." (Zayid 1979, p. 8). The 1971 Muslim Conference of Rabat further confirmed this position. In its final report it stated:

> The Conference tended to consider that family planning is for the spouses by mutual agreement and without compulsion, to use a safe and lawful means to delay or precipitate pregnancy in such a way as to suit their health, social and economic circumstances, within the framework of responsibility towards their children and themselves (Zayid 1979, p. 9).

The traditional Moslem family is strongly male oriented, with male dominance and responsibility prescribed by the Koran. Moslem women receive a minimum amount of education, except about domestic activities. Almost all Moslem women marry, and at an early age. The practice of polygamy, which is still somewhat prevalent among wealthier Moslems, increases the marriage opportunities for females (Kirk 1966). All of these factors combine to promote pronatalism among Moslems.

THE REALIZATION OF FAMILY SIZE GOALS

One of the most important decisions young couples must make is whether or not to have children. If the decision is affirmative, then couples must then decide how many and when. Realizing goals that are set is not always possible for many reasons.

In our discussion so far we have made the distinction between wanted and unwanted births. For instance, Catholics have more wanted births than non-Catholics, and blacks have more unwanted births than whites. Avoiding unwanted births helps a family to realize its family size goals, but it is not always easy to accomplish.

Unwanted Births

Many people find it difficult to argue against the principle that couples should be able to have only the number of children they desire. Many political leaders have endorsed this concept, and the United Nations has issued a public proclamation signed by the heads of state of thirty nations that couples have a "right" to have the number of children they desire, and only that number (Declaration on Population: The World Leaders' Statement 1968). Government-sponsored family planning programs are intended to help couples avoid having unwanted births.

There are humanitarian as well as demographic reasons for studying unwanted fertility. It has been estimated that the total economic cost of raising a child to age eighteen in the United States varies from about $100,000 for families with a low-cost standard of living to $140,000 for families with a moderate-cost standard of living (Espenshade 1980). Thus, unwanted births represent financial costs which the parents would have preferred to avoid and for which little or no anticipatory planning usually has been done. These economic costs may result in financial hardships for the parents and may reduce the amount of money available for the unwanted child's brothers and sisters and for improving the family's standard of living. The poor have more unwanted children than others, which contributes to the perpetuation of poverty (Weller 1978, p. 264).

Even in a society sophisticated in the use of contraceptives, such as the United States, the magnitude of unwanted childbearing can be

Box 5.4 The Meaning of "Unwanted Births"

An "unwanted" birth has a technical meaning among demographers. Although it may be measured in a number of different ways, usually an unwanted birth results from a conception to a woman who reports that, before she became pregnant, she did not want to have any more children. For instance, the National Center for Health Statistics contacted a probability sample of women having a legitimate birth in 1972 and asked them this question about their birth: "Thinking back, *just before you became pregnant* with your new baby, did you want to become pregnant at that time?" Mothers were given their choice of the following responses:

1. "I wanted this pregnancy *at an earlier time,* as well as at that time."
2. "I wanted to become pregnant *at that time.*"
3. "I did not want to become pregnant at that time, but I wanted another child *sometime in the future.*"
4. "I did not want to become pregnant at that time, or at any time in the future."

The resultant study classified births as "unwanted" only if the mother gave the fourth reply—that she did not want to become pregnant at that time or at any time in the future. All other births were classified as wanted (Weller and Heuser 1978, p. 3). Demographers frequently refer to unwanted births as "number failures." The wanted births can be subdivided into two categories: timing controlled (those who gave the second reply) and timing failures (those who gave the first and third replies).

The wording of the question asked can affect the responses that are given. Also, the intensity of the woman's desire to have no more children is seldom measured. The question given above as an example was asked only of mothers. The fathers of these children were not asked if they wanted that birth to occur. Husbands and wives do not always agree on whether they want more children. Collecting data from both of them is very expensive and poses methodological risks. Some surveys have asked wives about their husbands' desires, but often wives give incorrect responses and the data have only limited value. Also, questions such as the one cited above refer only to the woman's feelings *before* she became pregnant. Many children resulting from an "unwanted" birth subsequently are deeply loved by their parents and are completely unaware that they resulted from an unwanted pregnancy.

---

quite large. According to one recent study, U.S. women in their childbearing years in 1973 reported already having almost 9 million unwanted births. If these women had had only the births they wanted, their average number of children ever born would have been 2.1 instead of 2.6 (Munson 1977). On a cross-sectional basis almost 10 percent of all births in 1973 to women who were or had been married were reported as "not wanted" by the mother (Weller 1978, p. 263).

The available evidence suggests that the elimination of unwanted births would substantially lower the growth rate of the U.S. population. Many of the differences in fertility between various racial, educational, and economic groups would also disappear.

The probability that a birth is unwanted is distributed among categories of women in the following manner:

1. It increases with the mother's age.
2. It is higher among blacks than among whites.
3. It increases as the number of children already born to the mother increases.
4. It decreases as the mother's educational level increases.
5. It is higher if the mother conceived her first pregnancy before marriage than if she conceived it after marriage. This is true of later births as well as the first one (Munson 1977; and Weller n.d.).

The major cause of an unwanted birth lies in the birth prevention practices of the population. Failures can and do occur with every contraceptive method, but the failure rate is higher for some methods than for others. Thus, some women have unwanted births because they have contraceptive failures and do not terminate the pregnancy with an induced abortion or miscarriage. Other women have unwanted births because they do not practice contraception regularly, or at all. Substantial numbers of women are either unable or unwilling to prevent unwanted conceptions with the existing contraceptive knowledge and technology. Historically, the alternative of induced abortion has been available only under very special circumstances. Only recently have restrictions been relaxed in the United States, for example, and there are still many areas of the country in which getting a legal abortion is practically impossible (Weinstock et al. 1976).

Controlling the Timing of Wanted Births

So far, we have been dealing only with the failure to control the wanted number of births. Failure to control the timing of wanted births is also important. Timing failures, as noted previously, are births that are wanted but that occurred sooner or later than the parents wanted. More than 27 percent of the legitimate births in 1972 were reported by the mother to be wanted, but later. More than 20 percent were reported to be wanted, but sooner (Weller 1976). In the United States more timing failures occur than unwanted births.

The ability to control the timing of births is particularly important with respect to the first birth, because the birth of a child can change a woman's role. The first birth represents a transition to motherhood and its associated roles. For many, it even represents the cause of entry into marriage itself. Over 23 percent of the first births to women interviewed in the 1973 National Survey of Family Growth were reported as occurring before marriage or within seven months after marriage (Weller n.d.). Presumably in the latter case, those first-borns were conceived out of wedlock. If the timing of first births was planned, the incidence of illegitimate births and hasty shotgun marriages would be reduced considerably. For many women controlling the timing of their first birth would result in marriage and motherhood at a later age. The proportion of women who might—during their period of postponed childbearing—choose to remain single and/or childless is not known.

The timing of the first birth is also important to married women. Not having the first child until the time it is wanted can mean more child-free time to continue education and acquire occupational interests and skills that may be incompatible with motherhood. Postponing the first birth may also result in a reduction in desired family size. Even after the first birth occurs, the inability to control the timing of subsequent births may reduce a woman's ability to plan an orderly occupational career. This may greatly reduce the financial and psychic rewards associated with activities outside the family (Presser 1973).

Deficit Fertility

There are three possible outcomes to any comparison between desired and **completed family size.** The couple may have more children than desired, the same number desired, or fewer children than desired. This last outcome has been labeled "deficit fertility."

Deficit fertility is an undeniable fact. Over 23 percent of the currently married women age fifteen to forty-four in the United States in 1973 reported that they desired more children than they expected to have. Substantial numbers of women outside the United States have also reported such a desire.

Studies have shown that deficit fertility is more likely to be found among certain categories of women than others. For example, researchers have discovered the following:

1. Deficit fertility is inversely related to the number of children already born. That is, the fewer children a woman has, the more likely she will experience deficit fertility.
2. It is greater for women who work than for women who are not in the labor force.
3. It is greater for whites than for blacks.
4. It is greater among women who marry at age twenty-five or older than among women who marry at younger ages.
5. Its probability increases as the woman's educational attainment increases (Weller 1974).

Two causes of deficit fertility are physiological impairment and a disagreement between husband and wife on ideal family size. In addition, a substantial number of couples may be deliberately restricting their childbearing to a level lower than they desire it to be. One reason, of course, is that they perceive the economic costs of childbearing to be high. There are other "costs" as well—career opportunity costs, social costs, psychological costs, the trauma of playing the parent role, and life style costs. As Paul Demeny states: "Not satisfying a desire is rational if the costs are too high" (1970, p. 36).

Thus, not everyone succeeds in planning the number and timing of their births. Two phenomena having to do with fertility deserve special attention because they represent an increasingly important contribution to population growth in the United States and because of their adverse effects on the children and/or their mothers. These are illegitimate births and births to teen-agers. Although not all of these births are unplanned, they are much more likely than births to other categories of women to be unplanned.

Illegitimate Births

Births that are conceived and occur outside of marriage are commonly referred to as **illegitimate,** although this term is regarded as degrading by some women who desire children but do not wish to be married. National estimates of the number of illegitimate births are based on information reported on the birth certificates of thirty-seven states and the District of Columbia. During the 1970s the number of legitimate births decreased, while the number of births to unmarried women increased. For instance, in 1977 there were about 2.8 million legitimate births, a figure 16 percent lower than the number of legitimate births in 1970. By contrast, there were over 515,000 births to unmarried women in 1977, an increase of 29 percent since 1970.[3]

Illegitimate births are largely unplanned and indicate that some American women are not successfully controlling their fertility. Although it is difficult to separate cause from effect, illegitimacy appears to have negative consequences for the child, the parents, and society.

Infant mortality is higher in the case of illegitimate births than it is for legitimate births. Also, the health and emotional stability of children born out of wedlock may be impaired, particularly when the father does not live with the family. Only a small proportion of infants born to unmarried women are adopted or later legitimized by the marriage of the parents. Most often the biological father does not maintain any consistent relationship with the mother and the illegitimate child. Thus, the unwed mother is mainly responsible for raising the child. Yet unwed mothers tend to have more emotional problems than other mothers. Although the state may supply monetary support for the illegitimate child, this amount usually is less than a steadily employed father would earn. Finally, recent research on the "battered child syndrome" indicates that children born out of wedlock are the ones most likely to be reported as child abuse cases (Hartley 1975).

[3]See box 5.5 for methods of measuring illegitimacy.

Box 5.5 Measuring Illegitimacy

There are two commonly used measures of illegitimacy—the **illegitimacy rate** and the **illegitimacy ratio.** The formula for the former is:

$$\text{Illegitimacy Rate} = \frac{\text{Number of Illegitimate Births}}{\text{Number of Unmarried Women 15–44}} \times 1{,}000$$

For example, in the United States there were 515,700 births to unmarried women in 1977. In that same year, there were an estimated 19,834,615 unmarried women of childbearing age. Thus:

$$\text{Illegitimacy Rate} = \left(\frac{515{,}700}{19{,}834{,}615}\right)1{,}000 = (.0260)\ 1{,}000 = 26$$

In other words in 1977 there were 26 illegitimate births per 1,000 unmarried women of childbearing age in the United States. Illegitimacy rates may also be computed for smaller age groups (e.g., those in the age bracket fifteen to nineteen, etc.).

The illegitimacy ratio tells the number of illegitimate live births per 1,000 live births. The formula for this is:

$$\text{Illegitimacy Ratio} = \frac{\text{Number of Illegitimate Births}}{\text{Number of Births}} \times 1{,}000$$

In 1977 there were 515,700 illegitimate births in the United States and 3,326,632 total births (legitimate as well as illegitimate).

$$\text{Illegitimacy ratio} = \left(\frac{515{,}700}{3{,}326{,}632}\right)1{,}000 = (.1550)\ 1{,}000 = 155$$

In other words, in 1977 out of every 1,000 births, 155 were illegitimate. This is the same as saying that 15.5 percent of all births in the United States in 1977 were illegitimate.

Substantial numbers of unwed mothers in American society are young. Having a birth at that particular time of their lives may cause them to interrupt or even terminate their education. As a result they may not be prepared for certain careers or occupational pursuits which they may prefer, and they may be denied the opportunity of developing useful skills. Living alone and lacking a secure commitment from the fathers may have a negative effect on the mothers' self-esteem. Illegitimacy is an important issue to society because of its potential to lessen societal control over its members' choice of mates and because of the less than adequate conditions of childbirth and childbearing usually accompanying a premarital pregnancy (Hartley 1975, pp. 7–16). An attempt to relieve these effects of illegitimacy would involve costly social and economic programs. Yet not trying to do so involves substantial human costs.

Teen-age Childbearing

There are close to 15 million teen-age females in the United States; in 1977 the 571,000 births to teen-agers represented over 17 percent of all births.

Like the birth rates for women in their twenties those for older teen-agers (eighteen and nineteen years of age) have declined since 1966. However, the rates for teen-agers age fifteen to seventeen actually increased slightly between 1966 and 1972, before they also started to decline. And in absolute terms the number of infants born to mothers of that age group in 1977 was 15 percent larger than in 1966. Perhaps more disturbing is that the number of births to mothers ten to fourteen years of age increased by over 40 percent during the 1966–1975 interval. In 1977 there were over 11,000 births to mothers in this age group (Ventura 1977; Taffel 1977; National Center for Health Statistics 1978 and 1979).

Teen-age childbearing is at a relatively high level because of the rather high rate of nonuse of contraceptives, the prevalence of ineffective methods among users, and increased rates of sexual activity among teen-agers. For instance, in 1976 less than two-thirds of the sexually experienced, never-married women age fifteen to nineteen reported having used contraception the last time they had intercourse and over 53 percent of the users had used the relatively ineffective methods of douche, withdrawal, or rhythm. Also, the proportion of never-married women in that age group who have had sexual intercourse increased from 27 percent in 1971 to 35 percent in 1976 (Zelnick and Kantner 1976 and 1978).

Teen-age childbearing takes on additional importance because disproportionate numbers of teen-age births are illegitimate. From 1960 to 1977 the proportion of teen-age births occurring out of wedlock jumped from 15 to 44 percent. During this same interval, while the illegitimacy rate (or number of births per 1,000 unmarried women) declined for women over age twenty, the rate increased by over 50 percent for women age fifteen to nineteen. In actual numbers illegitimate births to teen-agers in that age bracket increased by 77 percent. Thus, illegitimacy is becoming more and more concentrated in the teen-age years. Indeed, recently about one-half of all illegitimate births in the United States have occurred to persons under age twenty (National Center for Health Statistics 1979; and Baldwin 1976).

Teen-age mothers tend to receive inadequate prenatal care and their children tend to be of low birth weight (Ventura 1977). Consequently, the risk of infant mortality is greatly increased. Children born to teen-age mothers also have higher mortality rates during early childhood than do other children. The intellectual and psychological development of children born to teen-age mothers is also more problematic than when they are born to older mothers. This does not mean that all births to teen-age mothers result in physiological or psychological problems. It is just that the risk of negative outcomes for the pregnancy, the birth, and the child's development is high when the mother is a teen-ager. Postponing a birth until a woman is in her twenties decreases these risks considerably.

Teen-age childbearing has a number of consequences for the mother. As mentioned earlier, pregnancy and motherhood generally terminate formal schooling. Since earnings and occupational advancement tend to be a result of formal schooling, teen-age mothers place themselves at a severe disadvantage in the job market. Teen-age motherhood may also be associated with a larger completed family size, which may not be desired by the mother (Baldwin 1976).

Voluntary Childlessness

Childlessness is viewed as desirable by only a small proportion of the U.S. population (Blake 1974). Data collected in 1978 by the U.S. Bureau of the Census show that only 10 percent of American women age thirty to thirty-four are childless and expect to remain so permanently (U.S. Bureau of the Census 1979*b,* p. 18). Because some of these women have involuntary reproductive impairments, the proportion that is voluntarily childless is even smaller. Until recently the proportion of women remaining childless declined steadily. However, in the past few years oral contraceptives and other artifical means of birth prevention have become readily available, antiabortion laws have been declared unconstitutional, family and sexual norms have changed dramatically, educational levels have increased, and the participation of females in the paid labor force has increased significantly. Because of these changes, the extent of voluntary childlessness increased during the 1970s (Poston and Gotard 1977; and DeJong and Sell 1977).

There is a positive relationship between income level and being voluntarily childless (Poston 1974 and 1976). Persons who are voluntarily childless are primarily from the middle and upper socioeconomic strata. Apparently changes in the structure of American society have encouraged an increasing proportion of American couples to select childlessness as their family size goal, and changes in birth control technology have made possible the realization of this goal.

Policies to Increase Realization of Family Size Goals

In chapter 11 we will discuss methods of lowering national birth rates. Many people assume that this is the same as helping individuals realize their own family size goals, but this is not necessarily true.

As stated earlier, a number of heads of state have publicly endorsed the principle that couples have a "right" to have the number of children they desire, and only that number. The means usually adopted to reach that goal is a government-sponsored family planning program which emphasizes the dissemination of contraceptive knowledge and supplies to the population. However, family planning programs are designed to permit women to avoid having unwanted births or having births sooner than they desire. They are not designed to accommodate the needs of women who have fewer children than they desire or of those who do not have births as quickly as they would prefer. Probably these women are overlooked when policy is being formulated because their failure to realize their own family size goals actually reduces the rate of population growth—a goal which many policy makers desire. Yet, ignoring the needs of these people goes against the principle that couples have a right to have the number of children they desire and at the birth intervals they desire.

What would a policy be like that helps all people realize their own family size goals? Let us consider first those people who have unwanted births or have them sooner than they desire.

A major cause of unwanted childbearing or having a birth sooner than it is wanted is contraceptive failure. Improving the contraceptive practices of all segments of the population is one way to deal with the problem. More effective contraceptives without undesirable side effects could also be developed. The extent and accuracy of beliefs and knowledge of currently existing contraceptives should be studied. The reasons why some segments of the population are unable apparently to control their fertility while other segments of the population can do so should receive high priority. Does the explanation lie in lack of motivation, education, communication, and/or distribution and access? It may be that to reach some segments of the population, such as teenagers or the poor, it will be necessary to develop and use a completely different communication and distribution system than currently exists. Making termination of unwanted pregnancies as socially and economically untraumatic as possible for all segments of the population is another approach to reducing the incidence of unwanted births.

But what about the women who have fewer children than they desire or who do not have them quickly enough? A policy to enable people to realize their family size goals could involve taking steps to reduce involuntary sterility and reproductive impairments. This might be done through the development of new drugs which would reduce the occurrence of spontaneous abortion, prevent diseases that cause sterility, or increase the male's sperm count; or it might require improved techniques to permit corrective surgery of the reproductive organs. In those cases in which sterility is not completely preventable, adoption of children would be the only viable alternative. This would involve a certain amount of social change. At the present time in many states children who are adopted are viewed as inferior to "natural" children and are not granted social and legal equality. And to the extent that deficit fertility is voluntary, measures would have to be taken which permit people to "afford" as many children as they want, when they want them. In addition to family allowances, such measures might include providing subsidized, quality child care for all women who wish to work and granting generous maternity leaves with pay and without the loss of benefits (such as seniority) usually caused by interrupting employment.

Eliminating unwanted childbearing and permitting people to realize their family size goals are thus not identical objectives. Attaining one will not necessarily mean attaining the other. Programs designed to attain replacement level fertility (a must on the global level) that are based solely on the principle that each couple should have the number of children it desires and only that number will succeed only if the family size that individuals desire exactly coincides with replacement levels. In other words, if people want more children than the replacement level, to be truly successful these programs would have to enable them to have that number.

SUMMARY

Social, economic, and psychological factors affect fertility only through the "intermediate" variables relating to the probability of having intercourse, conceiving, and successfully having a live birth. Both the societal birth rate and the fertility of individual women are produced by a combination of those factors.

Birth rates are considerably higher in the developing than in developed countries of the world. Likewise, different types of people have different patterns of fertility.

The higher a person's socioeconomic status, the smaller the number of children that person is likely to have. In industrialized societies women who work tend to have fewer children than women who do not work. Having a smaller family increases the wife's availability for employment. However, her employment also encourages a small family.

Levels of childbearing also are lower in urban than in rural areas. This is particularly true in more modernized countries, though in the past twenty-five years the difference between rural and urban childbearing rates has diminished.

Blacks who live in the United States have more children than whites. One reason is their overall lower socioeconomic status. Blacks are also more likely than whites to have unwanted births.

In the United States and other more developed countries, Catholics tend to have more children than non-Catholics, primarily because they desire more children. Among non-Catholics, Jews have fewer children than Protestants because of differences in socioeconomic status. Family size differences between Catholic and non-Catholic women living in developing countries tend to be small or nonexistent.

Substantial numbers of American women do not have the number of births they desire. They can be classified in two groups. One group has unwanted births. Women in this group apparently have spouses who prefer more children than they do; they also sometimes lack adequate means of birth prevention. The second group of women exhibits deficit fertility, which is apparently caused by three factors: physiological reproductive impairments, disagreement with the spouse over family size preferences, and deliberate restriction of family size because of the perceived costs of a larger family.

REFERENCES AND SUGGESTED READINGS

Abu-Lughod, Janet. 1965. The emergence of differential fertility in urban Egypt. *Milbank Memorial Fund quarterly* 43 (April):235–253.

Arnold, Fred. 1970. The relation of parents' education and educational aspirations for children to fertility in Taiwan. In *1970 social statistics section proceedings,* pp. 244–249. Washington, D.C.: American Statistical Association.

Baldwin, Wendy H. 1976. Adolescent pregnancy and childbearing—growing concerns for Americans. *Population bulletin* 31 (September): 3–34.

Barrett, John C. 1971. Fecundability and coital frequency. *Population studies* 25 (July):309–313.

Blake, Judith. 1974. Can we believe recent data on birth expectations in the United States? *Demography* 11 (February):25–44.

Bouvier, Leon F., and Macisco, John J. 1968. Education of husband and wife and fertility in Puerto Rico. *Social and economic studies* 17 (March):49–59.

Bouvier, Leon F., and Rao, S. L. N. 1975. *Socioreligious factors in fertility decline.* Cambridge, Mass.: Ballinger Publishing.

Chamie, Joseph. 1976. The Lebanese civil war: an investigation into the causes. *World affairs* 139, no.3 (Winter 1976–77):171–188.

David, Henry P. 1970. *Family planning and abortion in the socialist countries of central and eastern Europe.* New York: The Population Council.

Davis, Kingsley, and Blake, Judith. 1956. Social structure and fertility: an analytical framework. *Economic development and cultural change* 5 (April):211–235.

Day, Lincoln H. 1968. Natality and ethnocentrism: some relationships suggested by an analysis of Catholic-Protestant differentials. *Population studies* 22 (March):27–50.

Declaration on population: the world leaders' statement. 1968. *Studies in family planning* 26 (January):1–3.

DeJong, G.F., and Sell, R. R. 1977. Changes in childlessness in the United States: a demographic path analysis. *Population studies* 31 (March):129–141.

Demeny, Paul. 1970. Causes and consequences of excess fertility. Honolulu: East-West Population Institute Paper.

Espenshade, Thomas J. 1980. Raising a child can now cost $85,000. *Intercom* 8 (September).

Ford, Kathleen. 1978. Contraceptive efficacy among married women 15–44 years of age in the United States. *Advance data* 26 (April 6).

Freedman, Ronald, Whelpton, Pascal K., and Smit, John W. 1961. Socio-economic factors in religious differentials in fertility. *American sociological review* 26 (August):608–614.

Glass, David V., and Grebenik, E. 1954. *The trend and pattern of fertility in Great Britain.* London: Her Majesty's Stationery Office.

Goldberg, David. 1967. Fertility and fertility differentials: some observations on recent changes in the United States. In *Public health and population change,* eds. Mindel C. Sheps and Jeanne Clare Ridley, pp. 119–142. Pittsburgh: University of Pittsburgh Press.

Goldscheider, Calvin, and Uhlenberg, Peter R. 1969. Minority group status and fertility. *American journal of sociology* 74 (January):361–372.

Goyal, R. P. 1975. Shifts in age at marriage in India between 1961 and 1971. *Demography India* 4 (December):336–344.

Grabill, Wilson H., Kiser, Clyde V., and Whelpton, Pascal K. 1958. *The fertility of American women.* New York: John Wiley.

Greeley, Andrew M., McCready, William C., and McCourt, Kathleen. 1976. *Catholic schools in a declining church.* Kansas City: Sheed and Ward.

Hartley, Shirley F. 1975. *Illegitimacy.* Berkeley: University of California Press.

James, W. H. 1970. The incidence of spontaneous abortion. *Population studies* 24 (July):241–245.

Kerr, Melville G. 1971. Perinatal mortality and genetic wastage in man. *Journal of biosocial science* 2 (April):223–237.

Kirk, Dudley. 1966. Factors affecting Moslem natality. In *Family planning and population programs,* eds. Bernard Berelson et al., pp. 561–579. Chicago: University of Chicago Press.

Kuczynski, Robert R. 1936. *The measurement of population growth.* New York: Oxford University Press.

McFalls, Joseph A. 1979. Frustrated fertility: a population paradox. *Population bulletin* 34 (May).

Mendoza-Hoyos, Hernan. 1968. Research studies on abortion and family planning in Colombia. *Milbank Memorial Fund quarterly* 46, part 2 (July):223–234.

Miro, Carmen A. 1964. The population of Latin America. *Demography* 1:15–41.

———.1966. Some misconceptions disproved: a program of comparative fertility surveys in Latin America. In *Family planning and population programs,* eds. Bernard Berelson et al., pp. 615–634. Chicago: University of Chicago Press.

Munson, Martha Little. 1977. Wanted and unwanted births reported by mothers 15–44 years of age: United States, 1973. *Advance data* 9 (August 10).

Nag, Moni. 1962. *Factors affecting human fertility in nonindustrial societies: a cross-cultural study.* New Haven: Yale University Press.

———. 1967. Family type and fertility. *Proceedings of the world population conference,* vol. II, pp. 160–163. New York: United Nations.

National Center for Health Statistics. 1978. *Health, United States 1978.* Washington, D.C.: Government Printing Office.

———. 1979. Advance report final natality statistics, 1977. *Monthly vital statistics report* 27, supplement (February 5).

———. 1980. Advanced report final natality statistics. *Monthly vital statistics report 29* (April 28).

Nortman, Dorothy. 1974. Parental age as a factor in pregnancy outcome and child development. *Reports on population/family planning* 16 (August):2–51.

Petersen, William. 1969. *Population.* 2nd ed. Toronto: Collier-Macmillan.

Population Council. 1968. Roman Catholic fertility and family planning: a comparative review of the research literature. *Studies in family planning* 34 (October):1–27.

Population Reference Bureau. 1980. *1980 World population data sheet.* Washington, D.C.: Population Reference Bureau.

Poston, Dudley L. 1974. Income and childlessness in the United States: is the relationship always inverse? *Social biology* 21 (Fall):296–307.

———. 1976. Characteristics of voluntarily and involuntarily childless wives. *Social biology* 23 (Fall):198–209.

Poston, Dudley L., and Gotard, Erin. 1977. Trends in childlessness in the United States, 1910–1975. *Social biology* 24 (Fall):212–224.

Presser, Harriet B. 1970. Voluntary sterilization: a world view. *Reports on population/family planning* 5 (July).

———. 1973. Perfect fertility control: consequences for women and the family. In *Toward the end of growth,* by Charles F. Westoff et al., pp. 133–144. Englewood Cliffs, N.J.: Prentice-Hall.

Requena, Mariano B., and Monreal, Tequalda. 1968. Evaluation of induced abortion control and family planning programs in Chile. *Milbank Memorial Fund quarterly* 46, part 2 (July):191–218.

Roberts, Robert E., and Lee, Eun Sul. 1974. Minority group status and fertility revisited. *American journal of sociology* 80 (September):503–523

Ryder, Norman B. 1973. Recent trends and group differences in fertility. In *Toward the end of growth,* by Charles F. Westoff et al., pp. 57–68. Englewood Cliffs, N.J.: Prentice-Hall.

Ryder, Norman B., and Westoff, Charles F. 1971. *Reproduction in the United States 1965.* Princeton, N.J.: Princeton University Press.

———. 1972. Wanted and unwanted fertility in the United States: 1965 and 1970. In *Demographic and social aspects of population growth,* vol. I, eds. Charles F. Westoff and Robert Parke, Jr., pp. 467–487. Washington, D.C.: Government Printing Office.

Sly, David F. 1970. Minority group status and fertility: an extension of Goldscheider and Uhlenberg. *American journal of sociology* 76 (November):443–459.

Smith. T. E. 1960. The Cocos-Keeling Islands: a demographic laboratory. *Population studies* 14 (November):94–129.

Smith-Lovin, Lynn, and Tickamyer, Ann R. 1978. Nonrecursive models of labor force participation, fertility behavior and sex role attitudes. *American sociological review* 43 (August):541–557.

Stokes, C. Shannon. 1972. Religious differentials in reproductive behavior: a replication and extension. *Sociological analysis* 33 (Spring):26–33.

Taffel, Selma. 1977. Trends in fertility in the United States. *Vital and health statistics,* series 21, no. 28 (September).

Tietze, Christopher. 1957. Reproductive span and rate of reproduction among Hutterite women. *Fertility and sterility* 8 (January–February):89–97.

———. 1960. Probability of pregnancy resulting from a single unprotected coitus. *Fertility and sterility* 11 (September–October):485–488.

———. 1961. The effect of breastfeeding on the rate of conception. *Proceed-*

ings of the International Population Conference, New York 1961, vol. II, pp. 129–135. London: UNESCO.

Tsui, Amy Ong, and Bogue, Donald J. 1978. Declining world fertility: trends, causes, implications. *Population bulletin* 33 (October).

United Nations. 1973. *The determinants and consequences of population change,* vol. I. New York: United Nations.

———. 1977. *Demographic yearbook 1976.* New York: United Nations.

U.S. Bureau of the Census. 1973. *Census of population: 1970. Subject reports,* Final Report PC(2)-3A, Women by number of children ever born. Washington, D.C.: Government Printing Office.

———. 1978. Perspectives on American fertility. *Current population reports,* series P-23, no. 70. Washington, D.C.: Government Printing Office.

———. 1979*a*. Estimates of the population of the United States, by age, sex, and race: 1976 to 1978. *Current population reports,* series P-25, no. 800. Washington, D.C.: Government Printing Office.

———. 1979*b*. Fertility of American women: June 1978. *Current population reports,* series P-20, no. 341. Washington, D.C.: Government Printing Office.

Van Ginnekan, Jeroen K. 1974. Prolonged breastfeeding as a birth spacing method. *Studies in family planning* 5 (June):201–206.

Vaughan, Barbara et al. 1977. Contraceptive failure among married women in the United States, 1970–1973. *Family planning perspectives* 9 (November–December):251–258.

Ventura, Stephanie. 1977. Teenage childbearing: United States, 1966–75. *Monthly vital statistics report* 26 (September 8).

Waite, Linda J., and Stolzenberg, Ross M. 1976. Intended childbearing and labor force participation of young women: insights from nonrecursive models. *American sociological review* 41 (April): 235–252.

Weinstock, Edward, et al. 1976. Abortion need and services in the United States, 1974–1975. *Family planning perspectives* 8 (March–April):58–69.

Weller, Robert H. 1974. Excess and deficit fertility in the United States, 1965. *Social biology* 21 (Spring):77–87.

———. 1976. Number and timing failures among legitimate births in the United States: 1968, 1969 and 1972. *Family planning perspectives* 8 (May–June):111–116.

———. 1977. Demographic correlates of women's participation in economic activities. In *International Population Conference: Mexico 1977,* pp. 497–516. Liege, Belgium: International Union for the Scientific Study of Population.

———. 1978. Family size goals and their realization by American women. In *Fertility and contraception in America,* vol. I, *Hearings before the Select Committee on Population, Ninety-fifth Congress,* pp. 262–281. Washington, D.C.: Government Printing Office.

———. 1979. The differential attainment of family size goals by race. *Population studies* 33 (March):157–164.

———. n.d. The realization of family size goals by American women. *Vital and health statistics* (forthcoming).

Weller, Robert, H., and Heuser, Robert L. 1978. Wanted and unwanted childbearing in the United States: 1968, 1969, and 1972 national natality surveys. *Vital and health statistics,* series 21, no. 32 (September).

Westoff, Charles F. 1973. Changes in contraceptive practices among married couples. In *Toward the end of growth,* eds. Charles F. Westoff et al., pp. 19–31. Englewood Cliffs, N.J.: Prentice-Hall.

———. 1976. Trends in contraceptive practice: 1965–1973. *Family planning perspectives* 8 (March–April):54–57.

Westoff, Charles F. and Jones, Elise F. 1977. The secularization of U.S. Catholic birth control practices. *Family planning perspectives* 9 (September–October):203–207.

———. 1979. The end of "Catholic" fertility. *Demography* 16 (May):209–217.

Westoff, Charles F., and Potvin, Raymond H. 1967. *College women and fertility values.* Princeton, N.J.: Princeton University Press.

Westoff, Charles F., and Ryder, Norman B. 1977. *The contraceptive revolution.* Princeton, N.J.: Princeton University Press.

Zayid, Mahmud. 1979. Family planning in Islam. *People* 6, no. 4 (1979):8–10.

Zelnick, Melvin, and Kantner, John F. 1976. Sexual and contraceptive experience of young unmarried women in the United States, 1976 and 1971. *Family planning perspectives* 9 (March–April):55–71.

———. 1978. First pregnancies to women aged 15–19: 1976 and 1971. *Family planning perspectives* 10 (January–February):11–20.

6
Birth Prevention Methods

Any discussion of the demographic variable fertility would be incomplete without looking at the way people try to control their fertility. Almost all married couples in the United States and other industrialized countries try to limit their family size or to control the timing and spacing of their births. Substantial numbers of unmarried, sexually active persons also attempt to prevent births. However, in some of the developing countries relatively few persons are using a birth prevention method.

A variety of methods are available to prevent births. The most popular ones in the United States are contraceptives, sterilization, and abortion. Some birth prevention methods are more effective than others,[1] and each method has its advantages as well as its disadvantages. As a demographic actor, you should be able to select the method which is most appropriate for your particular circumstances.

This chapter deals first with the two immediate determinants of the use of birth prevention methods—motivation and availability. A brief description of the major birth prevention methods then follows. We conclude by examining the mortality risks associated with birth prevention.

WHAT DETERMINES THE USE OF BIRTH PREVENTION METHODS?

Birth prevention methods are a means to an end. Whether a person wants to avoid giving birth and how important avoiding the birth is to that person are major determinants of the use of birth control. In turn, they are influenced by social, economic, and cultural variables.

Under some circumstances the birth of an additional child may be perceived as "less costly" than under other circumstances. If so, the actors will be less likely to use birth control, more likely to use a relatively ineffective method, and less careful in using their method. Couples who intend to have another child but are using some method of birth control to delay this birth provide an example. Those couples have higher rates of contraceptive failure than individuals seeking to prevent the birth of any more children, even when the same methods are used. Presumably the couples who want another child (eventually) view the consequences of an unplanned birth less negatively than those who want no more children. They may be less conscientious in their contraceptive usage and more willing to take chances. Thus, they have more contraceptive failures.

However, motivation is not the entire story. The more effective methods of birth prevention may not be equally available to all segments of the population. Some segments of the population may not use contraceptives because they mistakenly believe they cannot become

[1]Box 6.1 discusses measures of birth prevention effectiveness.

Box 6.1 Birth Prevention Effectiveness

Birth prevention methods can be measured in terms of their theoretical effectiveness, use effectiveness, and extended use effectiveness. Theoretical effectiveness refers to the efficaciousness of the method when it is used exactly according to directions and when it is used all the time. Use effectiveness takes into account the fact that some users do not follow directions carefully or do not use the method all the time. Extended use effectiveness combines the effectiveness of a method with continuation of use by also taking into account the experience of persons who begin use of a method but subsequently discontinue use for some reason.

Because they are interested in the consequences of people's actual behavior, demographers have shied away from measures of theoretical effectiveness. The traditional method of measuring use effectiveness, and the one used by the U. S. Food and Drug Administration, involves computation of the **Pearl Index** (*R*), named after its formulator, Raymond Pearl. The Index is computed as follows:

$$R = \frac{\text{Total Number of Conceptions}}{\text{Total Months of Exposure}} \times 1{,}000$$

The numerator is the total number of conceptions to persons while they were using a particular method, and the denominator is the total number of months those persons used that method. The quotient is multiplied by 1,000 to produce an estimate of the monthly probability of becoming pregnant while using that method (Pearl 1932; and Tietze 1962).

Recently serious concern has been expressed about the validity of the Pearl Index. The index is a valid estimate of the monthly probability of becoming pregnant while using that method if and only if the monthly probability of failure is the same for all women and for all durations of use. Yet we know that this is seldom the case. Previous research has shown that the probability of a failure declines as the duration of use increases. Ineffective or careless users become pregnant and are assigned a shorter duration of use than the more careful, effective users. Thus, including all durations of use in the denominator may produce a misleading estimate of the monthly failure rate, and several noted demographers have recommended to the Food and Drug Administration that it stop using the Pearl Index to measure contraceptive effectiveness. Instead, some measure of effectiveness should be used that indicates effectiveness during a set period of time, such as a year, after the method is first used by the person (Vaughan et al. 1977; and Hatcher et al. 1978). Unless otherwise specified, in our text we will follow this suggestion by using a measure of extended use effectiveness which shows the proportion of persons who have a contraceptive failure within one year after they begin use of that method.

pregnant. This is the case among many unmarried teen-agers in the United States. A survey conducted in 1976 showed that less than half of the unmarried teen-agers who were sexually experienced correctly perceived that the period of greatest risk is about two weeks after the menstrual period begins (Zelnick and Kantner 1977, p. 58). Other segments of the population find certain methods unacceptable for religious and other reasons. Thus, those methods are, in effect, "unavailable" to them. Finally, some people simply lack knowledge of the various birth prevention methods and their relative effectiveness.

Methods of Birth Prevention

The concept of preventing birth appeared early in human history. For instance, Egyptian papyri dating to between 1900 and 1100 B.C. describe various contraceptive preparations—including pulverized crocodile dung mixed with a gelatinous substance made from seaweed—to be used at the entrance to the vagina (Noonan 1966). But until fairly recently most methods have been relatively ineffective—with the exception of induced abortion and withdrawal. Currently the various birth prevention methods may be grouped as follows:

1. Prevention of contact between the sperm and ova
2. Prevention of ovulation
3. Prevention of implantation of the fertilized egg into the uterine wall
4. Other methods—surgical sterilization, induced abortion, and menstrual regulation

Below we examine the major birth prevention methods. We describe the principle by which each method works, give a short history of its development, assess its effectiveness, and describe the advantages and disadvantages of the method.

PREVENTION OF CONTACT BETWEEN SPERM AND OVA

Rhythm

Avoiding intercourse around the time of ovulation, when the ovary expels the egg, prevents conception. Generally there is only one egg per menstrual cycle, which lives about twenty-four hours after ovulation. The sperm needed to fertilize the egg live only about forty-eight hours after ejaculation. Theoretically couples who avoid intercourse during this seventy-two hour period (one day before and after ovulation) should be able to avoid conception. This is known as the **rhythm method,** or periodic continence. The trick is finding out the exact interval during which to avoid intercourse.

The notion that females cannot conceive during most of the menstrual cycle is very old, but early ideas on which part of the cycle was not "safe" were incorrect. People believed that the woman was most likely to conceive immediately after her menstrual period ended. The rest of the cycle was considered safe because the woman was thought to be sterile. Consequently, those who used this technique experienced frequent pregnancies, and the method gained a poor reputation.

The modern form of the rhythm method was developed in the early 1930s and is based upon the fact that the egg is released about fourteen days (plus or minus two days) *before* the next menstrual flow. Unfortunately, it is not simple to calculate the "safe" period because the length of each menstrual cycle is not uniform for each woman. Some women's menstrual cycles vary greatly in length. To estimate the interval during which she might become pregnant, a woman should first subtract eighteen days from her shortest-known menstrual cycle (fourteen days to estimate ovulation, two days for the life of the sperm, and another two days in case ovulation occurs a little early). Then she should subtract eleven days from her longest-known menstrual cycle (fourteen days to estimate ovulation, minus one day for the life of the egg, minus two days in case ovulation occurs a little late). (These calculations are shown in table 6.1.) The interval between these two calculations is when she should abstain from intercourse.

The greater the difference between the shortest and the longest

Table 6.1 How to Calculate the Interval of Fertility

IF THE SHORTEST CYCLE HAS BEEN (NUMBER OF DAYS)	THE FIRST FERTILE (UNSAFE) DAY IS DAY	IF THE LONGEST CYCLE HAS BEEN (NUMBER OF DAYS)	THE LAST FERTILE (UNSAFE) DAY IS DAY
21	3*	21	10
22	4	22	11
23	5	23	12
24	6	24	13
25	7	25	14
26	8	26	15
27	9	27	16
28	10	28	17
29	11	29	18
30	12	30	19
31	13	31	20
32	14	32	21
33	15	33	22
34	16	34	23
35	17	35	24

*Day 1 = first day of menstrual bleeding
Source: Hatcher et al. (1978), p. 95.

menstrual cycles the woman has experienced, the longer should be the period of abstinence. Thus, among women whose shortest menstrual cycle has been twenty-seven days and whose longest has been twenty-nine days, the recommended period of abstinence lasts only from day 9 to day 18. But among women whose shortest menstrual cycle has been twenty-two days and whose longest cycle has been thirty-five days, the recommended period of abstinence lasts from day 4 to day 24—over twice as long as for women with menstrual cycles of more uniform length.

The estimated time of ovulation can also be calculated by use of a basal body temperature chart. This method applies the principle that ovulation produces a rise in the basic metabolic rate, causing a corresponding increase in body temperature of about .6°F. Thus ovulation may be determined by recording one's temperature daily. This technique greatly reduces the length of abstinence, but there are drawbacks. Changes in body temperature are slight and easily misinterpreted. Some women do not know how to use a thermometer properly. Oral temperatures may not be sufficiently accurate, and some women consider taking daily rectal temperatures either inconvenient or unacceptable.

Current research efforts are focused on the development of a special paper that can be inserted into the vagina daily. This paper changes color when ovulation occurs. Another method of estimating the time of ovulation involves interpretation of cyclical changes in the cervical mucus, although the reliability of this technique has not been established firmly. Researchers are also testing use of a small electrical device to measure the electrical charges that occur in the body when the ovum is released (Peel and Potts 1969, pp. 80–86; Ross and Piotrow 1974, pp. 7–8; and Segal and Nordberg 1977).

Effectiveness

The contraceptive effectiveness of the rhythm method is controversial. Correctly taught and practiced, it can be very effective, particularly among women with fairly regular menstrual cycles. Improperly taught or practiced, the rhythm method may be very ineffective. Data collected in the early 1970s show that 9.5 percent of couples using the rhythm method to prevent an unwanted pregnancy and 28.8 percent of those using it to delay their next wanted pregnancy failed in their goals within the first twelve months of use (Vaughan et al. 1977, p. 254).

Occasional disregard of the rules for calculating the safe period is the most common cause of failure. The importance of motivation (and regularity of use) is shown by the fact that persons using rhythm to space or delay wanted pregnancies were three times more likely to experience failure than were persons using rhythm to prevent an unwanted pregnancy.

Advantages and Disadvantages

Except for the pregnancies that result from failure of this method, no known serious side effects are associated with use of the rhythm method. No special equipment is necessary (except for a calendar and/or thermometer). Its use does not require interruption of sexual foreplay or the application of any mechanical or chemical devices. It is acceptable to the Roman Catholic Church. However, effective use requires a high level of motivation by both partners and an ability to estimate accurately the day of ovulation. Another disadvantage is the worry the users experience knowing in advance the probability of failure.

Withdrawal

Withdrawal (or *coitus interruptus*) consists of removal of the penis from the vagina before ejaculation. Withdrawal is one of the oldest known contraceptive practices. The Old Testament refers to it, and its use has been reported by field researchers in many parts of the world. Many demographers believe that withdrawal played a major role in the fertility declines that were part of the demographic transition in Europe during the eighteenth and nineteenth centuries. As described earlier in chapter 2, the changes in the social and economic structure that accompanied industrialization rewarded smaller families and made large families more costly. Modern contraceptives had not been developed yet and withdrawal was a culturally acceptable method that was known and available. This illustrates again how social, economic, and cultural factors affect use of birth control methods.

Effectiveness

Withdrawal is more effective than most people believe. Data from the 1955 Princeton Study indicate a **failure rate** (or number of pregnancies per hundred person years of use) comparable to those reported for users of the condom and diaphragm and considerably lower than the failure rates reported for rhythm and other methods popular in the early 1950s (Tietze 1962, p. 367). Similar results have been reported in other studies. Failures can result from the escape of semen before ejaculation, from semen deposited externally near the vagina, or from simple delay in withdrawal (Segal and Nordberg 1977).

Advantages and Disadvantages

Certain religious groups object to the use of withdrawal on moral grounds (they believe every act of intercourse must have the possibility of resulting in conception). Although many people believe that withdrawal is a physically and psychologically damaging technique, there is no evidence to support this view. However, it does require the complete cooperation of the male partner as well as practice and considerable motivation. On the positive side, withdrawal is inexpensive and requires no special preparation or equipment.

Vaginal Contraceptives

Unlike rhythm and withdrawal, **vaginal contraceptives** work to prevent the meeting of sperm and ova by placing a barrier between them.[2] Various mixtures (in paste, foam, or jelly form) are inserted into the vagina in order to prevent conception. In addition to creating a physical barrier to the movement of sperm, vaginal contraceptives frequently contain a spermicidal (sperm-killing) chemical that further reduces the chance of conception.

The idea of vaginal contraceptives is very old. Aristotle described the use of oil of cedar and frankincense in olive oil to block the cervical entrance. During the Middle Ages, rock salt and alum were frequently used as vaginal contraceptives. In 1732 a sponge moistened with diluted lemon juice and inserted into the vagina was described as an effective contraceptive. During the 1920s and 1930s numerous vaginal suppositories and foaming tablets were developed and sold widely. Today aerosol foams and creams are popular. Vaginal contraceptives are still used in many parts of the world (Belsky 1975, pp. 38–39).

Effectiveness

The effectiveness of vaginal contraceptives depends upon the particular method used. In general, vaginal methods tend to be less effective than other contraceptives. Aerosol foams and creams tend to be more effective than jellies and foam tablets. Foam compares favorably with rhythm and douching but produces more failures than several other methods. Data collected in the early 1970s show that 13 percent of women using foam, cream, or jelly to prevent an unwanted birth and 17 percent of those using foam, cream, or jelly to delay having a wanted birth became pregnant within the first year of use (Vaughan et al. 1977, p. 254).

Advantages and Disadvantages

The major disadvantage of vaginal contraceptives is their relative ineffectiveness. Moreover, the vaginal preparations must be administered almost immediately before intercourse, which interrupts foreplay and is often inconvenient. Vaginal contraceptives must be inserted high into the vagina to be most effective, but some women are reluctant to do this. Another disadvantage is that vaginal contraceptives must be reinserted for repeated acts of intercourse. On the other hand, their use does not require medical supervision. There are no known adverse side effects except for mild burning, which can be experienced by both females and males, and vaginal irritation, which usually can be corrected by switching to some other type of preparation. There are some positive side effects. They provide vaginal lubri-

[2] For this reason vaginal contraceptives, plus diaphragms and condoms, form a group of contraceptives known as "barrier methods."

cation. Laboratory tests on animals have indicated that vaginal contraceptives may also inhibit the growth of venereal disease organisms. Tests are now underway to determine whether this effect is present in humans (Belsky 1975).

The Diaphragm and Cervical Cap

The vaginal **diaphragm** represents another method of erecting a barrier between the sperm and the ova. The diaphragm is a soft rubber vaginal cup with a metal spring reinforcing the rim. It is inserted into the vagina to block the access of sperm to the cervix (the opening to the uterus), and it is held in place by the spring tension rim, the woman's vaginal muscle tone, and the pubic bone. Although the diaphragm acts as a barrier to most of the sperm, it does not fit tightly enough to prevent the passage of all the sperm. Therefore, it is recommended that diaphragms be used with a spermicidal cream or jelly.

A **cervical cap** is a small, thimble-shaped cup which blocks the cervix. Most are plastic. The cervical cap provides a more effective mechanical block against sperm than does the diaphragm. Thus spermicidal mixtures are not as necessary with cervical caps as with diaphragms. Cervical caps are used widely in Europe, but they are not generally available in the United States. Ortho Pharmaceutical Company used to make them but discontinued manufacture in the early 1970s. Testimony before the Health Subcommittee of the U.S. Senate indicates that Ortho discontinued manufacture because caps are a low-profit item which, Ortho feared, would cut into their spermicide sales ("Critic Says Profit Favored Over Birth Control" 1979).

Diaphragms and cervical caps were developed for contraceptive use during the nineteenth century. In combination with a contraceptive jelly or cream, they were the methods most often recommended by physicians in private practice and by birth control clinics throughout the United States and Europe during the 1930s and 1940s (Peel and Potts 1969, pp. 62–63). About one-third of American couples who tried to plan their families during the 1940s used this method.

Effectiveness

When properly used with a spermicide, the diaphragm's failure rate can be relatively low. When improperly (or irregularly used), much higher failure rates occur. During the 1970s about 10 percent of women using the diaphragm to prevent an unwanted birth and 16 percent of those using it to delay or space a wanted birth became pregnant within the first year of use (Vaughan et al. 1977, p. 254). Thus, the diaphragm is more effective than foam and several other methods. In addition to nonuse because of insufficient motivation, failures are due to lack of knowledge regarding proper insertion, an improper fit, displacement during intercourse, and defects in the diaphragm itself. The cervical cap is about as effective as the diaphragm (Wortman 1976).

Advantages and Disadvantages

There are no known serious physiological side effects. Use of the diaphragm or cervical cap does not require the cooperation of the male partner, and it is used only when needed. This makes them both convenient methods for women who engage in sexual intercourse infrequently and do not need continuous protection. Using a spermicidal cream or jelly also produces additional vaginal lubrication during intercourse.

Since the diaphragm or cervical cap should be inserted no more than twenty-four hours before intercourse, its use requires that the user know in advance when she will have intercourse or she will have to interrupt sexual foreplay to insert the device. Regular use requires much motivation. Some women do not like the process of insertion, and other women view it as messy because of the spermicide. Diaphragms and cervical caps must be fitted by trained personnel, who must teach the proper insertion techniques. Both seem particularly ill suited for use in many developing countries, where there is often a lack of privacy for insertion and removal as well as a convenient source of clean water to clean the devices after use. Moreover, there tends to be a shortage of medical personnel for fitting the devices, and the need for a constant supply of spermicidal creams or jellies makes this barrier method relatively expensive (Wortman 1976).

The Condom

The **condom** is a mechanical barrier which fits snugly over the penis and prevents the ejaculated sperm from entering the vagina. Its first recorded appearance was during the sixteenth century when it was recommended as a prophylactic against venereal disease. Any contraceptive effects were incidental. Since the early condoms were made of linen, they were probably ineffective as contraceptive devices. Condoms made from the intestines of sheep and other animals first appeared in the eighteenth century. But it was not until the vulcanization of rubber in the mid-nineteenth century that condom use on a large scale became possible. The introduction of liquid latex in the mid-1930s made possible the manufacture of condoms which have greater tensile strength and which last longer before decaying. Today the world market for condoms is extensive. Factories produce over 144 million condoms annually, and manufacturers are beginning to advertise their products vigorously.

Effectiveness

Condoms are very effective. Almost all failures result from nonuse rather than defects in the condoms themselves. If 100 fecund couples each had intercourse 120 times per year while using the condom, about 3 percent of the women would become pregnant (Tietze 1960, p. 44). Data from the National Survey of Family Growth conducted in

1973 show that 6.6 percent of couples using condoms to prevent an unwanted birth and 13.7 percent of couples using them to delay having a wanted birth experienced a contraceptive failure within the first year of use of the condom (Vaughan et al. 1979, p. 254). Thus, condoms, especially in combination with vaginal contraceptives, are more effective than most of the other methods we have discussed so far—rhythm; withdrawal; foam, jelly, or cream; and the diaphragm.

Advantages and Disadvantages

The condom requires some interruption of sexual foreplay. An even larger drawback is decreased sensitivity for the male. Because the condom is used by the male, the female must depend upon her partner for cooperation.

The major advantages of the condom are its effectiveness and the fact that it has no medical side effects. Condoms are easy to store and their use requires no special training. Medical examination, supervision, and follow-up are not necessary. In addition to providing visible postcoital evidence of effectiveness, condoms offer effective protection against venereal disease (Dalsimer, Piotrow, and Dumm 1973).

PREVENTION OF OVULATION

Oral Contraceptives

The search for an effective oral contraceptive dates far back into human history. In 1956–1957 the Chinese government circulated among its people a printed list of fifteen traditional recipes for making oral substances that would have contraceptive effects. One contained silkworm eggs and dated back to the seventh century, when Sun Ssu-mao included it among his "prescriptions worth a thousand pieces of gold." In 1956 a prominent member of China's National People's Congress recommended that the following contraceptive formula be studied:

> Fresh tadpoles coming out in the Spring should be washed clean in cold boiled water and swallowed whole three or four days after menstruation. If a woman swallows fourteen live tadpoles on the first day and ten more on the following day, she will not conceive for five years. If contraception is still required after that, she can repeat the formula twice and be forever sterile (Tien 1965, p. 225).

The person making this recommendation became the deputy director of the Department of Health in one of the Chinese provinces. Tests of the formula were conducted under his direction and were spectacularly unsuccessful. In one study group 43 percent of the women volunteers became pregnant within four months. Moreover, these women were also exposed to tapeworms, schistosomiasis, and other parasites that accompany the ingestion of live tadpoles. In April 1958 tadpoles were declared to have no contraceptive value (Tien 1965).

The most familiar oral contraceptive, the **birth control pill,** was developed in the late 1940s and early 1950s. This pill prevents conception primarily by preventing ovulation. There are two additional factors that contribute to its contraceptive effect. Because ovulation does not occur, the consistency of the cervical mucus is maintained in a state that the sperm cannot penetrate. Also, because the full secretory pattern is not reached, the inner lining of the uterus is not suitable for implantation.

The oral contraceptive pill has become very popular. It is estimated that 80 to 100 million women throughout the world are taking the pill regularly, and in the United States over one-fifth of all currently married women age fifteen to forty-four are taking oral contraceptives (Hatcher et al. 1978, p. 37; and Ford 1978).

Effectiveness

The pill is very effective. Most of the pregnancies that do occur with this method result from failure to take the pill regularly (Potts et al. 1975). Only 2 percent of the women using it experience a contraceptive failure within the first year of use (Vaughan et al. 1979, p. 254).

Advantages and Disadvantages

The major advantages of the pill are its effectiveness and the fact that its use does not interfere with the sexual act in any way. It is not necessary to interrupt foreplay, nor is it necessary to conclude abruptly after coition. Moreover, use of the pill allows the female to use contraception independently of any cooperation by the male (or even of his knowledge).

The major disadvantage of the pill is its possible side effects. Some of these are beneficial, but some are adverse. Figure 6.1 contains results from a British study, which indicates the major known side effects. Most of the beneficial side effects are associated with the physical and emotional aspects of menstruation. These include decreased incidence of menorrhagia (heavy bleeding), dysmenorrhea (cramps), iron deficiency anemia, and premenstrual tension. Thus, for the majority of women oral contraceptives produce more regular menstrual cycles which are shorter in duration, produce less bleeding and abdominal discomfort, and are accompanied by less premenstrual tension than is normally the case (Potts et al. 1975, p. 38). The pill also appears to protect users from thyroid disease (Frank and Kay 1978).

On the other hand, there are definite negative side effects to using the pill. Some are just a nuisance, such as headaches, weight gain, and morning nausea. Some people find those "nuisances" so discomforting that they discontinue use of the pill, and only 45 to 75 percent of any group of women who initiate use of the pill will still be using it after one year (Hatcher et al. 1978, p. 38; and Westoff and Ryder 1968). Use of the pill also interferes with milk production, which makes it unsuitable for use by women wishing to nurse young infants.

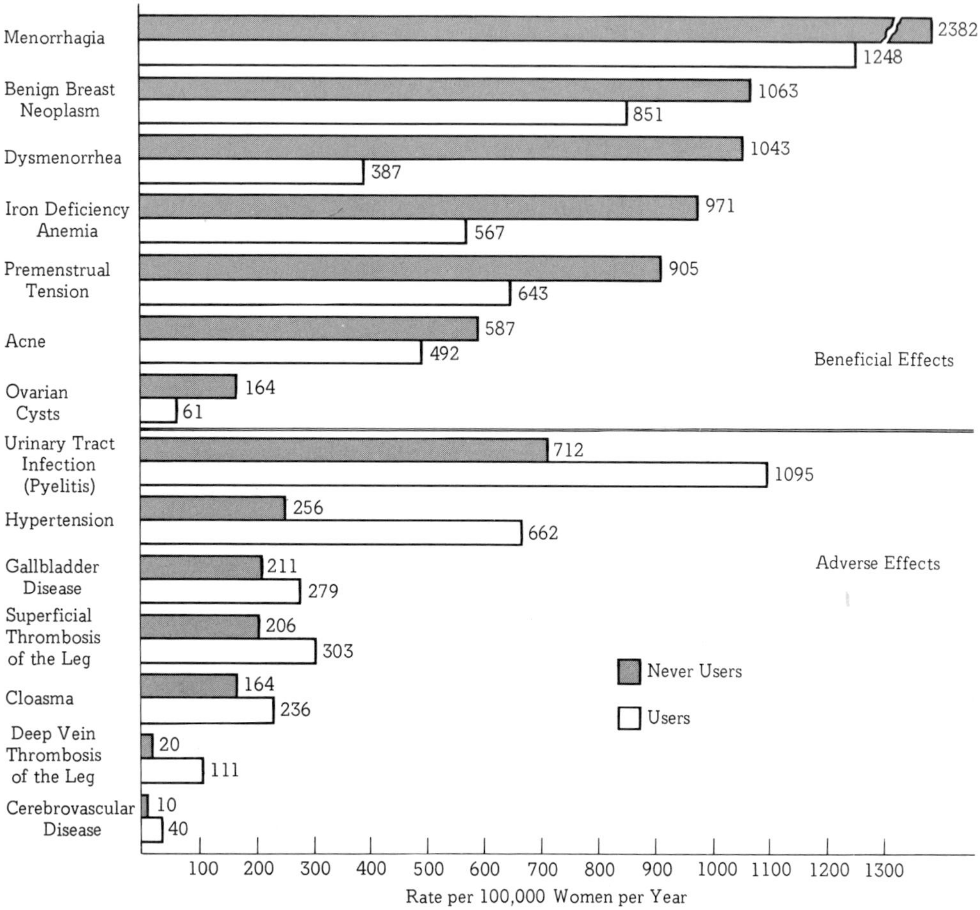

Figure 6.1 Comparison of the Incidence of Various Conditions Among British Users and Nonusers of Oral Contraceptives, 1968–1971

Note: This chart depicts the rates of occurrence of selected conditions in Britain per 100,000 oral contraceptive users and per 100,000 women who have never used oral contraceptives, standardized for age, parity, social class, and cigarette consumption. The conditions on the right occur more frequently among oral contraceptive users—that is, they can be considered adverse effects of pill use. The conditions on the left occur less frequently among oral contraceptive users—that is, pills have a protective effect against these conditions. The seriousness of these disorders, of course, varies greatly; cerebrovascular disease, although rare, is potentially life threatening, and iron deficiency anemia is a cause of continuing morbidity, whereas skin disorders are relatively minor.

Source: Potts et al. (1975), p. 31. Reproduced with permission of *Population Reports,* Series A, Number 2, Population Information Program, The Johns Hopkins University, Baltimore, Maryland.

Some of the side effects can be life threatening. Thromboembolic (blood clotting) disorders are one example. Although the more common superficial leg thromboses (or phlebitis) are not very dangerous, cerebrovascular diseases (strokes that are also thrombic) are potentially fatal. Figure 6.1 indicates that pill users are four times as likely as nonusers to suffer from this disorder. The estrogen content of the pills is primarily responsible for these thromboembolic problems. There is increasing evidence that estrogen may also be cancer causing (Marx 1976). In any case, the practice recently has been to prescribe pills that are low in estrogen content. In general, the mortality associated with pill usage increases sharply after age forty.

Heart disease is more frequent among women who use oral contraceptives than those who do not, although recent studies suggest that earlier research may have overestimated the cardiovascular risk associated with use of oral contraceptives (Belsey, Russell, and Kinnear 1979; and Tietze 1979). Smoking is also associated with heart disease. Those women over thirty-five who smoke *and* take oral contraceptives greatly increase their risk of heart disease. Similar interactive relationships for the increased risk of heart disease exist between taking oral contraceptives and being obese or diabetic, or having a history of high blood pressure (Segal and Nordberg 1977; and Beral and Kay 1977).

The presence of side effects—nuisance as well as serious—makes medical supervision imperative while the pill is being used to prevent conception. In situations where adequate medical supervision is not available and/or convenient, some other method of birth prevention may be desirable.

In the late 1960s researchers developed a "mini-pill" that contains no estrogen. First marketed in the United States in 1973, it consists of a small dose of progestin, which is taken daily, even during menstruation. This new product represents an attempt to reduce the side effects of pill use as well as to produce an oral contraceptive for women who breast feed their children or who should avoid estrogen for health reasons. The mini-pill has not been adopted widely. There are several major drawbacks to its use. One is that mini-pills are less effective contraceptives than are the pills which also contain estrogen. Moreover, use of the mini-pill also increases the incidence of menstrual disorders. Finally, forgetting to take just one or two pills (or failing to absorb a pill because of vomiting or diarrhea) may be enough to cause a contraceptive failure (Rinehart 1975).

PREVENTION OF IMPLANTATION

The Intrauterine Device (IUD)

The idea of placing devices in the uterus to prevent conception is fairly old. Casanova, the eighteenth-century Italian adventurer and libertine, recommended use of a gold ball for this purpose. The antecedent of the modern **intrauterine device** was the stem pessary, which was developed around 1868. This was a small button or cap which covered the opening of the cervix and was attached to stems extending into the cervical canal. In the 1920s a German named Ernst Grafenberg developed a silver ring to be placed within the uterus. In 1934 a Japanese named Ota introduced a gold ring. Both are still being used, although neither was accepted widely until the late 1950s (Peel and Potts 1969, pp. 128–129; and Huber et al. 1975, pp. 23–25).

Today a wide variety of intrauterine devices are available. Most are made of flexible plastic, although some IUDs also have copper wire twisted around them. Adding copper wire to the device increases its contraceptive effectiveness significantly. It is not known exactly how IUDs prevent birth. Prevention of proper implantation is thought to be the possible mechanism of action.

Effectiveness

IUDs are very effective. Only about 3 percent of women using IUDs to prevent an unwanted birth and 6 percent of women using IUDs to delay a wanted birth become pregnant within the first year of use (Vaughan et al. 1977, p. 254). Undetected expulsion of the device is the most common cause of pregnancy.

Advantages and Disadvantages

The major advantages of the IUD are that insertion of the device is necessary only once, it does not interfere with intercourse in any way, and it is effective. The major disadvantages are that IUDs are involuntarily expelled in 3 to 15 percent of the cases, and they have to be removed for medical reasons in an additional 5 to 20 percent of the cases. The IUDs that are expelled involuntarily generally may be reinserted successfully. Young women with few previous births have much higher rates of expulsion and pregnancy than older women who have more previous births. Excessive menstrual bleeding and pain are the major medical reasons that IUDs must be removed. Another disadvantage of the IUD is that trained medical personnel are necessary for insertion.

The long-term effects of IUD use are unknown. The short-term effects appear to be more a nuisance than a danger. The mortality rate associated with IUD use is estimated at between one and ten deaths per million women years of use and the majority of the mortality is related to pelvic infection (Huber et al. 1975).

The Morning-after Pill

A postcoital method of birth prevention would be convenient for women who have sexual intercourse infrequently or who—as is the case with rape victims—do not have an opportunity to use contraceptives before intercourse. The **morning-after pill** is a synthetic estrogen (DES or other synthetic estrogens) that serves this purpose. Approved by the Food and Drug Administration in 1975, the morning-after pill is available in many economically developed countries, primarily through private physicians and college health services. Although the morning-after pill is administered orally, it prevents pregnancy by interfering with the implantation of the fertilized ovum in the uterine lining, whereas the oral contraceptives described in the preceding section prevent pregnancy primarily by preventing ovulation.

Effectiveness

The morning-after pill is regarded as a very effective means of preventing birth. Those failures that do occur result from (1) an already established implantation, (2) an excessive lapse of time between unprotected intercourse and taking the pill, (3) inadequate dosages, (4) regurgitation of the pill, or (5) failure of the drug itself (Rinehart 1976, pp. 143–144; and Hatcher et al. 1978, p. 104).

Advantages and Disadvantages

The major advantages of the morning-after pill are its effectiveness and its suitability for use among women who had unexpected and unprotected sexual contact, particularly in rape situations.

The most common short-term side effects are nausea, headaches, menstrual irregularities, and breast tenderness. But some of the long-term effects may be dangerous. Female embryos that are already partially developed when they are exposed to DES have a higher than usual risk of developing genital cancer later in life, and male embryos exposed to DES tend to experience abnormalities of the reproductive organs (Hatcher et al. 1978, p. 105; and Rinehart 1976, p. 146).

Because of the possibility of these adverse effects on the fetus, the Food and Drug Administration has recommended that therapeutic abortion should be considered when a pregnancy occurs despite use of the morning-after pill. In general, not enough is known about the safety of morning-after pills to recommend their regular use, and the agency has approved use of the morning-after pill only in the case of an "emergency," to be determined by the prescribing physician.

OTHER METHODS

Surgical Sterilization

Surgical **sterilization** (called "tubal ligation") can be performed on both males and females. In the female, sterilization consists of cutting, tying, and removing a portion of the oviduct. In the male, sterilization (called **vasectomy**) consists of cutting, tying, and removing a portion of the spermatic duct, or vas deferens. As a contraceptive procedure surgical sterilization is a development of the twentieth century. It has become widely used in some countries, notably India, Puerto Rico, and the United States. Data from the 1976 National Survey of Family Growth reveal that over 19 percent of the currently married couples in the United States with a wife age fifteen to forty-four are surgically sterile for contraceptive purposes (Ford 1978). Surgical sterilization has become the method of contraception used most by American couples with a wife over age thirty. An important factor in the recent increased popularity of surgical sterilization has been the increase in male sterilization.

Effectiveness

The effectiveness of sterilization varies according to the techniques utilized by the physician and the gender of the patient. In general there are very few failures. Most failures result from inadequate surgical procedures or because the tubes grow together again. Some men who obtain vasectomies have unprotected intercourse soon after the operation. If this occurs before all the sperm that are already stored in the reproductive tract are expelled, then pregnancy may result. However, this is a short-term problem that is easily avoided (Wortman and Piotrow 1973*a* and 1973*b*).

Advantages and Disadvantages

Surgical sterilization is very effective. Because it must be performed only once, sterilization does not require continuous motivation. It does not interfere with sexual enjoyment in any way. However, it is extremely difficult to reverse sterilization, so it is not suitable for spacing births, nor is it suitable for persons who might change their minds about not wanting more children. Although the development and use of microsurgical techniques have greatly increased the chance of reversibility among vasectomy patients, most physicians still consider surgical sterilization a permanent form of contraception. Because sterilization is a surgical procedure, its practice requires adequate numbers of trained medical personnel. Moreover, there are some medical risks involved. In the female the major complications are hemorrhage, infection, and rectal or other bowel injury. The complication rates for vasectomy are very low, and most complaints are short term and minor. The most common complications are hematoma (a swelling or blood-filled tumor), infection, epididymitis (inflammation of the excretory ducts in males), and granuloma (an inflamed tumor). These occur in less than 5 percent of the vasectomies performed (Hatcher et al. 1978, p. 132).

Surgical sterilization does not lower the sexual drive or capabilities of the male or female. Several studies in economically developed countries such as Australia, Great Britain, and the United States even found that males who had vasectomies reported increased enjoyment of sex, which they attributed to freedom from anxiety about their partners' becoming pregnant (Ferber, Tietze, and Lewit 1967). There is no physiological basis for adverse psychological effects. Any psychological problems that do occur are usually symptomatic of problems that existed before the operation (Ferber, Tietze, and Lewit 1967; and Wortman 1975).

Induced Abortion

Induced abortion, or voluntary termination of a pregnancy, is one of the oldest known methods of preventing birth. Induced abortion is recorded in all societies with written histories and is known in virtually all contemporary primitive societies (Potts, Diggory, and Peel 1977, p. 154). The techniques currently utilized vary according to the preferences of the woman and her physician, the available technology and medical conditions, and the amount of time the woman has been pregnant. The major technique for inducing abortion is vaginal evacuation. This involves enlargement of the cervical canal and emptying the contents of the uterine cavity by either scraping (dilation and curettage) or suction (vacuum aspiration). Other procedures include saline (or other medication) injections into the uterus to stimulate preventive labor and, when all other methods have failed, surgical evacuation. These are generally attempted only when the woman has been pregnant for more than three months.

The demographic importance of induced abortion is clear. When abortion has been legalized and made widely available to the population, substantial declines in the birth rate have occurred. Jean van der Tak (1974) documents two additional facts about the demographic importance of induced abortion. First, no economically developed country achieved its past declines in the birth rate without considerable recourse to abortion (whether legal or illegal). Second, no countries now classified as developing can achieve fertility control without widespread use of abortion (whether legal or illegal). Worldwide, an estimated 30 to 55 million induced abortions occur annually (Tietze and Murstein 1975).

Effectiveness

Induced abortion is effective by definition. Unless the embryo or fetus is removed from the uterus, it is not an abortion, merely an attempted abortion.

Advantages and Disadvantages

The major advantage of induced abortion is that it is a completely effective method of preventing birth. However, there are several disadvantages. One is the fact that in many countries it is illegal to obtain an abortion except in very special circumstances. About 70 percent of the world's population live in countries where legal abortions are available, either on request or for socioeconomic reasons, but even in such countries (including the United States) abortions are not always available for financial reasons or because abortion services are not offered in the person's community.

When abortion is illegal it normally is not performed under sanitary conditions. Skilled medical personnel often are not available in such circumstances. Consequently, the risks of serious complications and mortality are high. Serious complications are relatively rare with legal abortions, and the mortality rate is quite low.

Generally, the mortality rate for abortions performed early in gestation and under sanitary conditions with medical supervision is very low—less than 5 per 100,000 abortions. Thus, the procedure is much safer than many familiar operations, including tonsillectomy. Because **maternal mortality rates** in countries with good obstetric services average about 20 per 100,000 births, induced abortion is much safer than its alternative—giving birth (van der Vlugt and Piotrow 1973). The mortality risks of obtaining an abortion increase sharply after the first three months of pregnancy. The medical implications of obtaining abortions repeatedly are not clear. Studies have found that having abortions may increase a woman's risk of having a subsequent miscarriage, premature delivery, or low-birth-weight infant. However, this increased risk of subsequent pregnancy complications appears to be associated with the technique used to perform the abortion. For example, dilation and curettage apparently causes problems in later pregnancies, but there is little evidence that this is true of abortions by vacuum aspiration (Maine 1979).

The ethics of obtaining an abortion are much debated. People disagree on the meaning of human life and when it begins. Some believe ability to live outside the uterus ("viability") defines human life. According to medical tradition viability is usually not attained until after twenty-eight weeks of gestation, but this is not a provable fact. Some people believe that the fetus becomes a human being at conception and that it has a "right to life" that no one, not even its mother, should violate.

Those who favor legalized abortion argue that it is practiced widely whether or not there are prohibitions against it. Legalization facilitates early (and hence safer) and nondiscriminatory access to abortion under sanitary medical conditions. This lowers maternal mortality and illness associated with illegal abortions. It is also argued that the legalization of abortion allows women to have complete control of their fertility and permits them to escape being mothers involuntarily.

Menstrual Regulation

When a woman's expected menstrual period is late in appearing, menstruation may be induced. This procedure is called **menstrual regulation** or "menstrual extraction." By producing a menstrual flow, this procedure prevents the development of any fertilized ova in the uterine wall, yet the woman may avoid the ethical dilemma of getting an abortion once pregnancy has been positively diagnosed.

Two basic procedures may be used in menstrual regulation. One uses a hand-operated plastic syringe and a narrow piece of flexible plastic tubing called a "cannula" to aspirate the uterus within fourteen days of a missed menstrual period. The other technique under study involves the administration of a massive dose of a substance called "prostaglandin" into the vagina. This creates an endocrinal imbalance, which results in the appearance of menstruation. Both procedures represent recent developments in birth prevention technology.

Effectiveness

The effectiveness of each method is difficult to establish, because not all women who undergo treatment are pregnant. Reliable pregnancy tests require a lapse of twelve days after a missed menstrual period, yet many women undergo menstrual regulation procedures before then. In two recent reports the failure rates (that is, when the suction technique fails to terminate an existing pregnancy) were too high to be accepted. Brenner et al. (1975) reported a 4.2 percent failure rate and only 54.8 percent of the patients were actually pregnant. Atienza et al. (1975) reported a 6 percent failure rate and a 27.1 percent non-pregnant rate.

Advantages and Disadvantages

In addition to being effective, menstrual regulation has no known mortality associated with it. Discomfort is mild, resembling a menstrual cramp. Complications are rare. However, the suction technique requires medical supervision by trained personnel, and the suppository technique, which is not available for clinical use yet, would not be suitable for use by women who strongly dislike the notion of inserting foreign materials into their vagina. Moreover, menstrual regulation by suction is effective only if it is performed soon after the missed menstrual period. Hence, it may not be suitable for use among women who are ambivalent about whether or not they want another child at that time.

The fact that menstrual regulation is usually performed before it can be determined that the woman is pregnant raises some interesting legal issues. Generally, women cannot be considered to have obtained an abortion unless it can be determined that they are pregnant. Given that menstrual regulation can also be used for diagnosing and treating menstrual problems or for other therapeutic purposes unrelated to pregnancy, it might even be difficult to establish legally that a woman had intended to obtain an abortion. Hence, menstrual regulation may be particularly suitable for use in situations where the legality of obtaining an abortion might be questionable (Lee and Paxman 1977).

THE MORTALITY RISKS OF BIRTH PREVENTION

The medical risks of using oral contraceptives or any other method of birth prevention occur in exchange for a reduced probability of becoming pregnant and giving birth, which are also associated with mortality risks. Generally, the risks of maternal mortality are higher than the mortality risks associated with a particular birth prevention method. However, because all the methods (except induced abortion) are not completely effective, it is necessary also to take into account the maternal mortality associated with the pregnancies that would result from the method's failure. Thus, the overall mortality associated with a method has two components. One is the mortality associated with use of the method itself. The other is the mortality that would occur in women who became pregnant while using that method.

For instance, if 1,000,000 women use the pill for one year, about 1,000 of them will become pregnant. Maternal mortality rates are so low in most developed countries that none of these women could be expected to die. However, twenty-one of the women who did not become pregnant could be expected to die because of side effects of pill use. This is a total mortality rate of 21 per million users. There are other methods of birth prevention that have no side effects that cause death. However, when deaths due to the pregnancies resulting from contraceptive failure are considered, the oral contraceptive is actually much safer. A good example of this is the diaphragm. People do not die directly from use of the diaphragm. Yet a sufficient number of pregnancies occur among diaphragm users that the overall mortality rate associated with diaphragm use is considerably higher than the overall mortality associated with pill use. Unprotected intercourse is an even better example. When deaths due to the complications of pregnancy and birth are taken into account, using no method of birth prevention is associated with higher mortality rates (238 per million women) than using the pill.

G. I. M. Swyer and his colleagues (1970)[3] caution that it is essential to keep the mortality risks of birth prevention methods in perspective by comparing them with the mortality risks associated with other activities. They point out that the known death rate associated with use of oral contraceptives is less than that associated with swimming. Also every English car driver could expect to be admitted to a hospital once every twenty years as the result of an auto accident. By contrast, a woman would have to use oral contraceptives for 2,000 years for a similar chance of being admitted to a hospital. Moreover, a comparison of consumption of cigarettes and oral contraceptives, along with their respective mortality risks, shows that using oral contraceptive pills are no more dangerous than smoking one-third of a cigarette once a day for three out of every four weeks (Swyer et al. 1970, p. 41). The combination of oral contraceptives and smoking is particularly dangerous.

Thus, although using a method of birth prevention may be associated with some known mortality risks, these generally are less than

[3]Swyer, a British endocrinologist, and his associates have made an excellent study of the mortality risks associated with the various methods of birth prevention. Their data were collected in England and Wales and are very similar to those presented in figure 6.2. Christopher Tietze (1977) has conducted a similar analysis on data collected in other economically developed countries.

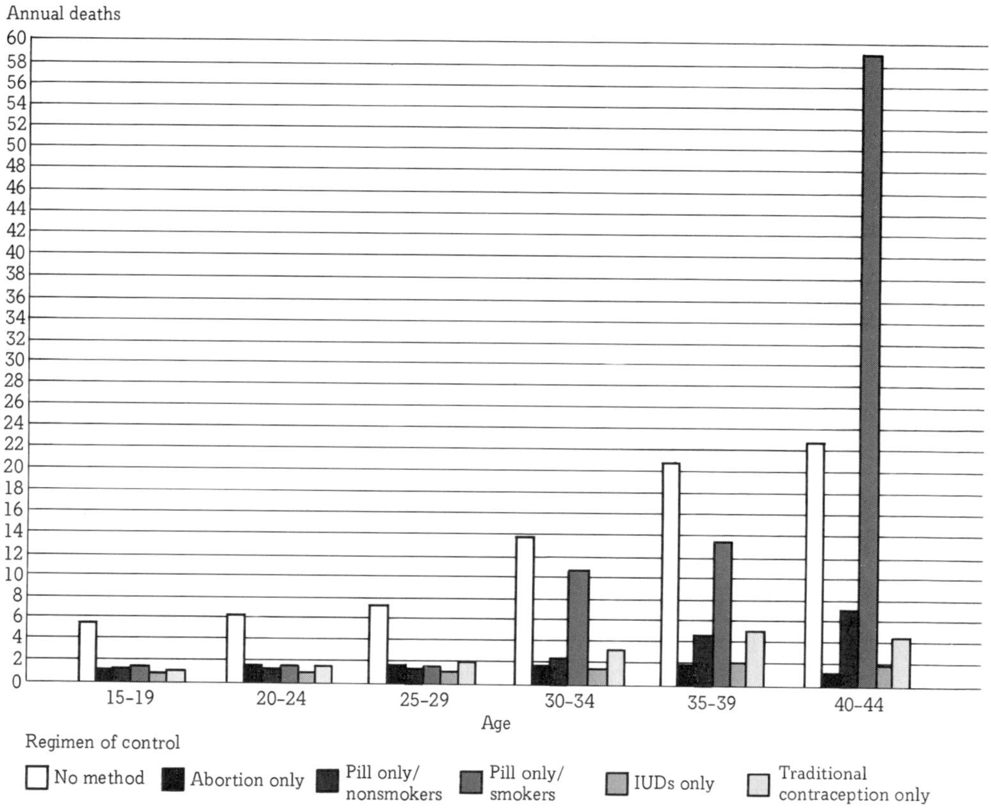

Figure 6.2 Annual Number of Deaths Associated with Control of Fertility and No Control per 100,000 Nonsterile Women, by Regimen of Control and Age of Woman
Source: Tietz (1977*b*), p. 76.

the mortality risks associated with fairly common activities. They are certainly less—except in very special circumstances—than the mortality risks associated with giving birth.

Figure 6.2 depicts overall risks of deaths associated with selected methods, cross-tabulated by age group of the mother. At the younger ages, the method used seems to make little difference. However, among older women the mortality risks of pill use rise rapidly, especially if these women are smokers. Indeed, among women age forty to forty-four who smoke, using no contraceptive is much safer than using the pill.

SUMMARY

A thorough understanding of a population's level of fertility requires knowledge of the extent to which people try to limit family size. Whether or not a person uses a birth prevention method and how effectively that method is used depend upon the person's motivation and the availability of the various methods. These, in turn, are influenced by social, economic, and religious factors.

The chief means by which people attempt to limit their family size are contraceptive techniques and devices, surgical sterilization, and induced abortion. Some methods are more effective than others. However, there is no perfect method of birth prevention. Each involves risks of failure or of adverse effects.

Although use of birth prevention may be associated with medical risks (including mortality), these are much smaller than the mortality risks associated with pregnancy and giving birth. Generally, they are also smaller than the mortality risks associated with many widely accepted activities.

REFERENCES AND SUGGESTED READINGS

Atienza, M. F: et al. 1975. Menstrual extraction. *American journal of obstetrics and gynecology* 121:490.

Belsey, Mark A., Russell, Yvonne, and Kinnear, Kay. 1979. Cardiovascular disease and oral contraceptives: a reappraisal of vital statistics data. *International family planning perspectives* 5 (March):2–7.

Belsky, Raymond. 1975. Vaginal contraceptives: a time for reappraisal? *Population reports,* series H, Barrier methods 3 (January):37–56.

Beral, V., and Kay, C. R. 1977. Mortality among oral contraceptive users. *The lancet* 2:727.

Birth control deaths. 1976. *Newsweek* (March 1):60.

Brenner, W. E., Edelman, D. A., and Kessel, E. 1975. Menstrual regulation in the United States: a preliminary report. *Fertility and sterility* 26: 289–298.

Chaudry, S. L., Hunt, W. B., and Wortman, J. 1976. Pregnancy termination in mid trimester—review of major methods. *Population reports,* series F, 1(September 1976):65–83.

Critic says profit favored over birth control. 1979. *Tallahassee Democrat* (August)2:4.

Dalsimer, Isabel, Piotrow, P. T., and Dumm, John J. 1973. Condom—an old method meets a new social need. *Population reports,* series H, Barrier methods 1 (December):1–19.

Ferber, A. S., Tietze, C., and Lewit, S. 1967. Men with vasectomies: a study of medical, sexual, and psychosocial changes. *Psychosomatic medicine* 29:254–366.

Ford, Kathleen. 1978. Contraceptive utilization in the United States: 1973 and 1976. *Advance data* 36 (August 18).

Frank, P., and Kay, C. R. 1978. Incidence of thyroid disease associated with oral contraceptives. *British medical journal* 2:1531.

Hatcher, Robert A., et al. 1978. *Contraceptive technology 1978–1979.* New York: Irvington Publishers.

Huber, Sallie Craig, et al. 1975. IUD's reassessed—a decade of experience. *Population reports,* series B, Intrauterine devices 2 (January):21–48.

Lee, Luke T., and Paxman, John M. 1977. Legal aspects of menstrual regulation. *Studies in family planning* 8 (October):273–278.

Maine, Deborah. 1979. Does abortion affect later pregnancies? *International family planning perspectives* 5 (March):22–25.

Marx, Jean L. 1976. Estrogen drugs: do they increase the risk of cancer? *Science* 191 (February 27):838–839, 882.

Noonan, John T. 1966. *Contraception.* Cambridge, Mass.: Harvard University Press.

Orlans, F. Barbara. 1973. Copper IUD's—performance to date. *Population reports,* series B, Intrauterine devices 1 (December):1–20.

Pearl, Raymond. 1932. Contraception and fertility in 2,000 women. *Human biology* 4:363–407.

Peel, John, and Potts, Malcolm. 1969. *Textbook of contraceptive practice.* New York: Cambridge University Press.

Piotrow, P. T., and Lee, Calvin M. 1974. Oral contraceptives—50 million users. *Population reports,* series A, Oral contraceptives 1 (April):1–26.

Potts, Malcolm, Diggory, Peter, and Peel, John. 1977. *Abortion.* New York: Cambridge University Press.

Potts, Malcolm, et al. 1975. Advantages of orals outweigh disadvantages. *Population reports,* series A, Oral contraceptives 2 (March):29–51.

Rinehart, Ward. 1975. Minipill—a limited alternative for certain women. *Population reports,* series A, Oral contraceptives 3 (September):53–67.

———. 1976. Postcoital contraception—an appraisal. *Population reports,* series J, Family planning programs 9 (January): 141–154.

Ross, Clara, and Piotrow, P. T. 1974. Birth control without contraceptives. *Population reports,* series I, Periodic continence 1 (June):1–19.

Segal, Sheldon, and Nordberg, Olivia S. 1977. Fertility regulation technology: status and prospects. *Population bulletin* 31 (March):1–25.

Shalita, Ronald. 1975. Prostaglandins promise more effective fertility control. *Population reports,* series G, Prostaglandins 6 (September):57–64.

Swyer, G. I. M., et al. 1970. The scientific basis of contraception. *Population studies,* supplement, Towards a population policy for the United Kingdom (May):37–47.

Tien, H. Yuan. 1965. Sterilization, oral contraception and population control in China. *Population studies* 28 (March):215–235.

Tietze, Christopher. 1960. *The condom as a contraceptive.* New York: National Committee on Maternal Health.

———. 1962. The use-effectiveness of contraceptive methods. In *Research in family planning,* ed. Clyde V. Kiser, pp. 357–369. Princeton, N.J.: Princeton University Press.

———. 1977*a*. Induced abortion: 1977 supplement. *Reports on population/family planning* 14 (December):2–19.

———. 1977*b*. New estimates of mortality associated with fertility control. *Family planning perspectives* 9:2 (March–April):69–81.

———. 1979. The pill and mortality from cardiovascular disease: another look. *International family planning perspectives* 5 (March):8–12.

Tietze, Christopher, and Murstein, Marjorie Cooper. 1975. Induced abortion: 1975 factbook. *Reports on population/family planning* 14 (December):1–75.

van der Tak, Jean. 1974. *Abortion, fertility, and changing legislation: an international review.* Lexington, Mass.: D. C. Heath.

van der Vlugt, Theresa, and Piotrow, P. T. 1973. Uterine aspiration techniques. *Population reports,* series F, Pregnancy termination 3 (June):25–48.

Vaughan, Barbara, et al. 1977. Contraceptive failure among married women in the United States, 1970–1973. *Family planning perspectives* 9 (November–December):251–258.

Westoff, Charles F., and Ryder, Norman B. 1968. Duration of use of oral contraception in the United States, 1960–1965. *Public health reports* 83 (April):277–287.

Wortman, Judith. 1975. Vasectomy—what are the problems? *Population reports,* series H, Sterilization 2 (January):25–39.

———. 1976. The diaphragm and other intravaginal barriers—a review. *Population reports,* series H, Barrier methods 4 (January):57–75.

Wortman, Judith, and Piotrow, P. T. 1973*a.* Colpotomy—the vaginal approach. *Population reports,* series C, Sterilization 3 (June):29–44.

———. 1973*b.* Vasectomy—old and new techniques. *Population reports,* series D, Sterilization 1 (December):1–19.

Zelnick, Melvin, and Kantner, John F. 1977. Sexual and contraceptive experience of young unmarried women in the United States, 1976 and 1971. *Family planning perspectives* 9 (March–April):55–71.

7
Mortality

People can choose to have children or not to have children; people cannot choose to die or not to die. Everyone has to die eventually. But some die sooner than others. For example, death comes earlier to males than to females, and generally to the poor than to the rich. Thus, while death is certain, the length of time a person lives is uncertain and depends on a number of factors.

Mortality can also be looked at from the societal point of view. Societies with high rates of mortality are very likely to exhibit high rates of **morbidity.** That is, diseases of various types are rampant. Such societies have very few elderly in their populations. While a few people live to be seventy or even eighty years old, they are rare indeed. Controlling mortality is perhaps the prime goal of any society; remaining alive is perhaps the prime goal of any individual.

Demographers who study mortality are interested in those factors that contribute to differences in length of life. They also are interested in studying the causes of death and societal mortality trends as well as the general life expectancy, or the average number of years a person can be expected to live in a particular society.

This chapter begins with an examination of the major causes of death, both in the past and in the present. Then we look at mortality trends on the international level and in the United States and examine the reasons for the declining mortality rate currently. We turn next to differences in mortality by sex, age, socioeconomic status, and race. The chapter concludes with a discussion of a special kind of mortality—that which occurs during infancy—and some speculation about future trends in mortality.

CAUSES OF DEATH

Historic Conditions

Mortality data before the Industrial Revolution are incomplete, but we do know that mortality was very high. Demographers use a statistical model known as a **life table** to measure mortality, survivorship, and life expectancy (see Appendix 2, pp. 333–336). A life table for ancient Greece prepared from burial records shows a life expectancy at birth of about thirty years.[1] As late as the eighteenth century life expectancy ranged from only thirty to forty years in Europe and the United States (United Nations 1973; and Dublin et al. 1949). Still, mortality levels were not constant from year to year. There were short-term fluctuations caused primarily by changes in the major causes of high mortal-

[1]Bear in mind that life expectancy figures take into account the death rates for infants (which in the past were quite high). Life expectancy should not be confused with the **life span,** which refers to the maximum expected length of life.

ity—famines, epidemics, and wars. Poor living conditions in urban areas have also contributed to high levels of mortality in the past.

Famines and Food Shortages

Preindustrial populations had much less control over their food supply than we have now. Agricultural output was limited by the inefficiency of manual labor, by plagues of insects or rodents, and by plant diseases. Abundant harvests could not be fully exploited because of inadequate food storage facilities. Since transportation was underdeveloped, isolated areas with a severe food shortage could not import food from other areas with a surplus.

The results were often disastrous. For instance, populations declined over large areas of Europe during the famine years of 1315–1317. In the 1690s one-sixth of the population in some regions of Sweden died after severe crop failures. In one Finnish province about one-third of the population died. Western Europe suffered very heavy mortality between 1740 and 1743 because of a series of bad harvests. During the Irish potato famine of 1846–1851 an estimated 850,000 people died from starvation and disease. As many as 19 million persons may have died in India between 1891 and 1910 as the result of famines (Wrigley 1969, p. 63; United Nations 1973; and Davis 1951, pp. 39–40). Even today millions of people are dying from lack of food in Southeast Asia and parts of Africa. However, these deaths result more from chronic food shortages than from short-term famine conditions. The demographic effects would be even more pronounced if these countries could not import limited amounts of food from other countries.

Epidemic Diseases

Europe's worst epidemic—the plague, or Black Death, of 1348–1350—killed between one-fourth and one-third of its population. There were other widespread plagues which also killed many people (Tuchman 1978), and there were other deadly diseases. People have been ravaged by epidemics of typhoid, smallpox, dysentery, malaria, pneumonia, tuberculosis, yellow fever, puerperal fever, and other infectious diseases. Infectious diseases spread rapidly among concentrations of people through personal contact, by community use of contaminated water and food supplies, and by the migration of persons and disease-carrying rodents and insects from one population center to another. Isolated areas stood a better chance in times of epidemics because isolation reduced these contacts. Entire areas were often unaffected by the epidemic, while other areas had very high mortality. For instance, the last important epidemic of the plague in western Europe (from 1720 to 1722) apparently followed communication routes. Moreover, the greater the concentration of population, the more the plague affected it (Goldscheider 1971, p. 109).

Until fairly recently, methods of treating infectious diseases were ineffective. For example, in the sixteenth century the main remedy against plague was bloodletting through leeches, which probably did more harm than good. Most people afflicted with infectious diseases in the seventeenth and eighteenth centuries received no medical attention. Those who did probably would have been better off if they had not. The only medical measure likely to have been effective before 1900 was vaccination against smallpox. Antibiotics and sulfa drugs had not been invented. The importance of segregating infectious patients in hospitals was not fully appreciated. Often people would be admitted to hospitals with one disease only to die from another disease contracted in the hospital itself. Puerperal fever killed a significant number of women because of unsanitary conditions surrounding labor and delivery. Finally, mortality following surgery was extremely high; techniques were crude and settings and equipment were not kept sterile (McKeown, Brown, and Record 1972; and United Nations 1973, p. 144).

War Losses

The effects of war on mortality are difficult to determine. In addition to military casualties, heavy civilian losses usually occur because of infection by diseases carried by soldiers, killing associated with plunder, famine following the destruction of farmland, and the hardships brought about by economic and social disorganization.

In the past war losses in particular countries engaged in fighting were often severe. In this century wars have involved a greater number of countries, and technological developments have increased the potential of war to kill, with correspondingly high war losses. In World War I there were about 10 million military and civilian casualties, whereas in World War II there were almost 55 million casualties. In Germany over 40 percent of the casualties were civilians, and in Russia about 60 percent of the casualties were civilians (Petersen 1975, p. 269).

The development of weapons such as the neutron bomb and new instruments of biological warfare will further blur the distinction between civilians and military personnel as legitimate targets in times of war. David Heer (1965) has concluded that a nuclear attack on the United States would kill between 18 and 30 percent of the total population, would be directed primarily at urban centers, and would greatly transform American society by creating labor shortages and disrupting the supply of goods and services.

Poor Living Conditions in Urban Areas

Before the twentieth century mortality levels in urban areas were generally higher than those in rural areas because urban living conditions were often wretched. Cities and towns were congested and unsanitary. Industrial waste and sewage often polluted the water supply. Sewage and refuse tended to be thrown into the street. Indeed, pedestrians had to be wary of chamber pots being emptied out of overhead windows. Fire and police protection often were absent, and indoor toilets were rare. Housing was inadequate. As late as 1850 about 5 percent of the population of Boston lived in damp underground rooms.

Unsanitary conditions attracted rats and lice, which spread diseases like the plague and typhus. Damp and poorly ventilated housing provided ideal breeding grounds for bacteria. The seepage of excrement into wells also spread disease. The absence of an adequate water supply made domestic cleanliness and personal hygiene impossible. As late as 1809 in London water was available only in the basement of most houses, and in some sections of town water could be turned on only three days a week (Thomlinson 1976, p. 96; and United Nations 1973, p. 146).

Under conditions such as these it is little wonder that mortality was high. However, mortality fluctuated widely for short periods of time. Mortality would decline following periods of sharp increase for several reasons. The conditions that caused the crisis would improve. The periods of crisis often eliminated from the population those persons who were most vulnerable physiologically and economically. A virulent disease would become less lethal because of changes in the disease itself or because of the development of natural immunities against it (Wrigley 1969, pp. 63–69).

Present-day Causes

Even today, data on causes of death are not complete. Some deaths are not registered. In many countries a large proportion of deaths occurs without a physician's presence, and the cause of death is therefore either unknown or poorly diagnosed. Some deaths result from multiple causes. The decisions about which specific factor caused death may not be made uniformly. Sometimes the cause of death is misrepresented if it is a socially unacceptable disease, like syphilis. International comparisons of cause-of-death data are difficult because countries differ in terminology, method of certification, diagnostic techniques, and the quality of the coding and data collection system.[2] Despite these shortcomings one can make some useful generalizations from the data we have.

Since there are too many causes of death to consider each one separately, the United Nations has grouped them into five major types. These are:

Group 1: infectious, parasitic, and respiratory diseases
Group 2: cancer
Group 3: diseases of the circulatory system
Group 4: deaths from violence (including accidents)

[2]For some commonly used measurements of cause of death, see box 7.1, p. 188.

Group 5: other causes, including gastrointestinal diseases, diabetes, and birth injuries

Figure 7.1 shows that the prevalence of each cause of death is strongly related to the overall level of mortality. As the average life expectancy of a population increases, the proportion of deaths due to Group 1 diseases declines. The proportion of deaths due to Groups 2 and 3 increases slowly until life expectancy is about sixty and then increases sharply. The proportion of deaths due to Group 5 diseases increases slightly until life expectancy reaches seventy years and then declines sharply. The extent of death directly attributable to violence (Group 4) appears unrelated to the overall level of mortality (United Nations 1963, p. 111).

The prevailing causes of death are different in the developing countries than in the developed ones, reflecting the fact that the average life expectancy in the developing countries is about twenty years less than that in the developed countries (fifty as compared to seventy years). The differences are illustrated by the data presented in table 7.1. Belgium and the United States are used as examples of de-

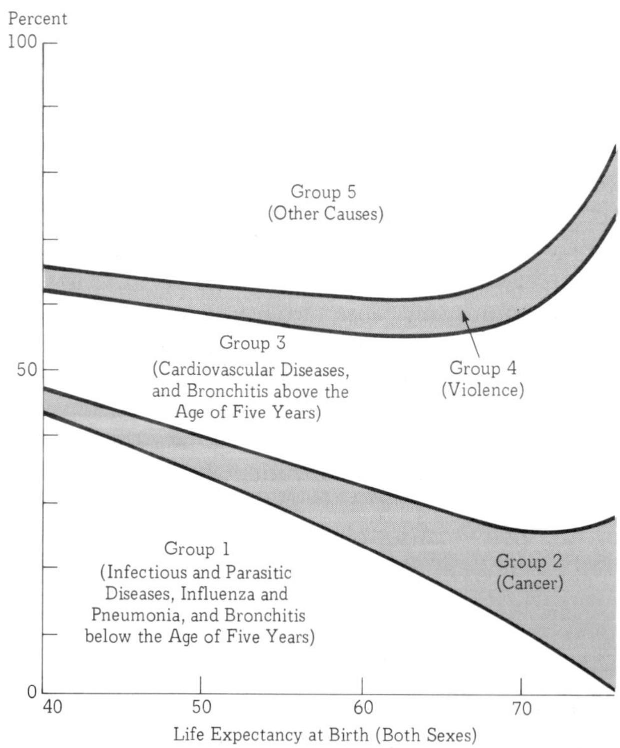

Figure 7.1 Distribution of Deaths by Cause-of-Death Groups for Different Levels of Life Expectancy at Birth
Source: United Nations (1963), p. 110.

Table 7.1 Percent of Deaths Due to Various Causes for Selected Countries, circa 1975

CAUSE	COLOMBIA	EGYPT	MAURITIUS	THAILAND	BELGIUM	UNITED STATES
Group 1						
Infectious and parasitic diseases	14.4%	2.3%	7.1%	10.3%	0.8%	0.8%
Diseases of the respiratory system	12.7	18.1	12.2	11.9	7.1	5.9
Group 2						
Neoplasms (cancers)	8.6	1.6	5.6	2.7	21.0	19.6
Group 3						
Diseases of the blood and blood-forming organs	1.7	0.5	2.1	0.0	0.2	0.3
Diseases of the circulatory system	23.4	13.0	29.7	4.7	43.0	52.2
Group 4						
Accidents, poisonings, and violence	10.8	3.6	6.2	10.2	6.5	8.3
Group 5						
Diseases of the nervous system and sense organs	2.0	0.8	2.5	1.7	1.1	0.9
Diseases of the digestive system	2.9	25.6	4.0	4.7	3.5	3.7
Certain diseases of perinatal infancy	5.3	4.8	5.8	2.0	0.8	1.4
Other group 5	8.8	3.3	8.3	3.1	7.2	5.2
Cause unknown	9.4	26.4	16.5	48.7	8.8	1.7

Source: World Health Organization (1978).

veloped countries, and Colombia, Egypt, Mauritius, and Thailand are used as examples of developing countries.

Bear in mind our earlier warnings about the quality of the data and the difficulty in making valid international comparisons concerning cause of death. One clue about the quality of the data lies in the proportion of deaths attributed to unknown causes. Note that it is higher in the developing countries than in the developed ones.

The pattern is fairly clear. As a society modernizes, the infectious and parasitic diseases are brought under control. The proportion of deaths caused by such diseases decreases dramatically as the overall levels of mortality decline. This decline is attributable not only to the discovery and diffusion of new medical techniques but also to the improvement of general living standards and changes in the environment such as improved housing, water supply, and drainage. At the same time the proportion of deaths caused by degenerative diseases (those associated with the deterioration of cells and organs) increases markedly. The older age structure of the population in the developed countries contributes to these differences because the incidence of degenerative diseases increases with age. In addition, medical technology has not been able to cure degenerative diseases; treatment is usually limited to postponing death. Medical advances increase the proportion of persons in the older age groups who experience these same diseases and subsequently die from them (United Nations 1963, p. 95).

INTERNATIONAL MORTALITY TRENDS

The crude death rate of the world's population is about 11 per 1,000. Life expectancy at birth is about sixty-one years. Of course, these are only averages, permitting variability. Generally, the higher a country's level of economic development, the lower its crude death rate and the greater the life expectancy. In the developed countries, the crude death rate is about 9 per 1,000 and life expectancy is seventy-two years. In the developing countries, these figures are about 12 per 1,000 and fifty-seven years (Population Reference Bureau 1980).

Although mortality levels are currently higher in the developing countries than in the developed countries, since 1920 mortality has declined very rapidly in the former countries. The causes of this rapid decline are different from those for the more gradual decline experienced by the developed countries, as we shall see next.

Causes of Mortality Declines in the Industrialized Countries

The onset of industrialization signaled a long-term decline in mortality in the Western world. Improvements in diet and living conditions resulted in improved health and resistance to disease. Between 1800 and

1850 life expectancy increased from thirty-five years to forty, and between 1850 and 1900 it increased from forty to over fifty years. This sharp increase in the last part of the nineteenth century occurred at a time when many cities started to clean up their water supplies.

Mortality continued to decline in the industrialized countries during the first half of the twentieth century. For instance, by 1950 life expectancy in England and Wales was over sixty-five years. Declines in mortality have been smaller since then, but by 1980 life expectancy had reached seventy-two years. The declines in mortality experienced during the twentieth century by England and the other industrialized countries have been caused mostly by improved medical treatment and technology.

Many social, technological, and economic changes accompanying industrialization also contributed to the decline in mortality. One of the changes was agricultural improvement. Beginning about the late seventeenth century, crop rotation, better fertilizers, and improved machinery and equipment were introduced. The quantity and variety of food increased. The addition of the potato to the staple foods available increased productivity (per acre) and decreased dependence upon cereal crops. The introduction of root vegetables and clovers allowed farmers to maintain large numbers of livestock throughout the winter. Nutritional levels went up. Transportation technology and networks improved, which reduced the effect of local food shortages.

The change from a home handicraft to a machine factory system increased the amount and variety of goods available to the public. Again, improvements in transportation facilitated their distribution and led to more intensive industrialization by creating ever larger markets. Coal (for heating), cotton (for clothing), and soap (for cleanliness) all became cheaper. Increased wages enabled workers to upgrade their living conditions and diets. At first, the working conditions in factories were poor. But eventually a number of social reforms brought laws fixing maximum working hours, setting minimum work ages, and regulating working conditions. Industrial employment thus became less harmful.

The quality of housing was upgraded partly because of higher wage levels and partly because of technological changes such as improved heating systems. Public utilities began to supply clean water and provide a system of sewage disposal that had been absent before industrialization (Wrigley 1969, pp. 164–180; and Thomlinson 1976, pp. 97–98).

Aside from smallpox vaccination, there were few improvements in medical practices that contributed to mortality declines until the twentieth century. Since the theory that germs transmit diseases was not accepted widely until the end of the nineteenth century, surgery remained unsterile and infectious diseases were spread by contamination. Louis Pasteur and Robert Koch did not master immunization until the late 1870s and 1880s. Since 1900 we have seen the development of immunizations against almost all infectious diseases—typhoid, scarlet fever, polio, influenza, tetanus, yellow fever, cholera, and so on. Drugs have been developed to cure or halt the progress of infectious diseases and respiratory infections. In the late 1930s we began to use sulfa drugs to sterilize wounds and to fight against infections. Penicillin has proven effective against a variety of infections. The most important antituberculosis drugs were introduced in the mid-1940s and early 1950s. Other important antibiotics also came into use after World War II. As we will see later in this chapter, mortality from many infectious diseases declined to insignificant levels. Insulin was developed for diabetics. New diagnostic techniques have made possible the detection of diseases at an early stage in their development. Surgical techniques have improved and become much more sanitary. Finally, the development of effective insecticides has greatly reduced mortality from insect-borne diseases, such as typhus and malaria (United Nations 1973, p. 151).

To summarize briefly, today's industrialized countries, especially in Europe and North America, experienced long-term declines in mortality as industrialization occurred. These declines were attributable primarily to improved standards of living and technological changes. Since 1900 a number of medical advances have occurred that have greatly reduced the risk of death from infectious diseases and have lowered mortality considerably.

Causes of Mortality Declines in the Developing Countries

Many developing countries have experienced substantial drops in mortality since 1920. In Trinidad and Tobago the crude death rate dropped from 22 in 1920–1924 to 7 in 1969. The crude death rate in Mauritius declined from 32 in 1930–34 to 8 in 1969. In Jamaica it dropped from 24 in 1920–1924 to only 7 in 1969 (United Nations 1973, pp. 113–114). These declines in mortality are noteworthy because they occurred much more rapidly than those in the developed countries that took place as they underwent industrialization. As a consequence of these rapid drops in mortality, the differences between developed and developing countries have diminished.[3]

What caused this rapid decline in mortality? Primarily it was due to technological advances in the prevention and control of infectious disease and the growth and expansion of public health and medical services. Increased communication and cooperation between countries have allowed developing countries to import health care technol-

[3]Some developing countries have even attained death rates lower than those in the developed countries. However, if the age structure of the population is taken into account, the mortality rates of the industrialized countries are still lower. As we will demonstrate in chapter 10, the high proportion of young persons in the developing countries lowers their crude death rates, because crude rates do not consider age composition.

ogy from industrialized countries. And international agencies have assisted them in establishing mass public health programs (Davis 1956). These factors are largely independent of the economic conditions of the population.

Public health programs for the control of disease and improved environmental sanitation have been extremely effective in reducing mortality in the developing countries. For instance, a sharp fall in the death rate in Egypt between 1945 and 1947 has been attributed to the nationwide DDT dusting program. Although this program was directed against typhus, it reduced mortality from a number of other infectious diseases borne by insects. In developing countries in general the introduction and increased use of antibiotics curtailed mortality from pneumonia, other respiratory diseases, typhoid fever, and a large group of intestinal diseases. A malaria control program and vaccination against whooping cough were important causes of a drop of more than 50 percent in the death rates of rural areas of New Guinea between 1949 and 1965 (United Nations 1973, p. 153).

Although public health programs and improved environmental sanitation may be extremely successful in bringing about short-term declines in mortality, social and economic factors are important in maintaining these reductions permanently. An increased level of living is essential for those countries to reduce mortality to the levels now present in the developed countries (Bourgeois-Pichat and Pan 1956; and United Nations 1973).

TRENDS IN THE UNITED STATES

The mortality declines that have taken place in the United States are consistent with the model of the demographic transition described earlier in chapter 2. Mortality started dropping gradually in response to those changes in social and economic conditions and the environment that were part of societal modernization. Such changes began taking place before any appreciable public health measures were applied. Abdel Omran (1977, p. 4) suggests that an epidemiological revolution occurred *alongside* the demographic transition. In addition to significant declines in the level of overall mortality in the United States, dramatic changes in cause of death have occurred in this century. Let us look at changes in mortality and then at changes in the prevailing causes of death.

Changes in Mortality

Systematic information for the entire country has been available only since 1933, although some local governments have maintained mortality data for quite a bit longer. For instance, as early as 1639 Massachusetts arranged for the recording of deaths, births, and marriages. From sources like this we can make informed guesses about the level of mortality during much of American history. In the period immediately preceding 1800 life expectancy was about twenty-five years in Philadelphia and about thirty-five years in Massachusetts and New Hampshire. By 1850 it had increased to about forty years in these states (Kitagawa and Hauser 1973, p. 2). Since then significant increases in the average length of life have been observed. Life expectancy for the U.S. population was 47.3 years in 1900. In 1978 it was estimated at 73.3 years. Most of this increase occurred before 1950, when it was 68.2 years. (U.S. Bureau of the Census 1960, p. 25; and National Center for Health Statistics 1979*d*).

Life expectancy has not increased uniformly at all ages. Most gains have taken place in the younger age groups. For instance, an infant born in 1860 could expect to live to age forty; by 1978 an infant could expect to live to seventy-three years—an increase of thirty-three years. For people in the older ages increased life expectancy has not been so dramatic. A sixty-year-old person in 1860 could expect to live another sixteen years. In 1978 a sixty-year-old person could expect to live another twenty years—a gain of only four years.

The gains in life expectancy at the younger ages occurred because we can largely control the diseases that cause death in those years. We have not been able yet to control the diseases that cause death at older ages.

As life expectancy has increased, the crude death rate also has declined impressively. Burial records of Boston in the late eighteenth century suggest a crude death rate of 33 per 1,000 among whites and 70 among slaves. In 1906–1909 the national crude death rate was about 15. It has declined steadily since then. In 1950–1954 it was 9.5, and in 1979 it was 8.7 (Omran 1977; United Nations 1973, p. 113; and National Center for Health Statistics (1980*a*).

Changes in Cause of Death

The pattern of cause of death in the United States is somewhat predictable. As mortality from infectious and parasitic diseases (Group 1) has dropped rapidly, mortality from degenerative diseases (Groups 2 and 3) has become more prevalent. Mortality from motor vehicle accidents has increased sharply, while deaths from other types of accidents have dropped. Figure 7.2 shows this pattern. The data in this figure are not percentages of death due to a particular cause. Instead, they are cause-of-death rates (see box 7.1). In 1900 infectious diseases (influenza, tuberculosis, and intestinal disorders) were the leading causes of death. Heart disease ranked fourth and cancer eighth. In 1978 heart disease and cancer were the two leading causes of death; influenza and pneumonia ranked only fifth, and tuberculosis was no longer a significant factor in mortality.

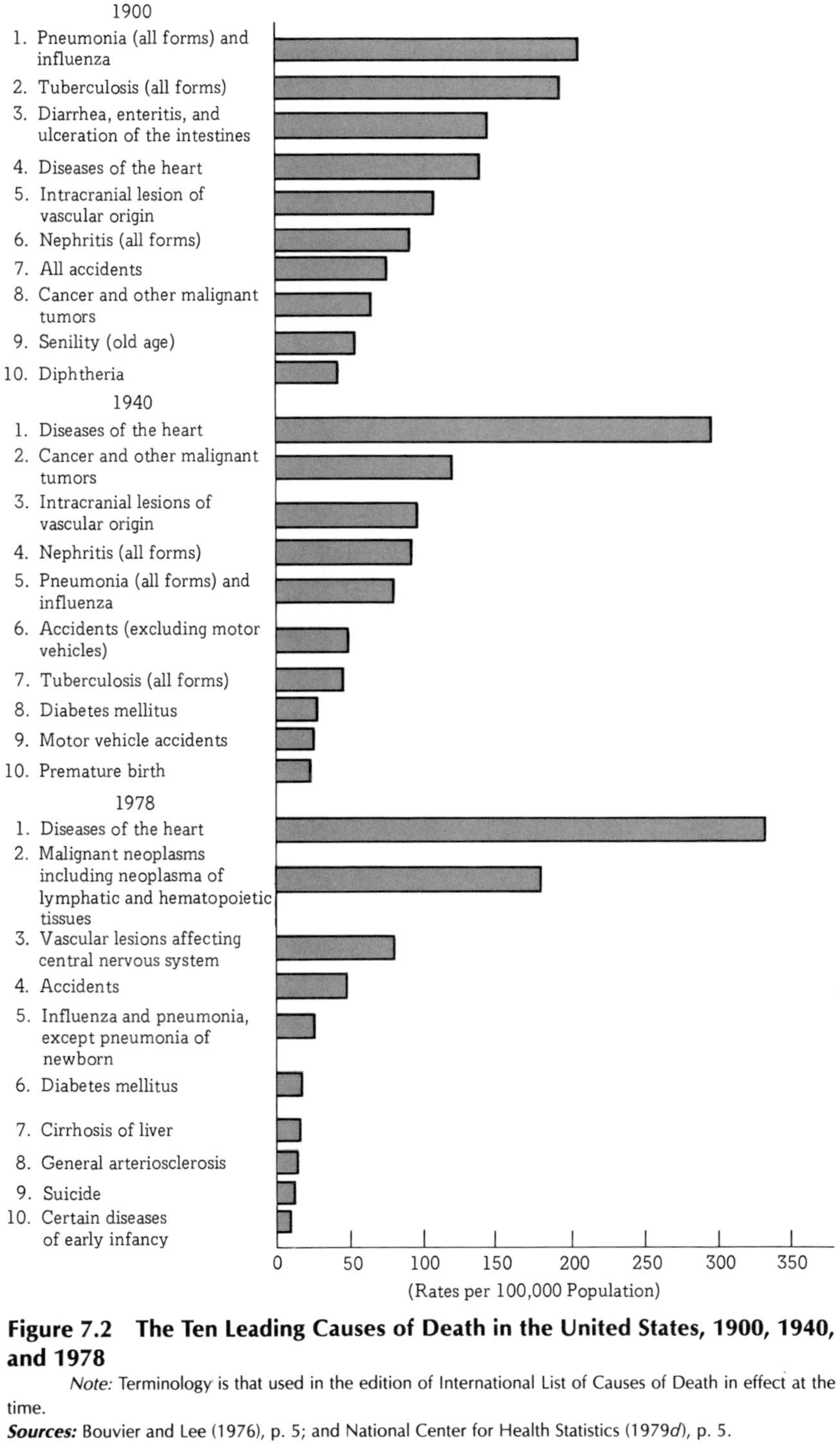

Figure 7.2 The Ten Leading Causes of Death in the United States, 1900, 1940, and 1978

Note: Terminology is that used in the edition of International List of Causes of Death in effect at the time.

Sources: Bouvier and Lee (1976), p. 5; and National Center for Health Statistics (1979*d*), p. 5.

Box 7.1 Measurements of Cause of Death

We use the percent of deaths from a certain cause of death, *x,* to measure its prevalence. It is calculated as:

$$\frac{\text{Total Deaths from Cause } x}{\text{Total Deaths}} \times 100$$

In 1977 cirrhosis of the liver accounted for 30,848 deaths in the United States. That same year, there were 1,899,597 deaths in the United States. Substituting these values in the formula above, we get:

$$\left(\frac{30{,}848}{1{,}899{,}597}\right)100 = .016\ (100) = 1.6\%$$

Thus, cirrhosis of the liver accounted for 1.6 percent of all deaths in the United States in 1977.

The **cause-of-death rate** measures the probability of dying from the cause within a given period of time such as a year. The rate is calculated as:

$$\frac{\text{Total Deaths from Cause } x}{\text{Total Population}} \times 100{,}000$$

Note that the numerator is the same as when we calculated percent of all deaths due to cause *x*. However, the denominator is different. Also, we use a multiplier of 100,000 to avoid having too many zeros in our rates. It is estimated that the total U.S. population on July 1, 1977, was about 216,863,000. Substituting this value in the formula, we get:

$$\left(\frac{30{,}848}{216{,}863{,}000}\right)100{,}000 = .000142\ (100{,}000) = 14.2$$

Thus, the cause-of-death rate for cirrhosis of the liver in the United States in 1977 was 14.2 per 100,000 population.

Sources: U.S. Bureau of the Census (1979); and National Center for Health Statistics (1979*a*).

To some extent the increase in mortality from degenerative diseases is a result of the declines in deaths from infectious diseases. New cures have made possible recovery from tuberculosis, pneumonia, and influenza, especially among the young. These people then live to be sixty or seventy years before succumbing to degenerative diseases such as cancer, stroke, and heart disease. Two-thirds of all deaths in 1978 were due to those causes. By the early 1970s cause-of-death rates due to heart disease and cancer had increased 2.5 times over their 1900 levels. However, death rates from heart disease and strokes are now dropping at all ages. Since 1930 the death rate due to cancer has increased dramatically among males but not among females—illustrating the effects of some changes in medical practice and technology which have benefited females more than males, such as widespread use of the PAP test to detect vaginal cancer (Bouvier and Lee 1976).

Further reductions in mortality probably could be achieved by altering the life styles of Americans, since many diseases are associated with patterns of living. For instance:

1. Heart disease and stroke are associated with smoking, obesity, cholesterol-rich diets, stress, and lack of exercise.
2. Various types of cancer have been associated with smoking, food additives, and environmental pollution.
3. Heavy consumption of alcohol causes cirrhosis of the liver.
4. About one-half of the deaths due to accidents in the United States involve automobile accidents. Many of these are due to careless driving and/or heavy consumption of alcohol.
5. Suicide has been related to stress.
6. Respiratory ailments are aggravated by smoking and air pollution (Population Reference Bureau 1977).

Thus, our life style contains a number of enemies to good health. Because of them, some people die at an earlier age than necessary. All these factors could be controlled if the American public wanted to control them and were willing to pay the social and economic costs necessary to do so.

DIFFERENCES IN MORTALITY

The timing of death varies among categories of people. In almost every society the mortality rate differs by sex, age, and socioeconomic status.

By Sex

Males typically have higher death rates than females at every age. Indeed, more male than female fetuses are spontaneously aborted. Exceptions to this pattern exist in some sections of Africa, Latin America, and Asia, where most instances of higher female mortality occur between the ages of one to thirty and levels of mortality are generally very high. The higher rate of female mortality may be due to the inferior status of women in those societies. Women who are ill may be neglected while medical care is concentrated on males. In those populations female death rates in the age bracket one to thirty are consistently higher than male rates for infectious diseases, especially respiratory tuberculosis. But in later life, males have greater mortality than females from every cause of death (except, of course, maternal mortality). Even in high-mortality countries females over age forty have lower death rates than males from infectious diseases. Thus, somewhere before age forty females switch from having higher mortality rates from infectious diseases to having lower rates. This crossover could be produced in two ways. The wives and mothers could have greater social value in these societies than younger females, leading to improvements in medical care with age. Or changing physical differences between the sexes during the process of maturation and senescence could explain the crossover.

The "physical differences" hypothesis seems more likely for two reasons. First, the sex difference favoring females is generally maintained even after age sixty, when the reproductive and social significance of women is lower. Second, it is also present in older age brackets in populations with low mortality, in which prevailing health practices are not overtly discriminatory against females (Preston 1976, pp. 121–123).

Generally as mortality levels decrease, females increasingly live longer than males. Table 7.2 shows this for the United States, but it is a general pattern. In 1900 females could expect to live two years longer than males. By 1940 mortality levels had declined considerably, and this difference was 4.4 years. Females born in 1978 could be expected to live 7.7 years longer than males born in that year. This difference, combined with the tendency of American females to marry males several years older than themselves, makes widowhood practically inevitable for the vast majority of American women.

Many people believe that females live longer because of differences in life style. In particular, males have more hazardous occupations and, in societies such as our own, may not seek medical care as readily as females. There are elements of truth in this line of reasoning. However, females live longer than males even when differences in living habits, tension, and self-care are controlled, or held constant (see box 7.2). Moreover, females survive almost all forms of disease better than males. The conclusion seems inescapable that females live longer because they are physiologically superior to males.

Table 7.2 Life Expectancy at Birth by Sex, United States, 1900–1978

	LIFE EXPECTANCY AT BIRTH			
DATE	Both Sexes	Males	Females	Difference Between Males and Females
1900	47.3	46.3	48.3	2.0
1910	50.1	48.4	51.8	3.4
1920	54.1	53.6	54.6	1.0
1930	59.9	58.1	61.6	3.5
1940	63.0	60.8	65.2	4.4
1950	68.5	65.7	71.3	5.6
1960	69.9	66.6	73.1	6.5
1970	71.0	67.1	74.8	7.7
1977	73.2	69.5	77.2	7.7

Sources: U.S. Bureau of the Census (1960), p. 25; and National Center for Health Statistics (1978), p. 14, and (1980 *b*), p. 19.

The basic cause of sexual differences in mortality may be physiological, but the importance of medical and sociocultural factors should not be neglected. Sexual differences in mortality increase as modernization occurs because of the interplay of sociocultural and medical factors. For example, in societies with a low level of economic development, infectious diseases are the predominant causes of death. Females are at a severe disadvantage because they are expected to carry out a variety of vital roles: wife, mother, nurse, cook, maid, (frequently) farm laborer, and producer of items such as soap and clothing. In addition, because of frequent births females are vulnerable to many illnesses, especially respiratory ailments, anemia, and diseases related to pregnancy and childbirth (such as puerperal fever). As modernization occurs, labor-saving devices become more prevalent, maternal mortality decreases, nutritional levels increase, effective treatment for infectious disease becomes available, and degenerative diseases become the leading causes of death. Females benefit more from these changes than do males.

Medical advances have changed mortality rates for females more than males. For instance, three common cancers in the male are those of the colon, the lung, and the prostate. These organs are concealed, they are not examined routinely, and cancers in these areas yield symptoms only in advanced stages. By contrast, the three common cancers in the female are located in the cervix, the uterus, and the breast. Cancers in these areas often yield symptoms in the early stages of the disease. Some methods of detecting them are so simple that the methods have been incorporated into routine screening and physical checkups (Omran 1977).

Environmental, or external, factors usually mentioned as influencing changes in sex differences in mortality are changes in working conditions, health technology, smoking, diet, body weight in relation to size, exercise, and stress. Although the changes in working conditions that have occurred with industrialization (in the United States, at least) have benefited males more than females, this effect has been outweighed by changes in health technology that have benefited females more than males. Also, per capita cigarette consumption increased dramatically during the period from 1900 to 1960. Although the differences between males and females have diminished lately, it is still true that a higher proportion of men smoke than women. Because smokers have higher mortality rates than nonsmokers, this factor would also increase the difference in mortality by sex (Retherford 1975, pp. 12–23; and Preston 1970).

By Age

Mortality is closely related to age. In general terms mortality rates decline until people reach about age fourteen, gradually increase until the forty-five to fifty-four age group is reached, and then increase

Box 7.2 Sex Differences in Mortality

Strong support was found for a biological explanation of sex mortality differences in a study conducted by Francis Madigan (1957). The subjects selected for this study were white, native-born American, Roman Catholic brothers and nuns (that is, members of religious orders) engaged in educational work. These subjects were selected because nuns and brothers have a similar life style and thus have the same diet, daily routine, and access to medical care. In addition, since this group of brothers and nuns was engaged in the teaching profession, the members were also subject to similar levels of stress. Thus, by selecting brothers and nuns in the teaching profession, Madigan was able to control (i.e., hold constant) socioenvironmental factors such as differences in stress and life style among men and women in the general population, which are some of the purported causes for sex differences in mortality. It must be mentioned, however, that all of the possible socioenvironmental differences between men and women were not controlled. For example, Madigan was unable to control for differences in obesity and smoking, two factors which are strongly related to cardiovascular disease and cancer. Also, social factors could have intervened before these people entered religious life. In spite of these limitations, however, Madigan did have two groups of subjects that were as equivalent in life style as any two groups of men and women found in a "natural" (i.e., nonexperimental) setting.

Twenty communities of brothers and forty-one communities of nuns were sampled. In each of these communities life records were collected for all members who had been in the community at least three years during the period 1900 through 1954. Nuns and brothers who had served abroad, had been married, or were over the age of twenty-seven before entering religious service were excluded from analysis. This procedure resulted in 9,813 life records of brothers and 32,041 for nuns. On the basis of those life records, life expectancies at specified ages for brothers and nuns were calculated and are shown below.

	AGES						
GROUP	15	25	35	45	55	65	75
Nuns	56.58	47.75	39.35	30.75	22.45	14.78	8.92
Brothers	54.00	44.80	35.62	26.71	19.09	12.27	7.14
Ratio of Nuns to Brothers	1.05	1.07	1.10	1.15	1.18	1.20	1.25

If socioenvironmental factors were responsible for the differences in life expectancy among men and women, then when these factors are nearly identical, as they were among the brothers and nuns in this study, the life

continued

Sex Differences in Mortality (continued)

expectancies for both sexes should be similar. But as the table reveals, the nuns could expect to live longer at each age than their male counterparts. In addition to this finding, the amount of the difference between the life expectancies of nuns and brothers was found to be nearly identical to that found between native-born, white females and males in the United States. On the basis of these findings Madigan concluded that biological, rather than socioenvironmental factors are responsible for sex differences in mortality.

---

sharply in the older age groups. Figure 7.3 presents data for 1900 and 1978 to illustrate the age-specific changes in mortality that have occurred in the United States during this century. Note that the largest decline has occurred in the age group composed of infants. Mortality during the first year of life, called "infant mortality," will be given special consideration in a later section. Other significant declines in mortality have occurred during early childhood (age one to four) and old age (sixty-five and over). These decreases in mortality can be explained by the reduction in death due to diseases of infancy and infectious diseases. These affect the very young and the aged more than other segments of the population. The changes that have occurred in age-specific death rates in the United States are typical of those that took place in other nations as they modernized. Indeed, the "age curve" for 1900 in figure 7.3 reflects the present mortality pattern in developing countries; the age curve for 1978 reflects the pattern for all developed countries.

By Socioeconomic Status

In general the higher the socioeconomic status, the lower the mortality—whether SES is measured in terms of income, occupation, or education (Stockwell, Wicks, and Adamchak 1978). Occupational differences are especially important because they also reflect differences in income, access to existing health facilities, environmental surroundings, and the amount of personal stress and strain that exist within the various socioeconomic strata. Of course, the type of work itself may be detrimental to health. But occupational differences in mortality are produced more by the life styles associated with membership in the various socioeconomic strata than by direct occupational risks.

English data from as early as 1850 show an inverse relationship between occupational status and mortality rates (Logan 1954). As access to medical care increases and nutritional levels and living conditions improve, differences in mortality due to SES may be expected to become weaker. However, data from the United States and a number

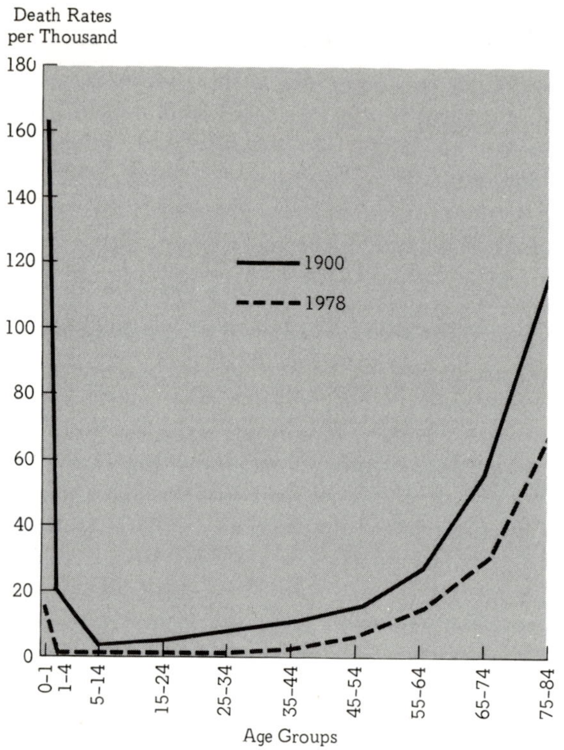

Figure 7.3 Age-Specific Death Rates for the United States, 1900 and 1978
Sources: U.S. Bureau of the Census (1975), p. 60; and National Center for Health Statistics (1980*b*), p. 16.

of other countries show that those differences have remained quite strong.

Equally significant differences owing to SES exist in statistics relating to cause of death. Research conducted in the United States shows that there is an inverse relationship between a person's educational attainment and the chances of dying from major cardiovascular-renal diseases, some forms of cancer, accidents, influenza and pneumonia, and tuberculosis.

However, educational attainment is associated with higher than average chances of dying from cancer of the prostate and breast cancer. It may be that the best-educated males are more likely to die from cancer of the prostate because they tend to survive the other causes of death. The positive relationship between mortality from breast cancer and education is probably attributable to the fact that women of high socioeconomic status have lower fertility and are less likely to breastfeed their infants (Kitagawa and Hauser 1973, pp. 78–83).

By Race

So far, we have been discussing differences in mortality that are observed in almost every society. In the United States differences in mortality by race are also pronounced. Although data are collected for "whites" and "nonwhites," almost all of the nonwhite category are blacks. In 1900 whites had a life expectancy 15.1 years greater than nonwhites, and they were twice as likely to survive to age sixty-five. Since then the differences have been reduced dramatically, but not erased. In 1978 white males had a life expectancy 5.2 years greater than nonwhite males. Among females the difference was 4.2 years (National Center for Health Statistics 1980*b*). At all ages under eighty-five years, age-specific death rates were higher for nonwhites than for whites. The smallest differences occurred among persons fifteen to nineteen and seventy-five to eighty-four years, where the mortality rate for nonwhites was only 1.03 times that of whites in 1978. The largest differences occurred in the age groups twenty-five to twenty-nine through forty to forty-four, where the mortality rates of nonwhites were at least twice as high as those of whites (National Center for Health Statistics 1980*b*). After age eighty-five nonwhites had lower mortality than whites. We do not know the reason for this change in pattern. Perhaps higher death rates in the younger age brackets allow only very healthy and hardy nonwhites to survive to old age. Also, the quality of the data at these older age ranges is poor, and nonwhites may be more likely than whites to report themselves as being older than they actually are.

Whites probably have an overall lower mortality than nonwhites because whites tend to have a higher SES. On the average blacks have less education, hold less prestigious occupations, and earn less than whites. Very little evidence exists to suggest that biological factors cause blacks to die younger than whites.

INFANT MORTALITY

Not all babies born in any given year live to reach their first birthday. As with general mortality a number of factors contribute to differences in infant mortality. In other words, all newborn infants do not have an equal chance of surviving to age one. The **infant mortality rate (IMR),** which measures deaths to persons during their first year of life,[4] tends to decrease along with overall levels of mortality, but there are several reasons for giving the IMR special consideration. In high-mortality populations the highest mortality rate is in the first year of life. Deaths during infancy are generally due to diseases and conditions to which

[4]See box 7.3 for ways of measuring such deaths.

Box 7.3 Measuring Infant Mortality

The infant mortality rate (IMR) indicates how many infants (defined as under one year) die in a given calendar year per 1,000 births in that year. Note that the denominator is the total number of births and not the total population in the age bracket zero to one year. The formula may be stated this way:

$$IMR = \frac{\text{Deaths of Infants}}{\text{Total Births}} \times 1{,}000$$

In 1977 there were 46,975 deaths in the United States to persons less than one year of age. In that same year there were 3,326,632 births. Substituting these values in the formula, we get:

$$IMR = \left(\frac{46{,}975}{3{,}326{,}632}\right) 1{,}000 = (.01412)\ 1{,}000 = 14.1$$

Demographers frequently separate **neonatal mortality** (deaths to infants zero to twenty-eight days old) from **postneonatal mortality** (deaths occurring from the age of twenty-nine days to one year). In each instance the denominator is the same as that used to calculate the IMR. Thus:

$$\text{Neonatal Mortality Rate} = \frac{\text{Deaths Zero to Twenty-eight Days}}{\text{Total Births}} \times 1{,}000$$

$$\text{Postneonatal Mortality Rate} = \frac{\text{Deaths 29–365 days}}{\text{Total Births}} \times 1{,}000$$

In 1977 there were 32,860 neonatal deaths and 14,115 postneonatal deaths. Substituting into the proper formulas, we get:

$$\text{Neonatal Mortality Rate} = \left(\frac{32{,}860}{3{,}326{,}632}\right) 1{,}000 = (.00988)\ 1{,}000 = 9.9$$

$$\text{Postneonatal Mortality Rate} = \left(\frac{14{,}115}{3{,}326{,}632}\right) 1{,}000 = (.00424)\ 1{,}000 = 4.2$$

The sum of the neonatal and the postneonatal mortality rates equals the infant mortality rate.

Sources: National Center for Health Statistics (1979*a* and 1979*b*).

other age segments of the population are less exposed or vulnerable. Since infant mortality may be directly and significantly affected by health programs, the IMR may change more rapidly than the general death rate, and it may vary independently of mortality rates at the older ages.

Infant mortality rates of 200 or more per 1,000 births were the rule as late as 1800, even in the presently industrialized countries. This means that at least one out of every five infants died before reaching age one. As late as the 1870s the IMR in European countries varied from 100 in Norway to nearly 300 in southern Germany (United Nations 1973, p. 124). In 1910 the lowest IMR recorded was for Norway (70). By contrast, in the United States in 1978 the IMR was 13.8 and the Swedish IMR was 8.2, the lowest in the world. That is, roughly 99 out of every 100 infants survive to their first birthday in Sweden.

IMRs vary considerably from country to country. In general, the more modernized a country, the lower its IMR. The range is from Sweden's 8.2 to over 200 in some African countries. For the global population as a whole, the IMR is about 102 (Population Reference Bureau 1980).

Causes

The causes of infant deaths can be divided into two types. There are **endogenous** causes, which are related to genetic disorders or the birth process itself, and **exogenous** causes, which are external to the birth process or genetic makeup. The major endogenous causes of infant death are immaturity of the infant, birth injuries, postnatal asphyxia and incomplete expansion of the lungs at birth, and congenital malformations. The major exogenous causes of infant mortality are parasitic diseases; pneumonia, influenza, and other infectious diseases; gastroenteritis (inflammation of the digestive tract) and diarrhea; and accidents.

It was long assumed that neonatal mortality (infant mortality during the first month) was due primarily to endogenous causes. Postneonatal mortality (deaths occurring in the first year but excluding the first month) was attributed primarily to exogenous factors. However, more recent research has led to the conclusion that the endogenous causes dominate infant mortality only during the first three to four days (Bouvier and van der Tak 1976).

The importance of the distinction between endogenous and exogenous causes of infant mortality lies in the relative difficulty of preventing each type. In general, given existing medical technology, little can be done to reduce the incidence of infant mortality caused by endogenous factors. But death by exogenous causes can be reduced through changes in a population's environment, nutritional level, health care, and sanitation facilities. In high-mortality countries public health measures that do not require economic development, such as widespread inoculation against disease, can cause relatively large declines in infant mortality. This is the primary reason that many of the less modernized countries have experienced the rapid declines in infant mortality since 1940 shown in table 7.3. The developed countries required much longer to achieve comparable reductions in infant mortality. However, in absolute terms, IMRs are still high in the developing countries. They will remain high until those countries experience

Table 7.3 Infant Mortality Rates for Selected Developing Countries, 1935–1939, 1960–1964, and 1977–1978

	AVERAGE ANNUAL RATES			
COUNTRY	1935–1939	1960–1964	1977–1978	% Decline 1935–1939 to 1977–1978
Sri Lanka	182	54	42	77
Taiwan	144	28	25	83
Costa Rica	144	73	28	81
El Salvador	125	70	51	59
Jamaica	127	48	15	88
Malaysia	149	58	44	70
Mauritius	151	61	35	77
Puerto Rico	123	45	20	84
Trinidad and Tobago	104	41	29	72

Sources: United Nations (1973), p. 125; and Population Reference Bureau (1980).

extensive economic development and attain the same levels of medical care, nutrition, sanitation, and overall well-being that are present in the developed countries. As for the developed countries, it is unlikely that IMRs will decline very much below current levels unless unforeseen medical breakthroughs occur or the health care delivery system during the prenatal and early postnatal periods is changed drastically.

Differences in Infant Mortality

Certain characteristics are strongly related to infant mortality. These include the infant's birth weight, sex, birth order, the mother's age, the mother's reproductive history, the mother's marital status, socioeconomic status, and race. Variations in these factors account for many differences in infant mortality rates.

Birth Weight

A birth weight of 2,500 grams (about 5.5 pounds) or less correlates most strongly with infant death. In 1977 about 7 percent of all babies born in the United States weighed 2,500 grams or less at birth. The greater the infant's birth weight (up to a point), the lower the risk of infant mortality. There is a positive correlation between birth weight and survival even when length of gestation is controlled (Shapiro, Schlesinger, and Nesbitt 1968, p. 53). Nonwhites have an IMR that is almost twice as high as the rate for whites, but when birth weight is controlled, this difference is present only among infants weighing *more* than 2,500 grams. We will discuss racial differences in infant mortality later in this section.

Sex

More male than female infants die in their first year. Sex differences in infant mortality begin in the very first hour of life and continue throughout the first year. In 1977 the neonatal mortality rate for males was 26 percent higher than the rate for females (National Center for Health Statistics 1979*a*). No single cause of death is responsible for this difference: all major causes of death produce higher mortality rates for male infants than for females (Shapiro, Schlesinger, and Nesbitt 1968).

Birth Order and Maternal Age

Infant mortality rates increase as the **birth order** of the infant (the numerical order in which he or she was born) increases. This is especially true among younger mothers. Among mothers age thirty and older, the relationship between an infant's birth order and infant mortality rates is U-shaped instead of linear—that is, it gradually decreases and then gradually increases. Mortality rates are highest for infants born to teen-age mothers because the mothers tend to receive inadequate prenatal care, are less likely than other mothers to have adequate prenatal nutritional levels, are more likely to be members of the lower socioeconomic strata, and have infants that tend to be of low birth weight or are illegitimate. The rates decline sharply for infants whose mothers are in the intermediate age ranges and rise to high levels among infants whose mothers are age forty or older.

Chances for surviving the first year are best for first infants whose mothers are in their twenties and best for second and third infants whose mothers are age twenty-five to thirty-four. Among infants whose mother's age is thirty or older, mortality is higher for first births than for subsequent births (Vavra and Querec 1973).

Previous Reproductive Loss

Previous fetal or reproductive loss increases the risk that a pregnant woman will lose a subsequent birth. Infants of mothers who have had a prior child die during infancy have a mortality rate that is 2.5 times as high as that for infants whose mothers do not have such a history. This relationship is independent of maternal age, birth order, and SES (MacMahon 1974, pp. 203–204).

Mother's Marital Status

In every nation for which data are available, mortality rates are higher for infants born to unwed mothers than for infants whose mothers are married (Hartley 1975, p. 8). For example, during the mid-1960s in the United States infant mortality rates were 73 percent higher for children of unmarried mothers than for legitimate children (National Center for Health Statistics 1971). Part of the difference in these rates may be due to the medical care received by the mother during pregnancy. Single women make fewer visits for medical care during the twelve months preceding the child's birth than do married women. This inequality is present for all geographical regions, in metropolitan as well as nonmetropolitan areas, and regardless of income (National Center for Health Statistics 1971). Another factor that helps to explain why illegitimacy is associated with higher infant mortality rates is that illegitimate infants are more likely than other infants to have a teen-age mother, to have a low birth weight, and to have lower socioeconomic characteristics.

Socioeconomic Status

The higher the SES of the mother, the lower the infant mortality rate. This difference is very pronounced. For instance, data for the United States for 1964–1966 show that mortality rates among infants born to married women with no more than an elementary education were 76 percent greater than mortality rates among infants born to married women with four or more years of college. Comparable differences have been reported in a number of countries. The differences are stronger for deaths after the first week of life than for those in the period immediately following birth, which suggests that the upper classes are better able to avail themselves of proper prenatal and postnatal services than are the lower classes (Bouvier and van der Tak 1976, pp. 20–21). There is no evidence that the relationship between SES and infant mortality has become weaker through time, either in the United States or in other industrialized countries (Adamchak and Stockwell 1978).

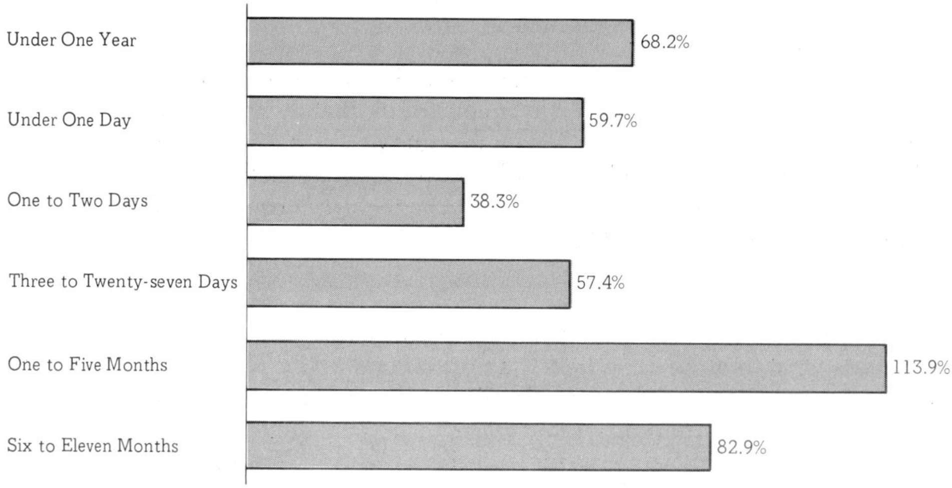

Figure 7.4 Excess of Nonwhite over White Infant Mortality Rates by Age at Death, United States, 1974
Source: Bouvier and van der Tak (1976), p. 19.

Race

In 1978 infant mortality was about 76 percent higher among nonwhites than among whites (National Center for Health Statistics 1980*b*). Figure 7.4 shows that nonwhite infant mortality is higher at all ages of infancy. These differences are more pronounced during the postneonatal period than during the first two days following births. Racial differences in infant mortality are actually greater now than they were in 1940 (National Center for Health Statistics 1979*a*).

Why do blacks have higher infant mortality rates than whites? First, they are more likely than whites to be in lower socioeconomic strata; as stated earlier, SES and infant mortality rates are inversely related. Second, black infants are more likely than white infants to have a birth weight of 2,500 grams or less. Nutritional and socioeconomic factors are the main reasons for the higher proportion of underweight black newborns. There is an inverse relationship between SES and birth weight that is produced primarily by differences in nutrition, prenatal care, maternal age, and the spacing of births (Bouvier and van der Tak 1976).

FUTURE TRENDS IN MORTALITY

Declining mortality has a number of social and economic implications. The efficiency and productivity of the labor force are increased because healthier adults can work better. More surviving children mean more potential workers. Improved childhood survival may also weaken some of the social, emotional, and economic rationales for high birth rates (see chapter 2). At the same time, declining mortality has the direct effect of increasing rates of population growth and may influence the population's age structure. Because of these social, economic, and demographic implications of declining mortality, there is considerable speculation concerning future levels of mortality.

Because the crude death rate is influenced so greatly by changes in age composition, we have discussed future mortality trends in terms of what will happen to life expectancy. On the global level life expectancy will surely increase. Three-fourths of the world's population live in developing countries. Those countries have experienced substantial declines in mortality since 1920, but they still have relatively high levels of infant mortality and relatively low life expectancies. Infectious diseases remain a dominant cause of death in developing countries, and modern medical and public health techniques can bring about further substantial reductions in mortality from these causes.

The developing countries have a very young age composition—and the young rather than the old have benefited from reductions in infectious disease. Consequently, further declines in mortality can be expected in many developing countries.

Added to these sources of change is the economic growth currently being experienced by several developing countries (e.g., South Korea, Taiwan, and the OPEC countries). Historically, life expectancy has increased as a result of economic growth because levels of living have increased. This pattern should continue. However, developing countries will continue to have lower life expectancies than the developed ones. Also, some developing countries with rapid population growth and abject living conditions are experiencing almost no economic growth (e.g., Bangladesh). Those countries probably will experience only very small decreases in mortality in the future and many will even experience *increases* in mortality. It is to be hoped that these will constitute only a minority of the developing countries and the overall trend will be toward increasing life expectancy.

A different picture emerges when the developed countries are considered. The level of mortality there is already so low that future reductions are likely to be minimal. Some reductions in mortality could be attained by changing the life style in the industrialized countries. However, that is not very likely. People will continue to smoke, to drive fast, and to exercise irregularly. The economically disadvantaged segments of the populations of the developed countries have relatively high mortality that could be reduced. However, this change would not greatly affect overall levels of mortality in those countries because disadvantaged groups form only a minority of the population.

Degenerative diseases are the major causes of death in the developed countries, yet the existing medical technology is directed primarily at delaying death from the degenerative diseases rather than preventing their occurrence altogether. Some progress has been made in reducing mortality due to heart disease and strokes (in the United States, at least). However, mortality rates from cancer have continued to increase. Future improvements in the treatment of degenerative diseases may be expected because of continuing research effort. However, only a basic breakthrough in the area of the physiological process of aging will increase substantially the length of time persons in developed countries will live. Even the complete elimination of a specific degenerative disease, such as cancer, would not greatly increase life expectancy there.

The increases in life expectancy derived from the elimination of a specific cause of death are small because the degenerative diseases all occur primarily in the older age groups. Elimination of a specific degenerative disease would merely shift the cause of death from one degenerative disease to another, perhaps as little as one or two years later. For instance, according to one estimate the elimination of cancer would increase the life expectancy of American males by only 2.26 years (Preston et al. 1972, p. 769).

This does not mean that people will not live longer. They will. However, without some unforeseen development in the near future, people in the developed countries will not live much longer than they do now. As Nathan Keyfitz points out: "Mortality data give the impression that underlying the stated cause is a basic process of aging. Unless and until something is done about this, one must expect small and decreasing returns from a war on cancer, heart disease . . . or any other individual cause" (1977, p. 501).

SUMMARY

The crude death rate of the global population is about 11; life expectancy is about sixty-one years. Countries vary considerably, but in general the more developed a country, the lower its mortality rate.

Historically the major causes of high mortality have been famines and food shortages, epidemic diseases, wars, and poor living conditions. Mortality has declined as countries industrialize. The factors causing mortality to drop in the developed countries in the nineteenth and twentieth centuries were generated internally by improvements in levels of living.

Since 1920 mortality has declined rapidly in the developing countries. These declines have been caused primarily by public health measures and medical technology imported from the developed countries. As overall levels of mortality drop, the proportion of deaths due to infectious and parasitic diseases decreases sharply, and the proportion of deaths due to degenerative diseases (such as cancer and heart disease) increases.

The three major factors related to differences in mortality are sex, age, and SES. Females outlive males because they are biologically superior and because of differences in their life style and utilization of medical care. After childhood (ten to fourteen years), mortality rates increase gradually until age forty-five to fifty-four and then increase sharply. SES is inversely related to mortality because of differences in working conditions, life style, and the utilization of health care technology.

Infant mortality rates vary inversely with a country's level of modernization. Death during the first few days following birth seems unpreventable despite existing medical technology. But infant mortality following that period can be reduced greatly by changes in nutrition, the environment, and the health care delivery system.

The characteristics most strongly related to the risk of infant mortality are the infant's birth weight, sex, and birth order, and characteristics of the mother such as her age, whether she has experienced reproductive loss before, her SES, and her marital status at the time of the birth.

Mortality will continue to decline in most developing countries as levels of living increase and as infectious diseases are brought under control. However, future reductions in mortality will be minimal in the developed countries.

REFERENCES AND SUGGESTED READINGS

Adamchak, Donald J., and Stockwell, Edward G. 1978. Trends in the relationship between infant mortality and socioeconomic status. *Sociological focus* 11:47–52.

Bourgeois-Pichat, Jean, and Pan, Chia-Lin. 1956. Trends and determinants of mortality in underdeveloped areas. In *Trends and differentials in mortality,* pp. 11–25. New York: Milbank Memorial Fund.

Bouvier, Leon F., and Lee, Everett S. 1976. The health of Americans: trends in illness and mortality. In *Population profiles.* Washington, Conn.: Center for Information on America.

Bouvier, Leon F., and van der Tak, Jean. 1976. Infant mortality—progress and problems. *Population bulletin* 31 (April).

Davis, Kingsley. 1951. *The population of India and Pakistan.* Princeton, N.J.: Princeton University Press.

———. 1956. The unpredicted pattern of population change. *The annals of the American Academy of Political and Social Science* 305 (May):53–59.

Dublin, Louis, et al. 1949. *Length of life.* New York: Ronald Press.

Goldscheider, Calvin. 1971. *Population, modernization, and social structure.* Boston: Little, Brown.

Hartley, Shirley F. 1975. *Illegitimacy.* Berkeley: University of California Press.

Heer, David M. 1965. *After nuclear attack: a demographic inquiry.* New York: Praeger.

Keyfitz, Nathan. 1977. Cause of death in future mortality. In *International Population Conference: Mexico 1977,* pp. 483–503. Liege, Belgium: International Union for the Scientific Study of Population.

Kitagawa, Evelyn, and Hauser, Philip M. 1973. *Differential mortality in the United States.* Cambridge, Mass.: Harvard University Press.

Logan, W. P. D. 1954. Social class variations in mortality. *Public health reports* 69 (December):1217–1223.

MacMahon, Brian. 1974. Infant mortality in the United States. In *Mortality and morbidity in the United States,* eds. Carl L. Erhardt and Joyce E. Berlin, pp. 189–209. Cambridge, Mass.: Harvard University Press.

Madigan, Francis C. 1957. Are sex mortality differentials biologically caused? *Milbank Memorial Fund quarterly* 35:202–223.

McKeown, Thomas, Brown, R. G., and Record, R. G. 1972. An interpretation of the modern rise of population in Europe. *Population studies* 26 (November):345–382.

National Center for Health Statistics. 1971. National natality and infant mortality surveys: 1964–66. *Monthly vital statistics report* 20:5, supplement (August 2).

———. 1973. Summary report—final mortality statistics, 1970. *Monthly vital statistics report* 22:8 (November 14).

———. 1979*a*. Advance report final mortality statistics, 1977. *Monthly vital statistics report* 28:1, supplement (May 11).

———. 1979*b*. Advance report final natality statistics, 1977. *Monthly vital statistics report* 27:11, supplement (February 5).

———. 1979*c*. Provisional statistics, births, marriages, divorces and deaths for 1978. *Monthly vital statistics report* 27:12 (March 15).

———. 1979*d*. Provisional statistics, annual survey for the United States, 1978. *Monthly vital statistics report* 27:13 (August).

———. 1980*a*. Provisional statistics, births, marriages, divorces and deaths for 1979. Monthly vital statistics report 28:12 (March 14).

———. 1980*b*. Advance report final mortality statistics, 1978. Monthly vital statistics report 29:6, supplement (September 17).

Omran, Abdel. 1977. Epidemiologic transition in the U.S. *Population bulletin* 32 (May):3–42.

Petersen, William. 1975. *Population*. 3rd ed. New York: Macmillan.

Population Reference Bureau. 1977. American way of life: a way of death? *Interchange* 6 (November):1–3.

———. 1980. *1980 world population data sheet.* Washington, D.C.: Population Reference Bureau.

Preston, Samuel H. 1970. *Older male mortality and cigarette smoking.* Berkeley: Institute of International Studies, University of California.

———. 1976. *Mortality patterns in national populations.* New York: Academic Press.

Preston, Samuel H., Keyfitz, Nathan, and Schoen, Robert. 1972. *Causes of death: life tables for national populations.* New York: Seminar Press.

Retherford, Robert D. 1975. *The changing sex differential in mortality.* Westport, Conn.: Greenwood Press.

Shapiro, Sam, Schlesinger, Edward R., and Nesbitt, Robert E. L., Jr. 1968. *Infant, perinatal, maternal, and childhood mortality in the United States.* Cambridge, Mass.: Harvard University Press.

Stockwell, Edward G., Wicks, Jerry W., and Adamchak, Donald J. 1978. Research needed on socioeconomic differentials in U.S. mortality. *Public health reports* 93 (November–December):666–672.

Thomlinson, Ralph. 1976. *Population dynamics.* 2nd ed. New York: Random House.

Tuchman, Barbara W. 1978. *A distant mirror.* New York: Knopf.

United Nations. 1963. *Population bulletin of the United Nations no. 6—1962.* New York: United Nations.

———. 1973. *The determinants and consequences of population change,* vol. I. New York: United Nations.

U.S. Bureau of the Census. 1960. *Historical statistics of the United States, colonial times to 1957.* Washington, D.C.: Government Printing Office.

———. 1975. *Historical statistics of the United States, colonial times to 1970.* Washington, D.C.: Government Printing Office.

———. 1979. Estimates of the population of the United States, by age, sex, and race: 1976 to 1978. *Current population reports,* series P-25, no. 800. Washington, D.C.: Government Printing Office.

Vavra, Helen M., and Querec, Linda J. 1973. *A study of infant mortality from linked records by age of mother, total-birth order, and other variables.* Washington, D.C.: U. S. Department of Health, Education, and Welfare.

World Health Organization. 1978. *World health statistics annual,* vol. I. Geneva, Switzerland: World Health Organization.

Wrigley, E. A. 1969. *Population and history.* New York: McGraw-Hill.

8
Migration

Migration combines with the other demographic variables, fertility and mortality, to produce changes in population size and distribution. Migration patterns may affect greatly both the individuals involved and the society in which they live. Like fertility and mortality, migration does not occur randomly. Some people do not migrate at all. Others migrate many times. Some types of people are more likely than other types to migrate. Reasons for migration also differ. Many people migrate because they are forced to do so as a result of natural disasters or political upheavals; others do so because they want to migrate.

Migration is more difficult to measure than fertility and mortality. Conceptually, migration is a special type of geographic mobility containing four key elements: movement, a permanent change of residence, a change in the physical and social environment, and distance. Measuring those properties involves subjective judgments. To reduce ambiguities and to maximize the comparability of data, demographers use crossing a political boundary as the criterion of when a change of residence constitutes migration. Moves across political boundaries are called migration; moves within political boundaries are called **local movements.** The amount of migration plus the amount of local movement equal the total **geographic mobility** of the population. Thus all cases of migration are cases of mobility, but all cases of mobility are not necessarily cases of migration.

Two types of political boundaries are used: national and subnational. As mentioned previously, movement into a country is called immigration, while movement out of a country is called emigration. Movement within a country that involves crossing political boundaries is called **internal migration**. In the United States counties are the relevant subdivisions. Movement into a county is in-migration; movement out is out-migration.

Classifying population mobility in this way can result in misinterpretations because of the arbitrary nature of the measurement techniques. For instance, if you moved one hundred miles, you might have to change jobs and make new friends but you would not be classified as a migrant if you did not move out of the county. If you live on one side of a street that coincides with the county line you might be classified as a migrant if you moved across the street. Sometimes even moves from one state to another may not result in as substantial a change of environment as a relatively small move in distance. For instance, movement from an upper-middle-class suburb of Chicago to an upper-middle-class suburb of New York may result in a much smaller change in a person's social environment than would a move from the center of Chicago to its fringe area.

There are also problems of enumerating the population. It is costly to collect complete migration histories. Instead, demographers tend to rely on census data which compare a person's current residence with the residence of a year ago or perhaps with the state or county in which that person was born (see box 8.1). Despite its imperfections,

Box 8.1 Measuring Migration

There are inherent difficulties in measuring migration that are not generally encountered when dealing with fertility or mortality. Births and deaths are registered at the time of occurrence, but generally the movement of a person is not. Although a few countries—for example, those in Scandinavia—require people to register at city hall when they move from one place to another, it is necessary to rely upon other means of measuring the extent of migration in the United States and most other countries.

The U.S. census of population contains two useful items—state of birth and place of residence five years prior to the census. By comparing state of birth with place of residence at the time of enumeration, it is possible to divide people into the following categories:

1. Those living in a given state and born there
2. Those living in a given state but born somewhere else
3. Those born in a given state but living in some other state

People in the first category are called "nonmigrants," or "natives." People in the second and third categories are classified as "lifetime migrants."

Data concerning people in these categories can be used to estimate the presence (and size) of **migration streams** (rather large movements of persons from one state or region to another). It is also possible to estimate the proportion of a state's population that was born elsewhere. The "holding power" of a state (or region) can be estimated by calculating the percent of the people born there who still live there when the census is taken.

Knowing residence five years before the census data makes possible the determination of the proportion of a state's population which moved into the state within the past five years. People in this category are known as "recent migrants." Consider these data, which are for persons living in the state of Maine in 1970:

		TOTAL NUMBER	PERCENT OF TOTAL
Born in Maine		683,395	75.2
Lived there in 1965	647,902		
Lived elsewhere in 1965	35,493		
Born in the United States, but not in Maine		145,818	16.0
Lived there in 1965	87,821		
Lived elsewhere in 1965	57,997		
Foreign born		42,715	4.7
Lived there in 1965	36,150		
Lived elsewhere in 1965	6,565		
Other*		37,214	4.1
Totals		909,142	100.0

*Includes persons born in outlying areas or abroad or at sea of American parents, as well as native persons for whom state of birth was not reported.

Source: U.S. Bureau of the Census (1973*a*), p. 55.

continued

Measuring Migration (continued)

These data show us that at least 20.7 percent of Maine's 1970 population was not born there. Of these, about one-fourth were foreign born. Data from another tabulation (U.S. Bureau of the Census 1973*b*, p. 7) show that 32.9 percent of the 1970 U.S. population born in Maine were living in some other state in 1970.

When residence in 1965 is examined, we see that 100,055 persons (35,493 + 57,997 + 6,565), or 11 percent of the total population, are recent migrants. Of these, 35,493 were born in Maine but lived elsewhere in 1965. These persons may be classified as "return migrants" because they are returning to their state of birth. The other 64,562 recent migrants were born either abroad or in some other state.

The Census Bureau also aggregates the data for states in order to measure migration between regions.

---

this mode of classifying changes of residence has definite advantages. Respondents can recall their recent moves easily. There are few ambiguities about whether a move crossed county lines, since county lines do not change very often. Finally, the data collected are easy to manipulate statistically.

In this chapter we discuss the major trends and patterns of international migration as well as internal migration within the United States. We examine how geographic mobility differs by such variables as age, race, and socioeconomic status. The chapter concludes by dealing with the ways that migration affects the lives of individual migrants as well as the community they leave and the community they join.

MAJOR INTERNATIONAL MIGRATIONS

Most people living in the Americas are descendants of immigrants. Some of your ancestors came to America voluntarily seeking religious toleration, political freedom, or improved living conditions and economic betterment. Some of your ancestors came involuntarily as slaves. Even those of you who are Native Americans are descended from immigrants; the first people to reach the Western Hemisphere probably migrated from Siberia to Alaska over a land bridge that existed from 26,000 to 8,000 B.C.[1]

[1]Chapter 3 discusses the history of immigration to the United States.

Migration Patterns Through History

The movement of large numbers of people from one nation to another goes far back into human history, even before the foundation of nations. The early movements were across land areas and over short sea routes. Migration of a people was preceded by an invasion of their armies. Sometimes the invaders would occupy the new lands permanently, perhaps intermarrying with the subdued population. The Norse peoples from Scandinavia illustrate this. They carried out numerous raids in Europe during the ninth century and then settled in England, Ireland, and France (where they were known as Normans). Sometimes the invaders would occupy the new lands only briefly and then return to their original territory, leaving only a few members in the occupied region.

Often the invasions were accompanied by the enslavement of the defeated people and their forced migration to the land of the conquerors. For instance, a single Roman military campaign might bring in as many as 50,000 prisoners. During the height of the Roman Empire, the population of Rome probably reached 1 million persons—a large number of them slaves who had immigrated involuntarily. Earlier, during the fifth century B.C., the population of Athens included between 75,000 and 150,000 slaves, from both Europe and Asia, representing between 25 and 35 percent of the population (Davis 1974, p. 95).

Exploration also played a role in making migration possible. In the fifteenth and sixteenth centuries, men like Marco Polo, Columbus, and Magellan set out to satisfy the curiosity of governments, eager to know what riches lay over the horizon. Some brought back treasures; all who survived and returned brought back information about new lands. Settlement often followed in later centuries. The Portuguese started colonies in Africa, the Spaniards, English, Dutch, and French in the Americas, and the English in Australia and New Zealand.

The greatest period of European migration overseas was from 1840 to 1930. At least 52 million people emigrated during that period, primarily to North America. This number equaled one-fifth of the population of Europe in 1840 and exceeded the number of Europeans already abroad after more than 300 years of settlement (Davis 1974, p. 98).

Compared to the massive movements out of Europe, intercontinental migration from Asia was slight before World War II. East Indians went to such places as British Guiana, East Africa, Fiji, Mauritius, and Trinidad; Japanese and Filipino migrants went to Hawaii; the Japanese settled in Brazil.

Intercontinental migration from Africa was different from other types of movements. The mass outpouring of Africans was involuntary. An estimated 9.6 million slaves were transported to the New World from 1651 until the abolition of slavery in the nineteenth century.

Since mortality during voyages was great—perhaps as high as 25 percent—the total number enslaved was probably well over 11 million. This was the greatest slave migration in history, in terms of distance and numbers moved (Curtin 1969).

Such massive migrations have had a number of consequences for the world. An increase in world population occurred after 1750 because in the regions of origin the emigration relieved the pressures of population on land and resources, postponing an inevitable change in birth or death rates. In general, the greater the rate of emigration, the later the birth rate of a European country declined. In France, which exhibited very low emigration, the birth rate began to fall as early as the mid-eighteenth century; in Italy, on the other hand, a significant fertility decline did not start until early in the twentieth century. At the area of destination, the immigrants had very high birth rates and were widely cited as illustrating the biological maximum of human increase. Some of the highest birth rates ever recorded were noted in French Canada in the latter part of the seventeenth century. Rates as high as 65 per 1,000 were common among these immigrants to the New World (Sabagh 1942; Henripin 1954; and Bouvier 1965).

Another consequence of those migrations was a geographic redistribution of the global population. Between 1750 and 1930 the population of the main areas of destination for European emigrants increased 14.0 times, while the population of other areas of the world increased only 2.5 times. In 1750 those areas of destination contained less than 3 percent of the world's population; by 1930 they contained 16 percent. The geographic distribution of races also was altered dramatically. By 1930 about one-third of all whites no longer lived in Europe, and more than one-fifth of all blacks no longer lived in Africa (Davis 1974, p. 99).

Migration Patterns Since 1930

Beginning with the unrest that preceded World War II, the earth's population took part in substantial international movements. These were some of the major migrations:

1. During Hitler's rise to power in the 1930s, millions of Jews and political refugees fled Germany. At the end of World War II there were compulsory large-scale transfers of population in Europe as the result of repatriation. The uprooting of 20 million eastern and central Europeans by flight, expulsion, transfer, or population exchange represented a drastic solution to the problems of ethnic minorities in these regions (Bouvier, Shryock, and Henderson 1977).
2. After the end of World War II about 3 million Japanese were returned by decree to Japan from other Asian nations.
3. When India and Pakistan were partitioned in 1947, more than 7

million Moslems fled from India to Pakistan, and a comparable number of Hindus fled from Pakistan to India. In the Punjab area of Pakistan those who fled (**refugees**) made up 68 percent of the population.

4. In 1948 thousands of Palestinians were displaced from the territory that now is Israel, which today represents a classic example of an immigrant country drawing a population from dozens of other countries.
5. In the 1970s millions of Southeast Asians as well as Africans were uprooted because of both political and economic upheavals, resulting in one of the most tragic refugee problems in history. Ten million refugees migrated from what had been East Pakistan (now Bangladesh) to northern India in 1971. More recently additional millions of Asians have escaped from Cambodia, Vietnam, and Laos into neighboring Thailand and elsewhere.

There are two special features about the migration since 1930. One is the large numbers of people involved. The second is that a significant portion of the migration was involuntary. In the period from 1946 to 1955 alone, roughly 50 million people emigrated from their homelands (Cook 1957). Many of these people were forced to leave—usually at an economic disadvantage. They normally experienced severe difficulties in attempting to resettle elsewhere, partly because of their disadvantageous economic situation and partly because of political and cultural considerations. The "boat people" of Vietnam and Haiti illustrate this experience.

Within the last few decades the flow of voluntary migration has changed directions somewhat. The nations of western Europe are now experiencing net immigration instead of net emigration, as may be seen in table 8.1. Increasingly, voluntary international migration has flowed from the relatively less industrialized countries into the more developed ones rather than simply from one industrialized country to another. The developed countries have more jobs and offer higher wages, economic opportunities which attract both legal and illegal immigrants from developing countries. Their immigration is facilitated by modern means of travel and communication and often by the assistance of international organizations (Davis 1974, p. 103).

In addition to creating a potential "brain drain" in the developing countries, this immigration contributes to population growth in the developed countries and gives them a sizable foreign population. The effect of immigration upon the economy is not clear. Some people believe that the immigrants take jobs away from the native population. Others believe that the immigrants tend to fill jobs that the more highly trained native workers would not want anyway.[2] In any case con-

[2]Immigrant status in the United States varies. See box 8.2.

Table 8.1 Estimates of Net Migration in Selected Countries of Europe, Northern America, and Oceania, 1950–1970

REGION AND COUNTRY	NET MIGRATION (THOUSANDS)	REGION AND COUNTRY	NET MIGRATION (THOUSANDS)
Europe	−3,028	Northern Europe	−698
		Denmark	−32
Western Europe	+8,748	Finland	−214
Austria	−103	Ireland	−558
Belgium	−211	Norway	−10
West Germany	+4,780	Sweden	−297
France	+3,258	United Kingdom	−181
Luxembourg	+22		
Netherlands	−50	Northern America	+8,698
Switzerland	+630	Canada	+1,802
		United States	+6,896
Southern Europe	−7,301		
Greece	−651	Oceania	+1,857
Italy	−1,958	Australia	+1,712
Malta	−81	New Zealand	+145
Portugal	−1,958		
Spain	−1,377		
Yugoslavia	−1,282		
Eastern Europe	−3,777		
Bulgaria	−178		
Czechoslovakia	−174		
East Germany	−2,488		
Hungary	−161		
Poland	−526		
Romania	−250		

Source: United Nations (1974).

cern has been great enough that the developed countries have erected political barriers to prevent the massive movement of persons from economically disadvantaged countries. These barriers tend to limit the number of immigrants in any one year and place restrictions on the characteristics of the immigrants so that only persons with socially and economically useful characteristics are admitted legally. (Such laws will be discussed in chapter 11 dealing with population policy.)

Some people believe that the developed countries could relax these political barriers against immigration and serve as a repository for the excess population growth taking place in the developing countries. Aside from the potentially undesirable economic and cultural effects of attempting to do this, the demographic effects would be devastating. Davis (1974, p. 105) estimates that the developed countries would have to accept at least 53 million immigrants a year if they tried to absorb the excess population growth of the developing coun-

Box 8.2 Classifying U.S. Residents

The United States government classifies its residents into two groups—citizens and aliens. There are two types of citizens:

1. **Nationals:** persons born in the United States or certain persons born overseas of United States citizens.
2. **Naturalized citizens:** permanent immigrants who have become citizens.

Aliens are persons living in this country who are not citizens. There are several types of aliens:

1. **Immigrants:** persons who are admitted into the United States to reside there permanently. These persons may eventually qualify for citizenship. They are permanent immigrants.
2. **Nonimmigrants:** persons who are admitted into the United States for specific and temporary periods of time, such as tourists or foreign students.
3. **Refugees:** conditional entrants who are allowed to remain in the United States for indefinite periods. If Congress passes enabling legislation, such persons may become permanent immigrants and eventually qualify for citizenship.
4. **Illegal immigrants** (or "undocumented" migrants): persons who are in the country illegally, through entry without inspection (EWI), as visa abusers, or through use of fraudulent documents.

tries. Combining this source of population growth with the amount of reproductive change already present in the developed countries would double their population every eleven years.

As we enter the 1980s it is clear that international migration is far from abating. Similarly, the number of refugees from various forms of political and economic oppression is growing, as exemplified by the recent exodus out of Cuba. A special Library of Congress report recently estimated that as many as 13 million people are now homeless, and the situation is far broader and more serious than the highly publicized plight of the Vietnamese boat people (Committee on the Judiciary, U.S. Senate 1979). Where these millions of unfortunate people eventually will settle remains a big question. Humans have always migrated "in search of a better life." Perhaps the words of the late President Houari Boumedienne of Algeria are a prophecy for the future: "No quantity of atomic bombs could stem the tide of billions . . . who will some day leave the poor Southern part of the world to erupt into the relatively accessible spaces of the rich Northern Hemisphere looking for survival" (quoted in Reiss 1977, p. 27).

INTERNAL MIGRATION IN THE UNITED STATES

Each year since 1947 the U.S. Bureau of the Census has conducted a sample survey of the population to determine place of residence one year before the survey date. The most remarkable aspect of the statistics collected is their stability over time. There have been no upward trends and no downward trends. Each year about one out of every five Americans moves from one house to another, and one out of every fourteen Americans migrates by moving from one county to another. About one-half of those migrants move from one state to another.

The cumulative effect of this mobility is striking. For instance, more than 36 percent of the population age three or older in 1978 lived in a different house in 1975, and 14 percent lived in a different county (U.S. Bureau of the Census 1978).

Some people move many times during their lives; others do not move at all. Americans average about thirteen changes of residence and four moves across county lines during their lifetimes (Wilbur 1963; and Long and Boertlein 1976). The rates of geographic mobility in the United States are comparable to those in Canada and Australia but are much higher than the rates for several other developed countries, such as Sweden, Ireland, and Japan.

It is unlikely that the rates of geographic mobility will increase in the future. The effects of rising income levels and declining family size, which tend to increase the mobility rate, will be offset by the effects of increased female labor force participation and changes in the age composition of the population. An increased commitment of wives to their careers should reduce the readiness with which couples can relocate. And the prevailing low fertility levels will increasingly concentrate population in the older age groups, which are less mobile (Long and Boertlein 1976).

Interregional Flows

As mentioned earlier in chapter 4, until recently the major interregional flows of internal migrants in the United States have been from east to west and from south to north. During the nineteenth century there was a steady movement westward as the new areas beyond the Mississippi were settled. With the exception of California migration into the western states diminished and was minimal during the first half of the twentieth century. Since then it has accelerated considerably. Between 1970 and 1978 the western region of the United States had a net in-migration of 1.4 million people. This was sufficient to account for almost one-half of the population increase in that area during the interval.

Labeled the "seedbed of the nation," the South was an exporter of people from late in the nineteenth century into the 1960s. Long the most underdeveloped and rural area of the nation, the South lagged behind as industrialization surged in the North (Biggar 1979). Both poor whites and blacks left the region in search of jobs. The movement from the South to the North, in addition to being an interregional flow, offered an example of rural-urban migration. Blacks often left behind very limited economic opportunities in rural areas of the South to find jobs in northern cities.[3] The adjustment problems facing these migrants from the rural South were enormous as they tried to conform to big-city norms. The move also contributed to the development of the urban ghetto and its attendant problems.

Recently the trend of movement from the South has been reversed; today there is migration into the South. The region gained 2.6 million people through migration between 1970 and 1975 compared to only 400,000 in the previous five-year period (Biggar 1979). The trend is continuing: over 1 million more people moved into the South than left the region between 1975 and 1978.

Three demographic factors contributed to the South's changeover from net out-migration to net in-migration: increased return migration of persons born in the South, decreased out-migration of native southerners, and increased in-migration of persons born outside the South. Table 8.2 illustrates some of these factors.

Note that the percentage of migrants choosing to remain within their own region is highest for the South (79.9 percent). Also note that more than half of the interregional migrants from the Northeast and the North Central region and more than two-fifths of the interregional migrants from the West chose the South as their destination.

These changes were true of blacks as well as whites. From 1965 to 1970 the number of blacks leaving the South was about 2.3 times greater than the number of blacks coming in, but between 1970 and 1975 the number of black out-migrants was slightly smaller than the number of black in-migrants (U.S. Bureau of the Census 1975). This dramatic turnaround is continuing to the present day. Between 1975 and 1978 net in-migration of blacks into the South amounted to 26,000.

The entire southern region is gaining migrants, whereas before only the large numbers of migrants into Florida offset net out-migration from the rest of the region. However, since 1970 Florida's net in-migration has almost been matched by a large in-migration to the rest of the South. Since 1976 migration to Florida has declined considerably, while other Sunbelt states, such as Louisiana and Oklahoma, have continued to experience increased in-migration.

The return migration pattern can also be documented. Between 1955 and 1960 about 2.7 percent of the former black out-migrants re-

[3]C. Horace Hamilton (1964) contains an interesting history of black out-migration from the South and its basic reasons.

Table 8.2 Destination of Migrants Between 1975 and 1978 Within the United States, by Region: Total, Elderly, White, and Black

REGION OF ORIGIN	TOTAL NUMBER OF MIGRANTS* (THOUSANDS)	PERCENT WHO STAYED IN REGION	DESTINATION OF THOSE WHO LEFT THEIR REGION			
			Northeast	North Central	South	West
Total migrants						
Northeast	5,134	69.3	—	17.7%	57.3%	25.0%
North Central	7,593	71.4	11.4%	—	52.3	36.3
South	9,282	79.9	23.8	37.8	—	38.4
West	6,125	75.1	12.0	32.7	55.3	—
U.S. total	28,134	74.6	12.3	20.8	40.3	26.6
Elderly migrants†						
Northeast	295	61.7	—	7.1	77.0	15.9
North Central	309	71.5	6.8	—	46.6	46.6
South	317	83.3	32.1	43.4	—	24.5
West	255	81.2	12.5	35.4	52.1	—
U.S. total	1,176	74.3	9.6	15.9	50.7	23.8
White migrants						
Northeast	4,578	70.3	—	17.3	56.1	26.7
North Central	7,082	78.3	11.0	—	53.1	35.8
South	8,221	80.4	25.2	37.2	—	37.6
West	5,613	74.8	12.1	33.6	54.3	—
U.S. total	25,494	75.1	12.5	20.6	40.6	26.3
Black migrants						
Northeast	467	62.0	—	15.8	67.8	15.8
North Central	411	60.8	8.1	—	56.5	35.4
South	985	75.2	16.0	44.7	—	39.3
West	261	67.4	10.6	20.0	69.4	—
U.S. total	2,124	68.6	9.2	23.1	40.5	27.2

*All persons age three or more who moved across at least a county line.

†Migrants age sixty-five years or more.

Source: U.S. Bureau of the Census (1978), table 7.

turned to the South; between 1965 and 1970 about 3.9 percent returned (Campbell, Johnson, and Stangler 1974; and Long and Hansen 1975). The white rate of return in the 1965–1970 period was even higher, amounting to almost 12 percent. Data for 1975–1980 are not available as yet, but the indirect evidence suggests that this pattern is still true.

Many reasons can be cited for this altered pattern of interregional migration. Economic change has occurred such that wealth and economic opportunity are now more evenly distributed throughout the country. The severe northern winters have made the mild southern climate appear attractive, especially to retirees who are also looking for less expensive places to live. Widespread air conditioning has changed "oppressive" heat to "balmy" weather. The South has been transformed politically as well, and race relations have improved significantly. A lot of the return migrants are "coming home" to take advangage of the changed situation.

CAUSES OF MIGRATION

What lies behind these flows of people from one place to another? What makes people migrate? Several reasons can be cited. As we stated earlier, migration sometimes is involuntary: people are forced to migrate by oppressive governments or because they fear for their lives. Others migrate voluntarily in search of economic opportunity or different climates. Children have to migrate because their parents choose to do so.

Most people migrate because they believe they will be better off in the new environment than in the old one. As Donald Bogue has stated, "Ultimately, all migration (if it is voluntary) results from a subjective response to two subjectively perceived and subjectively interpreted environments—the one presently occupied and another that is a possible alternative" (1969, p. 754). The key word in this generalization is "subjective." Not everyone ends up being better off as a result of migration. The costs and benefits of remaining in a particular location are difficult to weigh, and the advantages of going to a new place are even more difficult to calculate. A young executive may migrate to another community because of a *belief* that, taking all things into account, he or she would be better off by accepting employment in a new firm there, but this may not prove to be the case.

The costs and benefits of living in various locations are not always economic. Friendships, familial ties, alternative life styles, and social and physical environments are noneconomic factors that people consider when comparing alternative locations.

Whenever streams of migration occur, generally the causes may be found in some characteristics of the area of origin and/or the area of destination as well as in the nature of intervening obstacles to movement between the two areas (Lee 1966). These three factors are presented in figure 8.1. The characteristics of the areas of origin and destination may be divided into two types: (1) factors that, other things being equal, are conducive to leaving an area; and (2) factors that, other things being equal, are conducive to moving into a particular area. The former are known as "push factors" and are represented by minus signs at the place of origin in figure 8.1. The latter, known as "pull factors," are represented by plus signs at the place of destination. To be sure, both places also have other factors that make the decision to move or not to move more difficult. There are plus factors at origin and minus factors at destination.

Declines in an employment base and oppressive, repressive, or discriminatory treatment are major push factors in the place of origin. For example, jobs may be eliminated because a natural resource is depleted, demand declines, or a job is mechanized (as frequently happens in agriculture). Likewise, persons may migrate to another area because they feel persecuted on the basis of their ethnic origin or political/religious orientation. The westward trek of the Mormons in the latter part of the nineteenth century typifies such a migration. Environmental factors may also be important. The occurrence of a catastrophe such as a flood, fire, drought, or earthquake may provide a strong incentive to leave an area. John Steinbeck's *Grapes of Wrath* lucidly illustrates the movement of "Okies" to California in the 1930s. On a more personal level, people may be fired, feel alienated from the community because of their values, or believe they have few or no opportunities for personal development such as marrying, professional fulfillment, or an active social life.

On the other hand, potential migrants may be "pulled" to another area by opportunities for desirable employment, a larger income, or a larger measure of freedom. Employment opportunities account for a considerable amount of migration into the urban areas of the developing countries. An area may also offer the opportunity to obtain specialized training or education, desirable living conditions, and a favorable environment where one can experience new or differ-

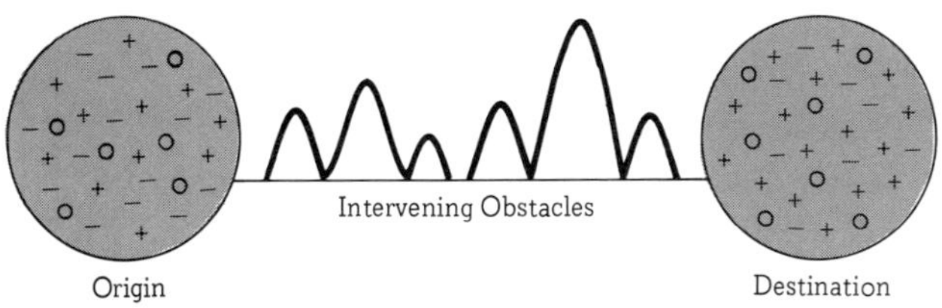

Figure 8.1 Origin and Destination Factors and Intervening Obstacles in Migration
Source: Lee (1966), p. 50.

ent activities, milieus, or people (Bogue 1969, pp. 753–755; and Bouvier, Shryock, and Henderson 1977, pp. 32–33).

At the same time, a simple calculus of pluses and minuses does not always determine the act of migration. Between every two points there are intervening obstacles. In some instances they may be great. Distance must be taken into account. Inertia must be overcome. Physical and political barriers such as the Berlin Wall or the Florida straits

Table 8.3 Reasons for Moving Given by Household Heads Moving Between States in 1974, 1975, and 1976

DETAILED REASON FOR MOVE	DISTRIBUTION OF PERSONS
Employment	
Job transfer	27.6%
Entered or left U.S. Armed Forces	4.9
Retirement	3.0
New job or looking for work	23.4
Commuting reasons	0.9
To attend school	3.9
Other	2.6
Family	
Needed larger house or apartment	1.1
Widowed	0.3
Separated	1.2
Divorced	0.8
Moved to be closer to relatives	7.1
Newly married	1.4
Family increased	0.1
Family decreased	0.1
Wanted to establish own household	1.2
Other	2.8
Other	
Neighborhood overcrowded	0.4
Change in racial or ethnic composition of neighborhood	0.1
Wanted better neighborhood	1.2
Wanted to own residence	1.0
Lower rent or less expensive house	0.8
Wanted a better house	0.4
Displaced by urban renewal, highway construction, or other public activity	0.1
Displaced by private action	0.4
Schools	0.9
Wanted to rent residence	0.1
Wanted residence with more conveniences	0.1
Natural disaster	0.1
Wanted change of climate	4.8
Other	5.5
Not reported	1.7
Interstate migrants (thousands)	16,332

Source: Long and Hansen (1979), p. 6.

may exist. Immigration laws may restrict the free movement of people into a country. The importance of a particular intervening variable may vary from one person to another. What appears trivial to some people may be very significant to others (Lee 1966, p. 51).

The reasons that people give for moving reveal the variety of factors that contribute to migration. The data in table 8.3 were collected from interstate migrants in the United States in 1974–1976. The most commonly expressed reasons for moving were job transfers and the taking of a new job or looking for work. Yet only a bare majority of the respondents selected a job-related reason for moving. As Larry Long and Kristin Hansen note, "Attempts to explain or predict interstate migration solely on the basis of economic variables may fail to account for the movement of a sizeable proportion of the population (1979, p. 7). Other reasons for moving included "moved to be closer to relatives." In one out of twenty households "change of climate" was the main reason for moving.

The reasons for migration are various and may change over time. More hedonistic reasons, like the desire for a warmer climate, appear to be increasingly important factors in moving. Similarly, the reasons for movement are likely to vary among persons in different occupations and socioeconomic circumstances. The basic general principle is that in any move, regardless of the particular reason, a decision has been reached that the area of destination offers advantages over the area of origin which outweigh the disadvantages of movement. Many people may make the comparison and decide not to move at all. A number of people may not even give serious consideration to movement, even though it may be advantageous to do so. Whether those choices seem correct or incorrect to the outside observer is not important. The point is that perceptions outweigh reality as determinants of migration.

DIFFERENCES IN MIGRATION

Let us now look at the ways that migration varies by age, race, and socioeconomic status. As will be shown, migration is definitely not randomly distributed among populations.

By Age

Age is strongly related to mobility—whether the distance is short or across county lines. Table 8.4 shows the selectivity of mobility by age in the United States between 1975 and 1978. Young adults between twenty and twenty-nine were more likely to have moved during that three-year period than other people. This is the age at which people leave their family home to seek out new employment or higher education. It is also the age at which most people marry, and at least one

Table 8.4 Mobility Status of the U.S. Population Three Years Old and Over, March 1975–March 1978

AGE	THOSE WHO LIVED IN THE SAME HOUSE	THOSE WHO MOVED IN THE SAME COUNTY	THOSE WHO MOVED TO A DIFFERENT COUNTY IN THE SAME STATE	THOSE WHO MOVED TO A DIFFERENT STATE	THOSE WHO LIVED ABROAD IN 1975
All ages	64.5%	20.5%	7.4%	6.4%	1.3%
Under 5	44.9	33.2	11.0	9.2	1.7
5–9	57.1	25.1	8.3	8.0	1.6
10–14	68.8	18.6	5.9	5.5	1.1
15–19	71.3	17.3	5.4	4.8	1.2
20–24	38.6	34.3	13.5	11.2	2.3
25–29	34.0	36.7	14.8	11.9	2.6
30–34	50.9	27.9	10.2	9.2	1.7
35–44	67.7	18.2	6.4	6.2	1.5
45–54	78.9	12.4	4.4	3.5	0.8
55–64	82.9	10.0	3.8	2.9	0.5
65+	86.3	8.4	2.9	2.3	0.1

Source: U.S. Bureau of the Census (1978), p. 17.

of the spouses is likely to change residence at that time. After age thirty-five there is much less mobility, since people are more likely to be settled in their livelihoods. But what explains the relatively high rate of movement of very young persons under age ten? Their parents tend to be in the highly mobile age group of those twenty to twenty-nine, and the children simply are accompanying their parents. Similar differences among age groups have been observed in other countries.

By Race

Blacks are slightly more mobile than whites. But, compared to the movement of whites, their mobility is more likely to be in the form of local movement (see table 8.5). Data over time, beginning in 1950,

Table 8.5 Mobility Status of the U.S. Population Three Years Old and Over, by Race, March 1975–March 1978

	BLACK	WHITE
Lived in same house	63.8%	64.6%
Moved in same county	26.3	19.7
Moved to different county in same state	4.5	7.7
Moved to different state	4.5	6.6
Lived abroad in 1975	0.9	1.4
Total	100.0	100.0

Source: U.S. Bureau of the Census (1978), p. 7.

show the same pattern. When the migration of blacks is examined by age, young adulthood is an even more popular time for migration than it is among whites.

By Socioeconomic Status

In general, the greater a person's education, the greater the amount of migration (see table 8.6). The percent moving to a different county is 2.5 times as great among college graduates as it is among those with less than an eighth-grade education. The percent moving to a different state is over 4 times as great among college graduates. This suggests that the longer the distance of movement involved, the stronger the role that education plays in a person's propensity to move.

As the educational differences would lead us to suspect, white-collar workers are the most migratory occupational group. Manual workers tend to be as mobile as white-collar workers, but their moves are local ones for the most part. Farm and service workers generally are the least mobile occupational group. The occupational differences are most pronounced in the age groups seventeen to twenty-four and twenty-five to thirty-four. And they are much more pronounced for interstate migration than for general geographic mobility.

Persons who are not in the labor force have high mobility. These may be persons who have left school recently, who have married (or divorced) recently, or who have poor health and are seeking medical care or a more favorable environment.

The occupational differences emphasize that, at present, unskilled jobs are generally filled locally by nonmigrant residents, while the more technical and skilled jobs tend to be filled on the basis of regional or even nationwide competition and recruitment. Without skills a laborer has little incentive to migrate to another job. One of the complicating features of poverty is that little can be gained without also ac-

Table 8.6 Mobility Status of the U.S. Population, by Educational Attainment for Persons Eighteen Years of Age and Older, March 1975–March 1978

	YEARS OF SCHOOL COMPLETED					
MOBILITY STATUS	0–8	9–11	12	13–15	16+	All Years of School
Lived in same house	76.3%	67.7%	64.6%	58.2%	55.3%	64.7%
Moved in same county	15.3	20.8	21.0	22.4	19.9	20.1
Moved to different county in same state	4.3	6.4	7.2	9.8	11.0	7.6
Moved to different state	2.8	4.4	6.0	8.2	11.8	6.3
Lived abroad in 1975	0.3	0.7	1.2	1.4	2.1	1.3
Total	100.0	100.0	100.0	100.0	100.0	100.0

Source: U.S. Bureau of the Census (1978), p. 45.

quiring the training to change occupations. Moreover, it takes money to move long distances. By definition, the poor have a shortage of money.

Up to a certain point the higher one's income, the more likely one is to migrate. Lower-income groups tend to make local moves. The difference in local mobility and migration rates by income are sharper among whites than among nonwhites. They are also less consistent and more blurred than are the differences by education and occupation. Migrants tend to enter the lower rungs of each occupational category, where salaries are somewhat lower.

In summary, then, migration is not randomly distributed. Certain kinds of people are more likely to move than others; some move short distances; others move long distances. To some extent the number of times you move and where you move are determined in part by your characteristics—your age, your race, your socioeconomic background. Whatever the nature of the move, there are certain consequences for the areas involved.

CONSEQUENCES OF MIGRATION

The consequences of migration can be studied both from the total population's point of view at the areas of origin and destination and from the point of view of the individual migrant. Often the consequences for the individual migrants differ from those for the aggregate populations. For instance, as we mentioned previously, some people are concerned about a "brain drain" from the developing countries, as professionally trained persons migrate to take advantage of economic opportunities in the developed countries. If such movement happened on a large scale, the developing countries would suffer from the loss of these skilled persons. But the individual migrants themselves could experience great benefits by migrating. Likewise, the area of destination (the developed country) might find the immigrants' skills beneficial. Indeed, America's national development and cultural heritage would probably be quite different if it were not for the immigration of such talented persons as Arthur Rubinstein, Enrico Fermi, Harry Belafonte, and Joseph Pulitzer.

Earlier, in chapter 4, we discussed some of the negative consequences of middle-class migration out of the central cities. Yet most people move from the central city because they believe it will improve their living conditions. Thus, when we discuss the consequences of migration, it is necessary to distinguish consequences for the individual migrant from those for the larger population. Moreover, we must distinguish consequences for the sending area from those for the receiving area.

Impact on the Area of Origin

One way that migration affects the area of origin is by reducing its potential for population growth. This occurs in two ways. Persons who move out of an area represent negative entries in the demographic equation that we discussed in chapter 1. (The use of the demographic equation to calculate net migration is shown in box 8.3.) This loss may at least partially compensate for any reproductive increase that occurs. But those who move out of an area tend to be in the young childbearing age groups, which reduces the reproductive potential of the population of origin.

Many large cities in the United States owe their population declines to out-migration (see chapter 4). On the national level, perhaps the classic example of population loss due to net emigration is Ireland. Its population declined from over 5 million in 1851 to less than 3 million in 1926 because emigration far exceeded reproductive increase (United Nations 1973, p. 246). Barbados, Cuba, and Jamaica are also countries in which the rates of population growth have been lowered because of large-scale emigration.

The area of origin is affected as well by what type of people migrate. The question of who migrates partially depends on whether the migration is largely a response to pull factors or to push factors. Migrants responding to pull factors at the place of destination tend to be "positively" selected. They generally have more education than those

Box 8.3 Estimating Net Migration

In box 1.1 we illustrated the demographic equation: $P_2 - P_1 = (B - D) + (I - O)$. Using the same equation, we can derive the vital statistics method of estimating net migration. It is:

$$I - O = (P_2 - P_1) - (B - D)$$

For example, DeKalb County, Georgia, had a population of 256,782 in 1960 (P_1) and 415,387 in 1970 (P_2). Over this period there were 69,891 births and 19,471 deaths. To determine net migration ($I - O$), we substitute these values. Hence:

$$(415{,}387 - 256{,}782) - (69{,}891 - 19{,}471) = 108{,}185$$

A refinement of this method allows the calculation of net migration by age and sex. For example, the female population age ten to fourteen in 1960 is compared to that age twenty to twenty-four in 1970. The deaths that occurred to that cohort during the decade are subtracted from the total for the age group ten to fourteen. Any remaining difference is attributable to net migration.

who remain (Bouvier, Macisco, and Zarate 1976). Hence, their departure tends to lower the overall levels of educational attainment and may deprive the area of origin of persons with skills that would be very useful. Pull factors also may select persons with high aspirations for social mobility. For example, those who migrate from rural areas in many developing countries are often motivated by pull factors in urban areas. Such migrants may be more oriented toward achievement and active interaction with their environment than persons who remain. They tend to be better planners and more innovative. They see alternative modes of behavior (such as moving to the city) and explore them. To the extent this selectivity is present, the area of origin loses a valuable segment of its population (Macisco, Bouvier, and Weller 1970). The degree of positive selection increases with the difficulty of any intervening obstacles.

On the other hand, migrants responding to push factors in the area of origin tend to be "negatively" selected. They are the people who cannot seem to succeed, either because of poor education or lack of needed talents. They are almost forced to leave. They have fewer of the positive characteristics valued in their society. Other things being equal, the area of origin is changed positively by the out-migration of these people (Bouvier, Shryock, and Henderson 1977).

Impact on the Area of Destination

Migration increases the population of the area of destination in two ways. The net number of in-migrants represents the direct effect. The number of children born to the in-migrants after their arrival is the indirect effect. The magnitude of the direct effect depends on the relative size of the migrant and receiving populations, and the magnitude of the indirect effect depends on the relative levels of reproductive behavior among the migrants and the receiving population.

Until the latter part of the nineteenth century, net immigration was a major cause of population growth in some of the overseas countries of European settlement, such as Argentina, Australia, and Brazil. In the United States for every one hundred persons added to the population between 1850 and 1900 through reproductive change, the gain through net migration ranged from twenty to forty in each decade (United Nations 1973, p. 245). The current volume of immigration is not large relative to the American population, but levels of reproductive behavior are so low in the United States that immigration represents an increasingly important component of national population growth.

Urban areas have experienced substantial growth because of net in-migration. As we saw in chapter 4, almost half the growth in the metropolitan population of the United States between 1940 and 1950 was caused by net in-migration from nonmetropolitan areas. Elizaga

(1965, p. 156) estimates that in-migration is frequently as important as urban reproductive change in producing the growth of Latin American cities. Comparable conclusions have been reached for cities in other parts of the world.

The indirect effects of in-migration are harder to estimate because normally the proper data are not available. Moreover, it is not known whether massive in-migration affects the fertility of the receiving population. Francis Walker, a director of the U.S. Bureau of the Census in the late nineteenth century, suggested that the declining fertility of native-born Americans reflected their concern with having their children brought up among so many foreigners (Walker 1891). But such a theory is far from being accepted, and it is more likely that the fertility of the natives of the receiving area is not affected by the size of the in-migration. There is reason to believe that the indirect effect of in-migration may be substantial since migrants tend to be concentrated in the young childbearing age groups. In Lima, Peru, over 60 percent of the currently mated women age fifteen to forty-nine in 1965 were in-migrants. About 20 percent of the total population increase between 1950 and 1960 in Guanabara State, Brazil, was due to reproductive change among the in-migrants after their arrival (Weller, Macisco, and Martine 1971, pp. 230–231). The effect of the age composition of the in-migrants is magnified if the in-migrants have higher fertility levels than those of the receiving population. Normally this is true. Occasionally it is not when those who migrate have high status or originate in communities very similar to the area of destination.

Each person added to the population means an additional person who must be fed, clothed, transported, housed, and given at least occasional medical care. Massive in-migration can put a severe strain on the ability of the receiving area to deliver those services. The extent to which the strains become real problems depends on the socioeconomic characteristics of the in-migrants and the extent to which the labor force can absorb the migrants.

In-migration affects the size of the labor force in two ways. First, because of the age-sex composition of the migrants, in-migration may increase the ratio of the economically active persons to the total population. This has been the case for the United States and several other industrialized countries (United Nations 1973, p. 250). Second, within the same age-sex categories the in-migrants may have higher rates of labor force participation than the receiving population. Both these effects seem to depend on the socioeconomic characteristics and the occupational skills of the in-migrants, however.

When persons with different cultural backgrounds migrate to an area, cultural heterogeneity develops. Cultural factors ultimately determine the tolerable levels of in-migration. Only a certain number of migrants can be absorbed without the receiving population feeling that their social institutions and value system are threatened. After

World War I the point was reached in the United States where people widely feared that continued large-scale immigration from southern and eastern Europe would "undermine" the American way of life. This fear led to restrictive legislation—a common development when the receiving population feels threatened by the massive immigration of persons from a different culture (Borrie 1970, pp. 114–115).

A similar situation is perhaps unfolding at the present time, not only in the United States but in other developed countries as well. The large influx of Hispanics and Asians is causing some Americans to wonder what the social institutions will resemble in another few decades. Great Britain is reassessing its immigration laws as the number of nonwhites living in England increases significantly. The issue is complex indeed and must be addressed in a rational manner. Consideration must be given to the responsibility of the United States and other developed countries to the rest of the world on one hand, and the institutions and values of the receiving countries on the other.

Impact on the Individual Migrant

One important consequence for the migrant is the opportunity to live in an environment with the social, economic, political, or physical characteristics that he or she believes to be preferable to the old environment. Whether or not this is the case depends on the accuracy of the migrant's perceptions of the circumstances in both the old and the new environments and the migrant's ability to utilize the advantageous features of the new environment. The latter, in turn, depends on whether the migrant possesses useful skills and how rapidly he or she is assimilated into the prevailing culture.

Actually, there are two types of assimilation—structural and cultural. The first refers to the extent to which migrants fit into the prevailing opportunity structure, such as the labor market. Cultural assimilation is more concerned with the extent to which the migrant adopts prevailing value orientations and ways of life. Traditionally it has been assumed that cultural assimilation is a consequence of structural assimilation (see Duncan and Schnore 1959). Yet people may occupy similar positions in the social structure and still have quite different value systems.

In general, the difficulty that migrants experience in being assimilated depends on how different they are from the receiving population. Early migrants to the United States had Anglo-Saxon or Germanic backgrounds and were easily assimilated into the society. However, when the source of immigration shifted to eastern and southern Europe, the background of the new immigrants varied considerably from that of the native-born United States population—in ethnicity, in language and culture, and in religion. Assimilation proved to be more difficult but not impossible. The election in 1960 of John

F. Kennedy, a Catholic of Irish origin, symbolized the "coming of age" of non-WASP Americans.

Nonwhite groups have found it much more difficult to be assimilated into the mainstream of American life. Despite having been here over 300 years, the American black is only just now beginning to be accepted by the whole society. One can only speculate on the problems of assimilation that the newest Americans of Hispanic and Asian nationality may confront.

While the immigrant Americans perhaps face more dramatic problems, the individual moving within the country must also adapt to new situations as he or she joins the residents of a new urban or rural area or leaves the Northeast for the South or Far West. Customs vary somewhat from region to region, and some "assimilating" is sometimes necessary if a newcomer is to adjust to the unfamiliar surroundings.

SUMMARY

Migration is a permanent shift of residence of such duration and distance that a change of physical and social environment occurs. It usually is measured as a change of residence across political boundaries.

People have always been mobile. Some kind of international migration has occurred as long as nations have existed. The extent of international migration increased significantly over the last three centuries as transportation and communication networks improved.

During the period immediately preceding and following World War II the amount of international migration was probably larger than ever before. Much of that migration was involuntary and involved severe personal and economic hardships for most of those involved.

There is a great deal of geographic mobility within the United States, much of it created by persons who move repeatedly. The annual rates of geographic mobility have been stable since 1947, when reliable data were first collected. On the average each year one person in five changes residence. One person in fourteen migrates by moving from one county to another.

A large part of the interregional migration has been from east to west and from south to north. Since 1970 the latter flow has been reversed. Both whites and blacks are now moving into the South.

There are marked differences among those who migrate in terms of age, race, and socioeconomic status. Young adults are the most likely to move as are very young children, who move with their parents. Migration rates fall sharply after age thirty and pick up a little among the elderly. Whites are somewhat more likely to move than blacks, although the latter move locally more often. There is a positive relation between education and likelihood of moving: the better educated are more likely to move than the less educated.

Migration is seldom explained in terms of the characteristics of only one place or factor. In any move, a decision has been reached that the area of destination offers advantages over the area of origin which outweigh the disadvantages of movement.

Economic reasons seem more important as causes of migration than as causes of moving locally. Generally, it can be stated that people move to "better themselves" in life. This is happening today and will continue to happen as long as people believe that opportunities and living conditions are better elsewhere.

Migration reduces the population and reproductive potential of the sending area and increases the population and reproductive potential of the area of destination. Migration may also affect the size of the labor force and contribute to social and cultural change.

REFERENCES AND SUGGESTED READINGS

Biggar, Jeanne C. 1979. The sunning of America: migration to the Sunbelt. *Population bulletin* 34 (March).

Bogue, Donald J. 1969. *Principles of demography.* New York: John Wiley and Sons.

Borrie, W. D. 1970. *The growth and control of world population.* London: Weidenfeld and Nicolson.

Bouvier, Leon F. 1965. A genealogical approach to the study of French-Canadian fertility 1650–1950. *Sociological analysis* 26 (Fall):148–156.

Bouvier, Leon F., Macisco, John J., and Zarate, Alvan. 1976. Toward a framework for the analysis of differential migration: the case of education. In *Internal migration: the New World and the Third World,* eds. Anthony H. Richmond and Daniel Kubat, pp. 24–36. Beverly Hills, Calif: Sage Publications.

Bouvier, Leon F., Shryock, Henry S., and Henderson, Harry W. 1977. International migration: yesterday, today, and tomorrow. *Population bulletin* 30 (September):3–24.

Campbell, Rex R., Johnson, Daniel M., and Stangler, Gary J. 1974. Return migration of black people to the south. *Rural sociology* 39 (Winter):514–528.

Committee on the Judiciary, U.S. Senate. 1979. *World refugee crisis: the international community's response.* Washington, D.C.: Government Printing Office.

Cook, Robert C. 1957. World migration, 1946–55. *Population bulletin* 13 (August):77–94.

Curtin, Philip D. 1969. *The Atlantic slave trade.* Madison: University of Wisconsin Press.

Davis, Kingsley. 1974. The migrations of human populations. *Scientific American* 231 (September):92–105.

Duncan, Otis Dudley, and Schnore, Leo F. 1959. Cultural, behavioral, and ecological perspectives in the study of social organization. *American journal of sociology* 65 (September):132–153.

Elizaga, Juan C. 1965. Internal migrations in Latin America. *Milbank Memorial Fund quarterly* 43, part 2 (October):144–161.

Gutierrez, H. 1977. Evolution de la population de l'Amerique Latine. *Population* 32 (Mars–Avril):461–466.

Hamilton, C. Horace. 1964. The Negro leaves the South. *Demography* 1:273–295.

Henripin, Jacques. 1954. *La population Canadienne au début du XVIII siècle.* Paris: Presses Universitaire de France.

Lee, Everett S. 1966. A theory of migration. *Demography* 3:47–57.

Long, Larry H., and Boertlein, Celia G. 1976. The geographic mobility of Americans. *Current population reports,* series P-23, no. 64. Washington, D.C.: Government Printing Office.

Long, Larry H., and Hansen, Kristin A. 1975. Trends in return migration to the south. *Demography* 12 (November):601–614.

———. 1979. Reasons for interstate migration. *Current population reports,* series P-23, no. 81. Washington, D.C.: Government Printing Office.

Macisco, John J., Jr., Bouvier, Leon F., and Weller, Robert H. 1970. The effect of labor force participation on the relation between migration status and fertility. *Milbank Memorial Fund quarterly* 48 (January):51–69.

Reiss, Bob. 1977. The melting pot. *Potomac magazine* (July 17):20–32.

Sabagh, Georges. 1942. The fertility of French-Canadian women during the 17th century. *American journal of sociology* 47 (May):680–689.

United Nations. 1973. *The determinants and consequences of population change,* vol. I. New York: United Nations.

———.1974. International migration trends, 1950–1970. *Conference background papers.* New York: United Nations.

U.S. Bureau of the Census. 1973*a*. *Census of population: 1970. Subject reports,* PC(2)-2D, Lifetime and recent migration. Washington, D.C.: Government Printing Office.

———.1973*b*. *Census of population: 1970. Subject reports,* PC(2)-2A, State of birth. Washington, D.C.: Government Printing Office.

———.1975. Mobility of the population of the United States: March 1970 to March 1975. *Current population reports,* series P-20, no. 285. Washington, D.C.: Government Printing Office.

———. 1978. Geographical mobility: March 1975 to March 1978. *Current population reports,* series P-20, no. 331. Washington, D.C.: Government Printing Office.

Walker, Francis A. 1891. Immigration and degradation. *Forum* 11:637–644.

Weller, Robert H., Macisco, John J., Jr., and Martine, George R. 1971. The relative importance of the components of urban growth in Latin America. *Demography,* 8, no. 2 (May):225–232.

Wilbur, George. 1963. Migration expectancy in the United States. *Journal of the American Statistical Association* (June):444–453.

Part IV

Determinants and Consequences of Age and Sex Composition

Although fertility, mortality, and migration are the three demographic variables that combine to produce population change, the age and sex composition of a population is equally important to demographers. At any given point in time, the age and sex composition of a population reflects past levels of fertility, mortality, and migration and sets limits on the levels each of these variables may assume in the near future. Chapter 9 explores these interrelationships.

The age and sex composition of a population may also influence nondemographic factors, such as the spending patterns of a society and the provision of services to its members. Chapter 10 looks at some of the interrelationships between age composition and nondemographic factors. Changes in the age composition of the U.S. population, which have resulted from fluctuations in fertility, have affected the demand for child care services, the provision of educational services, the rate of household formation, and the level of unemployment. These effects will continue to be felt in the future, along with a severe strain on the social security system caused in part by an aging U.S. population.

9

Age and Sex Composition and the Demographic Variables

Almost any characteristic of a population's composition can be of interest to a demographer if it affects a demographic variable. For example, a population's socioeconomic composition might be very important if it contributes to patterns of fertility, mortality, or migration. Racial composition and marital status can also be extremely important if they can be related to one or more of the demographic variables. We have noted that in the United States such relationships do in fact exist with fertility, mortality, and migration. Of course, socioeconomic factors, religious and racial differences, and the other characteristics of a population's composition are not always related to the demographic variables. It is only after considerable research that conclusions can be reached regarding the extent, if any, of any such relationships.

There are two characteristics of a population's composition that deserve special attention, however, because they are strongly related to each of the variables of fertility, mortality, and migration. These are age and sex. It is impossible to do any kind of demographic analysis without referring to the age and sex distribution of the population in question. Differences in fertility, mortality, and migration between societies or between groups are meaningless unless age and sex are considered. You should always bear this in mind when making demographic comparisons. The basic question to be asked is: Are the age and sex distributions of the societies being compared similar and, if not, what is the impact on the demographic analysis?

This chapter will show how the demographic variables of fertility, mortality, and migration determine the age and sex composition of a population. It will also demonstrate how the age and sex composition of a population, in turn, affects the current (and future) levels of each of these variables.

HOW AGE AND SEX COMPOSITION IS DETERMINED

Sex Composition

The **sex ratio,** the number of males per one hundred females, measures a population's sex composition. It can be computed for the entire population or for specific age groups. The larger the number, the greater the number of males in proportion to females. Table 9.1 presents the sex ratio for the entire population of selected countries around the year 1975. There was a relatively wide range reported, the high being Pakistan's sex ratio of 114 and the low being 86 for the Soviet Union.

The sex ratio of the total population is determined by the levels of fertility and mortality, sex-selective patterns of migration, and the *sex ratio at birth*—the ratio of male to female births. The higher the sex ratio at birth, the higher the entire population's sex ratio tends to be. Although the sex ratio at birth may vary from one population to

Table 9.1 Sex Ratios for Selected Countries, Circa 1975

COUNTRY	SEX RATIO
Soviet Union	86
West Germany	91
Colombia	94
Brazil	95
Czechoslovakia	95
United Kingdom	95
United States	95
Benin	96
France	96
Indonesia	97
Japan	97
Zambia	97
Argentina	100
Canada	100
Mauritania	100
New Zealand	100
Australia	101
Mexico	102
Gambia	103
Cuba	104
India	108
Pakistan	114

Source: United Nations (1977), pp. 166–201.

another, it is usually about 105—that is, there are about 105 males born for every 100 females born. The sex ratio at birth is lower when the conditions of gestation, such as adequate prenatal care, are poor and fetal mortality is high. This explains why populations with relatively low standards of living have lower sex ratios at birth than other populations and why, in the United States and other developed countries, there is a lower sex ratio for illegitimate than for legitimate births (United Nations 1973, p. 270). Single, teen-age women, who are most likely to have illegitimate babies, are also most likely to have inadequate prenatal care. Among whites in this country the sex ratio at birth in 1977 was 105.8, but among blacks (who had lower standards of living and hence poorer conditions of gestation and higher fetal mortality), the sex ratio at birth was only 102.6 (National Center for Health Statistics 1979*b*). One symptom of poor conditions of gestation is a low birth weight—less than 3,001 grams (6.6 pounds). Data from the United States in 1975 show that the sex ratio was only 80.8 for infants with a birth weight less than 3,001 grams, 95.0 for those weighing 3,001 to 3,500 grams at birth, and 114.9 for those with a birth weight greater than 3,500 grams (National Center for Health Statistics 1978, p. 226). Clearly, male fetuses are weaker than female fetuses.

The sex ratio for the entire population (all age groups) is seldom as high as the sex ratio at birth. For instance, in 1978 there were about

Table 9.2 Sex Ratio by Age Group, U.S. Population, July 1, 1978

AGE GROUP	SEX RATIO
Under 5	104.6
5–9	104.2
10–14	104.0
15–19	103.2
20–24	101.4
25–29	99.2
30–34	98.3
35–39	95.7
40–44	95.2
45–49	95.2
50–54	93.0
55–59	91.3
60–64	88.1
65–69	79.7
70–74	73.0
75–79	64.1
80–84	54.9
85+	45.4
All ages	95.1

Source: U.S. Bureau of the Census (1979), pp. 5–6.

106.5 million males living in the United States and about 112 million females—a sex ratio of 95. One important reason for this difference between the sex ratio at birth and the sex ratio for the entire population is that mortality differs by sex. As we noted in chapter 7, mortality tends to be higher among males than among females, and thus in each successive age category the sex ratio tends to fall. Eventually there are more females than males, an inequality that increases with age, as table 9.2 shows. In 1978 the sex ratio for the total U.S. population was 95.1. It was 104.6 for those under five and declined thereafter. At age twenty-three the number of males and females was equal, and after that there were more females than males. At the older ages the sex ratio is quite low: 64.1 for those seventy-five to seventy-nine and only 45.4 among persons eighty-five or older.

Because mortality is so strongly related to sex, any sex-selective change in mortality levels will alter the sex ratio. Changes in health technology in this century have benefited females more than males and so have contributed to lowering the sex ratio of the total population. War can also alter the sex ratio by increasing male mortality. For instance, in the 1959 census of the Soviet Union the sex ratio for the entire population was only 81.9. Among those age forty to forty-nine (who were age twenty to thirty years old during World War II) the sex ratio was under 60.

Fertility influences the sex ratio through its effect on age composition. In general, the higher the level of fertility, the younger the age composition. A younger age composition produces a higher overall sex ratio because the sex ratio is higher at younger ages than at older ones. This partially explains why in table 9.1 the sex ratios of the developing countries (which have a relatively young age composition) tend to be higher than those in the developed countries.

Sex-selective migration also affects the sex ratio. Normally, more males than females migrate from one country to another. Countries that receive a large number of immigrants have a higher sex ratio than they would have otherwise. Countries sending a large number of emigrants have a lower proportion of males than they would have otherwise. Until 1910, the sex ratio of immigrants into the United States exceeded 120. Because of the large volume of immigration, the sex ratio of the entire population was increased somewhat (Bogue 1959, pp. 152–156). More recently the flow of immigrants has been considerably smaller, and males no longer predominate. The sex ratio among legal immigrants has been about 88, which reflects the large number of war brides of U.S. servicemen. Consequently, immigration today has only a minimal effect on the sex ratio of the total U.S. population, and the effect is to lower the ratio a little.[1]

Internal migration also tends to be sex-selective, on the female side. In many areas migrants from rural to urban areas are predominantly female. This is especially the case in many developing countries, where there are few opportunities for paid employment outside the home for females living in rural areas. If the volume of migration out of rural areas is sufficiently large, women may outnumber men in urban areas, and the opposite may be true in rural areas. For example, in 1974 the sex ratio for the entire population of Ecuador was 99.9. In urban areas there were more females than males, and the sex ratio was only 92.3. In rural areas, where there were more males than females, the sex ratio was 105.5 (United Nations 1977, p. 150). Sex-selective migration can also significantly affect the sex ratio of individual cities in a country. For instance, migrants to Washington, D.C. are disproportionately female, and the sex ratio of the entire city population is only about 86.

Age Composition

Because age is so strongly related to fertility, mortality, and migration, as well as to patterns of consumption and life style, demographers are particularly interested in the age composition of a population. The **median age** (the age at which half the population is younger and half is older) is one way to measure the age composition of a population. But because it is only one figure, the median age can conceal significant variations in the age composition above or below this age. More de-

[1]Other examples of the potential effect of international migration on the sex ratio are reported in United Nations (1973), p. 272.

Box 9.1 Measures of Age Composition

In 1978 the median age of the U.S. population was 29.7. That figure can be obtained easily. First, however, the population should be arranged into equal size age groups. Thus:

AGE GROUP	NUMBER OF PERSONS	CUMULATIVE NUMBER
0–4	15,361,000	15,361,000
5–9	16,885,000	32,246,000
10–14	18,557,000	50,823,000
15–19	21,057,000	71,880,000
20–24	20,441,000	92,321,000
25–29	18,041,000	110,362,000
30–34	15,895,000	126,257,000
35–39	13,065,000	139,322,000
40–44	11,319,000	150,641,000
45–49	11,359,000	162,000,000
50–54	11,825,000	173,825,000
55–59	11,236,000	185,061,000
60–64	9,432,000	194,493,000
65+	24,055,000	218,548,000

The equation for calculating median age is:

$$Md = l_{Md} + \left(\frac{N/2 - \Sigma f_X}{f_{Md}}\right) i$$

where

$Md =$ median age of the population
$l_{Md} =$ the lower limit of the age group containing the middle person
$N/2 =$ the middle person (the total population divided by two)
$\Sigma f_x =$ the sum of all the persons in all the age groups preceding l_{Md}
$f_{Md} =$ the number of persons in the age group containing $N/2$
$i =$ length of age interval

On July 1, 1978, the total U.S. population was about 218,548,000. Thus, $N/2 = 218{,}548{,}000 \div 2 = 109{,}274{,}000$.

The middle person falls somewhere between twenty-five and thirty, because that is the age group which contains the number 109,274,000. Substituting the values from the table in the formula given above, we get:

$$Md = 25 + \left(\frac{109{,}274{,}000 - 92{,}321{,}000}{18{,}041{,}000}\right) 5$$

$$= 25 - \left(\frac{16{,}953{,}000}{18{,}041{,}000}\right) 5$$

$$= 25 + (.93969)\ 5 = 25 + 4.7 = 29.7$$

continued

Measures of Age Composition (continued)

It is also possible to use age data to calculate the dependency ratio and the index of aging. The dependency ratio is obtained by dividing the number of young persons (under fifteen) and old persons (sixty-five and over) by the number of persons in between those age brackets and multiplying that figure by one hundred. In the example above, the dependency ratio is

$$\left(\frac{50{,}823{,}000 + 24{,}055{,}000}{143{,}670{,}000}\right)100$$

$$= \left(\frac{74{,}878{,}000}{143{,}670{,}000}\right) 100 = 52.1$$

There are 52 "dependent" persons per 100 "active" persons.

The index of aging is calculated by dividing the number of persons age sixty-five or older by the number under age fifteen and multiplying by one hundred. Using the 1978 figures we get:

$$\left(\frac{24{,}055{,}000}{50{,}823{,}000}\right) 100 = 47.3$$

There are 47 "elderly" persons per 100 "young" persons. Changes in the index of aging roughly measure whether a population's age structure is becoming older or younger. The larger the index, the older the population's age structure.

[1]See box 3.2 for additional details.

---

scriptive detail may be obtained by calculating the percent of the population in various age groups. Data arranged in this way may be used to calculate the dependency ratio and the **index of aging.** Box 9.1 shows how to calculate these measures.

Table 9.3 presents all these measures for the United States from 1900 to 1978. The median age increased until 1950, decreased until about 1970 (because of the baby boom), and has increased since then. The index of aging has increased substantially during this century. In 1978 the index was over four times as large as in 1900. Although the proportion aged has increased, the total dependency ratio today is smaller than that in 1900. It decreased until 1940, increased in 1950 and 1960, and then began to decrease again because of declines in the percent of the population below fifteen.

Construction of an age-sex pyramid (also called a population pyramid) yields even more detailed information about the age (and sex) composition of a population. The pyramid, which may be based on numbers or percentages, is one of the most useful graphic devices in demography. Its shape yields clues concerning past levels of demogra-

Table 9.3 Age Composition of the Population of the United States, 1900–1978

YEAR	MEDIAN AGE	PERCENT OF POPULATION 0–14	15–64	65+	INDEX OF AGING	DEPENDENCY RATIOS Total	Youth (0–14)	Aged (65+)
1900	22.9	34.4	61.5	4.1	11.8	62.6	56.0	6.6
1910	24.1	32.1	63.6	4.3	13.4	57.3	50.5	6.8
1920	25.3	31.8	63.5	4.7	14.6	57.5	50.2	7.3
1930	26.5	29.4	65.2	5.4	18.4	53.4	45.1	8.3
1940	29.0	25.1	68.1	6.8	27.3	46.8	36.8	10.0
1950	30.2	26.9	65.0	8.1	30.2	53.9	41.4	12.5
1960	29.5	31.1	59.7	9.2	29.7	67.6	52.1	15.5
1970	28.1	28.4	61.8	9.8	34.6	61.7	45.8	15.9
1978	29.7	23.3	65.7	11.0	47.3	52.2	35.5	16.7

Sources: U.S. Bureau of the Census (1975), pp. 15, 91; and U.S. Bureau of the Census (1979), pp. 5–6.

phic behavior as well as information concerning current age and sex composition, as box 9.2 explains. It also tells about the kinds of social and economic problems a society can perhaps expect in the future (see box 2.2 back on page 45).

Figure 9.1 (page 245) presents an age-sex pyramid for West Germany in 1975. Beginning with age fifty to fifty-four, the number of females greatly exceeds the number of males, primarily because of the high mortality of males during World War II. Persons from fifty to fifty-four in 1975 would have been age fifteen to nineteen in 1940. The number of males increases sharply with the age group of those sixty to sixty-four. These persons, who were age twenty-five to twenty-nine in 1940, were less likely to be in the front lines than the younger persons and subsequently experienced lower wartime mortality.

It is also possible to examine the effects of changes in fertility, mortality, or migration on age composition by comparing population pyramids for the same country at two different points in time. Figure 9.2 (page 245) superimposes the 1978 pyramid for the U.S. population on the 1970 population pyramid. Notice that the 1978 population had fewer persons under age fifteen than the 1970 population, despite the fact that the total 1978 population was larger than the total population in 1970. The decline in fertility that has occurred since the early 1960s accounts for this difference. Also notice that the 1978 population had more persons age fifteen to thirty-nine than the 1970 population. The baby boom was responsible for this difference. The difference in the age bracket forty to forty-nine was caused by the low fertility levels during the early years of the Great Depression (when people age forty to forty-nine in 1978 were born). Beyond age forty-nine, the number of persons in 1978 generally outnumbered those in 1970.

Many people believe that reductions in mortality cause the aging of a population. After all, reductions in mortality increase the average

Box 9.2 Fertility and Age-Sex Pyramids

Distinctive population pyramids emerge from the various levels of demographic behavior. Note the effects of fertility on the shape of the pyramids presented below.

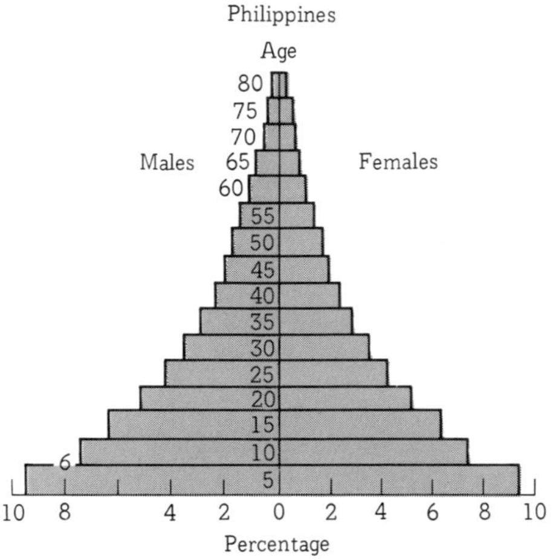

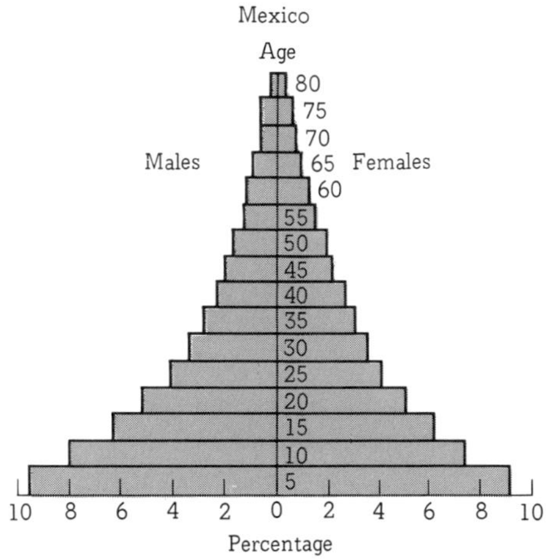

The pyramids for Mexico and the Philippines are typical of many developing countries where fertility is high and fairly constant. These pyramids have broad bases and steeply sloping sides, illustrating the large numbers of children and young people, and the small percentage of old people in the population.

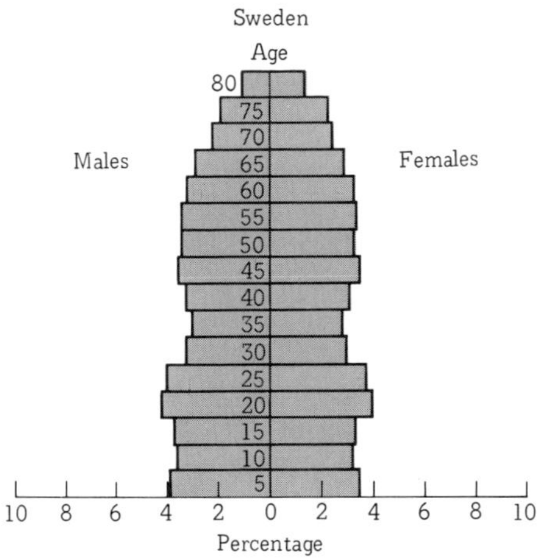

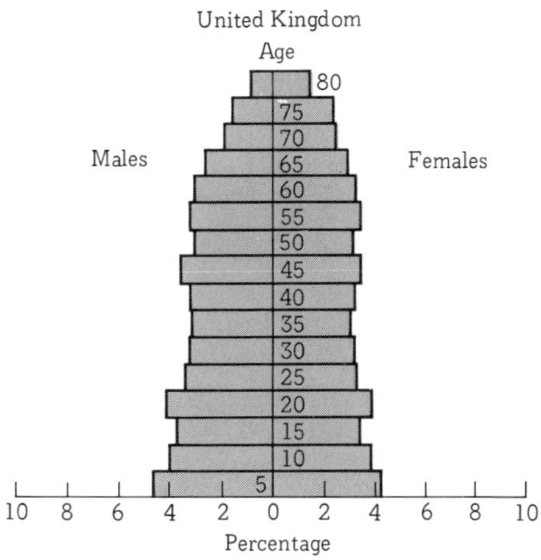

The age-sex structures of Sweden and the United Kingdom shown above reflect two populations of longstanding low fertility. Their population pyramids are almost rectangular in shape, with a slight sloping at the oldest age groups.

continued

Fertility and Age-Sex Pyramids (continued)

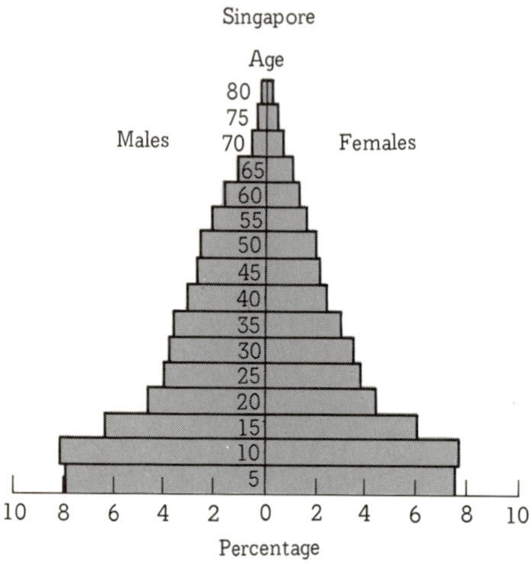

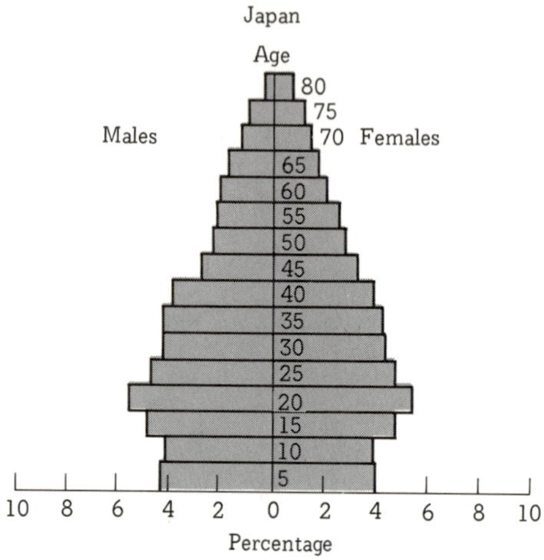

The pyramids of Singapore and Japan represent transitional populations where fertility has declined more recently. In Singapore fertility decline has been very recent and is reflected only in a narrowing at the base of the pyramid. In Japan, where fertility has been falling for several decades, the large cohorts born when fertility was much higher have moved progressively into older age groups creating a bulge. The shape of this type of pyramid has been variously described as a "beehive," "Chinese lantern," or "barrel."

Source: United Nations (1973), pp. 266–267.

age of death and increase the number of old people. Isn't it reasonable, therefore, to conclude that reductions in mortality would cause the population to "age"? The surprising answer is no. Ansley Coale (1964) points out that the average age of a population is the average age of living persons, not their average age at death. Moreover, reduced mortality has increased the number of young persons more than it has increased the number of older persons because typical improvements in health and medicine reduce mortality more among the young than among the old. He concludes that if the mortality levels prevailing in 1900 had continued unchanged, and the levels of fertility and immigration also remained constant, the age of the U.S. population would actually be greater than it is. In other words, the reduction in the death rate has produced a *younger* American population.

In the United States and several other developed countries death rates currently are so low among people under age forty that any further reductions in mortality would tend to occur among the older population. Although this would lead to a slight increase in the median age

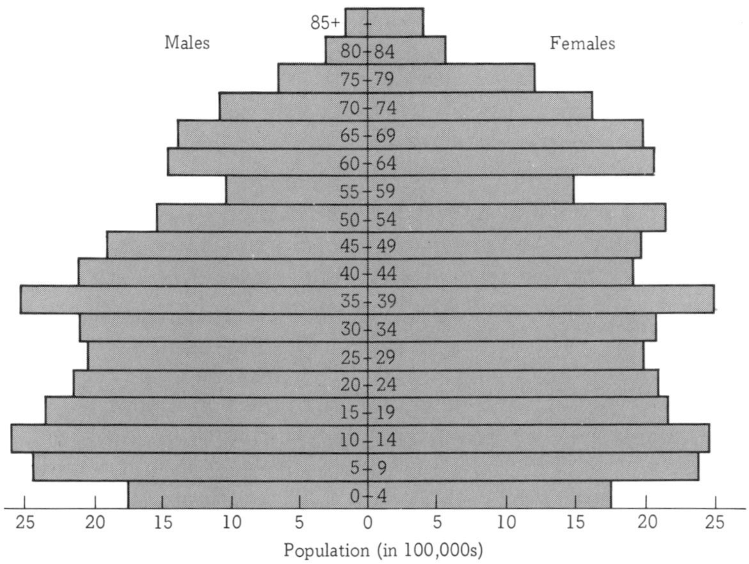

Figure 9.1 Age-Sex Pyramid for West Germany, 1975
Source: United Nations (1977)

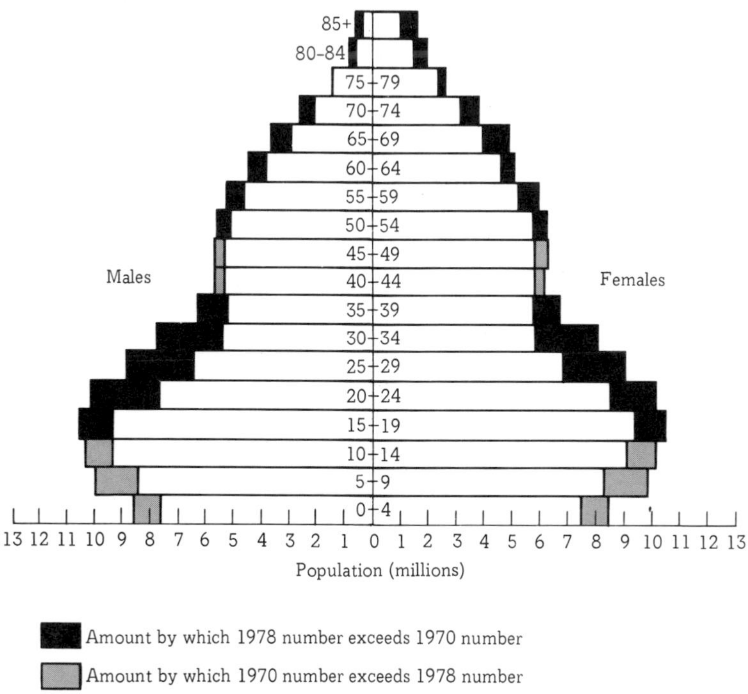

Figure 9.2 Age-Sex Pyramids of the United States, 1970 and 1978
Sources: U.S. Bureau of the Census (1972) and (1979).

of the population, its effect should not be exaggerated; only a small proportion of the population can benefit from such improvements (see box 9.3).

Low fertility is the principal ingredient in the aging of a population. With fewer children being born, the proportion of older persons in the population increases. A. I. Hermalin (1966) has clearly demonstrated that a decline in fertility contributed to an increase in the median age of the U.S. population during the early part of the twentieth century. On the other hand, a high level of fertility would tend to lower the median age of the population.

Net migration patterns also influence the age composition of a population. Because the immigrants to the United States have been disproportionately young, immigration contributed to a younger age distribution among the American population during this century than would otherwise have been the case. These influences should continue unless older immigrants start coming—an unlikely event.

Internal migration may play an important role in determining the age composition of the political subdivisions of the nation. An area like Pinellas County in Florida (which contains St. Petersburg) has a very old population because of a massive in-migration of older Americans from the rest of the nation. Certain counties in the Great Plains states also have a disproportionately old population, but for opposite

Box 9.3 Aging and the Mass Media

Too often the mass media have exaggerated the extent to which the age composition of the U.S. population is changing. In the late 1950s much was made of the fact that "half of the population is under age twenty-five." Although this figure was fairly accurate, the assumption that the drop in the median age would continue indefinitely was inaccurate. More recently, the number and proportion of elderly persons have increased, and the media have tended to exaggerate the aging of the population. So much incorrect demographic data about the aged have been presented in the media that a government report stated:

> Obviously statements sometimes made in the press and elsewhere that over one-third of the population of the United States will be over 65 years in another quarter to half a century are unfounded. This would be "possible" only if fertility continued at replacement or subreplacement levels and death rates at the higher ages were reduced to zero or near zero in the next few years (U.S. Bureau of the Census 1976, p. 10).

The report goes on to project that, with replacement-level fertility and a net immigration of 400,000 persons annually, the proportion of the population over sixty-four years old in 2000 would be 11.5 percent with constant mortality, 11.7 percent with slightly declining mortality, and 12.2 percent with rapidly declining mortality.

reasons: these areas have experienced a massive out-migration of young people, particularly young adults, leaving behind a much older population. Moreover, childbearing in such a population is diminished considerably.

Thus the demographic variables all contribute to changes in the age composition of a population but not necessarily in the manner commonly assumed. Low fertility tends to increase the median age of a population. To date, both immigration and decreases in mortality have had the effect of decreasing the median age of the population. But the effects of migration and mortality are dependent on what ages are most affected, as well as the age composition of the initial population (Bouvier 1974). Hence, it is risky to make sweeping generalizations.

THE EFFECTS OF AGE COMPOSITION ON FERTILITY AND MORTALITY

We have seen some of the ways that changes in demographic behavior can produce changes in the age composition. But age composition also affects the levels of fertility and mortality. In fact, demographic comparisons that do not take differences in age composition into account often produce misleading or invalid results (see box 9.4).

How Fertility Is Affected

At several points in this volume we have discussed the baby boom that occurred following World War II. One of the factors explaining the baby boom is the greater than normal proportion of women in the childbearing years as a result of the relatively high fertility of the 1920s. Throughout the 1970s and early 1980s severe upward pressures have again been exerted on the birth rate because of increases in the number of women in the childbearing years—the result of the baby boom. Fertility rates did not actually increase during the 1970s because couples delayed getting married and starting their families. If they had not done so, the age composition of the population was so favorable to high fertility that another baby boom would have occurred.

How Mortality Is Affected

Differences in age composition often help explain unexpected differences in death rates. For instance, in 1974 Sweden's crude death rate was 10.6 and Mexico's crude death rate was only 8.5. Yet Sweden is more advanced economically than Mexico, and mortality usually declines as economic growth occurs. Differences in age composition provide the answer to this paradox. Sweden has experienced many years of low fertility, creating a relatively old population. Only 20.7 percent

Box 9.4 Standardization

By now you are no doubt aware of the weakness inherent in crude rates. Because the crude rate's denominator includes the entire population, any variations in age composition will affect the rate itself. To get a better comparison of the demographic levels of two or more groups, the effect of differing age distributions should be eliminated. Demographers use a technique called **standardization** to do this. This important technique "accounts for" the peculiarities in population composition that may be "contaminating" the crude rate.

There are two basic methods of standardization—direct and indirect. Only the direct methods will be illustrated here. Direct age standardization calls for the selecting of a "standard" population and using its age distribution as a base. The age-specific death rates for the population under analysis are applied to the age distribution of the standard population. The final result of the computation is an **age-adjusted death rate.** It tells us what the death rates for the populations under analysis would be if they each had the age distribution of the standard population.

As an illustration, consider the mortality of whites and nonwhites in the United States in 1977. The crude death rate for whites in 1977 was 8.9 and that for nonwhites was 8.1. As the "standard" population, we can use the total U.S. population (all races) in 1977. (Almost any population may be used as the standard.)

(1) AGE GROUP	(2) AGE-SPECIFIC DEATH RATES White	(3) Nonwhite	(4) STANDARD POPULATION	(5) EXPECTED DEATHS White	(6) Nonwhite
1	12.7	25.5	3,164,000	40,183	80,682
1–4	0.6	1.0	12,078,000	7,247	12,078
5–14	0.3	0.4	36,372,000	10,912	14,549
15–24	1.1	1.4	41,245,000	45,370	57,743
25–34	1.2	2.6	33,161,000	39,793	86,219
35–44	2.1	4.8	23,544,000	49,442	113,011
45–54	5.7	10.3	23,392,000	133,334	240,938
55–64	13.6	21.3	20,402,000	277,467	434,563
65–74	29.9	37.1	14,590,000	436,241	541,289
75–84	71.6	73.8	6,834,000	489,314	504,349
85+	152.9	96.0	2,084,000	318,644	200,064
All ages	8.9	8.1	216,866,000	1,847,947	2,285,485

Sources: National Center for Health Statistics (1979*a*); and U.S. Bureau of the Census (1979).

To standardize using the direct method, we need the age-specific death rates (the number of deaths in a year per 1,000 people in a particular age group) for each population being compared (columns 2 and 3), and the number of persons in each age group in the standard population (column 4).

continued

Standardization (continued)

Each age-specific death rate (columns 2 and 3) is multiplied by the age group of the standard population (column 4) to determine the number of deaths that would occur in the standard population if it had the age-specific death rate present in the population being compared. Thus, there are 3,164,000 persons under one year of age in the standard population. Among whites in 1977 the age-specific death rate for this age group was 12.7 per 1,000. *If* this age-specific death rate were present in the standard population, then we could expect 40,183 deaths in this age group. The number of expected deaths in each age group are added together for each population and then divided by the sum of column 4, which is the total size of the standard population, and then multiplied by 1,000. This yields an age-adjusted death rate for that population.

Using the data provided above, the age-adjusted death rate for whites is:

$$\left(\frac{1{,}847{,}947}{216{,}866{,}000}\right)1{,}000 = 8.5$$

For nonwhites, it is:

$$\left(\frac{2{,}285{,}485}{216{,}866{,}000}\right)1{,}000 = 10.5$$

Comparisons of the crude death rates indicate that nonwhites (8.1) have lower mortality than whites (8.9). Yet when differences in age composition are controlled through standardization, it can be seen that nonwhites have higher mortality than whites.

Standardization may also be used for fertility or migration rates as well as for other factors, such as educational attainment or marriage duration. However, it is chiefly used to control for differences in age composition between populations. Because age is so strongly related to levels of fertility, mortality, and migration, standization is a valuable demographic tool.

of Sweden's population is under age fifteen. Almost 15 percent is over age sixty-five. By contrast, Mexican fertility is high and the population is relatively young. Over 46 percent of the population is age fourteen or younger. Only 3.4 percent is sixty-five or older. The young age distribution of the Mexican population produces a low crude death rate, while the older age composition of the Swedish population produces a somewhat higher crude death rate. When differences in age are controlled by examining age-specific death rates, the Swedish rates are lower than the Mexican rates in each instance.

Clearly, changes in age and sex composition have serious demographic impact. We have seen how crude birth and death rates are affected by age composition. It follows that crude rates of growth are also "contaminated" by such variations. Sophisticated demographic techniques have been developed to solve these problems. These are described in appendix 3 at the end of the book.

Changes in age and sex composition can have social and economic consequences as well. We will deal with this topic in chapter 10.

SUMMARY

The sex composition of a population is determined by the sex ratio at birth, sex-selective changes in mortality and migration, and fertility levels.

The age composition is also determined by the levels of fertility and mortality. In general, high fertility produces a relatively young age composition and declining fertility causes the average age of the population to become older. Declining mortality tends to make the age composition younger because most of the improvements in mortality rates occur at the younger ages. The effects of migration on age composition depend on the relative ages of the migrants and nonmigrants, but generally in-migration produces a younger population.

Age composition has a significant effect on fertility because women can bear children only at certain ages. Generally, populations with a high proportion of persons in the childbearing ages have relatively high fertility.

Because age is also strongly related to mortality, changes in the age composition may produce changes in mortality rates, so it is necessary to control for differences in age composition when comparing populations. The demographic tool of standardization is used for this purpose.

REFERENCES AND SUGGESTED READINGS

Barclay, George W. 1958. *Techniques of population analysis.* New York: John Wiley & Sons.

Bogue, Donald J. 1959. *The population of the United States.* Glencoe, Ill.: The Free Press.

Bouvier, Leon F. 1974. The demography of aging. In *Aging: its challenge to the individual and to society,* ed. W. C. Bier, pp. 37–47. New York: Fordham University Press.

Coale, Ansley J. 1964. How a population ages or grows younger. In *Population: the vital revolution,* ed. Ronald Freedman, pp. 47–58. Garden City, N.Y.: Doubleday-Anchor.

Hermalin, A. I. 1966. The effect of changes in mortality rates on population growth and age distribution in the United States. *Milbank Memorial Fund quarterly* 44 (October):451–469.

National Center for Health Statistics. 1978. *Vital statistics of the United States 1975,* vol. I. *Natality.* Washington, D.C.: Government Printing Office.

———. 1979*a*. Advance report final mortality statistics, 1977. *Monthly vital statistics report* 28:1, supplement (May 11).

———. 1979*b*. Advance report final natality statistics, 1977. *Monthly vital statistics report* 27:11, supplement (February 5).

United Nations. 1973. *The determinants and consequences of population change,* vol. I. New York: United Nations.

———. 1977. *Demographic yearbook 1976.* New York: United Nations.

U.S. Bureau of the Census. 1972. *1970 census of population general population characteristics,* Final Report PC(1)-B1, United States summary. Washington, D.C.: Government Printing Office.

———. 1975. *Historical statistics of the United States, colonial times to 1970.* Washington, D.C.: Government Printing Office.

———. 1976. Demographic aspects of aging and the older population in the United States. *Current population reports,* series P-23, no. 59. Washington, D.C.: Government Printing Office.

———. 1979. Estimates of the population of the United States, by age, sex, and race: 1976 to 1978. *Current population reports,* series P-25, no. 800. Washington, D.C.: Government Printing Office.

10
Age Composition and Emerging Social Issues

Many social issues are affected by changes in age composition. Government policy makers as well as business leaders, educators, and the media have recently discovered the importance of what is popularly termed "demographics"—the age, sex, and (to a lesser extent) marital status of a population's members. When population matters are discussed today, the focus is not necessarily on growth. More likely, it is changes in age composition and what these changes mean for a particular business enterprise or a specific group of people. For example, denim manufacturers, aware that the teen-age market is shrinking, focus on ways to persuade middle-aged Americans to buy blue jeans. Some economists worry about the ability to fill jobs in the late 1980s. That is when the members of the **baby bust** cohort (those born in the 1970s, when fertility was relatively low) enter the labor force and the number of young potential workers becomes relatively smaller compared to those born in the immediately preceding period of high fertility.

The President of the United States formally recognized the importance of demographics in his 1980 Economic Budget to the Congress, when he noted that certain demographic changes have substantial effects on the budget which can be anticipated. He cited as an example the government estimate of the number of people reaching retirement age a few years hence (Carter 1979, p. 68).

In the preceding chapter we looked at the way the age and sex composition of a population is produced by fertility, mortality, and migration patterns. In this chapter we will examine some of the ways in which changes in the age composition affect a variety of nondemographic variables and thereby may contribute to a number of social problems facing the American public.

THE EFFECTS OF CHANGING AGE COMPOSITION

Variations in fertility are especially important determinants of the U.S. age composition. Over the past fifty years the age composition has changed because of three patterns of fertility:

1. The low fertility of the 1930s
2. The high fertility between the late 1940s and the early 1960s
3. The low fertility of the 1970s

Persons born in these periods have been labeled the "good times cohort," the "baby boom cohort," and the "baby bust cohort," respectively (Harter 1977).

The **good times cohort** got that label because it reaped the social and economic benefits of being smaller than the cohorts that preceded it. As Carl Harter notes:

> By virtue of their smaller number, the thirties cohort, upon encountering each important life cycle event, have experienced relative abun-

> dance—a legacy from the larger cohort that preceded them ... Relatively speaking, in all their important life cycle events the 1930s cohort has "had it made." In 1950, when the thirties cohort was age 11–20, there were about a quarter million fewer fifteen-year-olds than there had been in 1940.... Insofar as the number of high school classrooms, glee clubs, athletic teams, debate squads, class officers, etc. had not diminished, then the 1950 fifteen-year-old had a greater chance than did the 1940 fifteen-year-old of being in a smaller class, of being a class officer, of being a member of the glee club ... etc. Similarly, in 1960, when the thirties cohort was 21–30, they required fewer new jobs and housing units than did their predecessors ten years earlier (1977, pp. 3–4).

The baby boom cohort has not been as fortunate as its predecessor. This cohort, which has been likened to a watermelon swallowed whole by a snake, is large by any standards. Although the crude birth rate was at its peak in the 1947–1957 interval, the actual *number* of births peaked between 1954 and 1964, when there were more than 4 million births annually—the only period during U.S. history with yearly birth cohorts that large.

Because of its sheer size, the baby boom cohort can expect problems as it passes through the life cycle. The group born in the early 1960s is just now completing college, and its schooling has been marked by overcrowded classrooms and a shortage of teachers. Many have entered the labor force, only to discover there are not enough suitable jobs to go around. Some members of this cohort are now seeking housing, which is scarce and expensive. When they reach retirement age, the demands on the social security system may result in strains between this large cohort and the younger workers who have to finance the system. Clearly, it will not be an easy path through the many phases of the life cycle for the baby boom cohort.

The baby bust cohort, born in the 1970s, should have a much easier path through life. Only 33 million births occurred in the seventies, 10 million fewer than in the 1955–1964 interval. Even if the low levels of fertility of the last decade are maintained through the 1980s, the number of births might still increase to perhaps 40 million—the result of the baby boom cohort becoming the parents of the 1980s.

By following the enormous baby boom group, the members of the baby bust cohort will be in a favored position throughout their life cycle and will be in a somewhat similar situation to the members of the good times cohort of the 1930s. As Conrad Taeuber states:

> Not only will there be fewer of them competing for jobs, services, and attention, but there also will have been an increase in public services and provisions made to accommodate the demands of the larger number of people that preceded them. They will be the beneficiaries of the baby boom (1979, p. 11).

Education facilities should be adequate; housing should be at least available, if not inexpensive; jobs should be more attractive. Still, this cohort is likely to experience some difficulties in career advancement.

So many people only ten to fifteen years older will be employed that promotions may be long deferred. Taeuber has suggested that middle-level positions may have to be created as "holding patterns" until the field is cleared of the older occupants of high-level jobs. Once members of the baby boom cohort retire, the senior positions will be opened to those in their fifties. Finally, when members of the baby bust cohort approach retirement, they should benefit from the improvements in the old-age institutions created for the large elderly population that preceded them.

Being a member of the baby boom generation or of the baby bust generation can make a significant difference in one's chances for success in life. This is not to suggest any form of demographic determinism. Individuals can and do succeed or fail on their own. Nevertheless, being born as a member of a large or a small cohort does alter the odds for succeeding. Manuel Plotkin, former director of the U.S. . Bureau of the Census, summed up the issue by stating that during the next several decades, the major demographic factor will continue to be the aging of the baby boom population. The people born during the peak of the boom, the 1950s and early 1960s, will continue to be the largest population group throughout most of their lives. As this large group passes through each of its stages, the institutions that deal with populations of particular ages will undergo the strain of rapid expansion, and a decade or two later they will undertake the often more painful task of precipitous retrenchment (Plotkin 1978, p. 277). The expansions and contractions of the population are shown by means of age pyramids in box 10.1. In the rest of this chapter we will examine some of the institutions likely to be affected by the severe fluctuations that we know will occur in the age distribution of the U.S. population.

Child Care Services

The issue of child care services has taken on increasing importance in recent years, despite decreasing fertility. A gain in female labor force participation is a major contributing factor in the growing demand for child care services. The labor force changes, in turn, reflect declining fertility among American women over the past ten to fifteen years as well as the emergence of the women's movement.

It would be an exaggeration to argue that demographic changes are at the root of the women's movement. But it is true that low fertility has facilitated its development. Several events—low fertility, the women's movement, increased female labor force participation—have jointly contributed to the emerging crisis in child care services in the United States.

Since 1965 the number of preschool children with mothers in the labor force has increased by 65 percent. Today 34 percent of all preschool children now have mothers in the labor force, and that proportion will no doubt increase in this decade. Sandra Hofferth (1978,

Box 10.1 Birth Cohorts

The progress of birth cohorts through the various stages of the life cycle may be studied through the use of population pyramids. The pyramids shown below are based on projections of the U.S. population made by the Bureau of the Census. They assume a total fertility rate of 2.1. Note the indentation in the 1980 pyramid at age forty to forty-nine. The people represented here were born during the 1930s, when the birth rate was lower than it was during either the 1920s or the 1940s. Also note the bulge caused by the baby boom and the way the pyramid slopes inward at the bottom because of the baby bust of the 1970s.

Because these projections assume a total fertility rate equal to replacement level, the pyramid becomes more and more rectangular through time. The number of births increases slightly during the 1980s as members of the

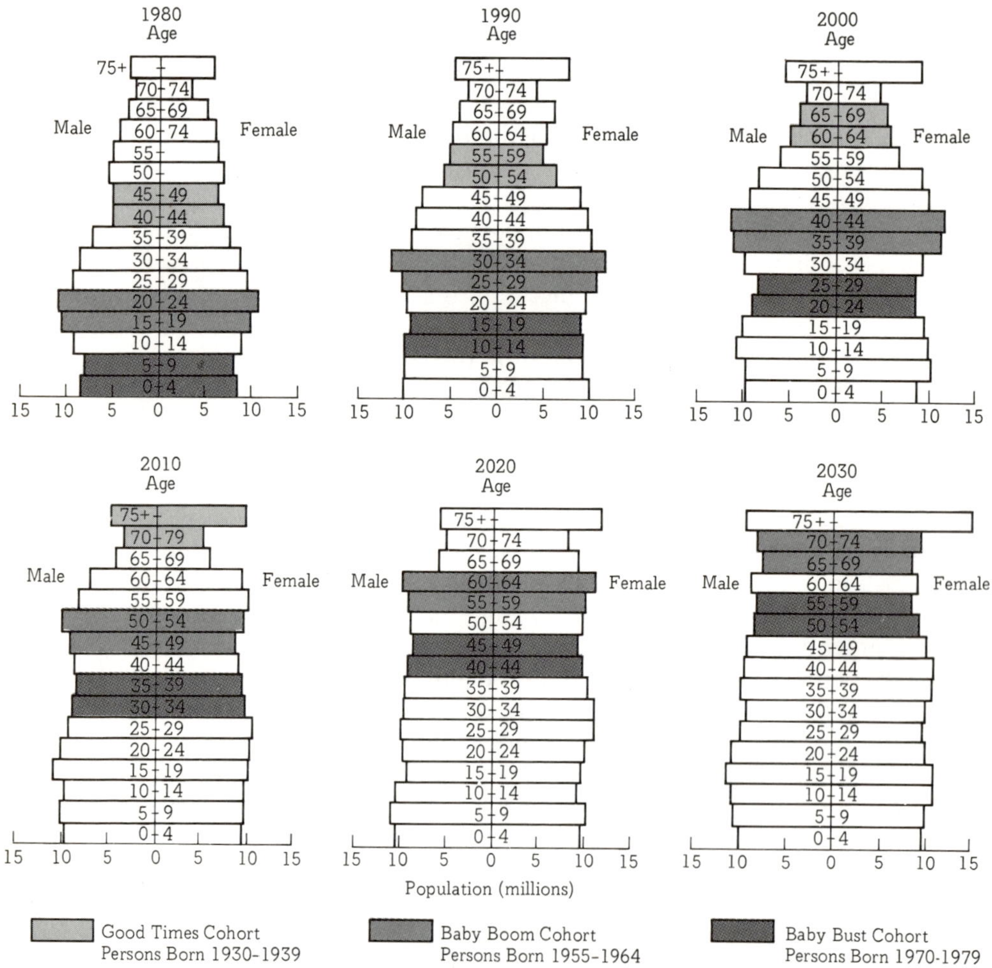

continued

Birth Cohorts (continued)

baby boom cohort pass through their twenties, which traditionally have been the prime years of childbearing. This increase is called an "echo" effect. The bulges represented by the baby boom and the echo effect continue to be present until the year 2030, when the baby boom cohort reaches age seventy and experiences very high mortality.

Source: U.S. Bureau of the Census (1977).

p. 528) projects that it will climb to 43 percent by 1990. Her projections are summarized in table 10.1. Note that the number of children under six with mothers in the labor force is projected to grow by 3 million in this decade alone.

Who takes care of these children? What is the quality of that care? In 1965 over 60 percent of such preschool children were cared for by a relative, usually in the child's home, and another 30 percent were cared for by a babysitter. By 1990 a smaller proportion will be cared for by relatives, because single parents are on the rise, and they are more likely to use child care services away from home than are married couples.

By 1990 possibly 4 million preschool children will be cared for by a nonrelative in or out of day-care centers. As the number of preschoolers needing day care grows, one can expect the emergence of franchises operated solely for the purpose of caring for preschool children. The quality of those services will have to be monitored very

Table 10.1 Number of Preschool Children in Day-care Arrangements, 1965–1990 (in thousands)

TYPE OF ARRANGEMENT	1965	1970	1975	1977	1980*	1985*	1990*
Family relative	1,227	1,789	2,055	2,001	2,410	3,015	3,345
Mother/father	1,146	1,677	1,927	1,876	2,260	2,826	3,136
Older sibling	81	112	128	125	150	189	209
Other relative	1,146	1,677	1,927	1,876	2,260	2,826	3,136
Child's home	582	838	963	938	1,130	1,413	1,568
Other's home	564	838	963	938	1,130	1,413	1,568
Nonrelative	1,180	1,733	1,991	1,938	2,335	2,921	3,240
Child's home	580	839	963	938	1,130	1,413	1,568
Other's home	600	894	1,028	1,000	1,205	1,508	1,672
Day-care center	212	307	353	344	414	518	575
Cares for self	18	28	32	31	38	47	52
Other	38	56	64	63	75	94	105
Total	3,821	5,590	6,422	6,253	7,532	9,421	10,453

*Based on projections.

Source: Hofferth (1978), p. 529.

carefully. While the right of every man and woman to seek gainful employment must be respected, we also need to be concerned about what will happen to the children who do not have the full-time care of one parent (Select Committee on Population 1978, p. 42).

Several suggestions have been offered to help us out of this dilemma. More flexible work schedules would help. Isabel Sawhill (1978, p. 753) has recommended more sharing of housework and child care by parents, with the division of responsibility reflecting the true preferences and abilities of the individuals involved rather than being culturally predetermined. The federal and state governments might increase their share of the cost of child care services. Underutilized schools could be converted to facilities for preschool children, and as the population of older persons increases, many "young old" persons (i.e., those between sixty-five and seventy-five) could serve as "babysitters" in these former school facilities.

Education

The problems for the educational systems caused in part by the baby boom and the subsequent baby bust have been discussed in chapter 3. Figure 10.1 illustrates these changes, as well as those we can expect in the next twenty years. In the mid-1950s and early 1960s there was an excess of students and a shortage of teachers and facilities, as the baby boom generation entered school and were taught by members of the good times cohort. Today there is a shortage of students and an excess of teachers and schools. Today teachers are numerous, not only because many of them come from the baby boom cohort but also because they were encouraged to become teachers by the teacher shortages they themselves experienced while in school. Many schools which were built to accommodate the baby boom children are not presently needed. Unless fertility increases sharply in the future, the number of students at the various levels will decrease by the end of the century. Policy makers are now pondering how best to turn the existing resources to more productive use.

We can see the demographic dimension of this problem, but what are some policy alternatives? Some have suggested very simply: have more babies. A larger school population would create more jobs for teachers. However, it would also cause an unparalleled population explosion—an unacceptable alternative. Another alternative would be to improve the entire educational system by allowing the decline in the number of students to result in more resources per student.

The present mood of the country, however, suggests that the reduction in the number of school-age children will be used as an opportunity to cut costs and reallocate resources rather than improve the existing educational system. Some observers consider this unfortunate, not only for children, but for society itself. The cohort born in the 1970s—composed of about 33 million children—will probably be the

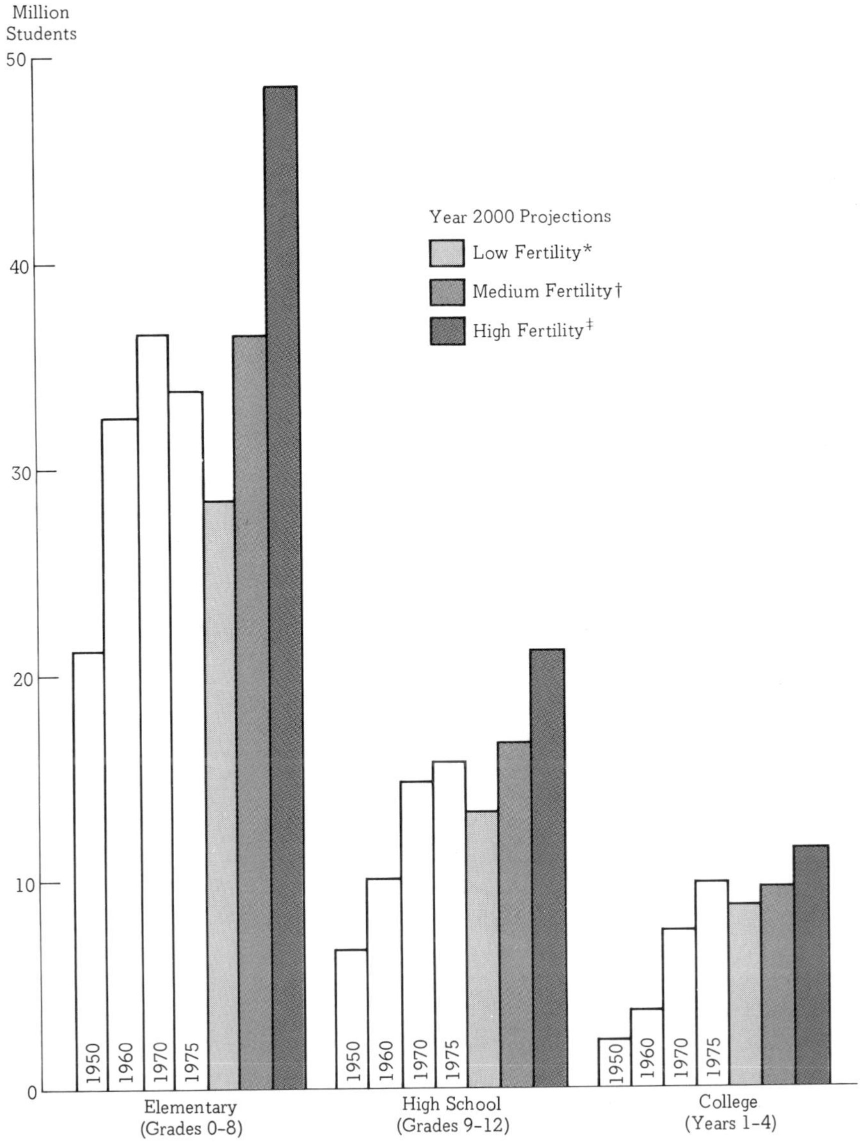

Figure 10.1 U.S. School Enrollment, 1950–2000

*Total Fertility Rate (TFR) of 1.7.

†TFR of 2.1. ‡TFR of 2.7.

Source: Population Reference Bureau (1977).

smallest in the second half of the twentieth century. It will follow the massive baby boom cohort and it will precede the "echo" cohort produced by the baby boom cohort as its members reach childbearing ages. Proportionately speaking, the number reaching the early stages of the professional-business part of the life cycle in about 2000 will be small. Many educators believe the nation cannot afford to waste any of this potential talent. It would be wise for society to ensure that this generation of the 1970s and the 1980s receives the very best education possible to train them for their adult responsibilities.

As Alan Pifer suggests, in an article entitled "Don't Forget the Children":

> Every child alive today or born in the years just ahead, whether male, female, black, white, Hispanic or otherwise, will be a scarce resource and a precious asset as an adult in the early part of the next century. At that time, the nation's standard of living, its capacity to defend itself—perhaps its very viability as a nation—will be almost wholly dependent on the small contingent of men and women who are today's children (1979, p. 34).

Household Formation

As people reach their twenties they usually begin to think about permanently leaving their parents' home. Young adults tend to break away from the parental nest in order to establish their own residence—to live with a new spouse, a live-in partner, or (as is increasingly the case) to live alone.

A **household** is simply an occupied housing unit, which can be owner occupied or rented. The housing unit is the physical side; the household is the human side of the same concept. There are two types of households: (1) family (a married couple, a man or woman with children, or any combination of relatives living together) and (2) nonfamily (a man or woman living alone or with unrelated persons). As we will see, both the number and the types of households have changed dramatically over the past few decades.

The actual number of households (occupied housing units) in the United States has grown by more than 17 million since 1970. In 1980 there were over 80 million households, representing an increase of 27 percent over the 1970 total. During the same period the population grew only about 10 percent.

A number of factors contributed to this large growth in the number of households. First, many of the baby boom generation are now young adults, setting up their own households. Second, fertility has been falling, and fewer married couples live with their parents. Third, there are more single adults. Young people are postponing marriage, yet leaving the parental home at an earlier age. In addition, divorce rates have been increasing, and there are more one-parent families. Fourth, people are living longer and more older people are maintaining their own homes (Norton and Glick 1979, p. 19). Thus demographic factors are having a serious impact on one of society's most important institutions—the home—and one of its most important industries—housing construction, and the many related industries, such as appliance manufacturing and hardware.

Many changes in household composition have occurred in recent years, attributable in large part to some of the factors listed above. As

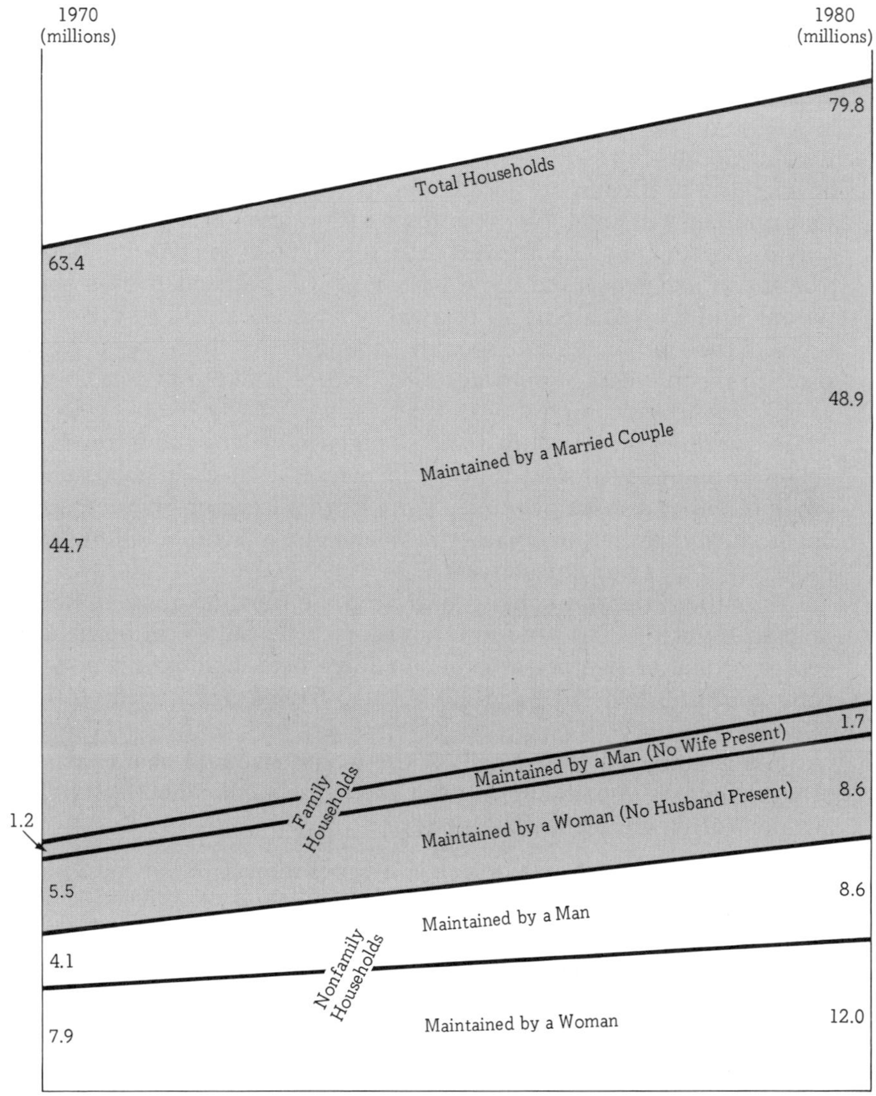

Figure 10.2 Number of Households by Type, 1970 and 1980
Sources: Norton and Glick (1979), p. 20; and U.S. Bureau of the Census (1979).

you can see from figure 10.2, nonfamily households have increased at a more rapid rate than have family households—72 percent compared to 15 percent over the past decade. Most of this increase among nonfamily households is accounted for by young people who have never been married or who are separated or divorced and by the emergence of households inhabited by two unmarried persons (Norton and Glick 1979, p. 20).

As a result of these changes over the past decade, a vastly different profile of households emerges as we enter the 1980s. In 1970, 81 percent of all households were family types (70 percent married couples and 11 percent single parent). Married couples now comprise 61 percent of all households, and 13 percent are headed by single parents. Over one quarter of all households are considered to be nonfamilial (U.S. Bureau of the Census 1979, p. 3).

The number of households will continue to increase fairly rapidly. The Census Bureau foresees over 96 million households by 1990—an increase of 21 percent in one decade. By the turn of the century that number will undoubtedly surpass 110 million. It is projected that only 57 percent of all households in 1990 will be of the type containing a husband and wife. Another 14 percent will be headed by a single parent, and the remaining 29 percent of households will be nonfamily types. These projections reflect the changes that have been taking place in recent years in marriage age, divorce, and family size, as well as changes in age composition.

In addition to reflecting basic changes in society, these trends are an important indicator to those who market consumer goods and a guide to public service planners. Many large purchases—homes, appliances, furniture, automobiles—are made on a household-unit basis rather than on a per person basis.

Another important change has been the rapid decrease in household size. For the first time in U.S. history, over half of all households consist of one or two persons. The average household size is now 2.8 compared to 3.1 in 1970 and 4.0 in 1940 (U.S. Bureau of the Census 1978*a*).

As is often the case, much of the future size and characteristics of households is dependent on what the baby boom cohort will do. As Arthur Norton and Paul Glick note:

> The behavior of this generation as it passes through its 20s and 30s, the traditional years for forming households, is not easy to predict. The decisions members of this group make about marriage, divorce and fertility should have a profound impact on what future households will be like (1979, p. 22).

The Labor Force

During the 1980 presidential campaign, candidate Ronald Reagan argued that the number of unemployed people had increased during the Carter years. The then-incumbent President, Jimmy Carter, pointed out that more people were employed during his administration than ever before in history. Many voters, not knowing whom to believe, saw this exchange as just another example of campaign rhetoric, but both candidates were telling the truth. More people are employed; more people are unemployed.

Population increases mean that more people are available for employment. Presumably most of them are actually working. However, the baby boom greatly expanded the proportion of the population between the ages of eighteen and thirty, an age group in which the unemployment rate tends to be greatest. Thus, the number of unemployed persons increased at the same time that the number of employed persons also increased.

As fertility declined in the late 1960s and 1970s, the labor force participation rates for women soared. In 1950, 28 percent of all women were in the labor force (i.e., working or actively seeking employment); by 1978 over half of all women were in that category. As we noted earlier, one outstanding feature of the entry of women into the labor force has been the increased participation of married women, particularly those with preschool children. In the past those women were least likely to be employed, yet since 1965 the most rapid increase in labor force participation has been among women with children under six years of age. Factors that once served as deterrents to the labor force participation of women, such as marital status and motherhood, are being offset by economic pressures on the family and the desire of some women for their own occupation and income.

When these two factors—the baby boom cohort entering the young adult years and the increased entry of women into the labor force—are taken into consideration, it is hardly surprising that unemployment rates have increased. The large number of potential new workers has created enormous pressure on the economic system, forcing it to absorb millions of new workers over the past decade. Indeed, it is surprising that unemployment rates are not higher than they are now.[1]

Future growth in the labor force may be expected. Ordinarily, this pressure could be expected to ease when the smaller baby bust cohort enters the years of young adulthood in the late 1980s and early 1990s, but projected increases in female labor force participation will more than compensate for that effect. Consequently, the U.S. labor force, which grew from 87.2 million in 1970 to 110 million in 1980, will grow to 120 million by 1990 and perhaps 135 million by the end of this century.

As table 10.2 shows, this growth will differ substantially by age and sex. Among males the increase (about twofold) will be largest in age groups thirty-five to forty-four and forty-five to fifty-four (the baby boom cohort). Among females substantial increases (three- and fourfold) will occur at all ages above twenty-four years.

[1]The impact of changes in age composition and the larger number of women in the labor force upon the aggregate rate of unemployment (that of all age groups) has been demonstrated by Joseph Anderson (1978, p. 791). Using the technique of standardization (see box 9.4), he states that the unemployment rate of 6.7 percent in the fourth quarter of 1977 would have been 13 percent lower if the 1977 labor force had had the same composition, in terms of age and marital status, as the 1956 labor force. This provides an excellent example of how standardization can be used in areas outside mortality analysis.

Table 10.2 Size of the U.S. Labor Force by Age and Sex, 1950–2000

MALES BY AGE GROUPS (IN MILLIONS)								
Year	14–15	16–17	18–24	25–34	35–44	45–54	55–64	65 and over
1950	.6	1.1	7.0	11.0	10.0	8.2	5.8	2.5
1960	.6	1.3	6.9	10.9	11.3	9.6	6.4	2.3
1970	.9	1.8	9.9	12.0	10.8	10.5	7.1	2.1
1977	.9	2.1	11.7	15.7	10.8	10.4	6.8	1.8
1980	.8	2.0	11.9	17.1	12.0	10.2	7.7	1.8
1990	.7	1.8	9.7	19.3	17.0	11.1	7.3	1.6
2000	.8	2.4	9.6	16.1	19.1	15.3	7.9	1.2
FEMALES BY AGE GROUPS (IN MILLIONS)								
Year	14–15	16–17	18–24	25–34	35–44	45–54	55–64	65 and over
1950	.3	.6	3.8	4.1	4.2	3.3	1.8	.6
1960	.3	.8	3.8	4.1	5.3	5.3	3.0	.9
1970	.6	1.3	6.8	5.7	6.0	6.5	4.2	1.1
1977	.7	1.7	8.8	9.2	6.8	6.7	4.3	1.1
1980	.6	1.7	9.3	9.6	7.4	7.1	5.2	1.3
1990	.6	1.7	8.3	12.7	11.7	8.8	6.2	1.4
2000	.9	2.5	9.2	12.2	15.0	14.6	8.0	1.4

Source: Anderson (1978), p. 802.

The accuracy of projections depends on continued low fertility and the continued participation of married women in the labor force. Changes in the volume or age composition of the immigration stream, in the economy, or in family formation could substantially affect both the size of the future labor force and its age composition, especially after 1990. But it is clear that there will be a need to generate enough jobs for millions of newly available job seekers over the next two decades. Given the current high rates of inflation and low rates of investment, meeting this need will prove difficult (Select Committee on Population 1978, pp. 51–55).

The Elderly and Social Security

In 1940 there were 9 million elderly people (age sixty-five and over) in the United States.[2] By 1980 the number had almost tripled to about 25 million. It will undoubtedly surpass 30 million at the turn of the century and reach 52 million by 2030. The elderly population has grown much faster than has the total population. During this century

[2]The terms "elderly," "aged," and "older people" will be used interchangeably in this section. While recent tendencies have been to elevate the age of retirement to seventy, we are following the conventional practice of using age sixty-five as the breaking point, in line with social security regulations.

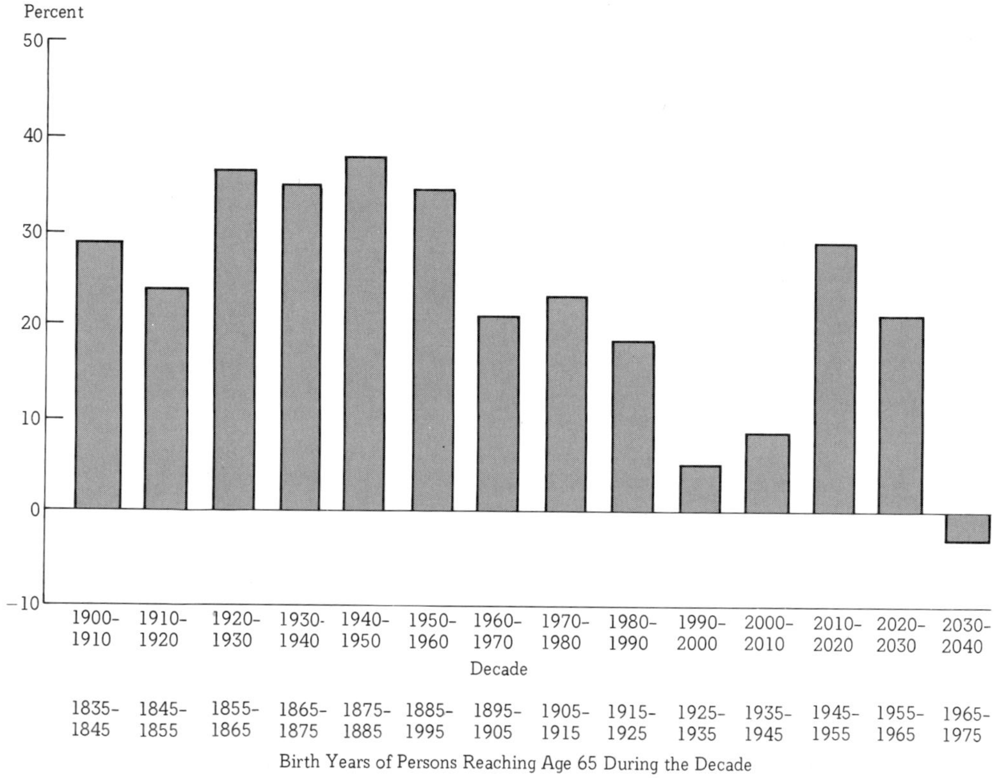

Figure 10.3 Decennial Percent Change of the Population Sixty-five Years and Older, 1900–2040
Source: U.S. Bureau of the Census (1976), cover.

the number of persons sixty-five and over will have increased tenfold, whereas the nation's total population will have increased only fourfold. The larger than average gains in the number of older people are the result of the high fertility of sixty-five and seventy-five years ago and lower fertility since then. Figure 10.3 shows the percent increase in the number of elderly for each decade since 1900. The birth cohorts of the last portion of the nineteenth century and the first decades of this century were quite large. Although mortality was high (relative to current levels), these cohorts were still large when they attained age sixty-five.

Fertility dropped sharply during the 1920s and 1930s. The effects of this decline will appear in 1990 when the rate of growth of the elderly population will drop to well under 10 percent. Fertility increased sharply during the baby boom. These cohorts will begin reaching age sixty-five about the year 2010. During that decade the elderly population will increase sharply—perhaps by as much as 30 percent. Because of the baby bust of the 1970s the size of the elderly population will actually be reduced between 2030 and 2040.

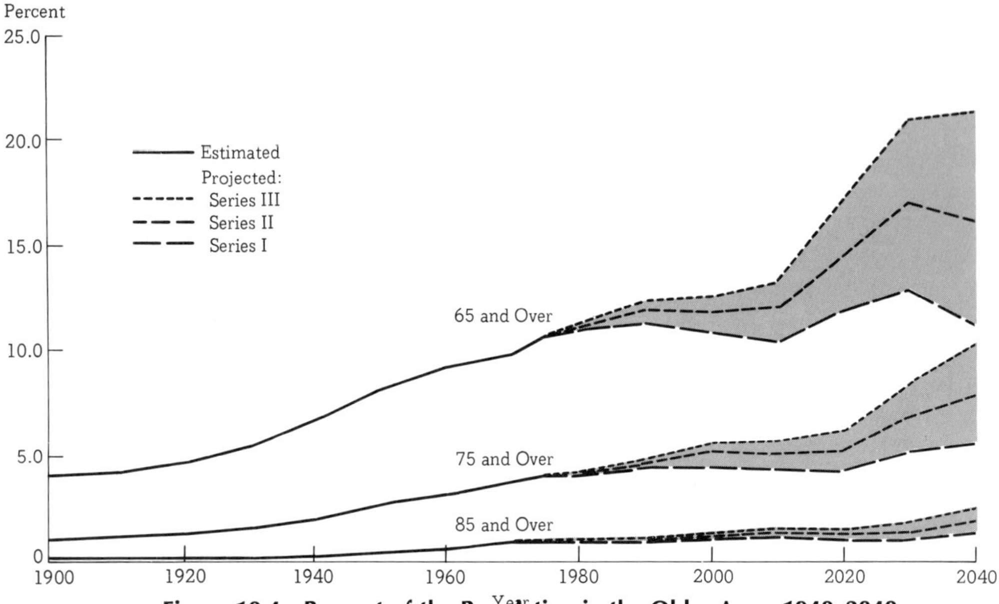

Figure 10.4 Percent of the Population in the Older Ages, 1940–2040
Source: U.S. Bureau of the Census (1976), p. 4.

So far we have been discussing increases in the *number* of older persons. We can project the increases in the numbers of the elderly sixty-five to seventy-five years into the future because these persons have already been born. It is much more difficult to project future *percentages* of the population age sixty-five or older. Those statistics depend on future levels of fertility. In general, higher fertility will mean lower percentages of the elderly, and lower fertility will mean higher percentages. Projections of the percent elderly using three different levels of future fertility are shown in figure 10.4. In all three projections the proportion aged will increase until at least 2020. By the turn of the century the elderly will comprise perhaps about 12 percent of the population and that proportion could climb to between 15 and 20 percent by 2030 if fertility does not increase.

Moreover, within the age group of those over sixty-five there will be growth in the proportion of persons over seventy-five and eighty-five. In other words, the elderly group will itself grow older as the baby boom cohort progresses through the final portion of the life cycle.

Increases in the proportion elderly will require changes in consumption patterns within our society as well as a vast reordering of public priorities. Signs of change are already visible. Youthfulness per se has been deemphasized, and the popular media increasingly refer to the "end of the youth culture." This change will be felt in other ways as well. For example, if we apply current utilization rates to project future use of nursing homes, in the 1980s the number of nursing home residents will increase by about 75 percent—from 1 to 1.73 million (Select Committee on Population 1978, p. 67). Other goods and services used more with advancing age—hospitals, physicians, pharmaceutical products, group housing arrangements, and the like—also will be in increased demand. Not only will total spending on the elderly rise, but *average* spending on elderly persons will go up because of the increasing age and dependency within the aged population.

Changes in public priorities are less visible but perhaps more dramatic. Knowledgeable persons speak of the "graying" of the U.S. budget because of the increased proportion of funds earmarked to serve the elderly. For instance in 1969 programs for the elderly received 19 percent of the federal budget. Nearly a fourth of the federal budget for fiscal year 1981 will go for such programs—an amount larger than requested for any other single category of expenditure, including defense. The demographic data we have discussed above suggest that the needs of the elderly will continue to grow rapidly in the 1980s.

The potential problems associated with the future growth of the aged population naturally lead to a discussion of the social security system. The federally operated system is funded by deductions from the wages of workers and employers; these monies are distributed to beneficiaries of a specified age, sometimes age sixty-two and most often sixty-five. If the number of workers equals the number of beneficiaries, there are no major problems. When the number of workers exceeds the beneficiaries (as will occur in the 1990s), a surplus of funds develops. And when the beneficiaries outnumber the workers who contribute to the system, a deficit emerges.

Currently social security is experiencing financial problems, in part because of the increasing elderly population. (A number of other nondemographic issues are also involved but do not concern us here.) These problems are expected to increase around 2010, when the baby boom generation begins swelling the elderly population. The middle-aged persons who will be working during that decade and paying into the social security pool will be those of the smaller baby bust generation. Thus, fewer economically active people will be paying for the "welfare" of an increased number of elderly. Because of this potential problem, some economists have argued for an increase in fertility to provide for a larger labor force in the next century. But most people agree that this "solution" would create more problems than it would solve.

Politicians have been quarreling for years over the proper funding of the social security system. On December 20, 1977, President Carter signed into law a new funding procedure, which, according to the President, "will guarantee that from 1980 to 2030, the Social Security fund will be saved" (quoted in Jackson 1977, p. 1). This somewhat optimistic statement was based on assumptions about future levels of demographic behavior that may not be valid.

The cost estimates used by President Carter assume that the total fertility rate will increase from the 1977 level of 1.8 to 2.1 by 1984. But if fertility does not increase, there will be fewer workers to pay for social security benefits. Unless the per capita level of benefits is decreased, each worker would have to pay a larger portion of his or her income in order to provide those benefits. If fertility rates continue at their current level, the projected long-term deficit would be twice as high as the President's officially projected deficit (Jackson 1977).

The official projection also assumes that future declines in mortality will be gradual and that the proportion of the population that dies in any given year will decrease by a total of 18 percent over the next seventy-five years. However, if mortality declines by 33 percent, the budget deficit would actually be increased by 42 percent. Thus, President Carter's optimism will be valid only if fertility rises somewhat and if mortality does not fall too rapidly. This is just one example of the extent to which knowledge of demographic processes is vital to the formulation of sound public policy.

Looking only at the elderly population overstates the argument for increased fertility and greatly oversimplifies the issue of dependency. As figure 10.5 shows, the massive growth in the elderly population in the early part of the next century does translate into a rapidly falling ratio of taxpayers (covered workers) to beneficiaries: from five in 1960 to just over two per beneficiary by 2030. But if fertility remains low, the proportion of children will decrease as will expenditures for their welfare. This will compensate for the increase in the elderly population. Rather than concentrate solely on the future proportion age sixty-five or older, economic planners should be looking at the total dependency ratio. Doing so yields a more complete picture.

In chapter 3 we defined the dependent years as fourteen or younger and sixty-five or older. In countries such as the United States, seventeen is a more realistic cutoff age for the young dependents. Because the necessary data are available, we have used age seventeen as the upper limit of the younger dependent age group and sixty-five as the lower limit of older dependents, with those eighteen to sixty-four representing the economically active age groups.

In 1980 there were 62.0 dependents per 100 active persons. If fertility continues at its present low level, by 2000 the dependency ratio will have *dropped* to 53.7. Even in 2020 (when members of the baby boom cohort begin to retire) the total dependency ratio will be only 57.9 per 100. Thus the total dependency load will not increase if fertility remains low. Instead, the number (and percent) of young dependents will decrease. Although the growing elderly population will present problems to society, a major problem after 2020 may well be that of developing the will and commitment necessary to balance our expenditures for the young with those for the aged.

Shifting the emphasis from one age group to another age group is far from simple. In economic, social, and political terms, the two age

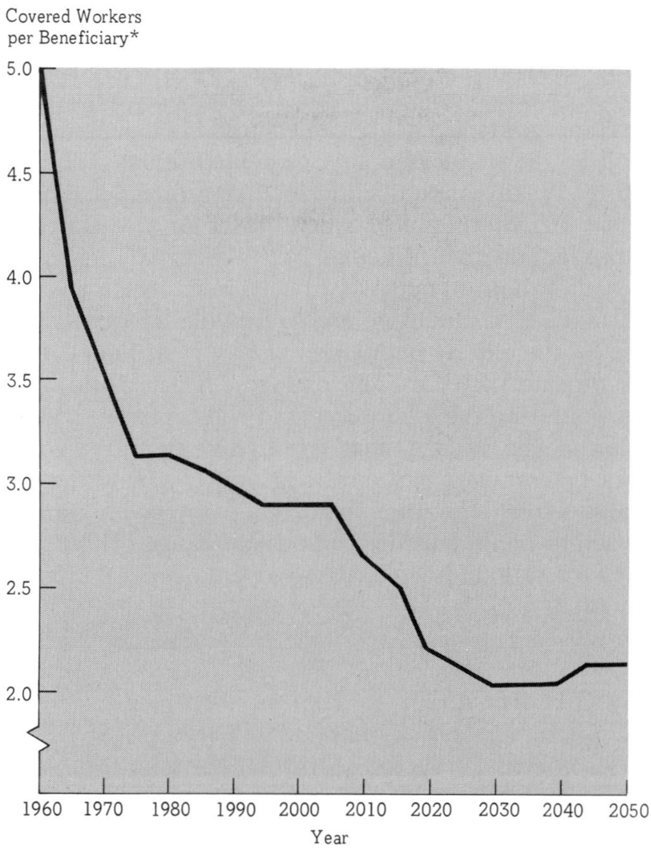

Figure 10.5 Number of Covered Workers per Beneficiary of Old-Age, Survivors', and Disability Insurance Programs, 1960–2050

*Based on Alternative II of 1978 *Trustee's Report:* total fertility rate = 2.1, unemployment rate = 5.0.

Source: Select Committee on Population (1978), p. 73.

groups are by no means equivalent. Still the decreased consumption of the young will considerably offset the increased consumption of the old. In 1976 health expenditures (public and private) totaled $120 billion. Of this, approximately $19 billion was spent on behalf of those under twenty and $35 billion by and for those sixty-five and over (Social Security Administration 1978). Total expenditures in 1976 for education were also $120 billion, of which about $90 billion was for the under-twenty age group (U.S. Bureau of the Census 1978*b*, p. 129). According to economist Alan Sweezy (1978), the total drain on the national product for those two items of consumption was $109 billion by the young and $35 billion by the aged. If, in 1976, we had had the age distribution projected for 2030–2050, these figures would have been $86 and $57 billion, respectively. Thus, the young would have consumed $23 billion less and the elderly $22 billion more of health and educational services.

Political difficulties in suggesting that these two age groups are interchangeable are foreseeable. Institutions are generally adamantly opposed to retrenchment. Managers are not trained in "managing decline." But this will be the situation many social institutions will have to face in the future. Finally, much of the financing for education is state and locally derived, whereas most expenditures for care of the elderly come from the federal government.

Clearly major alterations in our overall economic, social, and political systems will have to occur if we are to provide adequate care and proper shelter for the elderly population of fifty years hence. Fortunately, there is time to plan for such changes. Because the baby boom cohort is now entering the labor force and will continue to swell the ranks of the employed for the next twenty-five to thirty years, there will be no marked increase in the ratio of elderly to working-age population until after 2010. Only then, when the baby boom generation becomes the senior boom and the current baby bust cohort is in the job market, will the ratio of people sixty-five and over rise rapidly, reaching a peak in 2030.

SOME OPTIMISTIC FORECASTS

We have painted a somewhat troubled picture of the next fifty years in the United States. The society will be faced with complex problems that will emanate, at least in part, from erratic demographic behavior in the recent past. But with the recent "discovery" of demography by policy makers, a new awareness of these issues and their causes is emerging. Perhaps we will be able to plan for the predictable changes that will occur in the near future.

The changes in our age composition will have positive as well as negative effects. We have already noted how fortunate those born in the 1970s will be as they go through most of their life cycle. There are other positive effects. Everything else being equal, we can expect a decline in crime in the 1980s. Recent politicians have expressed concern with crime and have campaigned on so-called law and order platforms. Few have pointed out that, to a considerable extent, the high crime rate can be explained by the large proportion of teen-agers in the population, once again the result of the baby boom. Young people are more likely than older persons to commit crimes and be arrested for them. Of every one hundred persons arrested for burglary or auto theft, eighty-five are under age twenty-five. Seventy-seven of every hundred persons arrested for robbery and fifty-eight of every hundred arrested for rape are also under age twenty-five. A young population tends to push up the crime rate. If the birth rate remains low, the population will become older and crime rates should decline in the near future. As Timothy Schellhardt notes, "Crime analysts say that it is demography, the study of population, that provides the key to understanding the improving crime scene" (1977, p. 4).

For similar reasons, we can expect a decline in the rate of traffic accidents, another youth-related problem. Of course, factors such as improvements in driving and auto manufacture and better traffic control are also at work in lowering the rates. But, everything else being equal, as the proportion of teen-agers declines, the incidence of many similar youth-related problems can be expected to fall.

Finally, we can expect a reduction in society's preoccupation with the concerns of youth. There will probably be fewer fads in such areas as dress and popular music, along with a decline in youth-oriented "fast food" operations and what some critics call inane programming on television.

It is too early to determine the accuracy of the many projections posited in this chapter. One thing is certain: every part of American society will be affected by the changes that will occur in the age composition of the population. As we have noted, a built-in momentum exists in population change. The demographic behavior of one decade has repercussions for the entire society for many years in the future. In some respects that is unfortunate, because we can be adversely affected by the demographic behavior of previous cohorts without having had the opportunity to influence such behavior. But the built-in momentum also has some fortunate aspects. If we so desire, we can plan for future changes in the age structure of the population and be ready for them when they occur.

The changes in society that emanate from past as well as present population behavior have led to the "discovery" of demography. The term "demographics," as used by the mass media, has come to mean the impact of changing age and sex composition on various societal phenomena. This new acceptance of demography is vividly illustrated in box 10.2.

Box 10.2 The New "Demographics"

The ebb and flow of human population is endless. New babies delight couples. Deaths leave families in grief. Moves to new jobs stir excitement as well as doubts. Such everyday events are paid scant notice by economic analysts preoccupied with the topical issues of the day—inflation, trade balances, taxes, energy.

Yet the basic population changes of birth, death, and migration underpin many of today's troubling economic and business questions. Social Security taxes increase; can tomorrow's generations bear the burden? Middle

continued

The New "Demographics" (continued)

managers are in short supply; where can new executives be found? The West and South boom; is this the time to move to the Sunbelt?

Demographic considerations permeate today's business climate. Americans are watching less daytime television, perhaps because more women are working outside the home. Insurance companies find coverage purchased by young people declining, and they need to know whether corporate group policies fill the gap. The average age of American shareholders rises five years because housing begins to absorb a higher share of young families' investments. The number of people living alone has risen almost 50 percent in recent years, affecting markets from appliances to autos, from supermarkets to stereos.

Understanding these changes, whose implications vitally affect the future of business, demands the attention of executives these days.

When faced with uncertainties, executives often seek out specialists. They turn to a "new" type of expert—the demographer—to understand population changes and their impact on basic corporate decisions such as labor supply, location of facilities, the changing nature of markets, and the age make-up of consumer groups.

Utilities such as Pacific Gas & Electric and Chesapeake Potomac Telephone utilize demographers to help predict customer demand. Their key is household formations, the number of which is much confused by the late marriages, high divorce rates, and changes in fertility rates. General Motors employs a demographer to design equal employment opportunity policies; the company wants to know where to find minority and female workers. The American Medical Association has a demographer to study mobility of physicians, to identify what prompts doctors to move; are such decisions affected by the number of hospitals, or perhaps by state expenditures for medical care facilities?

Federal agencies spend millions of dollars for demographic studies. State governments call on population experts to help them compete for $35 billion of federal funds allocated on the basis of population. The Defense Department relies on demographic studies to plan its recruitment for the volunteer army. School districts justify school openings, and closings, on the basis of demographic projections.

Politicians can't escape demographic issues either. The Census Bureau recently estimated that 26 seats in Congress could change after the 1980 Census and 16 states could be involved. Florida would gain four seats; New York State would lose four.

The new members will join their colleagues in pondering an array of difficult population-related—thus business-related—issues: teenage pregnancy, illegal immigration, Social Security taxes, the Sunbelt-Frostbelt economic debate, aid to fast-growing underdeveloped countries, abortion, etc.

Source: Quoted from Hyatt (1979).

SUMMARY

Changes in age composition influence many aspects of society. They help determine patterns of consumption and expenditure of public funds.

During the twentieth century three shifts in fertility have influenced the current age composition of the U.S. population and will continue to do so until the middle of the twenty-first century. These shifts are: the lowered fertility of the 1930s; the baby boom between the late 1940s and early 1960s; and the lowered fertility of the 1970s.

Because of declining fertility, the birth cohorts of the 1930s were smaller than preceding cohorts. Persons born in the 1930s are said to belong to the good times cohort because they generally have experienced relative abundance—smaller classes in school, more opportunities to participate in various activities, and less intense competition for suitable jobs—when compared with the earlier, larger cohorts born when fertility was higher.

The baby boom occurred after World War II. Because this produced birth cohorts much larger than those of the 1930s, those born in the baby boom period have experienced relatively adverse circumstances—crowded schools and intense job competition—as they advanced through the various stages of the life cycle.

The baby bust cohort of the 1970s is much smaller and, like the good times cohort, will have a relatively easy time of it—up to a point. As school enrollments decline, pressures on the educational system will ease considerably, and there will no longer be a shortage of teachers and facilities. However, when those born in the baby bust reach their late thirties and early forties, occupational advancement will be slowed because of the backlog of personnel created by the baby boom. From 2010 to 2030 the baby bust cohort will feel the strain of an increased elderly population on the social security system.

Changing age composition also affects the demand for child care services, household formation, and unemployment rates. However, age composition is only one of many factors acting on those phenomena.

Some of the positive effects we can expect from the recent low fertility are less crime, lower traffic accident rates, and less emphasis on fads in the youth culture. Although demography cannot undo what previous decades of demographic behavior have wrought, it does enable us to plan for future changes in the age structure and their effects.

REFERENCES AND SUGGESTED READINGS

Anderson, Joseph. 1978. Population change and the American labor market: 1950–2000. In *Consequences of changing U.S. population: baby boom and bust*, vol. II, *Hearings before the Select Committee on Population,*

Ninety-fifth Congress, pp. 781–804. Washington, D.C.: Government Printing Office.

Carter, Jimmy. 1979. *1980 economic budget,* vol. 3. Washington, D.C.: Government Printing Office.

Harter, Carl L. 1977. The "good times" cohort of the 1930s. *PRB report* 3 (April).

Hofferth, Sandra. 1978. Family structure changes and child care. In *Consequences of changing U.S. population: baby boom and bust,* vol. II, *Hearings before the Select Committee on Population, Ninety-fifth Congress,* pp. 525–556. Washington, D.C.: Government Printing Office.

Hyatt, James C. 1979. Changing demographics and how they affect the future of business. Washington, D.C.: The Center for Strategic and International Studies, Georgetown University.

Jackson, Brooks. 1977. Despite rescue try, system still faces deficit. *Washington star* (December 20):A10.

Norton, Arthur J., and Glick, Paul C. 1979. What's happening to households? *American demographics* 1 (March):19–23.

Pifer, Alan. 1979. Don't forget the children. *American demographics* 1 (September):32–37.

Plotkin, Manuel. 1978. Future size and growth rate of the U.S. population. In *Consequences of changing U.S. population: baby boom and bust,* vol. II, *Hearings before the Select Committee on Population, Ninety-fifth Congress,* pp. 273–286. Washington, D.C.: Government Printing Office.

Population Reference Bureau. 1977. *Social education.* Washington, D.C.: Population Reference Bureau.

Sawhill, Isabel. 1978. Women in the labor market: prospects and policies. In *Consequences of changing U.S. population: baby boom and bust,* vol. II, *Hearings before the Select Committee on Population, Ninety-fifth Congress,* pp. 741–766. Washington, D.C.: Government Printing Office.

Schellhardt, Timothy. 1977. Maturing population will bring a decline in crime, experts say. *Wall Street journal* (October 3):4–5.

Select Committee on Population. 1978. Domestic consequences of United States population change. Washington, D.C.: Government Printing Office.

Social Security Administration. 1978. Age differences in health care spending. *Social security bulletin* (February).

Sweezy, Alan. 1978. The challenge of social security financing. *The national reporter* (June–July):3–7.

Taeuber, Conrad. 1979. A changing America. *American demographics* 1 (January):9–16.

U.S. Bureau of the Census. 1976. Demographic aspects of aging and the older population in the United States. *Current population reports,* series P-23, no. 59. Washington, D.C.: Government Printing Office.

———. 1977. Projections of the population of the United States: 1977 to 2050. *Current population reports,* series P-25, no. 704. Washington, D.C.: Government Printing Office.

———. 1978*a*. Household and family characteristics: March 1977. *Current population reports,* series P-20, no. 326. Washington, D.C.: Government Printing Office.

———. 1978*b*. *Statistical abstract of the United States, 1978.* Washington, D.C.: Government Printing Office.

———. 1979. Projections of the number of households and families: 1979 to 1995. *Current Population reports,* series P-25, no. 805. Washington, D.C.: Government Printing Office.

Part V

Population Policy

All governments influence demographic behavior. Sometimes this is the result of direct population policies, but sometimes the influence is unintentional or indirect. Part V is about those government policies that try to shape demographic behavior. Some of these attempts have been successful; others have not.

Usually, governments influence demographic behavior indirectly. Governments find ways of persuading people to act voluntarily in a "desired" manner. But since demographic behavior is heavily influenced by socioeconomic factors and the constitutional structure, mere propaganda is often insufficient. In certain instances, therefore, governments act directly to either limit or increase fertility, or to force people to move or not to move. Even death, as we will see, is at least indirectly related to various government policies, though we seldom refer to mortality policy in the same sense that we do fertility and migration policy.

The task of formulating population policy is complicated by the fact that frequently there is no consensus on the appropriate level of fertility and migration. For instance, some people believe that world population growth does not constitute a problem and that nothing should be done to limit it. Some people believe that rates of population growth in their own country should be even higher than they are now. Others, of course, believe that rates of population growth should be lower. In the United States, some believe that immigration should be eliminated, while others feel that the nation benefits from immigration.

Our concern in this part is not to make judgments about objectives, but to answer this question: In what ways may a government influence levels of fertility, mortality, and migration? In chapter 11 we will concentrate on government policies as they relate to fertility and mortality—the contributors to natural growth or decline. In chapter 12 we will discuss policies relating to migration, both domestic and international.

11
Policies Relating to Fertility and Mortality

Demographic behavior is of interest to all governments, and some even have a population policy. Hope T. Eldridge, has defined **population policies** as "legislative measures, administrative programs, and other governmental action intended to alter or modify existing population trends in the interest of national survival and welfare" (1968, p. 381). Not all population experts agree, however, on the exact definition of population policy. Here are some of the issues that demographers disagree on:

1. *Does there have to be an explicit statement by the government that a population policy exists?* The United States has no official population policy. Indeed, efforts to formulate one have been resisted strenuously by the legislative and executive branches of the government. Yet the federal government finances and sponsors programs designed to eliminate unwanted childbearing and to make contraception available to certain target populations (primarily the disadvantaged or the poor). These programs have a demonstrable demographic effect of lowering fertility, yet one could also argue that no official government policy exists.

2. *Does there have to be a planned course of action (or program)?* Some persons argue that the absence of specific measures to influence the population is itself a form of population policy. For instance, currently the U.S. birth rate is very low. If no measures are taken to raise the birth rate, some people would argue that the United States (by refusing to intervene) has a population policy favoring low fertility. But others would argue that the government intends no such policy and that some sort of official government action is needed before a policy exists.

3. *Do the goals have to be demographic, or may they be social and economic? And must the demographic effects be intended and direct, or can they be indirect and unintentional?* For ideological purposes China has attempted to increase the status of women, a measure which some believe has also had demographic effects. Does this deliberate attempt to increase the status of women for ideological purposes constitute a population policy on the part of the Chinese government? Consider, too, the situation of several Latin American governments, which have attempted to decrease the incidence of induced abortion in their countries by providing women with contraceptives. Do these countries then have a population policy favoring low fertility?

The point of raising these questions is to show that there are no "correct" answers. Governments may differ in their definition and formulation of population policy, and it is often very difficult to decide whether a specific country has a population policy.

In this chapter we will look at two types of population policies—those intended to affect fertility in order to change the rate of population growth and those intended to affect mortality.

ATTEMPTS TO INFLUENCE FERTILITY LEVELS

It is convenient to distinguish between measures designed to increase fertility and those designed to decrease it. The former are called "pronatalist" and the latter are called "antinatalist."

Pronatalist Policies

Most policies concerned with fertility trends before the twentieth century were pronatalist—that is, they encouraged fertility and population growth. Those policies usually assumed three general forms:

1. Pronatalist propaganda
2. Measures related to the family, such as family allowance programs, tax systems, and rewards to mothers
3. Restrictions on the distribution and use of contraceptives and abortion (United Nations 1973, p. 637; and 1972, pp. 17–48)

Some of the earliest known population policies were those of the Roman emperor Augustus, enacted between 18 B.C. and A.D. 9. Inheritance laws and rules concerning eligibility for office penalized the childless and favored parents. During the medieval period high mortality caused by the plague encouraged the development of pronatalist views and policies. In France tax exemptions and other privileges were used in the latter part of the thirteenth century to encourage immigration and fertility. A Spanish edict in 1623 granted tax exemptions to those who married young and raised large families (Glass 1940, pp. 86–91).

There have also been pronatalist policies in this century. Several of the developing countries believe that a larger population is necessary for economic growth or for settling sparsely populated regions. Brazil, Argentina, and many African nations have pronatalist policies. The objective of the Argentine policy, for example, is to double the size of the present Argentine population to 50 million by the end of this century (Schroeder 1974, p. 13).

Many Marxists and leftist Latin American leaders believe that problems in their countries are social and economic rather than demographic. They believe that if things get bad enough, a social revolution will occur. In their view population growth is a spur for the revolution necessary to achieve social, economic, and political change. They consider the idea that their countries should limit population growth a reactionary plot by the imperialist countries to continue exploiting the natural resources of Latin America.[1]

It is not just the developing nations that have wanted to increase their fertility levels in this century. The movement for population growth reached its peak in Germany, Italy, and Japan during the pe-

[1]This issue is explored in greater detail in J. Mayone Stycos 1971*a*.

riod between World War I and World War II. Intensive pronatalist propaganda, cash payments to families with children, the restriction of access to contraceptives, the regulation of emigration, and the enactment of "eugenic" laws (aimed at encouraging the reproduction of some genetic traits and discouraging others) reflected the attempts of those governments to have larger (and racially "pure") populations. Such measures were adopted because power and prosperity were equated with large numbers of people (Eldridge 1968, p. 382).

A number of other industrialized countries, such as France and Romania, also have adopted pronatalist policies at various times since World War I. Such policies represent a reaction to the low fertility and mortality rates that accompanied modernization in those countries. The nations fear that their national economic and political well-being will decline unless the population continues to increase. Because mortality is already very low and because these governments discourage massive immigration of persons from other countries as politically and culturally undesirable, the only method of increasing rates of population growth is to increase fertility.

Sometimes countries that have a pronatalist policy have also adopted measures with antinatalist effects. France provides such an example. In 1920 France prohibited the distribution of birth control propaganda and devices. In 1932 laws prohibiting induced abortion were tightened. In 1939 the French government adopted a *Code de la Famille,* which incorporated and enlarged existing family welfare and pronatalist measures. Allowances were extended to all economically active persons. Marriage loans, premiums on the birth of a first child, and other forms of aid for parents were provided (Glass 1940). The code was strengthened after 1945, when the birth rate was less than 15 per 1,000 population. In 1967 the distribution of contraceptives was legalized in response to public demand, but the regulation against commercial advertisement remained in effect. In 1969, partly to counteract relaxation of the laws, a revised family allowance scheme was approved which provided more support for large families (United Nations 1973, pp. 640–644; and Eldridge 1968). However, in 1974 a new statute was passed which provided for the distribution of free contraceptives, and another law lifted the prohibition on abortion. These measures were adopted to achieve the social goal of voluntary parenthood, but they illustrate how social policies with antinatalist effects can exist in countries with pronatalist population policies.

It does not appear that pronatalist measures in the industrialized countries have been very effective. In 1979 the French birth rate was still under 15 per 1,000 population. Birth rates in Belgium, Bulgaria, East Germany, and the other industralized countries with pronatalist policies are also quite low. Such policies have not been sufficient to offset the antinatalist aspects of social and economic policies and conditions that prevail. Of course, we cannot know what fertility levels would have been in these countries if there had been no pronatalist policies or if the policies enacted had been of a larger magnitude.

When abortion is the primary method used to prevent births, restricting access to it may cause fertility to increase sharply, at least in the short run. Romanian policy illustrates this. By 1956 the Romanian birth rate had fallen to 24.2 per 1,000 population, primarily due to widespread use of illegal abortion (David and Wright 1971). In 1957 the Romanian government legalized abortion to allow women to decide whether and when to have children and to reduce the incidence of illegal abortion (Mehlan 1965). At the same time the Romanian government did not encourage the use of contraception. Thus, induced abortion became the socially accepted means of birth prevention. The results were pronounced. The crude birth rate declined from 22.9 in 1957 to 14.3 in 1966 (Teitelbaum 1972, p. 405).

The Romanian government then became concerned with that decline in fertility, as well as with growing laxity in the medical practices used to induce abortion. In November 1966 Romania revised its abortion policy. It limited legal abortion to cases involving risk to the mother's life, risk of congenital malformation, evidence of rape, pregnancy of women over forty-five years old, women supporting four or more living children, and a rigorously defined set of physiological conditions. At the time the Romanian government took several additional pronatalist steps:

1. Official importation of oral contraceptives and IUDs was stopped. Some supplies remained available on the black market, and condoms and creams continued to be produced domestically.
2. Taxes on unmarried and married persons over twenty-five years old who were childless were raised by 10 to 20 percent.
3. Taxes on families with three or more children were reduced by 30 percent.
4. Parents of large families could send their children to health resorts free of charge.
5. Mothers of large families were promised early retirement from their jobs.
6. Substantial birth premiums were offered following the birth of every child after the second.
7. Divorces were made extremely difficult to obtain, and the required fees were raised to prohibitive levels.
8. A series of official awards, including such categories as "Mother Heroine," were established to reward mothers of large families (Teitelbaum 1973, pp. 80–81).

Figure 11.1 shows the results of these measures. The birth rate tripled in nine months, from 12.8 per 1,000 in December 1966 to 39.9 in September 1967. Since then it has declined fairly steadily. In 1980 the Romanian birth rate was 20 (Population Reference Bureau 1980).

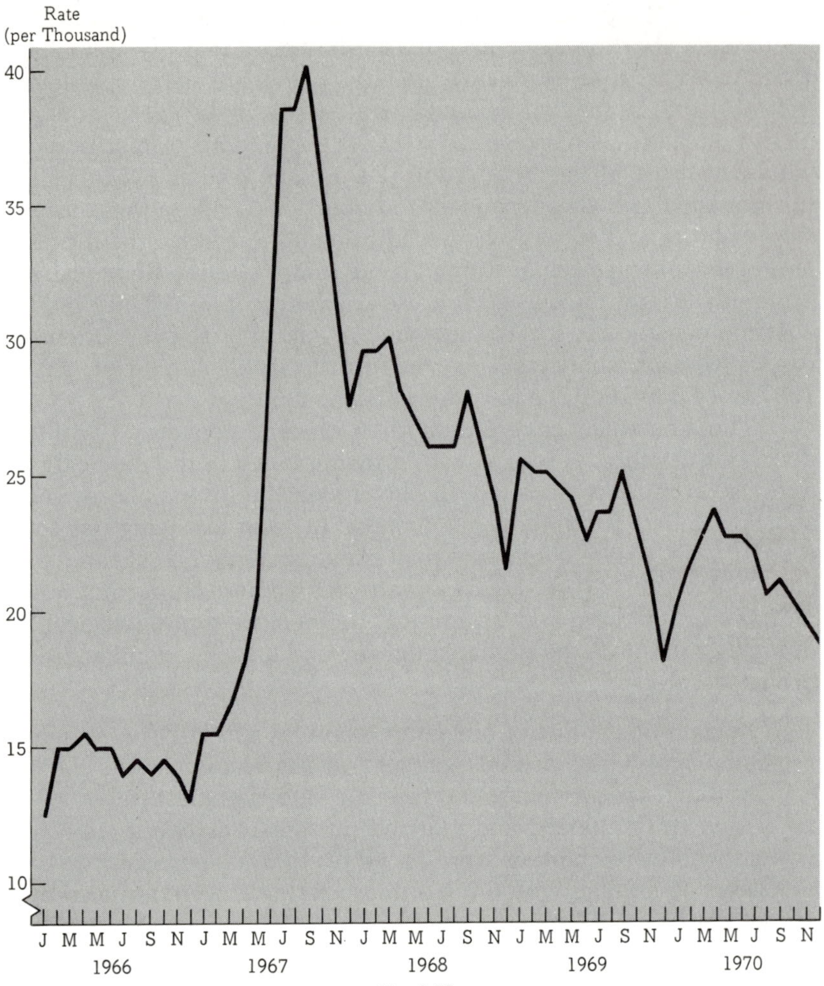

Figure 11.1 Monthly Birth Rates in Romania, 1966–1970
Source: David and Wright (1971), p. 207.

Apparently that decline occurred because of a strong preference for small families. But it took a little time for Romanian couples to make the sudden transition from primary reliance on legal abortion to other methods of birth prevention, including use of withdrawal, condoms, illegally imported contraceptives, and illegal abortion (David and Wright 1971). In that interval the birth rate had increased dramatically.

The Romanian experience indicates that in those situations in which one method is the primary means to prevent birth, severely restricting access to that method can result in higher fertility levels in the short run. Bernard Berelson (1979) concludes that the increase in

Romanian fertility following the 1966 decree may turn out to be almost as large, relatively, as the U.S. baby boom.

The long-run effect is less clear. Currently the Romanian birth rate is considerably higher than it was before the use of legal abortion was restricted. If the Romanian fertility level does not decline further, that will suggest that governments can increase fertility by adopting a number of pronatalist measures.

On the other hand, the decline in the birth rate since 1967 is very suggestive. Jean van der Tak uses it, along with the experience of other countries which have tried to restrict access to abortion, to conclude that "official restriction of legal abortion has only a temporary effect on birth rates where a small-family ideal is entrenched" (1974, p. 45). Henry David and Nicholas Wright (1971, p. 210) interpret the decline in the Romanian birth rate since 1967 as evidence that the traditional Romanian preference for a small family was not affected by the shift in legislation. They also conclude that, in the absence of a fundamental change in motivation for limiting family size and engaging in family planning, legal restrictions on abortion, coupled with more benevolent pronatalist welfare provisions, are unlikely to result in more than a short-term increase in the birth rate. If the Romanian birth rate continues to decline, their conclusions will be proven correct.

Antinatalist Policies

Antinatalist policies are aimed at reducing fertility. The two basic approaches are government-sponsored family planning programs and various non–family planning approaches.

National Family Planning Programs

Family planning programs aim at reducing fertility by providing contraceptive supplies, services, and information. The rationale is that the number of couples who want to limit their family size is sufficiently large that the birth rate will fall to acceptable levels within a reasonable period of time. As Donald Bogue states, "The family planning programs now underway . . . place great emphasis upon the 'knowledge and service' theory: If you inform people about the methods and give them good service, a significant number will accept" (1966, p. 727).

An appealing feature of this approach is its voluntary nature. Discussions of family planning programs focus on the right of parents to decide the number and spacing of their births. The emphasis is on voluntary parenthood and avoiding unwanted births. Changes in attitudes, values, and desired family size are not considered necessary in these programs. Rather, high fertility is viewed as a social malady that will disappear if enough contraceptive supplies, services, and information are made available to all segments of the population.

In addition to its voluntary nature, family planning is likely to be acceptable politically because it can be perceived (and marketed) as a health measure, has demonstrable humanitarian benefits, and promotes personal freedom by helping couples to have the number of children they desire. Moreover, it is a gradual effort and can be implemented relatively inexpensively (Berelson 1969).

It is true that the incidence of unwanted childbearing is high. Its elimination alone would cause substantial reductions in the birth rate, even in countries with sophisticated contraceptive technology, such as the United States. In 1972 in the United States there were about 234,000 legitimate births classified as unwanted by the mother (i.e., the pregnancy was not desired at that particular time). If these births had not occurred, the amount of population growth in the United States in that year would have been 14.5 percent lower than it actually was. If unwanted illegitimate births are counted, elimination of unwanted births would have had an even greater effect on population growth (Weller 1976; Bumpass and Westoff 1970).

Data collected in various countries in the mid-1970s show that in many developing countries a substantial proportion of fecund, married women want no more children. Moreover, many others did not want their last child or their current pregnancy (see table 11.1). Yet in each of those countries a large percentage of those women who want no more children are not using a modern method of birth prevention.

Table 11.1 Percentage of Currently Married Fecund Women Who Want No More Children or Who Did Not Want Their Last Child or Current Pregnancy

	WANTING NO MORE CHILDREN	NOT WANTING LAST CHILD OR CURRENT PREGNANCY
Asia and Pacific		
Bangladesh	61%*	NA
Fiji	50	27.7%
Indonesia	39	16.8†
Korea, Republic of	72	36.7
Malaysia	43	NA
Nepal	30	NA
Pakistan	49	NA
Sri Lanka	61	33.9
Thailand	57	NA
Latin America		
Colombia	61	42.0
Costa Rica	52	28.3
Dominican Republic	45	NA
Mexico	57	NA
Panama	63	33.3
Peru	61	46.1

*Some women were asked, "Do you want another child soon?"

† Ever-married women as base.

Source: Kendall (1979), p. 83.

Presumably, the provision of contraceptive services, supplies, and knowledge would facilitate lower fertility there.

On the other hand, the family planning approach has certain features which limit its potential to lower fertility. Most family planning programs concentrate on only one of the mechanisms that can affect family size—the use of contraception. Because of people's cultural or religious objections those programs often do not utilize all available means of contraception. This lowers acceptance rates and reduces the demographic effectiveness of the programs (Potter 1971). The fact that such programs frequently do not include unmarried persons further reduces their demographic impact.

In addition, some demographers have questioned the validity of responses to questions on desired family size in the developing countries (Hauser 1967; and Marino 1971). Some believe the responses are too low; others question the intensity of the responses. For instance, Ronald Ridker suggests that "if properly interpreted, evidence from attitude surveys suggests that desired family size is not much below actual family size" (1969, p. 281). The real question is whether there is sufficient motivation to endure the inconveniences and costs involved in attempting to limit family size. Finally, Riad Tabbarah (1964, p. 191) has shown that in many African countries the desired family size is higher than the number of children the average woman is physiologically capable of bearing. Under those conditions, the provision of family planning services would have little impact on the birth rate.

A government's fertility target may be lower than the family size desires of its population. For instance, under the mortality conditions usually present in developing countries, an average completed family size of 3.5 children would result in an annual growth of 1.2 percent. An average completed family size of 5.0 children would produce an annual growth rate of 2.4 percent. Thus some levels of desired fertility, even if realized, are not compatible with the attainment of reduced population targets (Weller 1973). Kingsley Davis maintains that "there is no reason to expect that millions of decisions about family size made by couples in their own interest will automatically control population for the benefit of society" (1967, p. 732).

Non–Family Planning Approaches

The shortcomings of the family planning approach to lowering fertility have led an increasing number of demographers to conclude that approaches that do not depend on family planning may also be necessary. Non–family planning approaches attempt to influence fertility by *motivating* people to desire—and have—fewer children.

Perhaps the biggest difference between family planning and non–family planning approaches is the treatment accorded to "desired family size." The family planning approach seems to view fertility as a "disease" that can be controlled by massive treatments with the proper vaccine (contraceptive). It ignores the possibility that desired family size may have to be altered, and it calls for minimal changes in the institutional structure of the society (perhaps one of its more attractive features to members of the government and/or the ruling class).

By contrast, a non–family planning approach to lowering fertility recognizes that family size may simply be a response to the way a person perceives the sociocultural world (Carlsson 1966; Chaplin 1971; and Salaff 1972). Judith Blake has written that "population replacement would not occur at all were it not for the complex social organization and system of incentives that encourage mating, pregnancy, and the care, support, and rearing of children" (1969, p. 528). Thus, the non–family planning approach emphasizes the importance of altering desired family size and attempts to accomplish this through changes in the institutional alignment and sociocultural environment of the population. In what follows we will focus on only a few of the many non–family planning methods frequently proposed and discuss their feasibility and demographic effectiveness.

Modernization

Perhaps the most reliable non–family planning method of reducing family size is societal modernization. Some scholars have taken the stance that modernization is a necessary condition for long-term declines in family size (Ovsienko 1966; Goldscheider 1971, p. 153; and Nortman 1972). At the same time, societal modernization may not be a sufficient condition for reductions in family size. A case in point is Mexico. By 1970 per capita energy consumption (an indicator of modernization) had increased to a level that was 4.1 times as great as the 1929 level, yet the crude birth rate declined by only 12.6 percent during that interval (Coale 1978).

The long-term effect of modernization may be declining family size, but the short-term effect may actually *increase* family size. As modernization occurs, better health conditions increase the probability that a woman will conceive and retain the fetus to term. Lowered mortality, which accompanies modernization, raises the proportion of persons who survive to the age of reproduction and reduces the probability of widowhood during the reproductive years (Davis 1967, p. 734; Bourgeois-Pichat 1967; and Bondestam 1972, pp. 43–48).

Because of the short-term effect modernization alone should not be depended on to lower family size. Indeed, one could scarcely recommend "modernization" to a nation as a means of reducing the birth rate. Most countries that are attempting to reduce rates of population growth are doing so in the belief that this will increase the rate of modernization.

In fact, there is a growing consensus emerging that argues for family planning and modernization being accomplished *together.* Reduced population growth does not necessarily lead to modernization; increased modernization does not automatically result in declining fertility. If a better way of life is desired, attempts to lower fertility and to encourage modernization should be combined.

Payments for not having children

One frequently recommended measure for reducing fertility involves payments to married couples for periods of time during which pregnancy and/or birth does not occur (Berelson 1969, p. 2). A large drawback to this approach is the substantial amount of money it requires. For instance, Marshall Balfour (1962) proposed providing national savings certificates to married women in their reproductive years who do not become pregnant for three or more years. Those payments were to be at the rate of $3 to $5 per year. Although this sum is too low to influence the reproductive behavior of many people, it would cost about $200 per year for each 1,000 inhabitants. A country with a population of 100 million would have to make annual payments of $20 million.

Of course, this cost is offset by the savings that result from each prevented birth (Enke 1966). The need for initial capital outlay could be reduced by deferring payments for four to five years. Moreover, most of the money subsequently would be recirculated in the economy, so that its effect would be similar to a redistribution of income. Morally, this approach seems preferable to one that features "disincentives." The latter involve financial penalties for giving birth or for having a family that is larger than the government desires.

The government of Singapore, which wants to attain zero population growth, enacted a series of disincentives in the late 1970s. Families with three or more children are subject to higher delivery fees in public hospitals, have a restricted choice of primary schools, do not get priority in public housing, lose certain maternity leave benefits, and give up income tax exemptions. The program has been combined with a comprehensive contraceptive program, an intensive propaganda campaign, and liberal abortion and sterilization services. Apparently that approach, which combines disincentives with a family planning program, has been relatively effective in reducing the number of couples having more than two children (Wong and Salaff 1977). By 1980 Singapore's total fertility rate was down to 1.9. As noted in box 11.1, China has tried a similar approach.

The reason that incentives are morally preferable to disincentives is that incentives for not having children can be used to improve the social and economic situation of the couple as well as any children that may already exist. Disincentives punish offspring and parents.

Increased female labor force participation

As we saw in chapter 5, research indicates that women who participate in the labor force in industrialized settings have fewer children than women who do not participate in the labor force. A number of studies

(text continues on page 292)

Box 11.1 Chinese Population Policy

The world's most populous country now has the world's most active program to reduce fertility. With a population rapidly approaching 1 billion, China is presently using every means possible to lower its birth rate to attain zero population growth before the turn of the century.

Since the present government came to power in 1949, the population restriction movement has had its ups and downs. On the one hand, China was determined to remain purely Marxist in all its policies, which meant that population growth could not be seen as being a negative factor in development. On the other hand, some realistic leaders were aware that China's awesome population size could not be allowed to grow indefinitely.

In 1949 Chairman Mao Tse-tung insisted that population growth presented no problem whatsoever, but by 1957 Mao advocated instant zero population growth (ZPG): "Steps must therefore be taken to keep our population for a long time at a stable level, say, of 600,000,000" (quoted in Tien 1963, p. 276). Mao was obviously not as astute demographically as he was politically. Instant ZPG, especially when the birth rate is relatively high, is an impossibility without massive increases in mortality.

Nevertheless, Mao's 1957 position led to the first birth control movement in China. When it was first launched, the obstacles were literally insurmountable. As a subcommittee of the U.S. House of Representatives noted, "The rural, largely illiterate population steeped in Confucian tradition that glorifies the big family ideal was not yet prepared even to listen to birth control propaganda—much less practice it; the urban population of some 80 to 90 million was only slightly more prepared to accept family planning practices" (Subcommittee on Planning 1979, p. 13).

The campaign peaked in 1957 with little evidence of success. The effort was abandoned during the Great Leap Forward from 1958 to 1960. For three years discussion of family planning disappeared from China's media until another campaign was launched in early 1962, only to be swallowed up by the Cultural Revolution in 1966 (Subcommittee 1979, p. 12). Both movements, the Great Leap Forward and the Cultural Revolution, advocated a return to pure Marxist ideology, which frowned on family planning.

While opposing ideologies were being debated, the population increased by perhaps 300 million. In 1969 the Chinese instituted a major birth control program that still continues to gain momentum. This campaign is not as likely to be affected by political and leadership changes as were the earlier campaigns. As might be expected, when the forces advocating massive family limitation programs finally succeeded on an apparently permanent basis, the pressure to go all out was overwhelming. As a result, today's policies regarding fertility reduction are perhaps the most extreme anywhere in the world, with the possible exception of those of Singapore.

According to recent reports, China's goal is to urge married couples to have *one* child, with two children being barely tolerated. Beginning in March 1980 salaries of families having had a third child were reduced by

continued

Chinese Population Policy (continued)

10 percent until the child reaches fourteen. The child is also denied free education and medical care. Housing priority is given to those with two or fewer children. Indeed couples with one child are given apartments for four-member families. Those who have no children at all are rewarded when they retire.

How does the Chinese government attempt to assure the success of such a rigid policy? Aside from the obvious social and economic advantages from lower taxes and better housing and schooling, peer pressure is also exerted. Each commune determines how many children will be born in any given year and all the women attend lectures on family planning. Other commune members see to it that they comply with the commune's goals. Women who become pregnant for the third time are urged to get an abortion, and most of them do. It is considered unpatriotic to become pregnant for a third time.

Pressure from the government and from peers does not guarantee a successful program. Birth limitation methods must be available at a reasonable price. In China, that is clearly the situation. Abortions are readily available throughout the country at no cost. During the 1970s there was an increase in the number of sterilizations—primarily for women over thirty-five. Without reliable statistics, it is difficult to determine which contraceptive method is most popular among the Chinese—the IUD or the pill. Both are used extensively.

Chinese scientists are working on new birth control techniques. They have developed the paper pill, or stamp contraceptive (edible sheets of paper with perforations like miniature postage stamps—22 to a sheet). More recently, the once-a-month pill has been introduced. The so-called vacation pill is another Chinese innovation. When Chinese laborers return to their sometimes distant homes for vacations, women can take the pill immediately after intercourse and again the next morning. This procedure is repeated throughout the brief vacation.

The combined contributions of government regulations, peer pressure, and the free availability of a wide range of innovative contraceptives are apparently having some success. Unfortunately, statistics emanating from China are few, and when they do exist are far from reliable. Crude birth rate estimates by Western experts on China range from 12 to 30. According to Deputy Prime Minister Chen Muhua, in 1978 the birth rate was 20 and the death rate was 8—resulting in a growth rate of 1.2 percent. On June 18, 1979, Premier Hau Kuo Feng declared to the National People's Congress that the government now aims for a natural increase rate of 1 percent in 1979, 0.5 percent by 1985, and zero growth by 2000 (Muhua 1979).

These goals are ambitious, to say the least, and the declines in fertility needed to attain such goals are unheard of in human history. On the other hand, no government has ever launched such a massive population limitation program and with such authority as China is presently undertaking.

depict a negative correlation between an area's rate of female labor force participation and its fertility rate. So perhaps one method of lowering fertility, particularly in the developing countries, would be to increase the rates of female labor force participation.

This idea has humanitarian appeal because it is consistent with the concept of sexual equality. And it offers the additional advantage of maximizing economic production and increasing family income, which would also enlarge the market for consumer goods and services.

But there are several reasons that this method may not be an effective means of reducing family size, particularly in the developing countries. One reason is economic: some of the developing economies are already characterized by high rates of male unemployment and underemployment.

The effectiveness of this measure is also questionable from a demographic point of view. Research conducted in developing countries has generally revealed that the association between female labor force participation and low fertility is either absent or perceptibly weaker than it is in industrialized settings. The woman who has a job in an urban industrialized area, is salaried, and works in a white-collar position is more likely to be willing to forgo or postpone parenthood than a woman who works in a rural area, is self-employed or unpaid, and works at menial tasks. Women's employment and fertility tend to be negatively related only when the women are engaged in the modern sector of the labor force, such as a factory. Such jobs are not available to many women in developing countries, especially in the nonmetropolitan areas (Weller 1977, p. 498). The social and economic context of employment in the developing countries favors parenthood over work.

Population education

Another measure frequently discussed in the context of non–family planning methods of reducing fertility is population education—essentially what you are studying now. Stephen Viederman offers a fairly broad definition of population education as "the process by which the student investigates the nature and meaning of population processes, population characteristics, the causes of population change, and the consequences of these processes, characteristics, and changes for himself, his family, his society, and his world" (1972, p. 337).

Presumably, if people knew the advantages of having smaller families and the disadvantages of having larger families, they would have fewer children. A great deal of demographic behavior is the result of socialization; that is, we learn attitudes about desirable family size from parents and teachers when we are children. By reaching the young and influencing motivation early, it might be possible to alter desired family size (Gustavus and Nam 1970). The vehicle for delivering a program of population education—the educational system—already exists.

But there are several problems with this approach. Most basic is a lack of consensus among population educators concerning the basic educational approach. The alternatives include sex education, education for family living, population awareness, and basic value orientation (Simmons 1970). Research is needed to determine which would be most effective under a particular set of circumstances.

The issue of whether population education should be one-sided or multisided in its approach to fertility behavior has yet to be resolved satisfactorily. Will the most effective program be one that is a propagandistic "Stop at two!" Or will it be one in which the advantages as well as the disadvantages of various sizes of families are explained to the student? Byron Massialas (1972, p. 353) observes that the idea of population control is antithetical to the proper role of the classroom teacher. It implies indoctrination of children and youth concerning the idea of limiting population size without allowing them to inquire into meaningful alternatives.

Another potential disadvantage of population education is the time lag involved. It does not allow society to adjust its demographic behavior promptly to changing conditions. In addition, there is the problem of reaching persons who are not regularly exposed to the school system, especially in the developing countries.

A more basic problem is that personal and societal goals do not necessarily overlap. If they did, then perhaps the entire issue of non–family planning approaches to reducing fertility would be meaningless. As Edward Pohlman and K. Seshagiri Rao state:

> A mass of research shows that people will not plan individual family size for [the] national good. . . . Population education, as we have defined it, includes also the meaning of larger or smaller families, and later or earlier marriages, to the *individual.* "If you marry too soon, these are the things that will happen to *you!*" "If you have too many children, here are the effects on *you!*" (1968).

But a great deal more basic research is needed that examines the relationship between family size and the social, mental, and economic well-being of individuals and families.

Some Generalizations

In most settings some reduction in family size can be achieved by providing birth prevention knowledge and services to the population. The provision of such family planning services also reduces the incidence of unwanted births, which are associated with social, economic, and psychological difficulties. Thus, a family planning approach to lowering fertility has both humanitarian and demographic effects, although the demographic effect is limited. If fertility needs to be reduced to even lower levels, the family planning approach must be supplemented by a non–family planning approach. The non–family planning approach would contribute to a reduction in the family size desired by the members of the population, and the family planning approach would provide the population with the means by which a smaller family size could be realized.

Some major gaps exist in our knowledge concerning the various non–family planning approaches to reducing fertility. Each approach apparently has disadvantages as well as advantages. Non–family planning measures should be tried on a provisional basis, with as much experimentation and research built into the programs as possible. Their effectiveness must be constantly assessed, in the realization that those particular methods may not be as effective as hoped. Governments would perhaps be wise to introduce several measures instead of relying on only one approach. Non–family planning approaches should be viewed as complementary to one another as well as to family planning programs.

ATTEMPTS TO INFLUENCE MORTALITY

Governments do not have explicit mortality policies in the same sense that they may have fertility or migration policies. The reduction of mortality is the goal of all governments, including those that wish to reduce their rate of population growth. It is frequently argued that measures which reduce mortality are in fact health policies, whose purpose is to improve the health of the population rather than to affect the rate of population growth or its geographic distribution (Eldridge 1968, pp. 383–384). But this would seem to be a narrow view of what constitutes population policy.

As we argued earlier, measures taken by governments can be viewed as population policies as long as they have a demographic effect. For example, the governments of most industrialized countries subsidize medical care; often medical clinics provide free care to the public. Although it can be said that these are examples of health policy, their overall effect is to increase life expectancy. Thus, it can be argued that mortality-related policies do exist. In what follows we will look at measures that affect mortality by causing it either to increase or to decrease.

Measures That Lower Mortality

The most attention-getting policies directly related to mortality are those supporting the development of medical knowledge with the potential to expand the life span—as, for example, through the development of new wonder drugs or organ transplants. Although some medical advances, such as heart and kidney transplants, have not had a significant impact on the mortality level of the entire society because few people can afford them, many scientists are convinced that life expectancy will increase significantly in the next thirty years as a result of such medical advances, which would not be possible without direct subsidization by the government.

Governmental policies aimed at reducing the incidence of specific diseases are clearly related to mortality. In 1971 then-President Richard Nixon declared a "War on Cancer," and millions of dollars have been spent for this purpose since then. We even have a federally financed National Cancer Institute, which sponsors research on new cures and treatments for cancer.

Thousands of lives are saved each year as a result of government regulations that require installation of safety features such as seat belts in new automobiles. The fifty-five-mile-per-hour speed limit was originally suggested by the federal government as a fuel conservation measure, but the argument for maintaining it has been that the lowered speed saves lives.

For instance, a report by the U.S. Department of Transportation in 1979 attributed an increase in traffic deaths during the preceding year to speeding, especially in the West, where many have ignored the lowered speed limit (Kramer 1979). The report noted that a total of 50,178 highway deaths were enumerated in 1978, the worst year since 1973, when more than 54,000 people died in highway crashes. The number of deaths dropped to 45,500 in 1975, at least partially because of the fifty-five-mile speed limit. The report also noted that only 8.4 percent of the people involved in serious automobile accidents were using their seat belts—a rate 40 percent lower than in the general population of drivers and passengers. Thus, it is clear that government policies regarding the speed limit and seat belts have affected the level of mortality caused by traffic accidents, regardless of their original intent.

Direct measures to lower infant mortality are occasionally put into law or advocated by various governments. Increasingly, low-cost clinics have made prenatal care available for pregnant women, and more attention is being directed to nutritional standards to reduce the proportion of low-weight infants. Information is made available to young couples concerning proper preparations for parenthood. Indeed, the U.S. government's pamphlet "Your Baby's Health" is by far the most popular of all government publications. Efforts are also being made at local levels to educate the public and thus reduce infant mortality (see box 11.2).

Perhaps the most publicized health policy that affects mortality relates to cigarette smoking. For over a decade the National Institutes for Health have been citing studies which show a strong positive relationship between cigarette smoking and the risk of lung cancer and certain cardiovascular diseases. For instance, the death rates for all causes combined among men thirty-five to forty-four years of age are twice as high for smokers as for men who have never smoked. Similar differences have been noted between smoking and nonsmoking older men and among women (Godley and Kruegel 1975). The World

Health Organization has also spoken out on the issue, concluding that "smoking-related diseases are such important causes of disability and premature death in developed countries that the control of cigarette smoking could do more to improve health and prolong life in these countries than any other single action in the whole field of preventive medicine" (1975, p. 12).

When he was Secretary of Health, Education, and Welfare, Joseph Califano spoke out forcefully on the issue of smoking and even went so far as to attempt to ban smoking in public buildings. Whether his propaganda campaign was effective in reducing smoking is difficult to determine, but the proportion of persons who smoke has declined substantially since the 1960s among adult males, although not among females.

The recent decline in deaths attributed to cardiovascular causes reflects, in part, the federally encouraged fitness and dietary programs originated in the Kennedy administration during the 1960s. Again the intent was not directly to save lives but to improve health. The end result has been a drop in coronary heart diseases. A recent government report concluded that "among the cardiovascular disease risk factors that may have declined in the U.S. population are two of the

Box 11.2 Infant Mortality in the District of Columbia

A specific example of governmental policy aimed directly at reducing infant mortality comes from the District of Columbia, which has traditionally had higher rates of infant mortality than the rest of the nation. Shortly after taking office in 1979, the mayor, Marion Barry, issued an order to the District's Department of Human Resources to devise a plan within ten days to reduce the District's infant mortality rate. On January 11, 1979, Mayor Barry stated:

> We must and we will regain our social conscience and consciousness in this city . . . and mount a Herculean effort to reduce this atrocious infant mortality rate. . . . We will be in the process of working to meet our objective of significantly lowering the District's infant mortality and bring it at least into line with that of the rest of the nation (1970).

On February 5, 1979, Mayor Barry released a comprehensive plan to reduce infant mortality in the District of Columbia. The plan contains sections on the following subjects: preventive health care and education; nutritional services; nursing services; prenatal care; neonatal care; and follow-up care of infants.

On May 7, 1980, Mayor Barry announced that the District of Columbia's infant mortality rate had dropped 16 percent in 1979 to the lowest level since the city began keeping records in 1912 (21.6 per 1,000 live births). Much of the improvement in infant mortality statistics was credited to greater attention by public and private hospitals to the problems referred to one year earlier by the mayor.

Table 11.2 Cases of Selected Diseases Before and After General Availability of Immunization in the United States, Selected Years, 1940–1976

	DISEASE						
YEAR	Rubella	Measles	Diphtheria	Tetanus	Pertussis	Polio	Mumps
1940	—	291,162	15,536	—	183,866	9,804	—
1945	—	146,013	18,675*	560*†	133,792*	13,624	—
1950	—	319,124	5,796	486	120,718	33,300	—
1955	—	555,156	1,984	462	62,786	28,985*	—
1960	—	441,703	918	368	14,809	3,190	—
1961	—	423,919	617	379	11,468	1,312	—
1962	—	481,530	444	322	17,749	910	—
1963	—	385,156*	314	325	17,135	449	—
1964	—	458,083	293	289	13,005	122	—
1965	—	261,904	164	300	6,799	72	—
1966	46,975	204,136	209	235	7,717	113	—
1967	46,888	62,705	219	263	9,718	41	—
1968	49,371	22,231	260	178	4,810	53	152,209*
1969	57,686*	25,826	241	185	3,285	20	90,918
1970	56,552	47,351	435	148	4,249	33	104,953
1971	45,086	75,290	215	116	3,036	21	124,939
1972	25,507	32,275	152	128	3,287	31	74,215
1973	27,804	26,690	228	101	1,759	8	69,612
1974	11,917	22,094	272	101	2,402	7	59,128
1975	16,652	24,374	307	102	1,738	8	59,647
1976	12,491	41,126	128	75	1,010	14	38,492

*Indicates year in which immunization became generally available.

†1947 was the first year tetanus was reported nationally; immunization became generally available in 1945.

Source: National Center for Health Statistics (1978), p. 249.

more important ones—uncontrolled hypertension and cigarette smoking among some age-sex groups—and two still relatively controversial ones—dietary consumption of saturated fats and physical activity" (National Center for Health Statistics 1978, p. 31).

The immunization of children against certain diseases has long been accepted practice in most countries. In some cases vaccines are available at little or no cost to the parents; in some areas vaccination is mandated by law. It is generally agreed that immunization against childhood diseases is one of the most successful forms of preventive medicine. Even so, about 40 percent of U.S. children age one to four remain unprotected against measles, rubella, diphtheria, tetanus, pertussis (whooping cough), and polio (Center for Disease Control 1977). Overall, however, the picture is bright. The tremendous impact of immunization can be seen in table 11.2. For example, the incidence of diphtheria fell from 18,675 cases in 1945 (when immunization became generally available) to 128 cases in 1976. Similarly, polio cases fell from 33,300 in 1950 to 14 in 1976.

Most governments are committed to improving the health of the

Table 11.3 Distribution of Personal Health Care Expenditures by Sources of Payment in the United States, Selected Years, 1929–1977

FISCAL YEAR	ALL PERSONAL HEALTH CARE EXPENDITURES (IN MILLIONS) OF DOLLARS)*	SOURCE OF PAYMENT						
		Direct Payment	Third-party Payment					
			Total¶	Private Health Insurance	Philanthropy and Industry	Government		
						Total	Federal	State and Local
Fiscal year ending June 30								
1929	$ 3,165	88.5%	11.5%	—	2.6%	8.9%	2.7%	6.2%
1935	2,585	82.6	17.5	—	2.7	14.8	3.4	11.3
1940	3,414	82.0	18.0	—	2.7	15.3	3.9	11.4
1950	10,400	68.3	31.7	8.5%	3.0	20.2	9.4	10.8
1960	22,729	55.3	44.7	20.7	2.3	21.7	9.2	12.4
1970	60,113	40.4	59.7	24.0	1.5	34.2	22.3	11.9
1971	67,228	39.1	60.9	24.9	1.4	34.6	22.9	11.6
1972	74,828	37.6	62.4	24.9	1.4	36.1	24.2	11.9
1973	82,490	36.8	63.2	25.4	1.4	36.4	24.5	12.0
1974	91,315	36.1	63.9	25.2	1.3	37.3	25.2	12.1
1975†	107,383	31.2	68.8	26.2	2.2	40.5	27.7	12.8
1976†‡	122,453	31.4	68.6	26.2	2.1	40.2	27.6	12.4
Fiscal year ending Sept. 30								
1975	110,665	31.4	68.6	25.8	2.2	40.7	27.4	13.3
1976	126,217	31.2	68.8	26.6	2.1	40.0	27.7	12.3
1977‡§	142,586	30.3	69.7	27.6	2.0	40.1	27.9	12.2

*Includes all expenditures for health services and supplies other than (1) expenses for payment and administration, (2) government public health activities, and (3) expenditures on fund raising by philanthropies.

†Revised estimates.

‡Federal fiscal year.

§Preliminary estimates.

¶Some columns do not add to totals because of rounding.

Source: National Center for Health Statistics (1978), p. 387.

population. In turn, this contributes to increased longevity and reduced mortality. Despite the failure to enact a national health insurance plan, such a commitment is apparent in the United States. As you can see from table 11.3, expenditures for personal health care increased from $3 million in 1929 to $122 million in 1976. In that time there has been a change in the source of payments. In 1929, 88.5 percent came directly from the individual person or family. By 1976 only 31.4 percent of the payments were direct. The government's share increased from 8.9 percent in 1929 to about 40 percent in 1976.

Measures That Increase Mortality

If we accept the fact that government measures or policies contribute to declining mortality, we must also accept the fact that some governmental policies can contribute to increasing mortality as well. Measures that endanger health, although unintentionally, can eventually raise mortality. Just as there are policies that decrease mortality, there are also policies raising mortality.

International warfare is the most obvious mortality-related governmental policy. Millions of human beings have been killed as a result of humans making war on each other. More than 50 million people died during World War II alone.

Governmental policies are sometimes deliberately aimed at increasing mortality. Genocide, as practiced in Nazi Germany, is the most tragic example of such a policy. Over 6 million Jews were put to death in a deliberate attempt to eliminate an entire ethnic group from the face of the earth.

Today as well we have several examples of government policies that contribute to increased mortality. Even while the secretary of Health, Education, and Welfare spoke out against smoking, his own government continued (and continues) to subsidize tobacco growers and benefit from cigarette tax revenues to the extent of $6 billion per year. The government continues to allow cigarette advertising in all media but broadcasting. Furthermore, decisions to smoke are not simply matters of individual choice. As the National Center for Health Statistics has reported:

> They take place in the context of a society that has glamorized such behavior through advertising and more subtle means and that continues to support industries producing unhealthful products, enacts or enforces laws against certain behaviors unevenly, has provided ambiguous messages about the kinds of behavior that are acceptable, and perhaps, more important, has not acted to ameliorate some of the socioeconomic and other stressful conditions that foster unhealthful decisions (1978, p. 36).

There is now mounting evidence that even the air in the immediate vicinity of smokers endangers the health of smokers and nonsmokers alike. Some businesses have started to limit smoking to certain areas, and some local jurisdictions are following suit, but no official federal policy bans smoking in public places. Indeed, a referendum on the issue was soundly defeated in California in 1978, in part because of a massive campaign financed by tobacco interests.

Cigarette smoke is but a minor contributor to air pollution. The growth policies of most developed countries have for decades resulted in increased degrees of smog and dangerous chemicals, which infect the environment—both air and water. Epidemiologists have found relationships between polluted air and water and the prevalence of certain respiratory and gastrointestinal diseases. Occupational exposure to certain chemicals is especially detrimental to health. For example, W. J. Nicholson (1976) has found that asbestos and textile workers with twenty years in the industry have more than four times the risk of cancer of the respiratory system as the general population. Indeed, there is also some evidence that exposure to asbestos can lead to lung cancer as late as thirty years after the incident (Patinkin 1978).

The March 1979 nuclear plant disaster at Three Mile Island in Middletown, Pennsylvania, has forced a rethinking of the government's energy priorities. Increasing concern is being expressed over the possible long-term effects of exposure to nuclear radiation. As with asbestos and lead, the "experiment" is of long duration—twenty to thirty years. Only then will we know if the government's energy policies will become the major killers of the early decades of the next century.

Some scientists foresaw radiation problems. In October 1958 Dr. Russell Morgan, at that time chief of the Johns Hopkins Hospital Department of Radiology, recommended that radiation safety standards and health research be centralized in a single agency, the Department of Health, Education, and Welfare. His suggestion was not followed. Pointedly, Morgan noted twenty-one years ago that it seemed "unwise" to give the Atomic Energy Commission (AEC) the dual role of "promotion and development of atomic energy on the one hand and regulation of radiation safety on the other." Morgan further predicted that "in its zeal to carry out its promotional activity, the AEC may lose sight of its responsibilities in operational safety." He then reported: "The long-range effects of ionizing radiation are identical to those experienced by individuals who are exposed to small, protracted doses. The effects were genetic changes, development of cancers, and a shortening of life expectancy" (quoted in Pincus 1979, p. 6).

Perhaps the strongest example of failure on the part of the U.S. government to do everything possible to improve health and longevity is its policy on medical assistance. For over thirty years there has been growing demand for some kind of national health program. The United States remains "the only great industrial country without a compulsory nationwide program of health insurance or sickness benefits. . . . There is ample evidence however of a shift of public opinion toward handling medical care as a predictable and insurable risk and collec-

Table 11.4 Infant Mortality Rates for Selected Countries, 1978

COUNTRY	RATE PER THOUSAND
Sweden	8
Japan	8
Denmark	9
Finland	9
Norway	9
Netherlands	10
Switzerland	10
Iceland	11
France	11
Luxembourg	11
Belgium	12
Canada	12
Singapore	12
Australia	12
East Germany	13
United States	13

Source: Population Reference Bureau (1980).

tive responsibility" (Woytinsky and Woytinsky 1953, p. 238). Interestingly, that statement was made in 1953! Since then the United States has instituted the Medicare and Medicaid programs to help the poor and aged, yet a comprehensive nationwide program of health insurance and health care is still being debated in Congress. Although it is gratifying to note that almost 90 percent of all Americans are covered by some kind of health insurance, such insurance is useful only when a disease is discovered; it does not encourage preventive medicine. As yet the concept of regular checkups—irrespective of health condition—is foreign to most Americans. National health programs encourage (and some countries insist on) such examinations.

For its degree of modernization the United States makes a poor showing on such health indices as life expectancy and infant mortality. For instance, despite recent improvements, the United States still has an infant mortality rate that ranks higher than fifteen other countries (see table 11.4). Perhaps the failure to institute a national health program that would provide better medical care can explain this poor showing.

SUMMARY

Population policies have been defined as legislative measures, administrative programs, and other governmental action which affect demographic behavior. All governments have such policies. Some government influences are deliberate, while others are unintentional.

There are two major approaches to influencing fertility levels.

One approach is to provide birth control knowledge and services through massive government-sponsored family planning programs. The other approach is to change the social and economic environment so that people are motivated to have fewer children. Examples of these non–family planning programs include modernization, payments for not having children, increased opportunities for the employment of women, and population education. The family and non–family planning approaches are seen as complementing each other.

Governments influence mortality primarily through their attempts to improve the health levels of the population. But there are several practices (such as war) which serve to increase mortality rather than lower it. Governmental failure to enact remedial laws and programs also may increase mortality.

REFERENCES AND SUGGESTED READINGS

Balfour, Marshall C. 1962. A scheme for rewarding successful family planners. Memorandum prepared for the Population Council.

Barry, Marion. 1979. Press release. Washington, D.C.: Office of the Mayor.

Berelson, Bernard. 1969. Beyond family planning. *Studies in family planning* 38 (February):1–16.

———. 1979. Romania's 1966 anti-abortion decree: the demographic experience of the first decade. *Population studies* 33 (July):209–222.

Blake, Judith. 1969. Population policy for Americans: is the government being misled? *Science* 164 (May 2):522–529.

Bogue, Donald J. 1966. Family planning research: an outline of the field. In *Family planning and population programs,* eds. Bernard Berelson et al., pp. 721–735. Chicago: University of Chicago Press.

Bondestam, Lars. 1972. The population situation in Ethiopia, part 2. *On family planning in Ethiopia* 2 (May):39–55.

Bourgeois-Pichat, Jean. 1967. Relation between foetal-infant mortality and fertility. In *World Population Conference, 1965,* pp. 68–72. New York: United Nations.

Bumpass, Larry, and Westoff, Charles F. 1970. The "perfect contraceptive" population. *Science* 169 (September 18):1177–1182.

Carlsson, Gosta. 1966. The decline of fertility: innovation or adjustment process? *Population studies* 20 (November):149–174.

Center for Disease Control. 1977. *United States immunization survey, 1976.* Atlanta, Ga.: Public Health Service.

Chaplin, David. 1971. Some institutional determinants of fertility in Peru. In *Population policies and growth in Latin America,* ed. David Chaplin, pp. 223–230. Lexington, Mass.: D. C. Heath.

Chavez, Cesar. 1968. *Muhammad speaks* (October 25).

Coale, Ansley J. 1978. Population growth and economic development: the case of Mexico. *Foreign affairs* 56 (January):415–429.

David, Henry P., and Wright, Nicholas H. 1971. Abortion legislation: the Romanian experience. *Studies in family planning* 2 (October):205–210.

Davis, Kingsley. 1967. Population policy: will current programs succeed? *Science* 158 (November 10):730–739.

Eldridge, Hope T. 1968. Population policies. In *International encyclopedia of the social sciences,* vol. XII, ed. David L. Sills, pp. 381–388. New York: Macmillan Company/The Free Press.

Enke, Stephen. 1966. Economic aspects of slowing population growth. *Economic journal* 76 (March):44–56.

Glass, David V. 1940. *Population policies and movements in Europe.* New York: Augustus M. Kelley.

Godley, Frank, and Kruegel, David. 1975. Cigarette smoking and differential mortality. Paper presented at the annual meeting of the Population Association of America.

Goldscheider, Calvin. 1971. *Population, modernization, and social structure.* Boston: Little, Brown.

Gustavus, Susan O., and Nam, Charles B. 1970. The formation and stability of ideal family size among young people. *Demography* 7 (February): 43–51.

Hauser, Philip M. 1967. Family planning and population programs: a book review article. *Demography* 4:397–414.

Kendall, Maurice. 1979. The world fertility survey: current status and findings. *Population reports,* series M, *Special topic monographs* 3 (July).

Kramer, Larry. 1979. Traffic deaths surge, past 50,000. *Washington post* (April 21).

Marino, Anthony. 1971. KAP surveys and the politics of family planning. *Concerned demography* 3 (Fall):36–75.

Massialas, Byron G. 1972. Population education as exploration of alternatives. *Social education* 36 (April):347–356.

Mehlan, K. H. 1965. Legal abortions in Romania. *Journal of sex research* 1:31–38.

Muhua, Chen. 1979. Realization of the four modernizations hinges on planned control of population growth, trans. John C. Chao. *Beijing people's daily* (August 11).

National Center for Health Statistics. 1978. *Health, United States 1978.* Washington, D.C.: Government Printing Office.

Nicholson, W. J. 1976. Case study 1, asbestos—the TLV approach. In *Annals of the New York Academy of Science, Occupational carcinogenesis,* eds. U. Saffioti and J. K. Wagoner 271 (May 28): 152–169.

Nortman, Dorothy. 1972. Population and family planning programs: a factbook. *Reports on population/family planning* 2 (September):1–87.

Ovsienko, V. E. 1966. Influence of social and economic factors on demographic characteristics. In *World Population Conference, 1965,* pp. 87–93. New York: United Nations.

Patinkin, Mark. 1978. Asbestos is killing Joe Ruggieri; but he's fighting—fighting well. *Providence journal* (April 21).

Pincus, Walter. 1979. Scientist in 1958 foresaw lack of concern for health risks of radiation. *Washington post* (April 16).

Pohlman, Edward W., and Rao, K. Seshagiri. 1968. Population education versus sex education. Paper presented at Family Planning Association of India Conference.

Population Reference Bureau. 1980. *1980 world population data sheet.* Washington, D.C.: Population Reference Bureau.

Potter, Robert G. 1971. Inadequacy of a one-method family planning program. *Studies in family planning* 2 (January): 1–5.

Ridker, Ronald G. 1969. Desired family size and the efficacy of current family planning programmes. *Population studies* 23 (July):279–284.

Salaff, Janet W. 1972. Institutionalized motivation for fertility limitation in China. *Population studies* 26 (July):233–262.

Schroeder, Richard C. 1974. Policies on population around the world. *Population bulletin* 29.

Simmons, Ozzie G. 1970. Population education: a review of the field. *Studies in family planning* 52 (April):1–5.

Stycos, J. Mayone. 1971*a*. Family planning and American goals. In *Population policies and growth in Latin America,* ed. David Chaplin, pp. 111–131. Lexington, Mass.: D. C. Heath.

———. 1971*b*. Opinion, ideology, and population problems—some sources of domestic and foreign opposition to birth control. In *Rapid population growth,* ed. National Academy of Sciences, pp. 533–556. Baltimore: Johns Hopkins.

Subcommittee on Domestic and International Scientific Planning Analysis and Cooperation, Committee on Science and Technology, U.S. House of Representatives. 1979. *The role of science and technology in China's population/food balance.* Washington, D.C.: Government Printing Office.

Tabbarah, Riad. 1964. Birth control and population policy. *Population studies* 18 (November):187–196.

Teitelbaum, Michael S. 1972. Fertility effects of the abolition of legal abortion in Romania. *Population studies* 26 (November):405–417.

———. 1973. U.S. population growth in international perspective. In *Toward the end of growth,* by Charles F. Westoff et al., pp. 69–83. Englewood Cliffs, N.J.: Prentice-Hall.

Tien, H. Yuan. 1963. Birth control in Mainland China: ideology and politics. *Milbank Memorial Fund quarterly* 41 (July):269–290.

United Nations. 1972. *Measures, policies and programmes affecting fertility, with particular reference to national family planning programmes.* New York: United Nations.

———. 1973. *The determinants and consequences of population change,* vol. I. New York: United Nations.

van der Tak, Jean. 1974. *Abortion, fertility, and changing legislation: an international review.* Lexington, Mass.: D. C. Heath.

Viederman, Stephen. 1972. Population education in the United States. *Social education* 36:4 (April):337–346.

Weller, Robert H. 1973. Non-family planning approaches to achieving population change targets. In *Seminar on demographic research in relation to population growth targets,* pp. 79–92. Paris: CICRED.

———. 1976. Number and timing failures among legitimate births in the United States: 1968, 1969 and 1972. *Family planning perspectives* 8 (May–June):111–116.

———. 1977. Demographic correlates of women's participation in economic activities. In *International Population Conference: Mexico 1977),* pp. 497–516. Liège, Belgium: International Union for the Scientific Study of Population.

Wong, Aline K., and Salaff, Janet W. 1977. *An exploratory study of the effectiveness of population disincentives in preventing higher-order births in*

Singapore. Ottawa, Canada: International Development Research Centre.

World Health Organization. 1975. Smoking and its effect on health. *Technical report series no. 568.* Geneva, Switzerland: World Health Organization.

Woytinsky, Wladimir S., and Woytinsky, Emma S. 1953. *World population and production.* New York: Twentieth Century Fund.

12
Policies Relating to the Movement of People

Throughout most of human history people have been free to move about in search of a better life. To a considerable extent, however, this freedom of movement has been restricted since late in the nineteenth century by a number of laws that infringe on the freedom to move. In some cases, people have been barred from crossing a country's border; in other instances, specific areas within a country have been declared "off limits" to certain people.

At the same time, governments have often taken measures to encourage movement into some areas and out of other areas. Again, there have been examples of such policies involving both nations and areas within a nation. Thus, when looking at policies related to the movement of people, both international and internal migration must be considered. First, we will examine policies concerned with international migration; later in the chapter, discussion will focus on policies regarding internal migration.

POLICIES ON INTERNATIONAL MIGRATION[1]

Some nations encourage immigration (movement into a country) in order to increase the rate of population growth. This was true of the United States during the nineteenth century. Canada and Australia have also done this. Today, Israel is a prime example of a country that actively seeks more immigration. Other nations, faced with rapid population growth, view emigration (movement out of a country) as a "safety valve" to relieve population pressure; some of the Caribbean countries are examples.

In addition to migration policies regulating the amount of population change, many countries also attempt to regulate the "quality" of the migrants. The social, economic, and cultural characteristics of the migrant population are important factors considered in formulating policies in those countries.

Since policies on emigration and, especially, immigration vary markedly from country to country, it is instructive to look at some of the variations.

Policies on Emigration

A number of countries discourage emigration through legal, social, and economic restrictions. Responses to a United Nations questionnaire distributed to member states attending the Bucharest World Population Conference in 1974 indicated that seventy-two countries "discourage" permanent emigration. Representatives from many other countries stated that their government had no specific policies on em-

[1]This section draws heavily on Leon F. Bouvier, Henry S. Shryock, and Harry W. Henderson (1977).

igration because the number was insignificant (Mauldin et al. 1974). Although no countries admitted that they encouraged emigration, a number of them, Cuba for example, do so.

Among those countries discouraging permanent emigration are the Soviet Union and the People's Republic of China. Until 1973 emigration from the Soviet Union was practically impossible for persons with university training. Those wishing to leave were subject to an educational exit fee ranging from $1,200 to $32,000, depending on the number of years of university training and the degree received. To this day, it is difficult for Jews to leave the Soviet Union.

Emigration from China has also been difficult. But today the Chinese government is following a somewhat more relaxed policy, partly as a result of the normalization of relations with the United States. Recently it has allowed an increase in legal emigration to Hong Kong and is less severe than before on those citizens caught trying to leave the country illegally.

Morocco, Tunisia, and Algeria tacitly encourage emigration as a partial and temporary solution to their unemployment problems. Egypt has a general policy that facilitates and encourages emigration for those who want to leave, but it does impose certain restrictions on the emigration of persons with skills needed by the country. Spain has also looked favorably on emigration—as evidenced by the net outflow of 1.4 million people between 1950 and 1970.

Emigration is also accepted by governments when transfers of populations are necessary because of religious or cultural differences. Such transfers occurred when Pakistan separated from India in 1947 and later when Bangladesh broke away from Pakistan in 1971. Similarly there have been exchanges of people between Turkey and Greece.

Some countries encourage emigration to rid themselves of politically troublesome citizens. Cuba presents the most dramatic example of such a policy. Cuba has encouraged emigration to the United States and elsewhere since 1962. The program peaked in 1980 when tens of thousands of Cubans took to the seas to seek refuge in the United States.

The victory by the North in Vietnam in 1975 has resulted in massive emigration from that country. The enormity of that movement is best reflected in the tragedy of the "boat people." These are mainly ethnic Chinese who fled their adopted land in small craft but were stranded on the high seas when other nations in the area refused to let them in. World opinion has since forced the Vietnamese government to downplay its policies that resulted in emigration. A special July 1979 U.N. Conference on Indo-chinese Refugees in Geneva resulted in an agreement by the Vietnam government that it would make every effort to stop unsanctioned departures of boat people for a "reasonable period."

Policies on Immigration

Barriers to immigration are more numerous than barriers to emigration. In the Bucharest survey 116 countries indicated that they restrict immigration and only 32 indicated they encourage it (Mauldin et al. 1974).

"Restrict" and "encourage" are relative terms. The Soviet Union and the United States each restrict immigration. Yet the Soviet Union admits virtually no foreigners, and the United States admits about 400,000 persons each year. In addition, of course, perhaps as many as 500,000 persons enter this country illegally, but they are not formally "admitted" by the government.

Immigration policies are subject to change in response to national demographic, economic, and political factors. Countries that admitted large numbers of immigrants at a time when there was empty land to be settled typically reduced the flow of immigrants as the population expanded and as the labor force became less able to absorb a large number of immigrants. The number admitted to the United States during the 1970s was 60 percent as large as the number admitted between 1905 and 1914. We will now take a look at the immigration policies of some countries that have received large numbers of immigrants in the past.

Australia

Few countries have depended on immigration for their very existence to the same extent as Australia. The settlement of that vast region by immigrants began in 1788 with 1,030 British subjects in the colony of New South Wales. Those settlers were predominantly bonded servants and former prisoners who had served time in English jails. Discovery of gold in the early 1850s attracted many additional migrants from the British Isles, New Zealand, Germany, Poland, the United States, the Scandinavian countries, and China. The Chinese immigrants caused resentment among many white Australians, leading to some racial unrest. Measures limiting their entry were introduced in the 1850s and 1880s, followed by a prohibition against the permanent settlement and naturalization of virtually all Asians. The Immigration Restriction Act of 1901, which gave immigration officials discretion to require immigrants to pass a written test in a European language, effectively excluded non-Westerners for over fifty years (Australian Population and Immigration Council 1977, p. 23).

Following its near invasion by Japan in World War II, Australia realized its defenseless position as a small population in a huge territory. It set for itself a goal of a 1 percent increase per year through net migration and another 1 percent through reproductive change. To stimulate settlement, the government spent up to $40 million a year to assist immigrants with traveling expenses, jobs, and accommodations.

Barriers against the immigration of non-Westerners began to crumble. Wartime refugees were allowed to stay, and persons with skills in short supply could enter for settlement and bring their families. In 1973 a policy of nondiscrimination on grounds of race, color, or nationality in the selection of migrants was adopted. However, certain measures still serve to qualify more Europeans than Asians for permanent residence. Since 1970 the number of immigrants into Australia from Asia has ranged from 7,000 to 9,000 persons each year, while the total annual immigration has fluctuated from 50,000 to 60,000 annually (Australian Population and Immigration Council 1977, p. 28).

Canada

In October 1974 the Canadian government announced it would tighten its system for admitting immigrants. Under the revision immigrants are graded on a scale that includes education, employment skills, presence of relatives in Canada, and a knowledge of either English or French. Partly as a result of that government action, immigration in all of 1975 amounted to only 187,881 persons—14 percent below that for 1974.

In 1977 the House of Commons enacted legislation that grants to the Minister of Manpower and Immigration broad powers to consider demographic goals such as geographic distribution in deciding whether to accept a person as an immigrant. Persons who may not be accepted otherwise will be admitted if they agree to settle in certain designated areas for at least six months. In addition to fulfilling demographic goals, the bill explicitly lists the aims of immigration as being the reunion of families, nondiscrimination, fulfillment of international obligations to help refugees, and economic growth (Population Reference Bureau 1977; *Ontario naturalist* 1977).

Canada has no quota system or limitations on the number of immigrants from a certain country. All immigrants come from the same pool. The new act does set a numerical limit, however, on immigration in a given year; that limit can be changed as conditions warrant.

United Kingdom

The United Kingdom has its own special immigration problems that stem from the large number of Commonwealth countries. It used to be that people living in countries belonging to the Commonwealth could freely immigrate to the "mother country," Great Britain. But as more and more immigrants came from India, the West Indies, and African nations, reaching fairly high levels in 1960–1962, Great Britain began to experience racial tension. In 1962 Parliament passed the Commonwealth Immigrants Act, which placed restrictions on migration from Commonwealth countries for the first time. Dependents of immigrants already resident in Great Britain as well as persons with specific job offers or special skills were the only ones permitted to enter. Although immigration from India and Pakistan was reduced immediately following passage of the act, it rose again in the late 1960s. Immigration from the West Indies, however, never returned to earlier levels.

The Immigration Act of 1971 also severely restricted the immigration of Commonwealth citizens. It favored the immigration of so-called patrials (persons who were either born or naturalized in Britain or who had at least one grandparent who was either born or naturalized in Britain). Not coincidentally, most people in that category are white. Under the new guidelines immigration into the United Kingdom from the Commonwealth countries in Asia, Africa, and the West Indies has dropped considerably. In 1968 the number of such immigrants was 74,300, while in 1973 the number was only 37,500. Indeed, in the past few years more West Indians have left Britain than have entered (Mrs. Thatcher touches a nerve 1978).

United States

Until 1875 the United States had no laws concerning the admission of aliens. (The Constitution did forbid the importation of slaves after 1838.) In 1875 a law was enacted which denied entry to persons suffering from certain physical and mental weaknesses. In 1882 a general immigration statute provided for a head tax of 50 cents and barred the immigration of convicts, mental incompetents, prostitutes, and persons likely to become public charges. The Chinese Exclusion Act, also passed in 1882, prohibited entry to Chinese emigrants except under rare circumstances.

Legislation prohibiting the entry of Orientals into the United States continued well into this century. The "Gentleman's Agreement" of 1907 called for Japan to refuse applications by laborers for passports to the United States. In 1917 Congress established an Asiatic barred zone that prohibited entry to any native of India, Burma, Siam (now Thailand), the Malay states, the East Indies, and the Polynesian islands. This policy of almost total exclusion of Orientals continued until 1943, when China was given a quota of 105 persons annually. The restrictions on the entry of other Asians continued until 1952 when "all countries were allowed a minimum quota of 100, with a ceiling of 2,000 on most natives of countries in the Asia-Pacific triangle, which broadly encompassed the Asiatic countries" (Congressional Research Service, Library of Congress 1979, p. 7).

Because of such restrictions, the Asian immigration has been insignificant compared to the European immigration. As we saw earlier (in chapter 8), the volume of immigration from Europe increased greatly in the late nineteenth and early twentieth centuries. At the same time, the source of these immigrants shifted from western Europe to southern and eastern Europe. Because these immigrants came from a different cultural and ethnic background than the predominantly white, Anglo-Saxon American population, pressures grew within the American political system to "solve the immigration problem." The first Quota Act of 1921 limited immigration from Europe to an annual quota equal to 3 percent of the number of each country's foreign-born residents in the United States at the most recent census. Those quotas were then reduced to 2 percent of the foreign-born population enumerated in the 1890 census. The reduction amounted to a flagrant act of discrimination against southern and eastern Europeans, most of whom had arrived after 1890.

The Immigration Act of 1924 (which went into effect July 1, 1929) lowered the overall quota from 357,803 to 154,000 immigrants annually. The annual quota of any nationality was "a number which bears the same ratio to 150,000 as the number of inhabitants in the United States in 1920 having that national origin bears to the number of white inhabitants of the United States in 1920, with a minimum quota of 100 for each nationality" (Congressional Research Service, Library of Congress 1979, p. 7).[2]

The new law functioned as it was intended: the quotas for southern and eastern Europe were cut from 45 percent of the total amount of immigration in 1921 to 15 percent in 1929. For example, Italy's quota was reduced from 42,057 to 5,802 (Petersen 1979, p. 30). Thus, Congress institutionalized racial and ethnic discrimination in the admission of immigrants and continued the process begun earlier with the imposition of restrictions on the admission of Orientals.

In 1952 Congress passed the McCarran-Walter Act over the veto of President Harry Truman. This act not only accepted the ethnocentric objective of the 1924 act ("keep America pure") but incorporated numerous "antisubversive" provisions. The annual quota for a country was set at one-sixth of 1 percent of the number of those inhabitants of the continental United States in 1920 whose ancestry or national origin was attributable to that country. Whereas natives of countries in the barred zones were generally inadmissible under the 1924 act, a few Asians were allowed into the United States under the 1952 act. Otherwise both acts were very similar (see table 12.1). However, persons of Asian ancestry were treated differently from others for immigration purposes. For example, according to Charles Keely, "a second-generation Brazilian of Japanese ancestry was to be counted against Japan's small quota, whereas a second-generation Brazilian of Italian ancestry was treated as a Brazilian, not as Italian" (1979, p. 16). Although both Presidents Eisenhower and Kennedy publicly criticized U.S. immigra-

[2]Congress originally tried to determine quotas based on the ancestry of the *entire* 1920 population. However, the geographic and ethnic ancestry of the resident population was often impossible to trace back to 1790, when the first census was taken. Hence, the decision was made to use the quotas described above (Petersen 1979).

Table 12.1 Annual Immigration Quotas by Country, 1929 and 1952

COUNTRY	QUOTA EFFECTIVE 1929	1952 IMMIGRATION AND NATIONALITY ACT
Europe	150,591	149,667
Austria	1,413	1,405
Belgium	1,304	1,297
Bulgaria	100	100
Czechoslovakia	2,874	2,859
Denmark	1,181	1,175
Finland	569	566
France	3,086	3,069
Germany	25,957	25,814
Great Britain	65,721	65,361
Greece	307	308
Hungary	869	865
Iceland	100	100
Ireland	17,853	17,756
Italy	5,802	5,645
Netherlands	3,153	3,136
Norway	2,377	2,364
Poland	6,524	6,488
Portugal	440	438
Romania	295	289
Spain	252	250
Sweden	3,314	3,295
Switzerland	1,707	1,698
Turkey	226	225
U.S.S.R.	2,784	2,697
Yugoslavia	845	933
Other Europe	1,538	1,534
Asia	1,323	2,990
Africa	1,200	1,400
Australia	200	600
All others	400	—
All countries	153,714	154,657

Source: U.S. Bureau of the Census (1958), table 103.

tion policy, it was not until 1965 that ethnic quotas were legislated out of existence.

A key amendment of the 1965 act was the provision that "no person shall receive any preference or priority or be discriminated against in the issuance of an immigrant visa because of his race, sex, nationality, place of birth, or place of residence" (Congressional Research Service, Library of Congress 1979, p. 57). An annual ceiling of 170,000 for the Eastern Hemisphere was established, along with a 20,000 limit per country. The annual ceiling for the Western Hemisphere was set at 120,000 with no limit per country.

In 1978 the act was amended to abolish the hemispheric ceilings.

Box 12.1 What Is Our Current Immigration Law?

The law governing U.S. immigration policy is the Immigration and Nationality Act of 1952, as amended. It is lengthy and complex legislation; a brief summary of its major provisions follows.

In recent years the United States has accepted about 600,000 immigrants* and refugees each year. A majority now enter under a fixed numerical limit of 270,000 a year. Many immigrants are exempt from this limitation, however. They include the husbands, wives, and minor children of U.S. citizens, the parents of adult U.S. citizens. In addition, 50,000 refugees can be admitted each year and provisions have been made to accept even more if the President and Congress agree.

Those immigrants who come under the annual ceiling of 270,000 are limited to 20,000 per year from any one nation. They also are subject to a visa allocation system of six preferences:

First: Unmarried sons and daughters 21 years of age or older of U.S. citizens (20 percent).

Second: Husbands, wives, and unmarried sons and daughters of permanent resident aliens (26 percent).

Third: Professionals and people of exceptional ability in the sciences and arts who will benefit the economy, culture, or welfare of the U.S. (10 percent).

Fourth: Married children of U.S. citizens (10 percent).

Fifth: Brothers and sisters of U.S. citizens 21 years of age or older (24 percent).

Sixth: Skilled or unskilled workers needed in the U.S. labor market who will not displace citizens or legal alien workers (10 percent).

Any visas not needed for the six preferences are available for other potential immigrants.

Tourists, travellers on business, and other temporary visitors do not need immigrant visas to come to the United States. During 1977, more than seven million nonimmigrants were admitted.

*An immigrant is a noncitizen who is allowed to settle permanently in the United States.

Source: Select Committee on Population (1978).

The overall limit of immigration was set at 290,000 per year, with a maximum of 20,000 people from any given country including those of the Western Hemisphere. In 1980 a new amendment lowered the annual limit to 270,000 but increased the refugee allocation from 17,400 to 50,000. Within these limits a preferential admissions system is in operation. Immediate relatives of U.S. citizens are accepted *outside* these limits (see box 12.1).

Illegal Immigration into the United States

Currently there is a great deal of concern over the volume of illegal immigration into the United States, which attracts most of the world's illegal migrants. Estimates of the number of illegal immigrants presently in this country range from 3 to 12 million persons. As figure 12.1 shows, about 1 million apprehensions take place every year, and close to 90 percent of those apprehended are Mexican. Of course, some people are caught several times in the course of a year. It is not known how many illegal immigrants plan to remain in the United States permanently and how many simply work for a brief period and then return to their homeland.

Illegal immigration is an emotional issue. Some people believe that the illegal immigrants take jobs from U.S. citizens. Others claim that the jobs they take are so arduous and pay so little that most Americans would not accept them. Some claim that the illegal immigrants place a strain on local, state, and national welfare systems. Others contend that most illegal immigrants are afraid to turn to government agencies because of fear of discovery.

Proposals to strengthen the laws against illegal immigration have met with some resistance. Certain agricultural interests want to maintain a supply of cheap labor. Some Hispanic rights groups, as well as

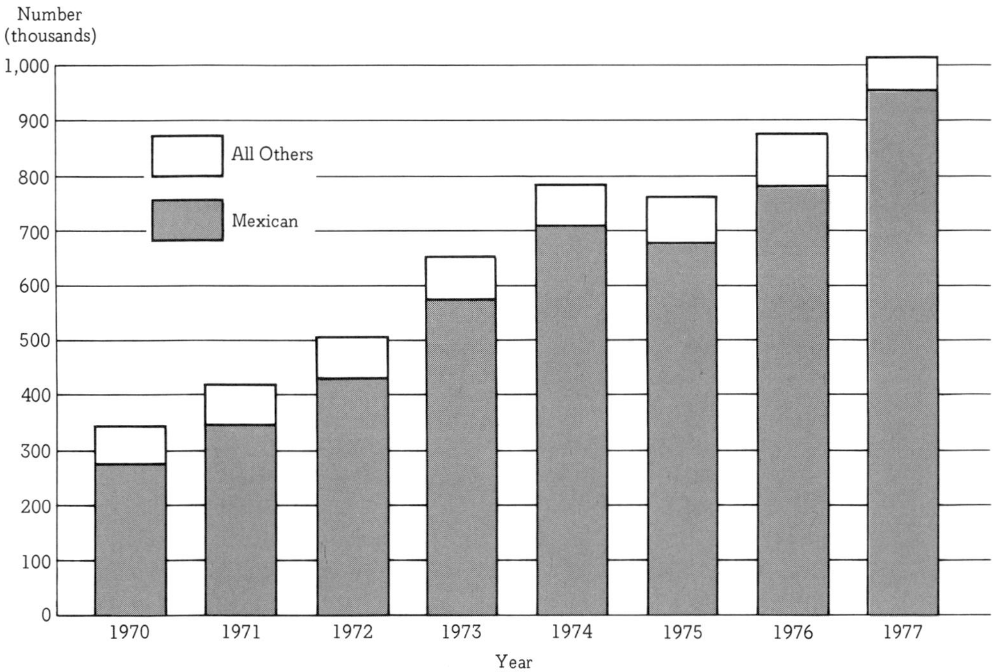

Figure 12.1 Illegal Aliens Apprehended in the United States, 1970–1977
Sources: Bouvier, Shryock, and Henderson (1977), p. 29; and U.S. Department of Justice (1979), pp. 92, 102.

the U.S. Catholic Bishops, are concerned that taking strong steps against illegal immigrants (many of whom are Latin American and Roman Catholic) would lead to discrimination against Latin Americans in general.

On the other hand, the AFL-CIO and other labor unions, along with the Urban League and other black organizations, fear increased job competition from illegal immigrants. Groups concerned about population growth point out that illegal immigration adds significantly to the numbers of people living in the United States.

In 1977 President Carter proposed (1) amnesty for all illegal aliens who have lived in the United States since 1970; (2) a temporary legal alien status for those who entered the country before 1977, which would allow them to work and travel but would not entitle them to any federal benefits; (3) penalties for employers who make a practice of hiring illegal aliens; (4) aid to countries that are sources of illegal immigration; (5) a complete review of immigration policy; and (6) increased guards on the Mexican border. The legislation was not passed by either house of Congress.

On October 5, 1978, President Carter signed a law which established the Select Commission on Immigration and Refugee Policy. This sixteen-member body was instructed to study and evaluate "existing laws, policies and procedures governing the admission of immigrants and refugees to the United States and to make such administrative and legislative recommendations to the President and the Congress as are appropriate." Little if any legislation dealing with immigration policy can be expected until after the commission makes its final report public in 1981.

The Refugee Problem

There have always been refugees. Whether for political or for economic reasons, people have always been forced to leave their native lands, sometimes simply to make a living, sometimes literally to remain alive. In recent decades, however, the number of refugees has grown significantly. Today there are more refugees than at any time since the end of World War II in Europe. While most attention is directed to refugees from Indochina such as the "boat people"—and the more recent exodus from Haiti and Cuba—the problem is worldwide. In contrast to the situation after World War II, when the refugees were located in a few countries in central Europe, refugees today are on all continents.

New concern with the problems of refugees has led to a serious reexamination of U.S. refugee policy. According to the Immigration and Nationality Act (INA), 50,000 refugees can be accepted each year. Those persons may obtain immigrant status after two years' residence if they so desire. But the definition of refugee has been limited. According to the INA, a refugee is one who has fled from a communist country or the Middle East because of persecution or who has been uprooted by natural disaster. The law makes no provision, for example, for persons fleeing from right-wing dictatorships in Latin America.

Additional refugees can enter the United States through the so-called parole provision of the INA, which has been used for the admission of large numbers of Hungarian, Cuban, and Indochinese refugees. The parole provision authorizes the attorney general, at his discretion and under conditions he prescribes, to let any alien into the United States temporarily in emergencies or for reasons affecting the public interest. Under certain circumstances those admitted may adjust their status to that of aliens lawfully admitted for permanent residence (i.e., an immigrant). Also, individual aliens temporarily in the United States may seek asylum on the ground that they would be subject to persecution in their home country. This was the legal basis for acceptance of several well-known Soviet ballet dancers in late 1979.

Considerable dissatisfaction has been expressed with the definition of the term "refugee" and with the power vested in the attorney general regarding the parole provision. On March 9, 1979, legislation was introduced in Congress to overhaul U.S. refugee policy and programs. The bill, which was signed by President Carter on March 10, 1980, accomplishes four basic objectives:

1. It repeals the current discriminatory treatment of refugees by providing a new definition of a refugee[3] that both recognizes the plight of homeless people all over the world and gives refugee admissions the same immigration status as all other immigrants.
2. It raises the annual limitation on regular refugee admissions from 17,400 to 50,000.
3. The bill provides an orderly but flexible procedure to meet emergency refugee situations and any other situations of special concern to the United States if the resettlement needs of the homeless people involved cannot be met within the regular 50,000 ceiling.
4. It provides for federal support of the refugee resettlement process and extends coverage to all refugees entering the United States (Congressional Research Service, Library of Congress 1979, p. 99).

According to Charles Keely, the 1965 Immigration and Nationality Act and its subsequent amendments have turned U.S. policy away from nativism: "The quota concept and its pseudo-intellectual baggage, scientific racism, were repudiated" (1979, p. 23). Current law emphasizes family reunion, the acceptance of some refugees, and labor protection balanced against admitting persons of needed skill. But

[3]According to the *Congressional Record,* the term "refugee" means any person who is outside any country of his or her nationality or, in the case of a person having no nationality, is outside any country in which he or she last habitually resided, and who is unable or unwilling to return to, and is unable or unwilling to take advantage of the protection of, that country because of persecution on account of race, religion, nationality, membership in a particular social group, or political opinion (U.S. Congress 1979, p. S2630).

there is some question as to whether the INA in fact achieves those goals and, indeed, whether the goals are now out of date. Consequently, the Select Commission on Immigration and Refugee Policy will review the entire immigration issue and make recommendations to the Congress in 1981 for possible new legislation.

We have seen in this section on international migration policy that governments (especially in those countries attractive to foreigners) are constantly passing new laws and reviewing older legislation dealing with immigration. Many of those measures represent direct steps to influence population size or national rates of growth. The concern over the ethnic, economic, and social characteristics of the immigrants shows that population composition is also important. Unless the various laws restricting international migration are relaxed, it is unlikely that international migration will be of sufficient magnitude to change the distribution of the world's population.

POLICIES ON INTERNAL MIGRATION

Programs and policies concerned with internal migration of people have the overall purpose of redistributing the population. In the process, growth in some areas is encouraged, while in other areas it is discouraged.

In many countries reproductive change has become negligible as a factor contributing to population growth. Differences in fertility and mortality between regions or states have become slight. As a result, net migration has assumed increased importance in determining changes in population distribution. Policies that implicitly or explicitly encourage (or discourage) movement of the population within a country have become important ways to affect population size, rates of local or regional growth, and population distribution.

In what follows we will discuss both government policies directly intended to regulate the size or growth of an area and those policies with unintentional and indirect effects. These latter policies may yield the same results as the direct policies.

Direct policies on internal migration are generally aimed at slowing urban growth, particularly in developing countries. At various periods in history some cities have sought rapid growth, but generally planners have been more concerned with regulating urban size and/or growth. In this connection four types of policies can affect population distribution:

1. Stopping the flow of migrants at the source by fostering rural development or social reform programs
2. Redirecting the flow of migrants to rural "frontier" areas
3. Developing urban growth poles and new towns
4. Limiting urban growth or encouraging migrants to return to their home area

Stopping the Flow of Migrants

Several Latin American countries have attempted to improve the living conditions of rural residents through land reform and community development programs. Farmers who own their land may be less likely to migrate to urban areas than those who rent it from a landlord. Some countries have attempted to discourage migration to the cities by providing essential social services to rural residents. For example, Venezuela has made an effort to improve rural housing. Other programs involve the erection of better schools and community facilities. Japan has established a number of rural development programs to diminish the massive migration into the Tokyo-Osaka metropolitan area.

Decentralization of industry is still another means of discouraging rural-urban migration. New factories are deliberately built in areas far from the large cities. Smaller towns which eventually may grow into small cities are developed. Hungary, Poland, and the Soviet Union have applied policies of decentralization and deconcentration of industry. Poland, for example, sets employment limits for the industrial plants in large urban areas and requires new plants in those areas to be licensed by the government. Moreover, some existing plants (or certain of their branches) have been transferred from Warsaw to quite distant small cities located in rural regions (United Nations 1973, pp. 220–221; and Fuchs and Demko 1979).

Redirecting Migrants to Frontier Areas

The development of remote areas of a particular country and the establishment of programs to upgrade living conditions in rural areas serve the double purpose of slowing down rural-urban migration and improving the socioeconomic conditions under which rural families live. The transmigration program in Indonesia is an example of governmental attempts to relocate some of the population into rural areas. Residents of Java are given financial incentives to move to the more sparsely settled island of Sumatra as well as other outer islands. According to Sumono Mustofa, the resettlement of millions of Javanese peasants represents "one of the biggest planned movements of people in history" (1978, p. 7).

Several Latin American countries have tried colonizing migrants with varying degrees of success. Brazil, for example, has not been too successful in getting people to migrate into the Amazon basin. The key to whether colonization schemes are successful is the amount of technical and financial backing the migrants receive from the government. Inadequate backing and the failure to provide ample technological and administrative assistance and services doom colonization efforts because the migrants simply move elsewhere (Simmons, Diaz-Briquets, and Laquian 1977, p. 106).

Growth Poles and New Towns

One approach to the geographic distribution of people is based on the growth-pole theory. Growth poles are already existing intermediate size cities that are intended to grow large enough to counter the continued growth of the largest cities in the country. It is hoped that these growth-pole cities will eventually develop their own suburbs and become industrial and commercial centers.

Both Japan and the Soviet Union have used this approach. Although no policies in the United States have been intended specifically for this purpose, the interstate highway system indirectly develops its own growth poles. Where two interstate highways intersect, commercial activities spring up and population grows. Often what once had been a small village develops into a medium-size town.

Another way to slow down growth in the large urban areas is to construct new towns in open areas. Such towns are generally intended to be self-sufficient in employment, shopping, community facilities, education, and the like. Because new towns need sources of employment, they go hand in hand with the policy of decentralization of industry.

The concept of new towns dates back to the nineteenth century in England. More recently, in 1946 Parliament enacted the New Town Act, which called for new, comprehensively planned cities to curb the growth of London, to provide a more effective pattern and method for metropolitan growth, and to prevent the depopulation of rural areas (United Nations 1973, p. 221).

The Brazilian government is based in Brasilia, a new town built to slow the growth of Rio de Janeiro. In the United States, Oak Ridge, the birthplace of atomic energy, grew out of the wilderness in the hills of eastern Tennessee during World War II. With the increased emphasis on energy research, its population rapidly rose to almost 100,000 persons before declining in the 1960s to its current level of 50,000 persons. The planned cities of Reston, Virginia, and Columbia, Maryland, are in the Washington, D.C., area. However, those cities are really only extensions of the suburbs of large metropolitan areas. Perhaps one could go back into history and argue that Washington itself was a new town—literally carved out of the wilderness. Probably the newest of new towns is in the state of Alaska. In December 1977 the Alaska Planning Council announced that a new capital city would be built between Anchorage and Fairbanks, near Mount McKinley.

The new-town approach to population redistribution has several drawbacks. For one, it is very costly. For another, the new cities must compete with already existing communities for migrants. To draw the volume of migration necessary to establish an urban center, a new city must be exceptionally attractive with respect to employment opportunities, wages, and social amenities.

Research shows that migrants tend to limit their choices of destination to places where friends and relatives have already settled. The earlier migrants serve as a source of information about the opportunities available in their new community and provide social support for the newer migrants. A steady flow of migrants into a locality becomes partially self-perpetuating. Initially, the new cities would not be able to take advantage of this type of information and support system. Several years, or even a decade, might be necessary for the "beaten path" effect to work in favor of new cities.

Finally, new cities are vulnerable to the effects of transiency. We saw earlier (in chapter 8) that a large proportion of people who migrate do so repeatedly. Because of this, the population base of a new city would most likely be heavily weighted with chronic movers. There would be high rates of subsequent out-migration. Consequently, large annual inflows of migrants would yield only moderate additions to the number of permanent residents.

The growth-pole approach to redirecting migration flows is more feasible than the new-town approach. It capitalizes on existing growth possibilities. The growth centers are in an advantageous position to command a large share of available migrants because local employment is expanding. And since they already possess a stock of migrants, growth-pole centers are favored by the spread of information by migrants to other would-be migrants (Morrison 1973).

Limiting Growth

Attempts to limit the size of individual cities are not new. The extension of Paris beyond certain limits was prohibited by law at various intervals between 1549 and 1672. During the time of the Tudors and Stuarts in England, from the fifteenth through the seventeenth century, proclamation after proclamation was issued forbidding the erection of new houses in London and requesting that rural immigrants return to their areas of origin (United Nations 1973, p. 218). Today governments still attempt to limit urban growth by restricting the construction of new residences. And they also try to convince rural migrants to return to their villages or even to dissuade them from leaving their villages in the first place. The current policy in the People's Republic of China strongly urges educated Chinese youth to return to the countryside and settle there.

In the United States zoning regulations and the issuance of building permits for water and sewage facilities can be used to encourage population growth or to restrict it. Prince George's and Montgomery counties in Maryland, both suburbs of Washington, once had high rates of net in-migration. Lately the rate has dwindled to almost nothing—largely because of moratoria on building permits. In 1972 the city of Petaluma, California, passed an ordinance which established a population-growth management policy. That policy links population growth to the expansion of facilities for education, water supply, and sewage disposal. The ordinance places an annual limit on the number of new housing units having five or more rooms in a subdivision or in a structure such as an apartment complex (Irwin 1977, pp. 8–9). Neighboring Marin County has established a similar policy.

More local actions like those taken in California can be expected as the public becomes more conscious of the problems that often accompany unplanned growth. Some local governments are imposing low-density zoning regulations. Others are restricting the operation of new industries that may threaten the area's ecological balance. Naturally there are conflicts between the proponents of growth and those favoring restrictions on population growth; they are bound to continue and become more heated. Policies will reflect that conflict, and the future population size of many local areas will be influenced by administrative decisions.

Indirect and Unintentional Effects of Policies

We have just looked at ways a government can attempt to control population distribution directly. But there are other ways that government policy can indirectly affect the way population is distributed. For instance, at one time segregation laws designed to separate whites from blacks were prevalent in the South. Those laws had the effect of determining where blacks could or could not live and distributing the population accordingly. The internment of Japanese-Americans during World War II is another example of a government policy that results in population redistribution, albeit temporary.

Today there are many "hidden" policies which unintentionally affect migration patterns. As Peter Morrison states:

> Agencies that build highways, award defense contracts, and choose locations for federal installations are simultaneously redistributing employment and altering incentive for private investment. These and other programs and activities, although uncoordinated, tend to accumulate and exert a powerful but undirected influence on migration (1975, p. 14).

He concludes that each such program or policy has probably had a greater impact on American cities than all the explicitly urban programs combined.

Some states have policies that are directed at increasing the state's population and economic base. Providing tax incentives for new industry is the method most used to achieve that objective. On the other hand, Oregon and Hawaii welcome visitors but not in-migrants. Of course, no state can actually prohibit in-migration, but states can make in-migration unattractive and expensive through tax practices.

Today the United States has no national policy specifically designed to affect population distribution. However, in 1978 the Select Committee on Population of the U.S. House of Representatives recommended that "Congress . . . investigate the impact of present laws and programs on the decisions of individuals and firms to locate or relocate within the U.S. Prior to enactment of new legislation, Congress should review [the] potential impact on population movements" (1978, p. 11). So far, no policy has been forthcoming from Congress.

Some people have argued that having no policy is itself a policy. They contend that the effect of having no distribution policies can be seen by driving through any metropolitan area in the United States. Suburbs give birth to additional suburbs. These so-called slurbs appear at various places within or even outside of congested areas. The result is urban sprawl and visual pollution.

Despite the absence of any stated national policies, population shifts have also occurred away from metropolitan areas in the direction of smaller places. New England is the best example of the decline in metropolitan growth. Almost every major city in that six-state region lost population between 1970 and 1980, while small cities grew substantially. The Ozark region of Arkansas now draws more migrants from California than it sends there (Morrison 1975, p. 12). On an even larger scale, the historic net out-migration of blacks from the South has been reversed. Between 1975 and 1978, 26,000 more blacks moved into that region than left it (U.S. Bureau of the Census 1979, p. 171). That has occurred as a result of economic and social change and not because of any explicit policies intended to reverse traditional migration flows.

If the United States remains without a comprehensive population distribution policy, in the future millions of people will move into those areas which appear most attractive to them. This attractiveness may be based on environmental, economic, social, or cultural factors. However, the migration patterns will continue to reflect the importance of hidden government policies. Those policies will help determine where the additional 50 million Americans that will be added to the population over the next few decades will live.

SUMMARY

Population changes result from variations in migration as well as in births and deaths. Those variations are not random. Governments are constantly passing measures that deal with international migration. Many of the laws represent direct efforts to influence national rates of population growth. However, a concern with "population quality" is also evident. Restrictions are established on the migration of persons with certain ethnic or economic characteristics. Because of those restrictions it is not likely that international migration will be a significant factor in determining the geographic distribution of the world's population in the foreseeable future.

Direct efforts intended to influence patterns of internal migration have been focused primarily on restricting urban growth by stopping the flow of migrants to cities, by redirecting migrants to frontier areas, by encouraging settlement of growth-pole cities and new towns, and by specific limitations on a city's growth. Migration patterns are also influenced by "hidden" policies. That is, they are affected indirectly (and often unintentionally) by governmental programs and measures intended to achieve other objectives. Examples of this indirect influence include highway construction programs, location of defense installations, and tax deductions for home owners.

As the world's population continues to increase, more policies designed to regulate demographic behavior on both local and national levels can be expected. Those policies, however, will not be completely successful unless they take into account the social, economic, and cultural milieu in which the demographic behavior occurs and unless they consider the indirect as well as the direct effects.

REFERENCES AND SUGGESTED READINGS

Australian Population and Immigration Council. 1977. *Immigration policies and Australia's population.* Canberra: Australian Government Publishing Services.

Bouvier, Leon F., Shryock, Henry S., and Henderson, Harry W. 1977. International migration: yesterday, today, and tomorrow. *Population bulletin* 30 (September):3–42.

Congressional Research Service, Library of Congress. 1979. *U.S. immigration law and policy: 1952–1979.* Washington, D.C.: Government Printing Office.

Fuchs, Roland J., and Demko, George J. 1979. Population distribution policies in developed socialist and Western nations. *Population and development review* 5 (September):439–467.

Irwin, Richard. 1977. *Guide for local area population projections.* Technical paper no. 39, U.S. Bureau of the Census. Washington, D.C.: Government Printing Office.

Keely, Charles B. 1979. *U.S. immigration: A policy analysis.* New York: The Population Council.

Mauldin, W. Parker, et al. 1974. A report on Bucharest. *Studies in family planning* 5 (December):357–395.

Morrison, Peter A. 1973. A demographic assessment of new cities and growth centers as population redistribution strategies. *Public policy* 21 (Summer):367–382.

———. 1975. *Toward a policy planner's view of the urban settlement system.* Santa Monica, Calif.: The Rand Corporation.

Mrs. Thatcher touches a nerve and British tension is suddenly a political issue. 1978. *New York times* (February 22).

Mustofa, Sumono. 1978. Indonesia steps up transmigration. *Populi* 5:7–13.

Ontario naturalist. 1977. (Spring).

Petersen, William. 1979. The census: constitutional right or neomercantilist tool? *American demographics* 1 (October):25–31.

Population Reference Bureau. 1977. Canada rewriting immigration law. *Intercom* 5 (June):11.

Select Committee on Population. 1978. Domestic consequences of United States population change. Washington, D.C.: Government Printing Office.

Simmons, Alan, Diaz-Briquets, Sergio, and Laquian, Aprodicio A. 1977. *Social change and internal migration.* Ottawa, Canada: International Development Research Centre.

United Nations. 1973. *The determinants and consequences of population change,* vol. I. New York: United Nations.

U.S. Bureau of the Census. 1958. *Statistical abstract of the United States, 1958.* Washington, D.C.: Government Printing Office.

———. 1979. Social and economic status of the black population in the United States: an historical view, 1790–1978. *Current population reports,* series P-23, no. 80. Washington, D.C.: Government Printing Office.

U.S. Congress. 1979. Proceedings and debates of the 96th Congress, 1st session. *Congressional record* 125:30 (March 13).

U.S. Department of Justice. 1979. *Immigration and naturalization service, 1977 annual report.* Washington, D.C.: Government Printing Office.

Epilogue

As we enter the eighties, it is appropriate that we review recent past events and speculate about the foreseeable future. Clearly the world is in flux—economically, politically, socially, and *demographically.* Experts in many fields agree that humankind is entering a new era. The Industrial Revolution is past and a new period is upon us—a period without a name, as yet.

We are witnessing massive upheavals in the Islamic world, the emergence of new economic power for Japan and West Germany, an unprecedented flow of wealth to the oil-exporting countries (OPEC), and demands by Third World nations for a new economic order. This is indeed a period of turbulence.

Interestingly, major planetary changes have their demographic counterparts. Thus, the Industrial Revolution and the demographic transistion occurred simultaneously in many parts of the Western world. It has even been argued that the demographic changes that occurred during the transition were a contributing factor in that most important of planetary revolutions.

As we have noted throughout this book, all three demographic variables are undergoing dramatic changes. These developments are occurring not only in the United States but all over the planet and perhaps herald the beginning of a new era.

In the developed countries, fertility has fallen to unprecedented lows. In several countries there are now more deaths than births. The number of such countries will increase during the 1980s and 1990s if current levels of fertility are maintained. At the same time a debate is currently waxing over whether the United States will experience a mini-baby boom starting in the mid-1980s. Given the unique ecological importance of the United States because of its high per capita levels of consumption, this is not an empty question.

Some of the developing countries are also experiencing rapid fertility declines—declines that exceed those which the now advanced countries had during their development period. The prime example, of course, is the People's Republic of China. Yet we should not exaggerate. Much more needs to be done if most developing countries are to attain the fertility levels achieved by the developed countries of the world. Nevertheless, it is apparent that something is happening. All over the world, more and more women are insisting on having only the number of children they desire.

A decline in the mortality rates in most regions of the world has also been noted. Even in the demographically advanced countries of Scandinavia, already extremely low death rates have fallen still more in the 1970s. Life expectancy in those countries is fast approaching eighty years—one whole decade more than the biblical "three score and ten." Great progress has also been noted in the United States, yet the nation cannot seem to catch up to other advanced countries on the various indexes of mortality. Progress is occurring in all the developed parts of the world.

Similarly, many developing countries are registering increases in life expectancy as improved health measures are instituted. Life expectancy is approaching seventy years in many such countries. But a caveat is appropriate. Famine and malnutrition can and do flare up in some of the poorest nations. Overpopulation as well as maldistribution of scarce resources contribute to the tragedy that is too often on the verge of erupting. Thus, the picture is not as cheerful as it should be.

People are on the move everywhere. The earlier pattern of east to west migration no longer predominates. Today people move from the developing to the developed countries—generally a south to north migration. Within the advanced regions people move from areas with fewer advantages to those with more; this is equally true within the developing regions. Thousands upon thousands of people are moving not only from Mexico and the Caribbean, Vietnam, and the Philippines to the United States; but also from North Africa to France; from the West Indies to Great Britain; from Italy and Turkey to Sweden and Switzerland; from China to Malaysia; from Yemen to Kuwait and Saudi Arabia; from Spain and Portugal to Belgium; from Angola and Mozambique to Portugal; from Chad and Mauritania to the Ivory Coast and Senegal. Many of these people remain in their new homes permanently.

The social changes accompanying this massive movement of people are incalculable. Immigration has greatly altered the cultural heritage and fabric of American society and probably will continue to do so. However, the United States is not unique in this respect. Other more homogeneous countries—Sweden, Switzerland, West Germany, Luxembourg to name but a few—are also becoming multiethnic in composition.

The world is changing before our very eyes. Western civilization as we have known it is undergoing a major transformation; Asian societies, especially China, are changing rapidly; the Islamic world is redefining its values; Africa and Latin America are awakening to the possibilities of material progress as the end of the twentieth century approaches. To a considerable extent these changes are independent of demographic factors. And yet, our demographic acts simultaneously reflect the past and help to determine what the world will look like in both the near and distant future.

Appendix 1
Determining Population Change—Past and Future

We have noted that the rate of growth for any given year can be estimated by subtracting the crude death rate from the crude birth rate (assuming no migration). However, other measures are needed to understand better past or future population changes.

A. PERCENT CHANGE OVER TIME

The question is sometimes asked: "How much has country *A* grown over the past ten years?" We could rely on the demographic equation to tell us the *numerical* increase. But we must also be able to indicate by what *percent* a country grew in *x* period of years. This can be done by expressing the amount of change as a percent of the initial population. The formula is:

$$\text{(1)} \qquad \frac{P_2 - P_1}{P_1} \times 100$$

For example, we can calculate the percent increase in the U.S. population between January 1, 1970 and January 1, 1978 as follows:

$$\left(\frac{217{,}739{,}000 - 203{,}849{,}000}{203{,}849{,}000}\right)100 = 6.8 \text{ percent}$$

This means that the population of the United States grew by 6.8 percent between 1970 and 1978.

B. AVERAGE ANNUAL RATE OF CHANGE

The population grew by 6.8 percent in eight years, but what was its average annual rate of growth? In the example given above, one could divide 6.8 by 8 and conclude that the average annual rate of growth was 0.85. But it is not quite that simple, for population grows geometrically (or exponentially). If there were 1,000 people at the beginning of year 1 and they increased by 10 percent every year, the population at the beginning of year 2 would be 1,100. But at the beginning of year 3, it would not be 1,200; it would be 1,210. The base on which the 10 percent rate is calculated gets larger all the time. This leads to a very important equation that allows us to determine growth:

$$P_2 = P_1 (1 + r)^n \tag{2}$$

Following the same hypothetical population, if $P_1 = 1{,}000$ and $r = .10$, the population at P_5 would be:

$$1{,}000\ (1 + .10)^5 \text{ or } 1{,}000\ (1.61051) = 1{,}611$$

In this example r is known. To solve for r we can use the following:

$$r = \sqrt[n]{\frac{P_2}{P_1}} - 1 \tag{3}$$

Such rates are sometimes easier to calculate with logarithms and today's calculators have common as well as natural logarithms. The following equation relies on common logarithms:

$$\log\ (1 + r) = \frac{\log P_2 - \log P_1}{n} \tag{4}$$

$$1 + r = \text{antilog of } \log\ (1 + r)$$

A more efficient method uses natural logarithms which assume continuous change as compared to annual change. The basic equations follow:

$$P_2 = P_1\, e^{rn} \tag{5}$$

$$r = \frac{\log\left(\frac{P_2}{P_1}\right)}{n\ (\log e)} \tag{6}$$

(This is the common log of e, or .43429.)

For example, using the data for 1970 and 1978 we can determine the average annual rate of growth according to the two methods just discussed:

$$\log\ (1 + r) = \frac{8.33794 - 8.30867}{8} = .003658 \tag{4}$$

$$1 + r = 1.00846$$

$$r = .00846 \text{ or } .846 \text{ percent}$$

$$r = \frac{\log\ (1.06814)}{8\ (.43429)} \tag{6}$$

$$= \frac{.02863}{3.47432}$$

$$= .00824 \text{ or } .824 \text{ percent}$$

The average annual rate of growth in the United States for the period between 1970 and 1978 was about .8 percent. Note that the exponential rate of growth is slightly lower than the geometric rate. This is because the exponential assumes continuous growth whereas the geometric assumes annual growth.

C. DOUBLING TIME

It should be clear why it does not take one hundred years for the population to double if its rate of growth is 1 percent. But how do we know that it would take seventy years? We can answer that question by solving for n rather than r in equations 2 and 6. We are looking for doubling time. Thus $P_2 - P_1 = 2P_1$; also we are assuming a growth rate of 1 percent (i.e., .01).

$$(2) \quad n = \frac{\log P_2 - \log P_1}{\log (1 + r)} = \frac{.30103}{.00432} = 69.68$$

$$(6) \quad n = \frac{\log 2}{r \log e} = \frac{.30103}{(.01)\,(.43429)} = 69.32$$

For rough estimates of how long it takes for a population to double at various rates of growth, we use 70 as our base. Thus, at .824 average annual rate of growth, the U.S. population would double in about eighty-five years, if such a rate were maintained (70 ÷ .824).

D. POPULATION PROJECTIONS

Projecting future population size is a complicated matter and most methods, such as the cohort-component method, are beyond our present level. Mathematical calculations are possible, however, and are based on the equations discussed above. Let us begin with the basic geometric growth equation:

$$P_2 = P_1\,(1 + r)^n; \text{ or } \log P_2 = \log P_1 + n \log (1 + r)$$

For example, given the January 1, 1978, U. S. population (217,739,000) and the average annual rate of growth (.846), if this rate is maintained indefinitely, what would the U.S. population be in the years 2000 and 2050? Using the above equations:

$$P_{2000} \text{ (using the geometric growth equation)} =$$

$$217{,}739{,}000\,(1.00846)^{22} = 262{,}075{,}917$$

$$P_{2050} \text{ (using the logarithm method)} =$$

$$\text{Log } P_{2050} = 8.33794 + 72\,(.0036587) = 8.601366$$

$$P_{2050} = 399{,}365{,}683$$

In the year 2000 the U.S. population would be 262 million; in 2050 it would reach 399 million, assuming a continued rate of growth of .846 percent.

We could also inquire how many years it would take to reach a certain population size. Equation 2 used to derive doubling time will give us the answer.

For example, how many years will it take for the United States to reach 300 million at the present average annual rate of growth?

$$n = \frac{8.47712 \text{ (i.e., log 300 million)} - 8.33794}{.00365} = 38.1 \text{ years}$$

It would take 38.1 years for the U.S. population to reach 300 million at present average annual rates of growth.

You could use the exponential growth methods to arrive at very similar results. Remember that these are mathematical projections. They have limited value in the long run, though they are useful for short-run projections. They are not intended as replacements for the more exact cohort-component method described in the text, which takes changes in fertility, mortality, and migration into consideration.

Appendix 2
The Life Table

To determine life expectancy, not only at birth but at any age, a life table must be constructed. One thing it tells us is the number of additional years a person can expect to live *if* the probabilities of dying at each age do not change. Like the total fertility rate, the life table is a hypothetical measure. It calculates life expectancy by taking a starting population of 100,000 (called a radix) as of January 1 in a given year, x, and following it "through life" assuming that at all times people die according to the age-specific rates of year x. The life table is the best measure of mortality and all that is needed for its calculation are the age-specific death rates for the year in question.

Table A2.1 on page 335 is called an "abridged life table" because it is calculated for five-year age groups rather than single years. Let us examine each of the columns in that table and do the necessary calculations.

Column 1 gives the age intervals. In the formula (x to $x + n$), x is the first year of the interval, and n is the length of the interval. Thus, 15–20 means the five-year interval between the fifteenth and twentieth birthdays.

Column 2 shows the proportion of persons alive at the beginning of the interval who die during the interval and is designated ${}_nq_x$. This is the basic column of the life table. The ${}_nq_x$ values represent probabilities that persons who enter an age interval will die before reaching the beginning of the next interval. Although the probability of dying resembles the age-specific death rate, there is a difference between the two. To arrive at ${}_nq_x$ from the age-specific death rate, a transforming equation must be used. It can be stated as follows:

$$ {}_nq_x = \frac{2(n)\,(nM)}{2 + (n)(nM)} $$

In the equation nM is the age-specific death rate (per person, not per 1,000), and n is the length of the interval. At the oldest age category, ${}_nq_x = 1.0$, since all who enter that interval will die. The probability of death for those in some of the other age categories can be calculated as follows:

AGE	$(_nM)$	CALCULATION	$_nq_x$
0–1	.01486	$\frac{2(1)\ (.01486)}{2+(1)\ (.01486)} =$	.0147
1–5	.000688	$\frac{2(4)\ (.000688)}{2+(4)\ (.000688)} =$	.0027
5–10	.000340	$\frac{2(5)\ (.000340)}{2+(5)\ (.000340)} =$	.0017
85 and over	.147259	no calculation	1.0

Column 3 shows the number of people still living at the beginning of the age interval and is designated (l_x). It is calculated by subtracting $_nd_x$ (column 4) from l_x (column 3) in the age interval immediately preceding the one being derived. For example, out of 98,264 persons entering the 5–10 age group, 167 die. Thus, for the next group, those age 10–15, there are 167 fewer people and the l_x is 98,097 (that is, 98,264 − 167).

Column 4 shows the number who die during a particular age interval and is designated $_nd_x$. It is arrived at by multiplying l_x (column 3) by $_nq_x$ (column 2). Thus, for age 10–15, 98,097 × .0018 = 177.

Column 5 shows the total years lived in the age interval by all the persons who enter that interval. It is designated as $_nL_x$. For example, 98,097 enter the 10–15 interval. If none die during those five years, they would live 490,485 years (98,097 × 5) in the interval. But 177 died in the interval. It is assumed that deaths are evenly distributed over the five-year period. Therefore $_nL_x$ is equal to $(l_x - ½\ d_x)\ (n)$. This equation is applicable to all age intervals after 0–1. During the first year it cannot be assumed that those dying will have lived six months on the average because most infant deaths occur within the first four weeks after birth. For present purposes (and if we consider only the developed countries) the following equation will suffice:

$$L_1 = l_0 - (.9 \times {_nd_x})$$

Thus, in our example:

$$L_1 = 100{,}000 - (.9 \times 1470) = 100{,}000 - 1323 = 98677$$

At the other age extreme (85+), another method must be devised. The $_nL_x$ for 85+ is calculated as follows:

$$\frac{l_x}{\text{Death Rate Per Person 85+}} = \frac{25{,}905}{.147259} = 175{,}915$$

Table A2.1 Abridged Life Table for the Total Population of the United States, 1977

(1) x to $x + n$	(2)* $_nq_x$		(3) l_x	(4) $_nd_x$	(5) $_nL_x$	(6) T_x	(7) $\overset{o}{e}_x$
0–1	0.0147	(14.860)	100,000	1,470	98,677	7,321,248	73.2
1–5	0.0027	(0.688)	98,530	266	393,588	7,222,571	73.3
5–10	0.0017	(0.340)	98,264	167	490,903	6,828,983	69.5
10–15	0.0018	(0.351)	98,097	177	490,043	6,338,080	64.6
15–20	0.0051	(1.016)	97,920	499	488,353	5,848,037	59.7
20–25	0.0067	(1.335)	97,421	653	485,473	5,359,684	55.0
25–30	0.0066	(1.321)	96,768	639	482,243	4,874,331	50.4
30–35	0.0070	(1.409)	96,129	673	478,963	4,392,088	45.7
35–40	0.0097	(1.955)	95,456	926	474,965	3,913,125	41.0
40–45	0.0151	(3.047)	94,530	1,427	469,083	3,438,160	36.4
45–50	0.0238	(4.823)	93,103	2,216	459,975	2,969,077	31.9
50–55	0.0370	(7.547)	90,887	3,363	446,028	2,509,102	27.6
55–60	0.0553	(11.381)	87,524	4,840	425,520	2,063,074	23.6
60–65	0.0854	(17.849)	82,684	7,061	395,768	1,637,554	19.8
65–70	0.1168	(24.804)	75,623	8,833	356,033	1,241,786	16.4
70–75	0.1755	(38.471)	66,790	11,722	304,645	885,753	13.3
75–80	0.2636	(60.730)	55,068	14,516	239,050	581,108	10.6
80–85	0.3612	(88.147)	40,552	14,647	166,143	342,058	8.4
85 or Over	1.0000	(147.259)	25,905	25,905	175,915	175,915	6.8

*The age-specific death rates *per 1,000* are included in parenthesis for your information.

Column 6 shows the total years lived in that age interval and all subsequent age intervals and is designated as T_x. To calculate T_x we merely sum up $_nL_x$ from the oldest age backward, thus:

$$175{,}915 + 166{,}143 = 342{,}058 + 239{,}050 = 581{,}108 \text{ and so forth}$$

Column 7 shows the average number of years of life remaining at the beginning of the age interval and gives us life expectancy at any age. It is designated $\overset{o}{e}_x$ and is calculated by dividing column 6 by column 3. At birth, one can expect to live

$$\frac{7{,}321{,}248}{100{,}000} = 73.2 \text{ years}$$

At age thirty-five, one can expect to live

$$\frac{3{,}913{,}105}{95{,}456}, \text{ or about forty-one more years}$$

From these instructions you should be able to construct an abridged life table, bearing in mind that these are shortcut methods that nevertheless yield close approximations of the actual complete life table.

Life tables can be used for many purposes besides studying mortality. Examples include estimation of the failure rates of contraceptives, analysis of progress through the educational system, and the measurement of marital formation and dissolution.

For instance, the $_nL_x$ column makes it possible to calculate the net reproduction rate briefly discussed in box 3.1. If no one died in any five-year interval, $_nL_x$ would equal 500,000. The difference between the number in the $_nL_x$ column and 500,000 reflects the deaths that occur up to a certain age. By multiplying the age-sex specific fertility rate by the appropriate $_nL_x$, the net reproductive rate can be determined.

Appendix 3
The Stable Population

In chapter 9 we noted how important age and sex composition are and how variations in age distribution can lead to misinterpretations of fertility and mortality rates. In earlier chapters we noted that many of the measurements of fertility and mortality were crude and of limited value for the demographic assessment of the fertility and mortality of societies.

The problems associated with fertility measures were partly solved by use of the total fertility rate. The processes of standardization and the life table serve as improved measures of mortality as compared to the crude death rate. In both instances the problem they solved stems from variation in the age distribution. Total fertility rates and life tables control for age; as a result, variations in age composition do not contaminate those measures.

However, neither process allows us to compute an annual rate of growth while controlling for age composition. The rate of growth is simply the difference between the crude birth rate and the crude death rate. The result is a *crude* rate of growth for a particular year. The contaminating effects of age composition on both the birth and death rates are not eliminated.

This problem is vividly illustrated using current U.S. data. In 1978 the crude birth rate was 15.2 and the crude death rate was 8.8. Thus, the *crude* rate of natural increase was 6.4. Yet the total fertility rate was 1.8—under the 2.1 needed for replacement. Obviously, the crude rate of reproductive change is misleading.

The demographic measure called the **intrinsic rate of growth** eliminates age composition as a factor in determining growth. This measure indicates what the growth rate would be if the age-specific fertility and mortality rates for a given year did not change. It reflects demographic behavior in a specific year and assumes an indefinite continuation of the rates of that year. The intrinsic rate of growth also serves as the first step in constructing a stable population—one of the most useful models in demography.

A **stable population** is the kind of population (that is, in regard to age and sex composition) that would result if a certain set of age- and sex-specific birth and death rates, observed for a specific year, continued indefinitely into the future. If this were so, a point in time would be reached where the age and sex composition of the population would become fixed and would no longer change. The concept "stable" refers to age and sex composition, not to size. A "stationary," or life table, population is a stable population in which the intrinsic birth rate is equal to the intrinsic death rate. Only in this special case is the size as well as the age-sex composition of the population unchanging.

In a stable population the rate of growth never changes, the crude birth and death rates are constant, the age structure is unvarying, and the sex ratio is always the same. What, then, does the stable population tell us? It tells us what a *real* population would eventually look like if its age-specific birth and death rates for a given year remained unchanged indefinitely. Generally it takes about seventy years to approach stability. The stable model tells us a population's intrinsic growth rate as well as its structure—assuming no change in fertility and mortality.

CALCULATING THE INTRINSIC RATE OF INCREASE

We determine the intrinsic rate of increase, r, from the age- and sex-specific fertility rates and ${}_nL_x$ from the female life table prior to calculating the stable population itself. The rate of increase is related to the net reproduction rate, which indicates the total number of daughters ever born, per woman, in a cohort of the stable population. The net reproduction rate is given by the formula:

$$\frac{F_2}{F_1} = e^{r\bar{a}}$$

Here $\bar{a}$ is the average interval of years between mother's and daughter's ages, or the mean length of generation. F_2 is the size of the second generation of females, and as here F_1 the size of the first generation of mothers.

Unfortunately there is no simple way to calculate $\bar{a}$ precisely because it represents the fertility of two cohorts. Thus, we begin by calculating $\bar{a}'$ (the average age of mothers in one cohort), then estimate the "real" length of generation, and then correct for the "error" involved. The estimate of $\bar{a}'$ is simply the average age of mothers *in one cohort* of the stable population. (Remember that we are looking for the average age of mothers at the birth of their daughters in the next generation.) The estimate of $\bar{a}'$ is computed and illustrated in columns 5 and 6 of table A3.1. First we total the number of births at all ages, multiply by the average age of mothers when their daughters were born, and then divide by the total number of births. Once we have calculated $\bar{a}'$, we can approximate the value of r' (the estimated value of the rate of growth). We then determine the extent of "error" and correct for it, thereby giving us a more reliable estimate of r.

EXAMPLE OF THE CALCULATIONS OF THE INTRINSIC RATE OF INCREASE, *r*

In this example we will determine the intrinsic rate of increase for the United States in 1976. The data needed include (1) 1976 age-sex specific birth rates; (2) ${}_nL_x$ values from the male and female life tables for 1976; and (3) sex ratio at birth. The calculations using these data are found in table A3.1.

Columns 1 and 2 of that table are self-explanatory. They show the age composition, by five-year age groups, of women in their childbearing years (age fifteen to forty-nine) and the midpoint of each age group.

Column 3 displays the age- and sex-specific birth rate per person (for females only). If the necessary data are not available, multiply the total number of births to each age group of females by the percent of all births that were female in the given year. The sex ratio at birth was 105.4 in 1976; thus the proportion of all births that were female is .4865. That is,

$$\frac{100}{100 + 105.4} = .4865$$

Column 4, Person-Years Lived, comes from the ${}_nL_x$ column of the female life table. That number is divided by 100,000.

Column 5, Expected Female Births, is derived by multiplying column 3 by column 4. The summation of this column gives us the net reproduction rate.

Column 6 shows the calculation of $\bar{a}'$. This is derived by multiplying column 2 by column 5. The summation of this column indicates the average age of women at the time they are averaging .85 female births. Thus, column 6 ÷ column 5 yields an estimate of the mean length of generation—25.76554—that is, the average age of women when they reproduce one female live birth. It is now possible to *estimate* the rate of growth, r':

$$r' = \frac{1}{\bar{a}'} \log e\ (\Sigma \text{ column } 5) = -.00611$$

Columns 7 through 9 represent adjustments. In column 7, multiply column 2 by the estimated rate of growth expressed in its negative form $(-r')$. Thus 17.5 (.00611) = .10693. In column 8, we take the exponential of the power expressed in column 7. Thus $e^x = e^{.10693} = 1.11285$; in column 9 multiply column 5 by column 8 and sum to determine the size of the estimating error. Without error this column would sum to 1.0. With error, the sum of the column is 1.00057 $(1 + E)$. It is now possible to correct for the original estimate of the rate of growth, r. The formula is:

$$r = r^1 + \frac{E}{\bar{a}' + \dfrac{E}{r'}}$$

Table A3.1 Calculation of the Intrinsic Rate of Increase in the United States, 1976

(1) AGE	(2) MIDPOINT	(3) BIRTHS PER YEAR (DAUGHTERS ONLY)	(4) PERSON-YEARS LIVED	(5) EXPECTED FEMALE BIRTHS (3) × (4)	(6) CALCULATION OF $\bar{a}'$ (2) × (5)	(7) $-r' \times (2)$	(8) $e^{-r} \times (2)$	(9) (5) × (8)
15–19	17.5	.02805	4.90037	.13745	2.40538	.10693	1.11285	.15296
20–24	22.5	.05586	4.88561	.27291	6.14048	.13748	1.14738	.31313
25–29	27.5	.05372	4.86899	.26156	7.19290	.16803	1.18297	.30942
30–34	32.5	.02586	4.84907	.12540	4.07550	.19858	1.21967	.15295
35–39	37.5	.00945	4.82131	.04556	1.70850	.22913	1.25750	.05729
40–44	42.5	.00224	4.77838	.01070	0.45475	.25968	1.29652	.01387
45–49	47.5	.00015	4.71029	.00071	0.03373	.29023	1.33673	.00095
				.85429	22.01124			1.00057

Substituting the values in table A3.1, we get:

$$\bar{a}' = \frac{22.01124}{.85429} = 25.76554$$

$$r' = \frac{1}{25.76554} \log e\ .85429 = -.00611$$

$$1 + E = 1.00057$$

$$E = .00057$$

$$r = -.00611 + \frac{.00057}{25.76554 + \left(\frac{.00057}{-.00611}\right)} = -.00609$$

The intrinsic or true rate of growth for the United States in 1976 was −0.6 percent.

CALCULATING THE STABLE POPULATION

Once the intrinsic rate of increase is derived, calculating the stable population by age and sex is the next step. Table A3.2 shows the calculations for the United States in 1976.

Column 1 lists the age composition in five-year age groups (from birth to age eighty-four) and groups together those over eighty-five.

Column 2 shows the midpoint of each age group. The midpoint for those over eighty-five is set at ninety.

Column 3 shows $e^{-r(x+2.5)}$. For example, in the age bracket 5–9, $e^{-(-.00609)(7.5)} = 1.04673$. Because the United States has a negative rate of increase, the double negative results in a positive number (.00609).

Column 4 is the ${}_nL_x$ column from the female life table for the United States in 1976.

Column 5 is the ${}_nL_x$ column from the male life table for the United States in 1976, but multiplied by the sex ratio at birth (1.054). That multiplication is done to make the two age distributions comparable.

Columns 6 and 7 are derived by multiplying column 5 by column 3 and column 4 by column 3. This gives us the actual age-sex distribution of the stable population.

Columns 8 and 9 standardize the total population to 100,000. Divide each entry in column 6 and column 7 by the sum of columns 6 and 7; then multiply by 100,000. Thus:

$$\left(\frac{525{,}368}{19{,}116{,}976}\right)100{,}000 = 2{,}748$$

Table A3.2 Calculation of the Stable Population of the United States, 1976

(1) AGE (x to x+5)	(2) MID-POINT (x+2.5)	(3) $e^{-r(x+2.5)}$	(4) STATIONARY POPULATION	(5)	(6) STABLE POPULATION	(7)	(8) STANDARD POPULATION OF 100,000	(9)
			Female	Male $(1.054)x_5L_x$	Male	Female	Male	Female
0–4	2.5	1.01534	492,643	517,431	525,368	500,200	2,748	2,617
5–9	7.5	1.04673	491,581	515,907	540,015	514,553	2,825	2,692
10–14	12.5	1.07909	490,983	514,954	555,682	529,815	2,907	2,771
15–19	17.5	1.11246	490,037	512,659	570,313	545,147	2,983	2,852
20–24	22.5	1.14685	488,561	508,172	582,797	560,306	3,049	2,931
25–29	27.5	1.18232	486,899	503,329	595,096	575,670	3,113	3,011
30–34	32.5	1.21887	484,907	498,979	608,191	591,039	3,181	3,092
35–39	37.5	1.25656	482,131	492,984	619,464	605,827	3,240	3,169
40–44	42.5	1.29641	477,838	484,979	628,732	619,474	3,289	3,240
45–49	47.5	1.33546	471,029	472,575	631,105	629,040	3,301	3,290
50–54	52.5	1.37675	460,741	453,608	624,505	634,325	3,267	3,318
55–59	57.5	1.41932	445,656	425,396	603,773	632,528	3,158	3,309
60–64	62.5	1.46320	423,811	384,610	562,761	620,120	2,944	3,244
65–69	67.5	1.50844	394,059	330,667	498,791	594,414	2,609	3,110
70–74	72.5	1.55508	352,288	264,603	411,479	547,836	2,152	2,866
75–79	77.5	1.60316	291,519	188,700	302,516	467,352	1,582	2,445
80–84	82.5	1.65272	213,866	115,357	190,653	353,461	997	1,849
85+	90.0	1.72996	226,823	87,998	152,233	392,395	796	2,053
					9,203,474	9,913,502	48,141	51,859

CALCULATING THE BIRTH AND DEATH RATES FOR THE STABLE POPULATION

We now have r and the stable age distribution. We also would like to know the birth and death rates implied by them. Remember that these are the rates that would result if the mortality and fertility of 1976 did not change. This calculation involves deriving the crude birth rates from the rates of increase. For females, the sum of column 7 in table A3.2 tells us the number of females in the stable population. Since there are always 100,000 female births per year, the crude birth rate for females is:

$$\left(\frac{100{,}000}{9{,}913{,}502}\right)1{,}000$$

For males it is:

$$\left(\frac{105{,}400}{9{,}203{,}474}\right)1{,}000$$

The crude birth rate for the entire population is:

$$\left(\frac{100{,}000 + 105{,}400}{9{,}913{,}502 + 9{,}203{,}474}\right)1{,}000$$

The rates are 10.09, 11.45, 10.74, respectively. Since the intrinsic rate of growth is $-.00609$, the death rate for females is $10.09 - (-6.09) = 16.18$; for males it is $11.45 - (-6.09) = 17.54$; for the total population it is 16.83.

You have now learned how to calculate a stable population by age and sex distribution, its intrinsic rate of increase, and its birth and death rates. These figures indicate what the U.S. population would look like if its 1976 age-specific fertility and mortality patterns remained unchanged in the future and there was no migration into or out of the country. Because the United Sates (in 1976) exhibited a negative rate of increase, the age-sex pyramid that would emerge looks quite strange. You should construct it and explain the implications it suggests for the future.

In sum, the stable population, though hypothetical, illustrates the structure of a closed population given no change in fertility and mortality. It also serves as a model that can be used when sufficient information is not available.

Glossary

abortion rate the number of abortions in a given year per 1,000 women age fifteen to forty-four (chapter 5).

abortion ratio the number of abortions in a given year per 1,000 live births in that same year (chapter 5).

age-sex composition the relative number of males and females in each age category of the population (chapter 1).

age-adjusted rate a rate (usually a death rate) in which the age distribution has been held constant (chapter 9). See *standardization.*

age-sex pyramid a vertical bar graph which depicts the relative number of males and females in each age category of a population; also called a "population pyramid" (chapter 2).

age-specific rates rates of fertility, migration, or mortality calculated for a certain age group (e.g., twenty to twenty-four, twenty-five to twenty-nine, etc.) (chapter 3).

alien any person living in a country who is not a citizen of that country (chapter 8).

baby boom the increase in fertility that occurred during the late 1940s and 1950s in the United States, Canada, Australia, and New Zealand, and briefly, in many Western European countries (chapter 2).

baby bust the decrease in fertility that occurred in the United States, Canada, Australia, New Zealand, and most Western countries in the 1970s (chapter 10).

birth control reducing the probability of conception through practices such as abstinence, use of contraceptives, and sterilization. Sometimes referred to as "contraception," "fertility control," and "family planning" (chapter 5).

birth control pill a contraceptive substance which is taken orally. Also called an "oral contraceptive" (chapter 6).

birth order the numerical order in which a person is born. For example, a person who was the second live birth of a mother has the second birth order. Also referred to as "parity"; thus, the second parity (chapter 7).

cause of death rate the number of deaths from a specific cause per 100,000 population. It can be specified for age, sex, race, and so forth (chapter 7).

center of population the point at which an imaginary flat, weightless, and rigid map of a specific area would balance if weights of identical value were placed on it so that each weight represented the location of one person at the census date (chapter 4).

central city the largest city in a metropolitan area (chapter 4).

cervical cap a small, thimble-shaped cup used to prevent conception by blocking the cervix (chapter 6).

child-woman ratio the number of living children under five years old per 1,000 women age fifteen to forty-four. This is often used as a measure of fertility when vital statistics data are not available (chapter 5).

city a place that is incorporated and has been granted certain powers, as defined in its charter, by the state in which it is located (chapter 4).

cohort a group of people who experience a major event in the same short period (e.g., one or five years). A birth cohort (persons born in the same year or five-year period) is an example (chapter 3).

cohort analysis examination of a cohort's demographic behavior over time (e.g., children ever born to a specific birth cohort of women); compare with *period analysis* (chapter 5).

completed family size the number of live births to a woman by the time she completes childbearing, usually defined as age forty-four or forty-nine (chapter 5).

condom a sheath designed to cover the penis during sexual intercourse for sanitary or contraceptive purposes (chapter 6).

conjugal union marriage or consensual union by one male and one female (chapter 5).

crude birth rate the number of live births in any given year divided by the midyear population and multiplied by 1,000 (chapter 2).

crude death rate the number of deaths in any given year divided by the midyear population and multiplied by 1,000 (chapter 2).

demographic equation the formula that explains the difference in sizes of a population P at two points in time: $P_2 - P_1 = (B - D)_{12} + (I - O)_{12}$ (chapter 1).

demographic transition a model of population change in which birth and death rates decline from high levels to low levels. Mortality usually falls first, resulting in rapid population growth (chapter 2).

demographic variables the three variables—fertility, mortality, and migration—that account for any change in population size (chapter 1).

demography the systematic study of populations, including their size, composition, and distribution and the causes and consequences of change in those factors (chapter 1).

dependency ratio the number of persons under fifteen years of age and sixty-five or older divided by the number of persons fifteen to sixty-four years of age (and then multiplied by one hundred). Occasionally those under seventeen and even nineteen is used rather than those under fifteen (chapter 3).

desired family size the number of children women would *like* to have, irrespective of other considerations (chapter 5).

developing countries those countries which have lower levels of per capita income and modernization than other countries (chapter 5).

diaphragm a contraceptive device which consists of a flexible disk that covers the uterine cervix (chapter 6).

doubling time the years required for a population to double in number at a specific rate. At a 1 percent rate of growth, the doubling time is 69.3 years (chapter 2).

effective family size the actual number of living children (chapter 5).

emigration the process of moving out of a country to live in some other country (chapter 3).

endogenous originating from within the body or genetic makeup (chapter 7).

ethnicity the quality of belonging to a particular national or racial group (chapter 1).

exogenous having a cause that is external to the body or genetic makeup (chapter 7).

expected family size the number of children that women expect to have in the future (chapter 5).

exponential growth a constant rate of growth applied to a continuously growing population base (chapter 2).

failure rate the number of pregnancies per hundred person years of use of a birth control method (chapter 6).

fecundity the physiological capacity to produce a live birth. A woman, man, or couple can be fecund or infecund (chapter 5).

fertility the actual number of live births of an individual, a group, or a population (chapter 1).

fetal mortality a stillbirth, spontaneous abortion, or miscarriage which terminates the life of the fetus before birth (chapter 5).

fetus the product of a pregnancy before birth (chapter 5).

foreign born that portion of a country's population born outside that country (chapter 3).

foreign stock those residents of a country who are either foreign born or native born, with at least one parent being foreign born (chapter 3).

general fertility rate the number of live births in any given year per 1,000 women age fifteen to forty-four; sometimes called simply the "fertility rate" (chapter 5).

gestation the carrying of a fetus in the uterus from conception to delivery (chapter 5).

geographic mobility any change in residence. It includes both local movements and migration beyond specific boundaries (chapter 8).

good times cohort persons born during the 1930s, when fertility was lower than the preceding and following decades (chapter 10).

Green Revolution a term coined in 1968 by William Gaud, administrator of the Agency for International Development, to describe the introduction and rapid adoption worldwide of high-yielding wheats and rices (chapter 2).

gross reproduction rate the average number of daughters that would be born to a female birth cohort if members completed their childbearing years subject to the age-specific fertility rates of a given year. See also *total fertility rate* and *net reproduction rate* (chapter 3).

growth rate the number of births plus the number of immigrants minus the number of deaths plus the number of emigrants in a given year, divided by the total midyear population, and multiplied by 1,000 (chapter 2).

high growth potential the first stage of the demographic transition, characterized by high birth and death rates. The potential for population growth is high if death rates are later lowered (chapter 2).

household all the people who occupy a particular housing unit (chapter 10).

householder technically the person listed in column 1 of the 1980 U.S. census of population and housing. Persons filling out the census form were instructed to place in column 1 a household member in whose name the house was owned or rented. If there was no such person, the instructions were to start in column 1 with any adult household member. Householder replaces the head-of-household concept used in earlier censuses (chapter 10).

illegal immigrant a person who is in a country illegally, through entry without inspection, as a visa abuser, or through use of fraudulent documents; sometimes called "undocumented alien" (chapter 3).

illegitimacy rate the number of illegitimate live births in any given year per 1,000 unmarried women age fifteen to forty-four (chapter 5).

illegitimacy ratio the number of illegitimate live births in a given year per 1,000 total live births in the same year (chapter 5).

illegitimate births births to women who are not married when the births occur and who were not married at the time of conception (chapter 5).

immigrant a person who is admitted into a country to reside there permanently (chapter 3).

immigration the migration of people into a country from any other country (chapter 3).

incipient decline the third stage of the demographic transition. It is characterized by low birth and death rates (chapter 2).

index of aging the number of persons age sixty-five and over per hundred persons under age fifteen (chapter 9).

infant mortality rate the number of deaths to infants under one year of age in any given calendar year divided by the number of births in that year and multiplied by 1,000 (chapter 7).

infecundity the physiological incapacity to produce a live birth. A woman, man, or couple can be fecund or infecund (chapter 5).

in-migration the process of moving into a specific political subdivision (e.g., a county or state) from another subdivision of the same country (chapter 1).

internal migration a change of residence from one civil subdivision (e.g., county or state) to another within the same country (chapter 4).

intrauterine device (IUD) a small device that is inserted directly into the uterus to prevent conception and/or implantation (chapter 6).

intrinsic rate of growth the rate of population growth which would occur if constant age-specific birth and death rates were applied for an indefinite period of time to an existing population (appendix 3); see *stable population.*

labor force that portion of the population which is employed or is actively seeking work (chapter 2).

life cycle the stages through which a person goes from infancy to old age (e.g., adolescence, adulthood, etc.) (chapter 3).

life expectancy the average number of additional years a person can be expected to live; also known as "expectation of life." Unless otherwise specified, it refers to life expectancy at birth (chapter 3); see *life table.*

life span the maximum number of years (about one hundred) a person can expect to live (chapter 7).

life table a statistical model used to study mortality which is generated from age-specific mortality, survivorship, and life expectancy rates (at various ages) (chapter 7).

live birth a fetus which shows signs of life after birth, according to certain indicators, such as breathing; indicators vary from country to country (chapter 5).

local movement change of residence which occurs within the political boundaries of a given area (e.g., within a county) (chapter 8).

maternal mortality rate deaths to women due to pregnancy or the process of giving birth, per 100,000 live births (chapter 6).

median age the age that divides a population into two equal groups, half younger and half older (chapter 9).

megalopolis a popular term referring to a group of contiguous or near contiguous metropolitan areas. For example, Boswash is the megalopolis extending from Boston, Massachusetts, to Washington, D.C. (chapter 4).

menstrual regulation a birth control method which consists of inducing menstruation, thus preventing the development of any fertilized ova in the uterine wall (chapter 6).

metropolitan area a central city and the surrounding counties that are economically integrated with that city. In the United States, a Standard Metropolitan Statistical Area (SMSA) consists of one or more contiguous counties, at least one of which has a city (or cities) with a population of 50,000 or more. All the counties included in the SMSA depend on the central city for economic activity (chapter 4).

migration a change of residence which is intended to be permanent and which involves crossing political boundaries. Migration may be international or internal (chapter 1).

migration stream the migration of a large number of individuals over a period of time from one particular place to another (chapter 8).

morbidity the incidence and prevalence of sickness in a population (chapter 7).

morning-after pill a birth control pill taken by the female. Composed of synthetic estrogen, it prevents implantation (chapter 6).

mortality the deaths occurring to a population (chapter 1).

national under U.S. law, a citizen born in the United States or born overseas of U.S. citizens (chapter 8).

natural increase the number of births minus the number of deaths in a population at two points of time; also known as "reproductive change." There can also be a natural decrease if deaths exceed births (chapter 1).

naturalized citizen a permanent immigrant who has been granted citizenship by the country into which he or she has immigrated (chapter 8).

neonatal mortality deaths occurring during the first twenty-eight days following birth (chapter 7).

net migration the number of persons moving into an area minus the number of persons moving out of that area (chapter 1).

net reproduction rate the average number of daughters that would be born to a female birth cohort if the members completed their childbearing years subject to the age-specific fertility and mortality rates of a stated year (chapter 3).

nonimmigrant a person admitted into a country for a specific and temporary period of time (e.g., a tourist or a foreign student) (chapter 8).

out-migration the process of moving out of a specific political subdivision to another within the same country (chapter 1).

parturition the act or process of giving birth. This term is sometimes used to refer to the process of labor (chapter 5).

Pearl Index a method of measuring the use effectiveness of a birth prevention method. It is calculated as the total number of conceptions to persons while they use a particular method per 1,000 number of months those persons used that method (chapter 6).

per capita the average units per person. This is one way of controlling for differences in population size when comparing figures such as energy consumption (chapter 2).

period analysis examination of the demographic behavior of a population at a specific point in time (e.g., the crude birth rate for 1980) (chapter 5); compare with *cohort analysis.*

population census the total process of collecting, compiling, and publishing demographic, economic, and social data pertaining, at a specified time or times, to all persons in a country or delimited territory (chapter 1).

population composition the structure of a population with respect primarily to age, but also including sex, race, economic status, and other social variables (chapter 1).

population density the number of persons per unit of land, usually a square mile or a square kilometer (chapter 3).

population distribution how people are spatially dispersed over a land area (chapter 4).

population explosion the sharp increase in the world's population brought about by declines in mortality that were greater than declines in fertility (chapter 2).

population momentum the growth of a population attributable to the high proportion of people in their childbearing years. Such growth continues to occur even after replacement level fertility has been attained (chapter 2).

population policies measures instituted by governments which influence demographic behavior (chapter 11).

population projection a systematic estimate of the future population of an area based on an assumed level of population growth and/or assumed levels of fertility, mortality, and net migration (chapter 2).

population register a mechanism which provides for the continuous recording of information about the population in such a manner that data on particular events each individual experiences, as well as selected descriptive characteristics, are maintained on a current basis (chapter 1).

postneonatal mortality deaths during days 29 to 365 (366 in leap years) following birth (chapter 7).

postpartum after a birth (chapter 5).

potential fertility the number of children a woman is capable of having (chapter 5).

progestogen a synthetic compound with a physiological effect similar to progesterone, which serves to prepare the uterus for the reception and development of the fertilized egg (chapter 6).

rate of reproductive change crude birth rate minus the crude death rate; also called "rate of natural increase" (chapter 3).

refugee a person outside any country of his or her origin who is unable or unwilling to return to and is unable or unwilling to seek the protection of that country because of persecution on account of race, religion, nationality, membership in a particular social group, or political opinion (chapter 8).

replacement level fertility (RLF) the level of fertility at which couples, on the average, are having only enough children to replace themselves (chapter 2).

reproductive potential the ability of a population to reproduce itself; it is affected by a relative concentration of persons in young childbearing ages (e.g., twenty to thirty-four) (chapter 2).

return migration the process of returning to one's earlier place of residence (chapter 4).

rhythm method a method of contraception based on abstinence from coition around the period when a woman is believed to be ovulating (chapter 6).

sample survey a collection of information, usually through interviews, from a sample of individuals or households (chapter 1).

sex ratio the number of males per hundred females (chapter 3).

stable population a hypothetical population with an unchanging birth and death rate, rate of growth, and age composition—all the result of constant age-specific birth and death rates (appendix 3).

standardization a statistical technique which controls for the effect of factors that may contaminate the comparison of populations with respect to demographic variables. Usually, age is the factor that is controlled (chapter 9).

standardized mortality ratio the ratio of actual mortality in a given category (e.g., occupation) to the mortality that would be expected if the age-specific rates for persons in all categories combined were present in that category (chapter 7).

stationary population a stable population in which the birth rate equals the death rate, resulting in no change in population size (chapter 9).

sterilization an operation performed on either a male or female to prevent conception (chapter 6).

suburb a residential or industrial area on the fringes of a city (chapter 4).

total fertility rate the average number of children a woman would have during her lifetime if her rate of childbearing was the same as that which prevailed in each age category in the year in question (chapter 3).

transitional growth the middle stage of the demographic transition, during which the population increases due to declines in mortality that precede declines in fertility (chapter 2).

urban places in the United States, incorporated and unincorporated places of 2,500 or more inhabitants (chapter 4).

urbanized area a central city, or cities, and surrounding closely settled territory (chapter 4).

urbanization an increase in the percent of the total population of a specific area that lives in urban areas (chapter 3).

vaginal contraceptives foams, jellies, or pastes that are inserted into the vagina to prevent conception by chemically immobilizing or destroying the sperm (chapter 6).

vasectomy the surgical excision of a part of the vas deferens which is performed as a means of sterilizing males (chapter 6).

vital statistics demographic data on births, deaths, marriages, and divorces (chapter 1).

withdrawal a birth control method which consists of removing the penis from the vagina before ejaculation. Also known as *coitus interruptus* (chapter 6).

zero population growth (ZPG) a population with a growth rate of zero because births plus immigration equal deaths plus emigration (chapter 2).

zygote a fertilized egg formed by the union of an ovum and spermatozoa (chapter 6).

Index